DESPISING SHAME
Honor Discourse and Community Maintenance in the Epistle to the Hebrews

SOCIETY OF BIBLICAL LITERATURE

DISSERTATION SERIES

Michael Fox, Old Testament Editor
Pheme Perkins, New Testament Editor

Number 152

DESPISING SHAME
*Honor Discourse and Community Maintenance
in the Epistle to the Hebrews*
by
David Arthur deSilva

David Arthur deSilva

DESPISING SHAME
Honor Discourse and Community Maintenance in the Epistle to the Hebrews

Scholars Press
Atlanta, Georgia

DESPISING SHAME
Honor Discourse and Community Maintenance in the Epistle to the Hebrews

David Arthur deSilva

BS
2775.2
.D47
1996

© 1995
The Society of Biblical Literature

Library of Congress Cataloging in Publication Data
DeSilva, David A.
    Despising shame : honor discourse and community maintenance
in the Epistle to the Hebrews / David Arthur deSilva.
        p.   cm.
    Includes bibliographical references and index.
        ISBN 0-7885-0200-X (cloth : alk. paper). — ISBN 0-7885-0201-8
(pbk. : alk. paper)
        1. Honor—Biblical teaching. 2. Bible. N.T. Hebrews—Criticism,
interpretation, etc. 3. Rhetoric in the Bible. I. Title.
    BX2775.2.D47   1996
    227'.8706—dc20   95-42324
                                                CIP

Printed in the United States of America
on acid-free paper

Contents

Abbreviations

AJT	*American Journal of Theology*
ANF	The Ante-Nicene Fathers: Translations of the Writings of the Fathers Down to AD 325 (ed. A. Roberts and J. Donaldson; 10 vols.; Grand Rapids: Eerdmans, 1951-53)
BTB	*Biblical Theology Bulletin*
CBQ	*Catholic Biblical Quarterly*
CBQMS	Catholic Biblical Quarterly Monograph Series
ICC	International Critical Commentary
JBL	*Journal of Biblical Literature*
JJS	*Journal of Jewish Studies*
JSNT	*Journal for the Study of the New Testament*
JSNTSS	Journal for the Study of the New Testament Supplement Series
JSP	*Journal for the Study of the Pseudepigrapha*
LCL	Loeb Classical Library (London: Heinemann, and Cambridge, MA: Harvard University)
MeyerK	H. A. W. Meyer, *Kritisch-exegetischer Kommentar über das Neue Testament*
NICNT	New International Commentary on the New Testament
NPNF[1]	A Select Library of the Nicene and Post-Nicene Fathers of the Christian Church, First Series (ed. P. Schaff and H. Wace; 14 vols.; Grand Rapids: Eerdmans, 1956)
NPNF[2]	A Select Library of the Nicene and Post-Nicene Fathers of the Christian Church, Second Series (ed. P. Schaff and H. Wace; 14 vols.; Grand Rapids: Eerdmans, 1956)
NTS	*New Testament Studies*
PG	Patrologiae Graeca (ed. J. P. Migne; 162 vols.; Paris, 1857-66)
SBLDS	Society of Biblical Literature Dissertation Series
SBT	Studies in Biblical Theology
SJT	*Scottish Journal of Theology*

SBLMS	Society of Biblical Literature Monograph Series
TDNT	*Theological Dictionary of the New Testament* (ed. G. Kittel and G. Friedrich; 10 vols.; trans. G. Bromiley; Grand Rapids: Eerdmans, 1964-76)
WTJ	*Westminster Theological Journal*
VC	*Vigiliae christianae*

Abbreviations of classical literature follow the *Oxford Classical Dictionary* wherever possible.

Acknowledgements

I wish to thank those who have been of inestimable help in the researching and writing of this dissertation. First and foremost, I am indebted to Dr. Luke Timothy Johnson, my advisor, who devoted many days to reading and critiquing drafts of my work from proposal to finished product. His contribution to this dissertation in terms of both scholarly acumen and emotional support has truly earned him the title *Doktorvater*. My debt of gratitude extends to the rest of my committee -- Dr. Carl R. Holladay, Dr. Vernon K. Robbins, Dr. Arthur Wainwright, and Dr. Louise Pratt -- who offered helpful suggestions both at the dissertation proposal and the final colloquium. I thank Dr. Robbins for taking the time to read and respond at length to an early draft of the dissertation.

Emory University has been most generous in its support of my education and research. That I have been freed from much financial anxiety by their support, especially by the additional fifth-year funding in the form of a Teaching Fellowship, has contributed much to the timely completion of this work.

Material in Chapters four, five, and six first appeared, in abbreviated form, in "Despising Shame: A Cultural-Anthropological Investigation of the Epistle to the Hebrews," *JBL* 113 (1994) 439-61. Material from chapter five has been published in abbreviated form in "Exchanging Favor for Wrath: Apostasy in Hebrews and Patron-Client Relationships," *JBL* 115 (1996) 95-120. The material is included here with permission of the Society of Biblical Literature. Material from chapter three first appeared in expanded form in "The Wisdom of Ben Sira: Honor, Shame, and the Maintenance of Minority Cultural Values," *CBQ* 58 (1996), included here with the permission of the Catholic Biblical Association, and in "The Noble Contest: Honor, Shame, and the Rhetorical Strategy of *4 Maccabees*," *JSP* 15 (1995), included here with the permission of Sheffield Academic press. I am grateful to Dr. Jouette Bassler, Father Joseph Jensen, and Mrs. Jean Allen for their generosity in allowing me to publish this material in this new context.

I wish finally to acknowledge the unwavering support of my wife, Donna Jean, whose love, encouragement, understanding, and commitment to this project helped me to keep my eyes forward and persevere.

for my parents,

J. Arthur and Dorothy deSilva,

with love and gratitude

CHAPTER ONE

Hebrews and Honor Cultures

The author of the Epistle to the Hebrews reflected deeply on the death of Jesus. For much of his exhortation, however, he speaks only of the positive effects of this death, and omits mention of Jesus' manner of death -- the form of execution and its negative connotations. Thus, Jesus' death is a tasting of death on behalf of all people (2:9) and is clearly the cause of the exalted position the Son enjoys (διὰ τὸ πάθημα τοῦ θανάτου δόξῃ καὶ τιμῇ ἐστεφανωμένον, 2:9). Jesus' death was a battle, in which the Enemy was destroyed and the slaves set free (ἵνα διὰ τοῦ θανάτου καταργήσῃ τὸν τὸ κράτος ἔχοντα τοῦ θανάτου, τοῦτ' ἔστιν τὸν διάβολον, καὶ ἀπαλλάξῃ τούτους, ὅσοι φόβῳ θανάτου διὰ παντὸς τοῦ ζῆν ἔνοχοι ἦσαν δουλείας, 2:14-15). Jesus' death was of great benefit, since through it he became the source of an eternal salvation to all who obey him (ἔμαθεν ἀφ' ὧν ἔπαθεν τὴν ὑπακοήν, καὶ τελειωθεὶς ἐγένετο πᾶσιν τοῖς ὑπακούουσιν αὐτῷ αἴτιος σωτηρίας αἰωνίου, 5:8-9). Finally, Jesus' death is a "better sacrifice" (9:23-24), which cleanses the heavenly sanctuary, institutes a new and "better covenant" (8:6), removes sins and cleanses consciences (9:14; 10:10) by opening up a new way to the throne of God (10:19-20). Again, the author links Jesus' death and his exaltation (οὗτος δὲ μίαν ὑπὲρ ἁμαρτιῶν προσενέγκας θυσίαν εἰς τὸ διηνεκὲς ἐκάθισεν ἐν δεξιᾷ τοῦ θεοῦ, 10:12).

Reading only so far, one might suspect the author of sublimating Jesus' death, of failing to deal with the realities of Jesus' execution in Palestine. But when Jesus, at the climax of a catalogue of faithful forebears, is held up as an example for the addressees' consideration, the author states boldly what he appeared to have avoided saying before. Prior and prerequisite to enthronement, Jesus "endured a cross, having despised shame" (ὑπέμεινεν σταυρὸν αἰσχύνης καταφρονήσας, 12:2). The author's words do not focus

1

on the obvious physical pain of crucifixion. Greater than the pain, he suggests, is the humiliation of the cross. But what does it mean for Jesus to have "despised shame"? How are we to understand this description against the background of Greco-Roman culture? Moreover, what does it mean to present such an attitude as exemplary?

Jesus does not stand within Hebrews as an isolated model for "despising shame." He is linked with the exemplars of faith in chapter 11, who in large measure are held together by a shared disregard for certain cultural norms of the honorable and shameful (11:13-16, 24-26, 35b-38). Indeed, the community addressed has itself been and is urged once more to be willing to bear social disgrace for the sake of the "confession" and the "hope" which lies before them. These preliminary observations suggest that language related to honor and dishonor is important for understanding at least one aspect of what Hebrews is attempting to accomplish for its readers/hearers. Attention to this dimension of language may in fact lead us closer to solving some long-standing riddles concerning the situation and purpose of Hebrews.

1 An Overview of Honor and Shame Language in Hebrews

Hebrews abounds in terms expressing honor, acts of honoring, and being honored. In the opening chapters δόξα and τιμή, the two words which most commonly refer to "reputation" and "honor" in Greek literature, appear several times.[1] In 1:3, Christ, the Son, is introduced as reflecting the δόξα of God;[2] in 2:9, Jesus is presented as having fulfilled the words of Ps 8:5, being crowned with "high repute" and "honor" (δόξῃ καὶ τιμῇ); in a comparison with Moses (3:3), the author claims that Jesus is "worthy of greater honor than Moses" (πλείονος γὰρ οὗτος δόξης παρὰ Μωυσῆν ἠξίωται) even as the builder of a house has greater honor (τιμή) than the house; the high priesthood is described as a τιμή, and Jesus' appointment to this office represents God's act of honoring him (5:5-

---

[1] For the close semantic relationship between these two terms, one may refer to Plutarch, *Roman Questions* 13 (*Mor.* 266F-267A, LCL): "Why do they also sacrifice to the god called 'Honor' with the head uncovered? One might translate Honor as 'renown' (δόξα) or 'honour' (τιμή). Is it because renown (δόξα) is a brilliant thing, conspicuous, and widespread, and for the reason that they uncover in the presence of good and honoured men, is it for this same reason that they also worship the god who is named for 'honour'?"

[2] The very presentation of Jesus as "Son" relates to honor, as the son shares in the honor of the father: ˊΗ γὰρ δόξα ἀνθρώπου ἐκ τιμῆς πατρὸς αὐτοῦ (Sir 3:11).

6) rather than a self-aggrandizement. The honor given to the Son is expressed in gestures: the angels prostrate themselves before him in acknowledgement of superior status (1:6); God anoints the Son (1:9) and crowns him (2:7, 9), two actions which, in honoring the head, honor the person; Jesus is invited to sit at the right hand of God, thus (by allusion to Ps 110:1) holding the place of honor and prestige *par excellence* in the Jewish and Christian cosmos-construction (1:13; 8:1; 10:12; 12:2). He awaits the final establishment of his position of ultimate and uncontested pre-eminence in the subjection of his enemies "under his feet," a place signifying submission (1:13; 2:8b; 10:13).

Hebrews' prominent use of the rhetorical scheme called *synkrisis* or "comparison," a feature of epideictic rhetoric, fits within such language concerning honor. Aristotle writes of the person whom one would praise in an epideictic speech:

And you must compare him with illustrious personages, for it affords ground for amplification and is noble, if he can be proved better than men of worth. Amplification is with good reason ranked as one of the forms of praise, since it consists in superiority, and superiority is one of the things that are noble. (*Art of Rhetoric* 1.9.38-39; LCL)

Jesus is consistently compared with eminent figures of the Jewish tradition -- angels in 1:4-13, Moses in 3:1-6, the Levitical priesthood and especially the High Priest in the extended comparison of 7:1-10:18 -- and in every case is shown to be superior. Indeed, the adjective κρείττων appears repeatedly throughout the letter (1:4; 7:7, 19, 22; 8:6; 9:23; 10:34; 11:16, 35, 40; 12:24), pointing to an epideictic element in the argument. Rhetorical theory confirms that the aims of these comparisons are the establishment of the superior worth (honor) of Christ as well as the greater expediency of Christ's mediation as High Priest.

The author of Hebrews also employs language of honor when speaking of those associated with Jesus. The destiny of the "many children" led by Christ is described as δόξα (2:10). Indeed, the very designation of believers as "children," who are called "partners of Christ" (μέτοχοι τοῦ Χριστοῦ, 3:14), the Son, points to a high level of honor. The association between Christ and the believers, as between God and the patriarchs, gives the lesser a share in the honor of the greater -- an association of grace, in that Christ "is not ashamed" (οὐκ ἐπαισχύνεται) to be called our brother (2:11), as God "is not ashamed" to be associated with the patriarchs as their God (11:16). Finally, there are a number of verbs and nouns related to the proper honoring of God: "worship" (λατρεύειν) in 9:14 and 12:28, and "piety and reverence" (εὐλαβεία and δέος) in 12:28.

Equally prominent in Hebrews are words and actions relating to dishonor. The addressees themselves have been the victims of the loss of their honor at the hands of a hostile society. At some point in the past they had been exposed to public shame (θεατριζόμενοι, 10:33). They have suffered both verbal assaults on their standing and physical abuse of their person (ὀνειδισμοῖς τε καὶ θλίψεσιν). Some of them, at least, also suffered the loss of their property (10:34), and with it an important measure of their status and means of maintaining and increasing their honor (e.g. through benefactions). Some of their group appear still to be afflicted with imprisonment or maltreatment (13:3), and the addressees are called to share with them in their time of degradation.

Just as a great deal of language is dedicated to affirming the honor of the Son, so also is there a substantial amount of admonition against dishonoring the Son (or God). This theme is announced in 2:3, as the author points out that greater honor implies greater punishment for affronts to that honor, such as disregarding (ἀμελήσαντες) the message brought by Christ. The example of the wilderness generation (chapters 3 and 4), and the exhortation proceeding from it, concerns the consequences of dishonoring God through lack of trust and disobedience. God's response of "wrath" (προσώχθισα, ὀργή, 3:10, 11) signals a response to an affront. Aristotle notes:

> Let us then define anger (ὀργή) as a longing, accompanied by pain, for a real or apparent revenge (τιμωρία) for a real or apparent slight (ὀλιγωρία). (Rh. 2.2.1)

> Men are angry at slights from those by whom they think they have a right to expect to be well treated; such are those on whom they have conferred or are conferring benefits (εὖ πεποίηκεν ἢ ποιεῖ)...and all those whom they desire, or did desire, to benefit. (Rh. 2.2.8)

Apostasy is equated with dishonoring Christ publicly (παραδειγματίζω, 6:6); such a willful act of "sin" is described more fully in 10:29 as a trampling underfoot of the Son of God, an estimation of the sanctifying blood as common, and an outrage to the Spirit of grace. The ultimate result of such an act is the complete degradation of the offender, who is "worthy" only of punishment.[3] Similarly, the addressees are warned, in

---

[3] "How much worse punishment do you think will be deserved by the one who tramples underfoot the Son of God, regards the blood of the covenant, by which he or she is sanctified, as profane, and outrages the Spirit of favor" (πόσῳ δοκεῖτε χείρονος ἀξιωθήσεται τιμωρίας ὁ τὸν υἱὸν τοῦ θεοῦ καταπατήσας καὶ τὸ αἷμα τῆς διαθήκης κοινὸν ἡγησάμενος, ἐν ᾧ ἡγιάσθη, καὶ τὸ πνεῦμα τῆς χάριτος ἐνυβρίσας;, 10:29).

the words of Prov 3:11, not to belittle the discipline of the Lord (μὴ ὀλιγώρει, 12:5) and not to disregard the One who speaks to them from heaven (Βλέπετε μὴ παραιτήσησθε, 12:25). More striking is the way language of dishonor attaches to Christ and to earlier heroes of faith. Hebrews presents the figure of the crucified Christ, who "endured the cross, despising shame, and sat down at the right hand of God (ὑπέμεινε σταυρὸν αἰσχύνης καταφρονήσας ἐν δεξιᾷ τε τοῦ θρόνου τοῦ θεοῦ κεκάθικεν)." In a culture sensitive to honor-rating and reputation, holding up as exemplary one who "despised shame" commands attention. Jesus stands, furthermore, as the *climactic* example. The author presents other figures who have chosen what was of less esteem in the world's eyes in their pursuit of the reward promised by God. Abraham left his homeland and embraced the status of "foreigner" and "sojourner" while awaiting the promise. But in so departing, he chooses dishonor from the world's point of view. Indeed, sojourning could be considered a reproach,[4] and the very terms "foreigner" and "immigrant" (τὸν ξένον καὶ τὸν μέτοικον) could be used as terms of abuse (Plutarch, *De Exilio*, 17 [*Mor.* 607 A]). Moses occupies a position of very high social standing as the son of a daughter of Pharaoh (11:24), a standing increased by his access to the θησαυροὶ Αἰγύπτου (11:26). He chooses, however, dishonor -- indeed, willingly relinquishes worldly honor -- in order to obtain God's reward. For him, the "reproach of Christ" (τὸν ὀνειδισμὸν τοῦ Χριστοῦ, 10:26) is accounted as a greater asset.[5] Finally, the author of Hebrews presents another group of low-status examples in 11:35b-38. These have suffered society's disgrace in the form of physical abuse and censure (11:36-38). This list parades those who by society's standards were utterly disgraced and without honor. Hebrews, however, introduces an ironic evaluation -- ὧν οὐκ ἦν ἄξιος ὁ κόσμος ("of whom the world was not worthy") -- which challenges the world's system of honor and values.

This presentation of the raw data concerning honor and dishonor in Hebrews is far from exhaustive, but serves to show how pervasive it is, and to stimulate some questions: What does the author seek to accomplish through the use of honor and shame language? Are the occurrences of such language unconnected, or do they connect with one another to form meaningful developments in argumentation? How can this language help the modern reader to uncover the strategy and program of Hebrews as directed toward first-century Mediterranean people who were, for the most

---

[4] Cf. Lucian, *My Native Land*, 8 (LCL): "for thus to sojourn is a reproach (ὄνειδος γὰρ τὸ τῆς ξενιτείας)!"

[5] The meaning of the problematic phrase "reproach of Christ" will be addressed later in this study.

part, concerned about honor (both their own and that of others)? Rather surprisingly, these questions have not previously been rigorously pursued in the history of interpretation.

2 History of Investigation of Honor and Shame Language in Hebrews

Commentaries generally are ill equipped to provide a coherent and connected interpretation of a text viewed from any particular perspective. The multiplication of minutiae prevents most authors of commentaries from pursuing such an enterprise. Hence it is not entirely surprising that no commentary has sufficiently explored the meaning of Hebrews from the perspective of an honor/shame culture. But neither has there been a monograph or article which attempts to construct an interpretation of Hebrews through examination of the language relating to honor and dishonor. Nevertheless, the present study does not move in a vacuum. The following paragraphs survey the contributions already made to the discussion.

The importance of shame and humiliation language has been explored at key places in the text. Most authors agree that humiliation or disgrace is a prominent component of the addressees' experience as Christians.[6] Moffatt even notes that shame was "an experience which our author evidently felt keenly."[7] Thompson relates this experience to the author's use of the contest imagery in 12:1-4, found also in Philo and 4 Maccabees. The image gives a positive interpretation of the persecutions and acts of violence suffered by a minority culture.[8] He further relates the experience of public shame to "the very nature of faith," parenthetically linking 10:33 to the other occurrences of ὀνειδισμός in 11:26 and 13:13.[9] John Chrysostom (d. 408) anticipates these insights. Trained in classical rhetoric and belonging to the honor/shame culture of the fourth-century

[6] Franz Delitzsch, *Commentary on the Epistle to the Hebrews* (2 vols. Tr. T. L. Kingsbury; Edinburgh: Clark, 1871), 192; Ceslaus Spicq, *L'Épître aux Hébreux*, (2 vols. EBib. Paris: Gabalda, 1952), 2.328-29; H. W. Attridge, *The Epistle to the Hebrews*, (Philadelphia: Fortress, 1989), 299; W. L. Lane, *Hebrews 9-13* (WBC, 47B; Dallas: Word Books, 1991), 299.

[7] J. Moffatt, *Hebrews* (ICC; Edinburgh: T. & T. Clark, 1924), 153.

[8] J. W. Thompson, *The Beginnings of Christian Philosophy: The Epistle to the Hebrews* (CBQMS, 13; Washington, DC: Catholic Biblical Association of America, 1982), 64.

[9] Thompson, *Beginnings*, 78; also Otto Michel, *Der Brief an die Hebräer* (12th ed. MeyerK 13; Göttingen: Vandenhoeck & Ruprecht, 1960), 273.

Mediterranean world, he sees nuances that would not be recognized again for fifteen centuries. Commenting on 10:32-34 he writes,

> Powerful is the exhortation from deeds [already done]: for he who begins a work ought to go forward and add to it....And he who encourages, does thus especially encourage them from their own example....Moreover he did not say 'temptations' but 'fight', which is an expression of commendation (ἐγκωμίου ὄνομα) and of very great praise.[10]

Chrysostom alerts the modern reader to the rhetorical practice (seen also in Tacitus' *Agricola* 34) of encouraging a group of addressees to pursue a task by citing their former investment in it. Chrysostom also notes that the author of Hebrews strategically uses a certain vocabulary, namely the imagery of the "contest" (ἄθλησις), to evoke images of noble and honorable activity, rather than vocabulary which either lacks this encomiastic connotation or possesses its opposite ("tribulations" or "trials").

A number of authors have also seen that the examples of faith in chapter 11 have some pertinence to the experience of suffering and shame on the part of the community.[11] Peterson notes that "the fact that Jesus 'despised the shame' of the cross and 'endured from sinners such hostility against himself' will have its own particular relevance for the readers, in view of their past experience (10:32-4), and what they may reasonably have expected again (10:35ff; 13:13)."[12] Moreover, several authors connect the examples of faith -- including the community's own past endurance -- with the hortatory intent of the author. John Calvin, another rhetorically trained interpreter, recognizes the hortatory character of 10:32-35:

> It is shameful, having begun well, to faint in the midst of the course; but baser still to go backwards when you have already made great progress....Moreover, he increases the effect of the exhortation by saying that they had performed glorious exploits even then when they

---

[10] Chrysostom, *Homilies on Hebrews*, in *NPNF¹* 14:461; Migne, *PG* 63.148-49.

[11] Thompson, *Beginnings*, 66; Lane, *Hebrews 9-13*, 374.

[12] David Peterson, *Hebrews and Perfection: An Examination of the Concept of Perfection in the 'Epistle to the Hebrews'* (SNTSMS, 47; Cambridge: Cambridge University, 1982), 170.

were as yet raw recruits: the more shame then would it be if they should faint now after having been exercised by long practice.[13]

Calvin's own choice of expression here, namely the phrase "It is shameful" (corresponding to the commonly encountered classical formulation, αἰσχρὸν δε), shows that his own training in classical rhetoric and literature has made him sensitive to the honor/shame dimension of biblical texts. H.-F. Weiß notes that Moses' choice of suffering with the people of God informs the paraenesis of 13:3, where the addressees are called to "remember those in prison".[14] Thompson proposes a correlation between the example of the pilgrims in chapter 11 and the pattern prescribed for the community in 13:13, a life which may involve shame.[15]

Finally, the example of Christ himself (which Weiß considers to have "a paraenetic potential"),[16] who "endured the cross, despising the shame," speaks to the community's own experience of dishonor. Christ's attitude, which the readers are called to emulate, is usually interpreted as "disdaining to shrink from shame,"[17] rising above the feeling of shame in order to perform one's duty,[18] braving or being unafraid of enduring the shame,[19] or stoically disregarding suffering and death.[20] Michel comes closest to the ancient meaning when he interprets αἰσχύνης καταφρονήσας as "consider as nothing, be unconcerned about" (my translation).[21] Here again, the most valuable guides to discerning the meaning of the text come from the third and fourth centuries, from readers of the text who are much closer to Hebrews in time, place, and culture. Gregory of Nyssa, for example, shows in *Contra Eunomium* 3.5 that Christ could despise the dishonorable reputation among human beings on account of his belonging to a higher court of reputation, indeed on account of his being the source of reputation (οὗτος ὁ τῆς ἐν ἀνθρώποις αἰσχύνης καταφρονήσας διὰ τὸ εἶναι τῆς δόξης κύριος).[22] Origen also recognizes two courts of

[13] John Calvin, *Calvin's Commentary on the Epistle to the Hebrews* (Tr. "by a beneficed Clergyman of the Church of England"; London: Cornish and Co, 1842), 32.

[14] Hans-Freidrich Weiß, *Der Brief an die Hebräer* (15th ed. MeyerK 13; Göttingen: Vandenhoeck & Ruprecht, 1991), 606.

[15] Thompson, *Beginnings*, 148-49.

[16] Weiß, *Hebräer*, 639 (au. trans.).

[17] Delitzsch, *Hebrews*, 306.

[18] Moffatt, *Hebrews*, 236.

[19] Lane, *Hebrews 9-13*, 414.

[20] Attridge, *Hebrews*, 358.

[21] Michel, *Hebräer*, 294: "für nichts achten, sich nicht kümmern um."

[22] Migne, *PG* 45.708 B 4-6.

reputation in a phrase taken from his *Fragmenta in Psalmos*, 37.12.4-5 (*TLG*): καταφρονήσας γὰρ τῆς παρ ᾿ ἀνθρώποις αἰσχύνης. John Chrysostom perceives that the author sets Jesus forward as an example specifically of disregarding reputation granted by the society: "But what is, 'Despising the shame'? He chose, he means, that ignominious death. For suppose that He died. Why also ignominiously? For no other reason, but to teach us to make no account of glory from human beings."[23] These authors, commenting directly on Heb 12:2, show that in the Greco-Roman culture one could appeal to the example of Jesus as a basis for distancing oneself from concern about one's honor rating in the eyes of society, and thus orienting oneself wholly to the approval of God and living solely according to what God praises and honors.

Several authors have also noted that the author uses the rhetorical device of shaming the audience at 5:11-14:

> About this we have much to say which is hard to explain, since you have become dull of hearing. For though by this time you ought to be teachers, you need some one to teach you again the first principles of God's word. You need milk, not solid food; for every one who lives on milk is unskilled in the word of righteousness, for he is a child. But solid food is for the mature, for those who have their faculties trained by practice to distinguish good from evil.

While some take this as a genuine description of the addressees,[24] others perceive that the audience would respond to the author's exhortations all the more forcefully after such an assault on their status as "mature Christians."[25] This is a step towards appreciating the ways in which the author designs his "word of exhortation" to catch the readers by their φιλοτιμία, their "love of honor."

Likewise in 2:10, the author describes the destiny of the "many sons" as "glory" (δόξα). Jesus' present honor will be the believers' honor at some future time.[26] L. D. Hurst has taken an important step in discerning that "the point of the extravaganza of chapter one is to lead the readers of

---

[23] *NPNF¹* 14:493; Migne, *PG* 63.194: Τί δέ ἐστιν, Αἰσχύνης καταφρονήσας; Τὸν ἐπονείδιστον, φησὶς, εἵλετο θάνατον. ῎Εστω γὰρ, ἀπέθνησκε· τί καὶ ἐπονειδίστως; Δι ᾿ οὐδὲν ἕτερον, ἀλλ ᾿ ἡμᾶς διδάσκων μηδὲν ἡγεῖσθαι τὴν παρ ᾿ ἀνθρώπων δόξαν.

[24] E.g. Delitzsch, *Hebrews*, 259; Michel, *Hebräer*, 140.

[25] E.g. Calvin, *Hebrews*, 58; Bengel, *Gnomon Novi Testamenti* (London: Nutt, Williams, and Norgate, 1862 [1773]), 828; Moffatt, *Hebrews*, 70; Attridge, *Hebrews*, 157; W. Lane, *Hebrews 1-8* (WBC 47A; Dallas: Word, 1991), 135.

[26] Delitzsch, *Hebrews*, 117; Moffatt, *Hebrews*, 24; Michel, *Hebräer*, 78; Lane, *Hebrews*, 48; Weiß, *Hebräer*, 205.

the epistle to the glory of mankind foretold in Psalm 8 and explored in chapter two."[27] The author's interest in expanding on the honor and status of Jesus is thus seen to be related not to a polemic against Judaism (as the potential choice of apostates within the community), but to the desire for honor on the part of Christians.

Another important function of the author's development of Christ's position is to heighten the effect of 10:29 ("How much worse punishment do you think will be deserved by those who have trampled upon the Son of God"). Many commentators[28] have noted the sharpness of this statement, and some have ventured to make connections with other passages speaking of Christ's exalted honor and the danger of God's satisfaction.[29] Héring notes the important parallel with the example of the wilderness generation in chapter three.[30] Indeed, the wilderness generation and Esau together present negative examples of those who have dishonored God and who therefore experienced God's anger rather than God's benefits. Such examples of despising God, in effect, are as important in the author's exhortation as the examples of "despising shame."

Finally, there are scattered comments in the literature which show some appreciation for the author's aim of overturning the dominant culture's evaluation of the honorable or disgraceful, and of the means by which a minority culture can maintain a counter-evaluation. While a few authors pass over the remark in 11:38 as "a splendid aside"[31] or parenthetical remark,[32] a number of commentators note the reversal of estimation in 11:38 -- those who were mistreated and who went about wandering in the margins of society were those "of whom the world was not worthy."[33] Weiß goes so far as to link this with 11:7 as "a condemnation of the world."[34] Thompson has noted that one who is "oriented to the unseen and abiding world," such as the person of faith would be (13:14) is able to assume "a stance of indifference to this

---

[27] L. D. Hurst, "The Christology of Hebrews 1 and 2," in L. D. Hurst and N. T. Wright, *The Glory of Christ in the New Testament: Studies in Christology* (Oxford: Clarendon, 1987), 163-64.

[28] E.g. Calvin, *Hebrews*, 132; Attridge, *Hebrews*, 294; Lane, *Hebrews 9-13*, 294.

[29] Delitzsch, *Hebrews*, 188; Michel, *Hebräer*, 236.

[30] Jean Héring, *The Epistle to the Hebrews* (Tr. A. W. Heathcote; London: Epworth, 1970), 94.

[31] Moffatt, *Hebrews*, 189.

[32] Attridge, *Hebrews*, 351.

[33] Delitzsch, *Hebrews*, 289; Spicq, *Hébreux*, 2.366; Michel, *Hebräer*, 283.

[34] Weiß, *Hebräer*, 623-24.

world."[35] While Thompson applies this to indifference with regard to one's material losses and sufferings in this world, it would be equally applicable to indifference with regard to the evaluation of the Christian by the representatives of this world.

These more or less unconnected remarks, together with some few attempts at coordination and linking, provide a background for the present study, which seeks to provide a thorough investigation of how the author of Hebrews constructs an alternate arena of honor and dishonor in order to allow his addressees to pursue honor and secure a sense of themselves as honorable specifically by continuing in their Christian commitments, and to inspire fear in the readers of dishonoring the One who is supremely the "significant other" by a misguided quest to attain approval of the transitory "court of reputation" of this world.

3 Honor, Shame, and New Testament Interpretation

This study also locates itself within continuing theoretical and methodological discussions. Recent years have seen a number of attempts to interpret the New Testament in the light of cultural-anthropological insights, particularly in light of the conception of the Mediterranean world as a culture in which honor and shame are "pivotal values."[36] The stronger proponents, indeed the pioneers, of this line of critical research claim that attention to the dimension of honor and shame in these texts allows the interpreter to "see as the natives see, ...value what they value; ...understand how and why they act the way they do."[37] Such zealous claims, however, have left other biblical scholars unconvinced of the utility of cultural- anthropological models. They question the adequacy of modern social-scientific constructions for the interpretation of ancient texts. Frequently, they suggest that forcing everything in the ancient literature into the one axis of honor and shame results in the suppression of other equally important dimensions of language.

A study of honor and shame language in an ancient Mediterranean text must therefore proceed critically on two fronts. It must first deal justly with the intricacies and complexities of the text under investigation. As E. R. Dodds said with reference to any investigation of Greek culture, it

---

[35] Thompson, *Beginnings*, 69.

[36] B. Malina, *The New Testament World: Insights from Cultural Anthropology* (Atlanta: John Knox, 1981), 25.

[37] J. Neyrey, "John 18-19: Honor and Shame in the Passion Narrative," *Semeia*, in press.

"must resist the temptation to simplify what is not simple."[38] At the least, determining the language which pertains to matters of honor or dishonor within the text must be accompanied by the recognition of other dimensions of language reflecting other concerns and values. Such discrimination will make it possible to investigate the relationship, if any, between these multiple dimensions, and to arrive at a more nuanced understanding of how honor and dishonor work as values in the text and in the culture more broadly. And, as with all "new" approaches to critical studies, the method and its models must be tested against the available data. In this case, the view of the first-century Mediterranean world as an honor/shame culture and especially the claim that honor and shame provide *the* "pivotal values" must be evaluated and modified in light of the rhetorical strategies of specific texts as well as the wider-ranging discussions of honor and shame in ancient Greek literature.

The present study takes up an investigation of ancient Greek culture already begun and not yet finished. Several classicists and cultural anthropologists have contributed to the understanding of the first-century Mediterranean world as an honor-shame culture. In his *Merit and Responsibility*, a work regarded by many biblical scholars as foundational for investigation of honor and shame in the Greek world, A. W. H. Adkins develops a picture of the Homeric world as a culture highly sensitive to, and competitive for, honor.[39] Honor as a pivotal value, he argues, persists into the world of fourth-century Athens (as seen especially in the tragedies of Aeschylus, Euripides, and Sophocles). Adkins shows also how the definition of honorable action changes in situations where cooperation (e.g., between host and guest) is called for rather than competition. Adkins acknowledges the importance of other axes of value, but stresses

---

[38] E. R. Dodds, *The Greeks and the Irrational* (Berkeley: University of California Press, 1966), 49.

[39] Aristotle himself thus characterizes the society of the Homeric epics (*Nicomachean Ethics* 3.8.1-3; LCL): "First, as most closely resembling true Courage, comes the citizen's courage. Citizen troops appear to endure dangers because of the legal penalties and the reproach attaching to cowardice, and the honours awarded to bravery; hence those races appear to be the bravest among which cowards are degraded and brave men held in honour (παρ᾿ οἷς οἱ δειλοὶ ἄτιμοι καὶ οἱ ἀνδρεῖοι ἔντιμοι). It is this citizen courage which inspires the heroes portrayed by Homer, like Diomedes and Hector.... This type of courage most closely resembles the one described before, because it is prompted by a virtue, namely the sense of shame, and by the desire for something noble, namely honour, and the wish to avoid the disgrace of being reproached (δι᾿ αἰδῶ γὰρ καὶ διὰ καλοῦ ὄρεξιν [τιμῆς γὰρ] καὶ φυγὴν ὀνείδους, αἰσχροῦ ὄντος)."

forcefully that the evaluation of some act as honorable/noble or dishonorable is a final verdict:

> The Chorus says of Apollo's advocacy of Orestes' killing of Clytemnestra that it was performed justly, *dikāi*; to which Electra replies, 'But not honourably', *kalōs d' ou*. Naturally...this settles the matter, for there is no higher term of value to invoke.[40]

Julian Pitt-Rivers' seminal essay, "Honour and Social Status,"[41] has also provided an essential foundation for modern cultural-anthropological reflection on honor and shame in the Mediterranean. The following excerpts from this essay provide a fairly coherent summary of the basic definitions of honor and how sensitivity to honor affects actions:

> Honour is the value of a person in his own eyes, but also in the eyes of his society. It is his estimation of his own worth, his *claim* to pride, but it is also acknowledgement of that claim, his excellence recognized by society....[I]n a complex society where consensus is not uniform, the individual's worth is not the same in the view of one group as in that of another....If honour establishes status, the converse is also true, and where status is conferred by birth, honour derives not only from individual reputation but from antecedence....The claim to excel is always relative. It is always implicitly the claim to excel over others. Hence honour is the basis of precedence....The victor in any competition for honour finds his reputation enhanced by the humiliation of the vanquished....We should [note] the intimate relation between honour and the physical person. The rituals by which honour is formally bestowed [e.g.] involve a ceremony which commonly centres upon the head of the protagonist....Public opinion forms...a tribunal before which the claimants to honour are brought, 'the court of reputation' as it has been called, and against its judgements there is no redress....Social groups possess a collective honour in which their members participate....[The] head is responsible for the honour of all its members.[42]

Pitt-Rivers sketches a picture of the Mediterranean person as one who knows and values the self only in connection with a social group and its ascription of status or reputation. Mediterranean culture appears as

---

[40] A. W. Adkins, *Merit and Responsibility: A Study in Greek Values* (Oxford: Oxford University Press, 1960). 185.

[41] Julian Pitt-Rivers, "Honour and Social Status," in J. G. Peristiany (ed.), *Honour and Shame: The Values of Mediterranean Society* (Chicago: University of Chicago Press, 1966), 21-77.

[42] Pitt-Rivers, "Honour," 21-25, 27, 35-36.

"agonistic:" people (particularly the males) engage publically in contests for honor.

Bruce Malina applies the definitions and descriptions of Pitt-Rivers directly to specific interactions described in the New Testament.[43] He claims that attention to markers of status, contests for honor, acts of naming and labelling, and so forth, open up the New Testament documents (particularly the Gospels) to an authentic first-century Mediterranean reading. He joins this conviction to a model of dyadic personality and the perception of limited goods. Malina, together with Jerome Neyrey, has restated the model and used it to describe how in Luke-Acts honor is ascribed or attained, displayed, held collectively, and divided between genders.[44] Reading Luke's narrative with special sensitivity to issues of honor and shame helps the interpreter to examine Jesus' life "more accurately," particularly as a "career fraught with conflicts."[45] The main benefit of this model, according to Malina and Neyrey, is that it "helps us to appreciate the agonistic quality of that world, and it offers us a literary and social form (challenge-riposte) to interpret the conflicts."

Neyrey further examines the passion narrative in John's gospel from the perspective of honor, dishonor, and the competition for honor. He interprets the motives, actions, and verbal exchanges as part of a plan on the part of the scribes and priests to regain their prestige (honor) by securing the utter humiliation of their opponent, who has been draining away a limited supply of honor. Most noteworthy, however, is Neyrey's sensitivity to the different evaluations of this contest from the perspective of the different characters within the narrative itself and the perspective of the readers, who know that Jesus' crucifixion was part of a "status-elevation ritual" rather than a "status-degradation ritual." He notes, "the gospel inculcates an ironic point of view that death and shame mean glory and honor. Thus the mock coronation of Jesus, which in the eyes of outsiders means shame, truly betokens honor from the viewpoint of insiders."[46] Neyrey claims that such a reading yields an impressive gain: "when we see through the lens of honor and shame, we truly see as the natives see. We value what they value; we understand how and why they act the way they do. We appreciate, moreover, what really drives these

---

[43] Malina, *World*, 25-51.

[44] B. Malina and J. H. Neyrey, "Honor and Shame in Luke-Acts: Pivotal Values of the Mediterranean World," in J. H. Neyrey (ed.), *The Social World of Luke-Acts: Models for Interpretation* (Peabody: Hendrickson, 1991), 25-66.

[45] Malina and Neyrey, "Honor," 64.

[46] Neyrey, "John 18-19," 17.

persons."[47] The lens of honor and shame has been subsequently applied to almost every document of the New Testament, either in the exploration of a narrow problem or in a wider exploration of an entire text.[48]

There are some widely recognized hazards in this line of research, particularly as it appears in the less careful application of these models to the New Testament texts by those who have not first familiarized themselves with the subtleties of honor and shame in the Greco-Roman world. Malina and Neyrey borrow extensively from classicists who have worked primarily with Homeric materials, and from cultural anthropologists who have worked in the study of modern Mediterranean cultures. The assumption of a static cultural system from Homer to present life in the Cypriot Highlands is at least open to question. Additionally, Malina and Neyrey work with narrative texts and apply their models largely to the social interactions described in those narratives, e.g. conflict stories between Pharisees and Jesus. When applied to narrative interactions -- especially the interactions of social equals -- the model appears to work fairly well. The model becomes somewhat less useful when one turns to the interpretation of epistolary literature, although one can readily see contests of honor *behind* some of the letters (such as 2 Corinthians). There remains the need for some reflection on how to approach the way honor and shame function in discursive texts, a need addressed by the present study of the discursive text of Hebrews.

Perhaps more basic is the complaint against the assumption of Mediterranean society as an undifferentiated honor culture in which "all groups are concerned about their honor."[49] Anthony J. Blasi observes that "when vastly different language groups, religions, systems of productive relations, nationalities, political structures, etc., are lumped together, the hypothetical unit ('Mediterranean culture') is a geographical prejudice in the eye of the beholder, not a scientific object."[50] Another basic objection to these analyses is the elevation of honor and shame above every other possible axis of value. Considerations of honor are often juxtaposed with considerations of expediency in deliberative speeches. The values of friendship and love frequently appear without reference to honor. E. R. Dodds explores the rise of guilt as a value comparable to and

---

[47] Neyrey, "John 18-19," 24.

[48] Jerome Neyrey has compiled an extensive bibliography on honor and shame, including several dozen studies in New Testament and Hebrew Scriptures. A noteworthy example is Moxnes' interpretation of this dimension of language in Romans (Halvor Moxnes, "Honour and Righteousness in Romans," *JSNT* 32 [1988] 61-77).

[49] Malina and Neyrey, "Honor," 26.

[50] Anthony J. Blasi, in a letter dated April 26, 1993.

surpassing that of shame in Greek culture. The cultures of the Greco-Roman world weave together a rich tapestry of many values, and one should not assume that in every interaction or consideration "honor" provides the stitch-pattern for the whole.

Abuse of a method does not disqualify the method. There clearly remains, however, the need to define a more careful and nuanced approach to the function and meaning of honor and shame language in New Testament texts, and more realistic expectations as to the results of honor/shame analysis in the interpretation of ancient texts. The present study takes into account the criticisms mentioned above in defining its aims. I will discuss them in reverse order.

First, other important values clearly exist in the Greco-Roman world, as demonstrated by the very existence of three rhetorical genres in both Greek and Latin treatises on rhetoric, each genre concerned with a separate axis of values. Only one genus -- epideictic -- is explicitly concerned with honor and dishonor, or praise and blame. The just and the unjust (forensic) and the expedient and harmful (deliberative) certainly claim positions of importance alongside honor and dishonor. The rhetorical handbooks show that considerations of security could be expected to motivate the hearers of a deliberative speech as well as considerations of honor (*Rhetorica ad Herennium* 3.3). Indeed, at times the orator would expect that considerations of security would triumph over considerations of honor (*Rhet. Her.* 3.4.8) as well as the reverse. Quintillian, while claiming to hold honor as the supreme end (and preferring to think of deliberative oratory as aiming at the honourable rather than the expedient), also affords evidence that people considered safety or advantage to be greater goods than honor:

> As we most often express our views before an ignorant audience, and more especially before popular assemblies, of which the majority is usually uneducated, we must distinguish between what is honourable and what is expedient and conform our utterances to suit ordinary understandings....For there are many who do not admit that what they really believe to be the honourable course is sufficiently advantageous, and are misled by the prospect of advantage into approving courses of the dishonourable nature (*Institutio Oratoria* 8.2-3; LCL).

Similarly, Aristotle describes "happiness" (εὐδαιμονία), the goal of deliberative rhetoric, as made up of a variety of components, "honor" and "reputation" (τιμή, δόξα; *Rh.* 1.5.3) are two among a number of such components, and are not even given first place:

If, then, such is the nature of happiness, its component parts must necessarily be: noble birth, numerous friends, good friends, wealth, good children, numerous children, a good old age; further, bodily excellences, such as health, beauty, strength, stature, fitness for athletic contests, a good reputation, honour, good luck, virtue (*Rh.* 1.5.4).

These same texts demonstrate, however, that considerations of honor and reputation were important factors in the decision-making process (that is, in leading the hearers to respond to a situation in the way proposed by the speaker) and were recognized as components of well-being. As such they deserve the same attention given to other factors which figure prominently in texts. While cases arose in which, against Adkins, a verdict of καλόν or αἰσχρόν did not form an ultimate value judgement against which there was no appeal, for certain people, such as a Sophocles or Quintilian, honor or dishonor were indeed ultimate values, and, generally speaking, considerations of honor or dishonor did play some part in the decision-making process of many inhabitants of the Greek world. The close relationship between epideictic and deliberative rhetoric in the handbooks demonstrates this:

Praise and counsels have a common aspect; for what you might suggest in counselling becomes encomium by a change in the phrase....Accordingly, if you desire to praise, look what you would suggest; if you desire to suggest, look what you would praise (Aristotle, *Rh.* 1.9.35-36).

And if epideictic is only seldom employed by itself independently, still in judicial and deliberative causes extensive sections are often devoted to praise and censure (*Rhet. Her.* 3.8.15).

The very label of καλόν or αἰσχρόν, however, would not be sufficient to motivate all to take a particular course of action.[51]

---

[51] Aristotle believes that only a minority are truly motivated by honor (*Nic. Eth.* 10.9.3-4): "But as it is, we see that although theories have power to stimulate and encourage generous youths, and, given, an inborn nobility of character and a genuine love of what is noble, can make them susceptible to the influence of virtue, yet they are powerless to stimulate the mass of mankind to moral nobility (τοὺ δὲ πολλοὺς ἀδυνατεῖν πρὸς καλοκαγαθίαν προτρέψασθαι). For it is the nature of the many to be amenable to fear but not to a sense of honour (οὐ γὰρ πεφύκασιν αἰδοῖ πειθαρχεῖν ἀλλὰ φόβῳ), and to abstain from evil not because of its baseness (διὰ τὸ αἰσχρόν) but because of the penalties it entails." While such a statement reflects Aristotle's anthropology as much as actual Greek society, his observations may not be wholly dismissed as the prejudice of the intellectual class.

With regard to the objection that honor/shame analysis make one generic "Mediterranean culture" out of the many and multiform cultures of that world, Pitt-Rivers himself argued that evaluations of the honorable or dishonorable vary between cultures, different groups within a culture, and different epochs. He would agree that nothing is gained by passing over the differences.[52]   Indeed, the heart of the present study lies in distinguishing between what the dominant culture evaluated as honorable and what the Christian minority group held up as honorable. Malina and Neyrey were also careful to include this important *caveat* in their presentation:

> Honor, then, is an abstract concept that becomes concrete only when a particular society's understanding of power, gender, and precedence is examined. Our abstract definition is based upon lumping together those common qualities that Mediterranean people label as honorable. What is honorable is what people consider valuable and worthy....Specific instances of valuable, worthy behavior are often quite local, variable, and ad hoc.
>
> Consequently, what might be deviant and shameful for one group in one locality may be worthy and honorable for another. Yet all groups are concerned about their honor.[53]

Some might accuse Malina and Neyrey of overstatement with regard to the last sentence of this excerpt, if one takes it to refer to a universal conception of honor and to mean that considerations of honor override all other considerations -- or else there would be no point to Theophrastus' characterization of the "shameless" person (as one who "despises a shameful reputation on account of gain," *Characters* 9.1; LCL) or to the rhetoricians' testimony that safety or advantage could be preferred to honor.   Nevertheless, one should bear in mind that people labelled "shameless," i.e. deviant, from the perspective of the dominant culture, may simply be pursuing honor differently defined. The acknowledgement of individuals or groups which were labelled as "shameless," and which were unconcerned with a dominant group's grant of reputation, leads to the question of how a group might indeed seek honor and express φιλοτιμία while being viewed as "shameless" by the dominant culture. In saying, therefore, that "all groups are concerned about their honor," Malina and Neyrey are not positing a single conception of honor as a universal value

---

[52] Pitt-Rivers, "Honour," 38. Much to his credit, Malina has included a small subsection clarifying this point in the revised edition of *The New Testament World* (Louisville, KY: Westminster/John Knox, 1993), 53-54.

[53] Malina and Neyrey, "Honor," 26.

within Mediterranean culture, but rather affirming that all groups, in defining their values or group boundaries, use the language of honor and shame to organize these values and motivate adherence to them.

The picture of first-century Mediterranean society as an agonistic honor culture suffers also from the failure of its proponents to follow the criticisms of Adkins and refinements of the picture of Homeric, Archaic, and Classical Greek society in the works of classical scholars such as E. R. Dodds and Bernard Williams. Dodds defines Homeric society as a "shame-culture":

> Homeric man's highest good is not the enjoyment of a quiet conscience, but the enjoyment of *tīmē*, public esteem: "Why should I fight," asks Achilles, "if the good fighter receives no more τιμή than the bad?" And the strongest moral force which Homeric man knows is not the fear of god, but respect for public opinion, *aidōs*....In such a society, anything which exposes a man to the contempt or ridicule of his fellows, which causes him to "lose face," is felt as unbearable.[54]

Nevertheless, Dodds contends strongly in the second chapter of his book that the Archaic and Classical ages of Greek culture witnessed the development of a guilt-culture alongside the older shame-culture. This began as a notion that the gods envied humans any success that might lift them, however temporarily, above their mortal condition. It developed into a doctrine of punishment for the *hybris* exhibited by mortals.[55] The development of a strong sense of fear of the gods brought in its train the "universal fear of pollution (*miasma*) and its correlate, the universal craving for ritual purification."[56] This in turn leads to the concern with conscience and purification from sins of ignorant (pollution) and willful transgressions (sins proper).[57] This background of shame-culture mingled with guilt-culture (mediated, of course, through Hellenistic Judaism and the distinctive Jewish understanding of sin and guilt) provides an interesting background to the text selected for analysis in this study, as the central chapters of Hebrews defy interpretation in terms of the model of an honor culture except as interpreted through the concepts of sin, sacrifice, and the purification of conscience.

Bernard Williams likewise helps refine the picture of how honor works within Greek culture. In particular, he questions Adkins' model of the

---

[54] E. R. Dodds, *The Greeks*, 17-18.
[55] Dodds, *The Greeks*, 33.
[56] Dodds, *The Greeks*, 38.
[57] Dodds, *The Greeks*, 35.

Greek world as essentially agonistic (thus also calling into question Malina's emphasis on this aspect of the model). Citing the work of Redfield, he speaks of αἰδώς and νέμεσις as a "reflexive pair," at work as early as Homeric society:

> It is natural, and indeed basic to the operation of these feelings, that *nemesis*, and *aidōs* itself, can appear on both sides of a social relation. People have at once a sense of their own honour and a respect for other people's honour; they can feel indignation or other forms of anger when honour is violated, in their own case or someone else's. These are shared sentiments with similar objects, and they serve to bind people together in a community of feeling.[58]

Perhaps indeed the fear of the gods discussed by Dodds arose out of the concept of *nemesis*, namely that violations of the honor of others placed one in a dangerous situation, that the triumph in a challenge-riposte scenario might incur the indignation of divinities who were themselves *aidaios* towards things *nemessētos* (worthy of indignation). At the very least, however, Williams provides a corrective to Adkins' view that "in the Homeric shame culture individuals were overwhelmingly concerned with their own success at the expense of others."[59] Rather, "the structures of *aidōs* and *nemesis* are essentially interactive between people, and they serve to bond as much as to divide."

This insight provides a significant bridge between the conception of the Greco-Roman world as an honor culture and the observation that patron-client relations formed an essential aspect of that world -- "the chief bond of human society," as Seneca claimed (*Ben.* 1.4.2). The cultivation of patrons gave the client access to the goods, services, and protection necessary for a safe and fruitful life; the cultivation of clients gave the patron prestige and power. It belonged to "gratitude" to honor one's patron, to act so as to enhance his or her reputation. To violate gratitude -- to act so as to bring dishonor to one's patron -- invited retribution. Honor is an important aspect of the cultural script of patronage and clientage. J.D. Crossan astutely notes that Mediterranean society is "located at the crossroads of, on the one hand, honor and shame, and, on the other, patronage and clientage, each with both vertical and horizontal, human and divine dimensions."[60] This link is also explicitly recognized

---

[58] Bernard Williams, *Shame and Necessity* (Berkeley: University of California Press, 1993), 80.

[59] Williams, *Shame*, 81.

[60] J. D. Crossan, *The Historical Jesus: The Life of a Mediterranean Jewish Peasant* (San Francisco: Harper, 1991), 73.

by Halvor Moxnes: "There is a strong element of *solidarity* in the relations, linked to *personal honor* and *obligations.*"[61] Just as it might be in one's interest to gain honor at the expense of another in a challenge-riposte setting, so it would often be in one's interest to gain goods and opportunities, which would also lead to the maintenance or increase of personal honor, through showing honor and respect for one's patrons or potential patrons. This is an essential aspect of the argument and exhortations in Hebrews, where Jesus and God now stand in the position of patrons.

Williams provides material useful as a corrective for another central tenet of Malina's construction of first-century Mediterranean reality, namely that personality was essentially dyadic rather than individualistic. This view of human personality is taken to be a correlate of an honor/shame culture. According to this model, Mediterranean people are "'other-oriented' people who depend on others to provide them with a sense of who they are."[62] Thus Jesus' questions in Matt 16:13 and 15 are viewed as sincere attempts on the part of Jesus to formulate his identity based on the feedback of significant others. The concern of these people "was how others thought of them (honor), not how they thought of themselves (guilt)."[63] This presents a picture of a system which is "immaturely heteronymous, in the sense that it supposedly pins the individual's sense of what should be done merely on to expectations of what others will think of him or her."[64] Williams' analysis of the actions of Ajax, Antigone, Neoptolemus, and Hippolytus in the Sophoclean and Euripidean tragedies demonstrates that a great deal depends on the internalizing of the values of the honorable or shameful, and that these characters act in accordance with their own sense of honor and shame. Furthermore, the dramatists can play morality in accordance with public opinion against morality in accordance with an inner sense of honor and disgrace. Violations of this internalized morality result not in losing face but in a sense of guilt. Those who prefer disgrace in society's eyes over violation of an internal norm clearly attach greater power to guilt than shame.

---

[61] H. Moxnes, "Patron-Client Relations and the New Community in Luke-Acts," *The Social World of Luke-Acts: Models for Interpretation* (ed. J. H. Neyrey; Peabody, MA: Hendrickson, 1991), 248.

[62] B. Malina and R. Rohrbaugh, *Social Science Commentary on the Synoptic Gospels* (Minneapolis: Augsburg Fortress, 1992), 113.

[63] Malina and Rohrbaugh, *Gospels*, 113.

[64] Williams, *Shame*, 81.

Williams concludes that the conception of "shame" or *aidōs* must contain something of what we would label as "guilt." He distinguishes the experiences of shame and guilt thus:

> What arouses guilt in an agent is an act or omission of a sort that typically elicits from other people anger, resentment, or indignation. What the agent may offer in order to turn this away is reparation; he may also fear punishment or may inflict it on himself. What arouses shame, on the other hand, is something that typically elicits from others contempt or derision or avoidance.[65]

This does not lead him to conclude that Homeric society was not a shame culture, especially since Greek societies "did not make of those reactions the special thing that they become when they are separately recognized as guilt."[66] Rather he wishes to expand the conception of shame culture to include the recognition of moral autonomy as well as the experience of [something like] guilt comprehended under the larger category of "shame." This, he argues, is closer to the reality of Greek culture, and, indeed, closer to the Jewish-Christian culture within which Hebrews emerges, in which the cleansing of conscience and the removal of sin play such a prominent part.

From the foregoing considerations it appears that, while the model of Mediterranean (and particularly Greek) culture is imperfect, it is not hopelessly marred. The greatest flaw is that Malina and his co-workers, in bringing the model of Pitt-Rivers to bear on New Testament texts, took for granted its direct applicability to Mediterranean cultures of two millennia ago. They have listened, in a sense, too trustingly to Pitt-Rivers and not demonstrated, through careful exposition of Hellenistic texts, in what modified manner Pitt-Rivers' model should be applied to ancient documents. Stronger documentation from ancient sources which illustrate their discussion of what honor was, how honor was measured, and how honor worked would have greatly strengthened the presentation as well as refined the model itself.

The groundwork of Adkins, the classicist, and Pitt-Rivers, the cultural anthropologist, has been helpfully supplemented by the critical studies of Dodds and Williams. These authors, together with an assessment of the place of honor in self-reflective classical texts such as the treatises on Rhetoric, assist the development of a new model which should prove more helpful for the task of interpreting New Testament documents, in particular

---

[65] Williams, *Shame*, 89-90.
[66] Williams, *Shame*, 91.

the Epistle to the Hebrews. Honor and shame are indeed retained as a pivotal axis of value, with the knowledge that other axes exist and may from time to time be expected to supersede honor and shame. A sense of honor (αἰδώς) may still be said to regulate human behavior, but not with an excessive emphasis on competition for attaining honor at the expense of others. Rather, αἰδώς is at once concerned with preserving one's one own honor as well as acknowledging the honor of others. People in this culture may be expected to be motivated not only by the quest for enhancing or preserving one's own honor but also by the imperative of showing honor appropriate to the status of others, particularly when one has entered or hopes to enter a patron-client relationship with those others. Additionally, all references to matters of sin, atonement, conscience, and the like, do not need to be interpreted solely in terms of challenges to the honor of divinity, but may still be related to "shame" in a broader sense which includes one's own awareness of wrongdoing. Finally, the concept of "dyadic personality" may be extended to include a sense of moral autonomy. For the inhabitants of the Mediterranean, reputation is indeed important as a component of happiness or well-being; notwithstanding this truth, one may speak of individuals acting on the basis of inner evaluations of what is honorable as well, even against the verdict of public opinion.

Having placed "honor" alongside other important values and rules of interaction in first-century Mediterranean society, we may now approach the task of applying this to the meaningful interpretation of a text from that world, namely the Epistle to the Hebrews. An analysis of this dimension of the text should provide insight into how the letter is strategically formulated to move the hearers in a certain direction. To use again the words of E. R. Dodds, "I do not expect this particular key, or any key, to open *all* the doors."[67] I do expect, however, that it will open a number of previously unopened doors in Hebrews without forcing the locks.

4 Method and Plan of the Present Investigation

Hebrews itself suggests the importance of honor and shame for the interpretation of New Testament texts as products of the Mediterranean world by so frequently using that realm of language. How, then, ought one to proceed in analyzing this dimension? First, it is important to determine exactly what is relevant to discussions of honor. This need not be limited to obvious lexical occurrences. We have already seen that the

---

[67] Dodds, *The Greeks*, 49.

rhetorical device of *synkrisis* also pertains to the establishment of prestige. Malina and Neyrey offer help by suggesting terms and concepts carrying connotations of honor or dishonor for a first-century Mediterranean audience. In order to avoid the charge of imposing a modern matrix on an ancient document, however, it is necessary to examine their claims regarding what terms and concepts express honor against the evidence from available Classical and Hellenistic texts. For example, we would not accept their opinion that "sonship" relates to honor if it were not for the fact that the classical rhetoricians include "descent" as a subheading under epideictic (illustrious parents and ancestors being a source of honor to the children); that Dio Chrysostom reflects this understanding when he claims honor and respect from the riotous Prusans based on his father's and grandfather's achievements (*Orations* 44.3-4; 46.3-4); that gnomic utterances in wisdom literature such as Sir 3:11 also uphold this view. Similarly, Malina and Neyrey claim that titles such as "high priest" serve as indicators of honor -- but this insight is only reliable insofar as it is reflected in statements such as Josephus, *Bellum Judaicum* 4.3.10 §164, in which the name of High Priest is called τὸ τιμιώτατον ... τῶν σεβασμίων ὀνομάτων ("the most honored of revered names"). Here, too, it will be important to determine in whose eyes the title would be so valued (e.g., the broader Greco-Roman population, or the subset of the Jewish people).

This study's analysis of honor and shame discourse in Hebrews is grounded in the exploration of the strategic use of honor as an instrument of persuasion in Classical and Hellenistic texts, and relies on primary evidence from this period for the determination of what is honorable or dishonorable. An important source for understanding how honor and shame function in discursive texts, although largely overlooked by scholars interested in honor/shame analysis, is the rhetorical handbook. Aristotle's *Art of Rhetoric*, the *Rhetorica ad Herennium*, and Quintilian's *Institutio Oratoria* all discuss how the orator is to use honor and dishonor in deliberative and epideictic speeches in order to persuade the hearers. These theorists also provide a more precise idea of the place of honor among the values of Greco-Roman society. After a brief summary of the rhetorical movement of Hebrews, which will provide a point of reference for the marshalling and analysis of primary evidence, chapter two will explore such rhetorical handbooks in detail as a means of gaining insight into the strategic use of honor and shame language. Since the rhetorical handbooks provide a window into the Greek culture out of which Hebrews is fashioned, such an approach will guard against the pitfalls of applying a modern social-scientific construct to an ancient text: rather, ancient texts will provide the framework for interpreting Hebrews.

For the sake of gaining a clearer understanding of how these values work rhetorically, as well as continuing to clarify the place of honor and shame in the Greco-Roman world, chapter two will also examine several speeches that reflect dominant cultural values. Such speeches assist the modern interpreter to see how honor and dishonor could be used to establish certain actions or orientations as desirable and impose sanctions against other actions or orientations. Investigation of ethical and wisdom literature will also provide insights into the power of the labels "honorable" and "shameful" to sustain the ethos and commitment to the central values of a culture.

As the next step in this investigation, chapter three will examine the use of honor and shame language among groups which have set themselves apart from the surrounding society, that is, who belong to self-avowed minority cultures and groups in tension with a dominant culture or cultures. An examination of Cynic/Stoic philosophical texts and Jewish texts written in times of social tension will show how dominant cultural evaluations of what is honorable or deviant are overturned in favor of the definitions of honor held by the members of the minority culture. An important aspect of both of these chapters is the dialectic between definitions of honor and the composition of the body of "significant others," who form the "court of reputation" which evaluates the behavior of the group members and assigns praise or blame on the basis of the groups's definitions of honorable activity.[68] Who makes up that body of significant others significantly determines what one will regard as honorable and shameful.

There is much discussion in the Hellenistic world concerning appropriate "significant others," and even criticism for choosing a certain group as one's "court of reputation." Some consider "public opinion" in its broadest sense their significant other, for whose approval they aim their actions; others respond only to their social equals and superiors as their "court of reputation," the opinion of the masses carrying no weight for them in their understanding of the honorable and of themselves as honorable people; others appeal to "higher" courts of reputation, by means of which they also set themselves off from full participation in the larger society. Examples of this latter group include those Jews who sought to preserve their distinctiveness in an increasingly Hellenized world, and certain philosophical schools which appealed to an inner guide or moral principle.

---

[68] Pitt-Rivers ("Honour," 27) speaks of the "court of reputation," namely, that body of significant others to whom one looks for approval (honor) or disapproval (shame).

Chapter three will thus provide specific support for Malina and Neyrey's claim that "what might be deviant and shameful for one group in one locality may be worthy and honorable for another."[69]   Language which aims at strengthening or defining the proper "court of reputation" -- the proper body to regard as one's significant others -- will be shown to serve the purpose of strengthening a group's norms and values.   Those who are not part of that body need not influence one's actions or goals with their "foreign," "misguided," or "deficient" ideas about what is truly honorable and therefore desirable.   Discussions of honor lead thus to discussions of social boundaries.[70]

The second half of this investigation turns at last to a detailed study of the Epistle to the Hebrews. The rhetorical handbooks and speeches suggest a number of angles from which to approach the letter, even as Hebrews itself exhibits a number of themes running throughout the work related to honor and dishonor. Chapter four will explore the experiences of the addressees from the lens of the dominant culture which disgraced and rejected them. The author's exhortation to the community comes to the fore as his choice of examples of desirable behavior are examined. These constitute the counter-definitions of honorable behavior, which the addressees are called to emulate. We will explore how the author seeks to detach the community from the outside world's evaluation of their honor, which enables him to strengthen their commitment to the group's values.

Chapter five explores the author's appeal to the addressees' sensitivity to the honor of others, specifically the honor of God. First, the author's attention to developing the supreme honor of Christ (as Son, Priest, and as the one "seated as God's right hand") is examined. Second, the role of Jesus as patron of the Christian community and as broker of the patronage of God, and the critical argument for the sole efficacy of Jesus' brokerage (as opposed to the Levitical priesthood's attempts at mediation) are developed. Finally, the warnings and exhortations in Hebrews are linked with the danger of violating the honor of the Patron, and thus exchanging God's favor (mediated through Jesus) for the wrath which seeks satisfaction. The only way to remain in God's favor, that is, to continue to receive God's benefactions and the promise of the inheritance, the "better possessions," and the glory of God's children, is to show gratitude

---

[69]   Malina and Neyrey, "Honor," 26.

[70]   Halvor Moxnes ("Romans," 63) has formulated a series of questions which reflects his awareness of the interrelationship of honor and social groups: (1) What is considered honorable or shameful within this particular culture or group? (2) On what basis is one recognized as honorable? (3) Who are the "significant others" in whose eyes one is granted honor?

-- by honoring God in Jesus, demonstrating loyalty, and showing solidarity with God's people.

Chapter six moves into the author's construction of an alternate court of reputation, building on the Jewish conviction that God is the ultimate significant Other. This constitutes an essential aspect of the author's strategies for motivating the addressees to pursue the course of action recommended in the letter. This chapter explores the role of the community as the visible counterpart to the divine court of reputation. Finally, the author's new construction of the basis of the believer's honor and his call to pursue honor before God's court of reputation is examined.

This investigation should thus provide a thorough description of the socio-rhetorical strategy of the letter as a whole,[71] and a clearer picture of the social situation envisioned and promoted in the letter through its counter-definitions of honor and disgrace: a presentation of the meaning of Hebrews as heard by readers sensitive to matters of honor (both receiving and showing honor), and a clearer picture of the effect and response which the author hoped to achieve in the addressees. As such this study seeks to contribute not only to interpretation of Hebrews but also to the understanding of how minority groups in the Hellenistic world could use the language of honor and dishonor to maintain their group cohesion and commitment.

---

[71] Socio-rhetorical criticism has been developed as an instrument of interpretation by Vernon K. Robbins. A recent statement of his work appears in his "Socio-rhetorical Criticism: Mary, Elizabeth, and the Magnificat as a Test Case," pp. 164-209 in *The New Literary Criticism and the New Testament* (ed. E. S. Malbon and E. McKnight; Sheffield: Sheffield Academic Press, 1994). The bibliography in this article refers to twelve other works by Robbins through which the development of this discipline may be traced.

CHAPTER TWO

Honor, Shame, and Dominant Cultural Rhetoric

The Epistle to the Hebrews has been recognized as deliberative rhetoric on account of the prominent place given to exhortation in the letter (2:1-4; 3:1, 7-13; 4:1, 11, 14-16; 6:1-3; 10:19-39; 12:1-13:19).[1] The passages of sustained argumentation serve the purpose of leading the addressees to heed the imperatives and cohortatives which appear in groups of varying lengths, clustered at the end of these arguments.[2] Hebrews also contains highly encomiastic language, for example in chapter 11, which lauds the heroes of "faith." The Greek and Latin rhetorical handbooks are an indispensable means of analyzing how Hebrews seeks to persuade its addressees, that is, for determining its socio-rhetorical strategy. These handbooks served as training manuals for those who sought to be orators in the court, the assembly, and the forum. Very few scholars have suggested that the authors of New Testament documents would have received formal rhetorical training. The New Testament letters

---

[1] Cf. C. P. Anderson (*The Setting of the Epistle to the Hebrews* [Ph.D. diss., Columbia University, 1969] 201, 202); T. E. Schmidt ("Moral Lethargy and the Epistle to the Hebrews," *WTJ* 54 [1992] 169); D. R. Worley, Jr., especially stresses the importance of the author's own designation of the work as a λόγος τῆς παρακλήσεως (*God's Faithfulness to Promise: The Hortatory Use of Commissive Language in Hebrews* [Ph.D. diss., Yale University, 1981] 52). H. Attridge (*Hebrews*, 14) also notes this self-designation, yet claims that it is "clearly an epideictic oration, celebrating the significance of Christ and inculcating values that his followers ought to share." While Attridge correctly emphasizes the aim of inculcating values, the following study will endeavor to demonstrate the supremacy of deliberative concerns in Hebrews (which are, of course, served by the author's ancillary use of epideictic rhetoric).

[2] William Lane, *Hebrews 1-8*, xcix-c.

nevertheless make use of rhetorical strategies discussed in these handbooks.[3] Whether these authors received formal training or gleaned the essence of the art of persuasion from hearing and reading the speeches of their day, the rhetorical handbooks illumine aspects of the argumentation of the New Testament documents and become especially valuable for the analysis of discursive texts such as the undisputed Pauline letters and Hebrews.

For the analysis of how the values of honor and shame are used in these letters, the rhetorical handbooks provide many clues. The handbooks are essentially textbooks on how to effect persuasion in one's hearers. They are therefore explicit about how the orator may use and manipulate dominant cultural values in order to stir the hearers to adopt one course of action over another. If honor and shame are important values within the Greco-Roman world, the handbooks should be expected to give attention to their potential as tools of persuasion. While there are indeed differences between the rhetorical traditions of Aristotle, Cicero, and others, and while the handbooks reflect significant developments in Greco-Roman oratory over the centuries,[4] our interest here is rather in what these handbooks reveal about honor and shame as motivators for the inhabitants of the Greco-Roman world. The proximity of the handbooks to the culture of the New Testament authors and their explicit purpose of teaching the art of persuasion make them a reliable guide to discovering the place of honor and shame in the process of evaluating and decision-making.

Our discussion begins with a brief presentation of the rhetorical character and composition of Hebrews itself, in order to demonstrate the appropriateness of treating Hebrews as an oration composed in accordance with the practices described in the classical rhetorical handbooks. This will include a brief statement of the rhetorical interests in Hebrews which guide this investigation in order to provide the reader with a point of reference from which to evaluate the analysis of other primary materials from the Greco-Roman and Jewish cultures in this and the next chapter. I will then

---

[3] See, for example, the discussion concerning the rhetorical structure and strategy of Galatians between Hans Dieter Betz, *Galatians* (Hermeneia; Philadelphia: Fortress, 1979) and Joop Smit, "The Letter of Paul to the Galatians: A Deliberative Speech" (*NTS* 35 [1989] 1-26. Ancient rhetorical theory has also been used profitably to analyze the strategies of persuasion in the Gospels, as for example in W. S. Kurz, S. J., "The Function of Christological Proof from Prophecy for Luke and Justin" (Ph.D. dissertation, Yale University, 1976).

[4] See, for example, G. Kennedy, *The Art of Persuasion in Greece* (Princeton: Princeton University, 1963); *The Art of Rhetoric in the Roman World* (Princeton: Princeton University, 1972); *Classical Rhetoric and Its Christian and Secular Tradition from Ancient to Modern Times* (Chapel Hill, NC: University of North Carolina, 1980).

begin marshalling support for my reading of Hebrews from the rhetorical handbooks, which sensitize the modern reader to how considerations of honor and shame functioned in persuasion and dissuasion. What the rhetorical handbooks prescribe concerning the strategic use of honor discourse will be further clarified by an analysis of several speeches by orators and authors who self-consciously appeal to dominant-cultural values. Finally, the use of honor and shame language as a vehicle for establishing and inculcating values will be explored through an examination of ethical and wisdom literature from both the dominant Greek culture and the dominant Jewish culture.

1 Hebrews as Ancient Rhetoric

Harold Attridge writes that "the body of [Hebrews], which the epistolary postscript styles a 'word of exhortation' (λόγος τῆς παρακλήσεως), is generally recognized to be a product of rhetorical art."[5] Indeed, Hebrews has been singled out among the New Testament documents as "the earliest example of Christian artistic literature."[6] While rhetorical criticism has been fruitfully applied to most every New Testament document, it is nowhere more appropriately applied than in the interpretation of this text which is so carefully and consciously crafted according to established ancient rhetorical conventions. I would not argue that the author received formal training in rhetoric: it is clear, however, that even if he received only the informal training common to all who heard speeches in the market places, synagogues, and theaters, he paid close attention to the art of persuasion behind such performances.

ELEMENTS OF RHETORICAL CRAFTING

Like many ancient texts, Hebrews appears to have been written with a view to oral delivery.[7] Given the liturgical setting of the reading of

---

[5] Attridge, *Hebrews*, 14.

[6] A. Deissmann, *Light from the Ancient East* (tr. L. R. M. Strachan; New York: Doran, 1927), 244.

[7] In the epilogue of 2 Maccabees, for example, the epitomator reveals the assumption that his work would be read aloud: "For just as ... wine mixed with water is sweet and delicious and enhances one's enjoyment, so also the style of the story delights the ears of those who read the work" (15:39).

letters from spiritual leaders of the early church, this makes perfect sense.[8]
William Lane has brought together a number of indications from within the
text that Hebrews is self-consciously an oration, that is, a text for oral
rather than visual communication.[9] The author uses verbs of speaking
when referring to his communication (2:5; 6:9; 8:1; 9:5; 11:32); he also
voices his concern for the addressees' attentive hearing of the message
(5:11). Awareness of the orality of Hebrews has opened the door for
scholars to examine its employment of many of the devices employed by
orators whose goal was not only to create an argument, but to deliver it "in
such a way as to *sound* persuasive to [their] audience."[10]

Hebrews affords many examples of a wide variety of the
embellishments, ornaments, and forms of argument recommended or listed
by the ancient rhetorical theorists. These elements of oratory point to the
rhetorical artistry and acuity of the author. Taking the first part of the
exordium (1:1-3a) as a demonstration, one may identify some commonly
used and skillfully employed rhetorical techniques already at work:

> In many and various ways God spoke of old to our fathers by the
> prophets; but in these last days he has spoken to us by a Son, whom he
> appointed the heir of all things, through whom also he created the world.
> He reflects the glory of God and bears the very stamp of his nature,
> upholding the universe by his word of power. (Πολυμερῶς καὶ
> πολυτρόπως πάλαι ὁ θεὸς λαλήσας τοῖς πατράσιν ἐν τοῖς προφήταις
> ἐπ᾽ ἐσχάτου τῶν ἡμερῶν τούτων ἐλάλησεν ἡμῖν ἐν υἱῷ, ὃν ἔθηκεν
> κληρονόμον πάντων, δι᾽ οὗ καὶ ἐποίησεν τοὺς αἰῶνας. ὃς ὢν
> ἀπαύγασμα τῆς δόξης καὶ χαρακτὴρ τῆς ὑποστάσεως αὐτοῦ, φέρων τε
> τὰ πάντα τῷ ῥήματι τῆς δυνάμεως αὐτοῦ....)

The Greek reveals the author's use of extended alliteration in the repeated
sounding of the phoneme |p| (five times in one clause).[11] Similarly,
one finds a repeated cadence between the two parallel clauses of 1:3a with

---

[8] Cf. Rev 1:3: "Blessed is the one who reads aloud the words of this prophecy,
and blessed are those who hear."

[9] Lane, *Hebrews 1-8*, lxxiv-lxxv.

[10] M. R. Cosby, *The Rhetorical Composition and Function of Hebrews 11* (Macon,
GA: Mercer University, 1988), 4. Both Cosby and G. H. Guthrie (*The Structure of
Hebrews: A Text-Linguistic Approach* [Leiden: Brill, 1994], 146) affirm the oral
character of Hebrews and take this into careful account in their respective analyses.

[11] Attridge cites 2:1-4; 4:16; 10:11, 34; 11:17; and 12:21 as other prominent
examples of alliteration (*Hebrews*, 20, n.157).

-στάσεως αὐτοῦ and -νάμεως αὐτοῦ.[12] The first period encompasses a complex of antitheses, or contrasts, frequently employed in oratory: "of old" stands in contrast with "in these last days"; "to the ancestors" stands in contrast with "to us"; "through the prophets" stands in contrast with "through a son."[13] Hebrews begins in what might be termed the "grand style," but frequently moves back and forth from grand to middle to plain styles, now forming fully embellished periods, now speaking in "lapidary and sometimes sententious phrases."[14] Thus the author displays the concern to vary style and sentence length that classical rhetorical theorists deemed necessary for effective composition and impact.

In addition to judicious use of alliteration, Hebrews provides the most extended example of anaphora in the New Testament. Both Cosby and Kennedy note the prominence of this rhetorical feature of chapter 11 with its repetition of πίστει.[15] Attridge has further identified several occurrences of assonance, asyndeton, brachylogy, chiasm, ellipse, hendiadys, hyperbaton, isocolon, litotes, and paronomasia.[16] The author's choice of metaphors also fits within the range of rhetorical commonplaces: education, agriculture, seafaring, law, athletic imagery, and cultic imagery.[17]

Hebrews also employs forms of argumentation which can be analyzed in terms of classical rhetorical theory. The sections of exposition abound in syllogistic and enthymematic arguments (e.g., 7:4-10); arguments "from lesser to greater" are observable throughout the oration (e.g., 2:1-4; 10:26-31). Hebrews also demonstrates its indebtedness to Jewish exegetical and rhetorical practice. It frequently employs *gezera shawa* (e.g., 4:1-11; 5:5-6) and *haraz* (e.g., 1:5-13), and uses the LXX as authoritative proof

---

[12] See Attridge, *Hebrews*, 20, nn.145-47 for this and other indices of attention to meter in the author's prose composition. Aristotle advises (*Rh.* 3.8.1, 3): "The form of diction should be neither metrical nor without rhythm.... Wherefore prose must be rhythmical, but not metrical."

[13] Calvin (*Hebrews*, 1) opens his commentary with a discussion of the careful rhetorical construction of this central proposition.

[14] Attridge, *Hebrews*, 20.

[15] Cosby, *Rhetorical Composition*, 3; G. Kennedy, *New Testament Interpretation Through Rhetorical Criticism* (Chapel Hill, NC: University of North Carolina, 1984), 156.

[16] Attridge, *Hebrews*, 20-21; cf. also Spicq, *L'Epître aux Hébreux*, 1.358-66. All of these rhetorical figures are discussed in Book 4 of the *Rhetorica ad Herennium*.

[17] Attridge (*Hebrews*, 21) provides several examples in each of these areas.

throughout the oration.[18]   Moreover, Hebrews contains discrete units which are identifiable as standard rhetorical forms. One finds in chapter 11 a complete *encomium* on "faith." Burton Mack has argued that 12:5-17 exhibits the characteristic form of elaboration on a theme, found in the *progymnasmata*.[19] The rhetorical device of *synkrisis*, or "comparison," figures prominently throughout the argumentation of Hebrews (e.g., the comparison of Jesus with Moses in 3:1-6 or with the Levitical Priesthood in 7:1-10:18). These kernels of argumentation and discrete rhetorical units are further linked together throughout the oration by means of connecting particles and phrases such as διό, τοιγαροῦν, διὰ τοῦτο and οὖν, as well as through frequent use of the device of *inclusio*,[20] foreshadowing of themes (e.g. the introduction of Jesus as High Priest in 2:17 and 3:1 before arriving at 4:14-16 which initiates the first actual discussion of Jesus' priesthood), summary statements (once explicitly in 8:1: Κεφάλαιον δὲ...), and transitional techniques involving linking words and key terms.[21] The question of whether or not Hebrews is a carefully crafted piece of rhetoric is answered roundly in the affirmative given this "overabundance" of "structural indices."[22]

RHETORICAL COMPOSITION

Scholars have been interested not only in identifying the smaller elements of rhetorical crafting in Hebrews, but more urgently in discerning its overall rhetorical structure, that is, the relationship of all its well-crafted parts within a unified whole. Investigations of this sort often begin with an attempt to determine the rhetorical genre of Hebrews. Early attempts to fit Hebrews into the form of a forensic (judicial) speech[23] gave way to the long-standing and as yet unresolved debate concerning whether Hebrews is epideictic or deliberative. The author calls his own work a

---

[18]   Its use of authoritative texts in this way distinguishes Hebrews from Greco-Roman speeches (cf. T. Olbricht, "Hebrews as Amplification," pp. 375-387 in *Rhetoric and the New Testament* [ed. S. E. Porter and T. H. Olbricht; JSNTSS 90; Sheffield: Sheffield Academic Press, 1993], 382-83).

[19]   B. Mack, *Rhetoric and the New Testament* (Minneapolis: Augsburg Fortress, 1990), 77-78.

[20]   Cf. Guthrie, *Structure*, 76-89.

[21]   Guthrie, *Structure*, 94-111.

[22]   Attridge, *Hebrews*, 16.

[23]   E.g., the work of F. von Soden, T. Haering, and H. Windisch, summarized in Lane, *Hebrews*, lxxvii.

λόγος τῆς παρακλήσεως (13:22), which Attridge takes as an indication of its epideictic character.[24]   While the term "word of encouragement" is suggestive of deliberation, epideictic oratory, as we shall show, certainly includes a strong element of inculcating values, virtues, and commitment to a certain way of life.   Olbricht has also proposed that the epideictic genre dominates Hebrews, and has outlined its structure according to the plan of a Hellenistic Funeral Oration.[25] W. G. Übelacker and Barnabas Lindars advance strong cases for regarding Hebrews as a deliberative speech, the former even analyzing the whole according to the five-part pattern found in Aristotle *Rh.* 3.13-19.[26]   These emphasize the exhortations which recur throughout Hebrews: the author is clearly concerned to urge the community to take a particular course of action in the present continuing into the future.

The problem of the genre of Hebrews arises from the nearly balanced sections of encomiastic exposition and exhortations, a feature which must be dealt with by any attempt to outline the structure and argument.   The argument of Hebrews moves largely within the sphere of *synkrisis*, "comparison," a device usually associated with encomia.[27] Hebrews thus gives the impression of being an epideictic speech in praise of Jesus' singular achievements.   Nevertheless, Hebrews is punctuated throughout by well-developed exhortations.   These are connected, moreover, by inferential particles such as διό and οὖν to the expositional sections which precede them, suggesting that each exposition serves to set up the following exhortation.

Lane shows proper restraint in affirming that "Hebrews cannot be forced into the mold of a classical speech.... Rhetorical devices are clearly discernible in Hebrews, but the presence of an identifiable rhetorical structure is less evident."[28]   This is not to deny our earlier observation that Hebrews exhibits great artistry in weaving together its discrete units into a coherent and persuasive whole: rather, the pattern for that whole is not to be sought through wooden application of the usual patterns of arrangement found in rhetorical handbooks.   Indeed, the overall pattern is

---

[24]   Attridge, *Hebrews*, 14.

[25]   Olbricht, "Amplification," 378.

[26]   W. G. Übelacker, *Der Hebräerbrief als Appel* (Stockholm: Almqvist & Wiksell, 1989), 214-229; B. Lindars, "The Rhetorical Structure of Hebrews," *NTS* 35 (1989) 382-406.

[27]   Thus Aristotle (*Rh.* 1.9.38) advises concerning how to develop the praise of one's subject: "And you must compare him with illustrious personages, for it affords ground for amplification and is noble, if he can be proved better than men of worth."

[28]   Lane, *Hebrews 1-8*, lxxix; cf. Guthrie, *Structure*, 32.

more suggestive of the so-called homily form -- a genre suggested by the author's own designation of the work as a λόγος τῆς παρακλήσεως. This term also appears in Acts 13:15, providing a term for the usual synagogue homily, of which Paul's speech in 13:16-41 is presumably an example.[29] Hebrews' frequent alternation between argument from Scripture (as authoritative text, and bearer of "first level rhetorical power"[30]) and application appears to reflect a macrostructure more in keeping with the text-centered synagogue oration.

Hebrews, then, exhibits characteristics of both epideictic and deliberative oratory, just as many Greek and Roman orators include other rhetorical genres in a single speech, always in the service of the aim of a dominant genre. Hebrews' structure, which is carefully crafted and connected, nevertheless is not clearly illuminated by a single Greek rhetorical form: its alternation between arguments based on interpretation of an authoritative text and exhortations based on inferences from and applications of that text place it more securely in the sphere of Jewish oratory, whose elements and strategies are fully derived from classical Greco-Roman rhetorical practice. Which genre dominates depends in part upon the individual hearer. For those who have remained committed in faith toward God in Christ, Hebrews maintains the values already inculcated and urges maintenance of those values: it thus functions more as epideictic rhetoric. For those who are contemplating apostasy from Christ in order to regain the favor of the non-Christian society, Hebrews takes on a more urgent, deliberative function.

Having shown that Hebrews incorporates many of the features of classical rhetoric in terms of argument, style, and, to a certain extent, form, it should be clear that analysis of Hebrews in light of classical rhetorical handbooks has much potential for providing fruitful insights into the strategy and purpose of the oration. While it may be wise to abandon the quest for a macrostructure in the usual patterns of rhetorical arrangement found in the theorists, there is certainly much to be gained from exploring smaller units as pieces of classical rhetorical discourse and, especially, allowing the ancient rhetorical theorists to inform us about the function of certain types of argument and to enlighten us as to the effect of certain rhetorical appeals on the hearer.

---

[29] See Lane, *Hebrews 1-8*, lxx-lxxiv for a discussion of research on this form. H. Thyen executes an in-depth analysis of Hebrews as a λόγος τῆς παρακλήσεως, taken as a technical term for the Jewish-hellenistic homily, in his *Der Stil der jüdische-hellenistichen Homilie* (FRLANT 47; Göttingen: Vandenhoeck & Ruprecht, 1955).

[30] Olbricht, "Amplification," 382.

The present investigation is interested particularly in how honor and shame are used in orations to motivate the hearers to choose a certain course of action. The rhetorical handbooks, as well as many surviving classical speeches, are full of helpful suggestions for where to look for honor discourse at work in an oration and what impact this discourse could be expected to have on the hearers. This will allow us to make a positive advance in our understanding of the rhetorical strategy of Hebrews. It will demonstrate that concerns about honor -- maintaining one's own and showing proper regard for the honor of the other -- provide a strong link between exposition and exhortation in Hebrews. The author develops the unique and exalted dignity of Jesus in order to set up his *a fortiori* warnings against offending Christ's honor, as well as to extend the hope to those who remain steadfast of sharing in Christ's honor. This allows us to explore the deep connections between the author's appeal to *logos* and the appeal to *pathos*, two essential aspects of a persuasive whole. The latter appeal, while stressed by rhetorical theorists as crucial to "victory," is often neglected by biblical scholars: attention to honor discourse opens up a window into the "logic" of the author's appeal to the emotions, especially his alternation between instilling confidence and fear. Finally, we shall be able to see how the cultural scripts of honor and shame, and of patronage and clientage, undergird the persuasive force of the expository sections as well as the connection between the expositions and exhortations, providing coherence and unity to the whole.

Having surveyed the rhetorical character of Hebrews and noted our chief interests in the author's strategic uses of honor and shame language, we are prepared to explore the wider literary resources of the Classical and Greco-Roman periods in an attempt to demonstrate that honor and dishonor did indeed carry the rhetorical weight and function in the strategic ways which the above analysis has posited. Furthermore, the connection between the individual's sensitivity to honor and the social construction and maintenance of values and culture will be explored as a means of demonstrating the social effect of the author's use of this language. A full exploration of this background requires first an analysis of the uses of this realm of discourse in dominant cultural rhetorical situations (chapter two) as well as an analysis of how honor and shame language are used by minority cultures (subcultures, countercultures) in order to create and maintain their values and group attachments within a dominant culture.

2 *Honor and the Art of Persuasion*

Of the three rhetorical genres discussed in treatises on rhetoric, the one most explicitly connected with honor and dishonor is epideictic.[31] Epideictic speeches praise the virtues and deeds of some particular person or group of persons, or censure the vices and deeds of a particular person or group. The occasions for the use of epideictic rhetoric by itself, however, are few in the ancient world, being limited to funerals and occasions for public memorial.[32] Nevertheless, elements of epideictic often appeared within the context of a judicial or deliberative speech.[33] Praise or blame of a particular person's character, virtues, and deeds makes up a large part of the forensic speeches which have come down to us, with epideictic rhetoric supporting other considerations for rendering a particular judgement for or against that person. Similarly, praise and blame of a person's or group's conduct could be expected to motivate the hearers to adopt or avoid a similar course of action. The relationship between epideictic and deliberative rhetoric was considered to be quite close:

> Praise and counsels have a common aspect; for what you might suggest in counselling becomes encomium by a change in the phrase....Accordingly, if you desire to praise, look what you would suggest; if you desire to suggest, look what you would praise (Aristotle, *Rh.* 1.9.35-36).

> But panegyric is akin to deliberative oratory inasmuch as the same things are usually praised in the former as are advised in the latter (Quintilian, *Inst.* 3.7.28).

---

[31] Cf. Aristotle, *Rh.* 1.3.5: "The end of those who praise or blame is the honourable and disgraceful."

[32] Burton L. Mack, *Rhetoric and the New Testament* (Philadelphia: Fortress, 1990), 34.

[33] Cf. *Rhet. Her.* 3.8.15: "And if epideictic is only seldom employed by itself independently, still in judicial and deliberative causes extensive sections are often devoted to praise or censure"; Quintilian (*Inst. Orat.* 3.4.16.) also stresses the use of topics of one genre within the framework of another genre, e.g. discussing the expedient within a forensic or epideictic speech, the just within a deliberative or epideictic speech, and so forth (see S. J. Kraftchick, "Ethos and Pathos Appeals in Galatians Five and Six: A Rhetorical Analysis" [Ph.D. Diss., Emory University, 1985], 99).

The orator's addressees were expected to desire what was praiseworthy, or set forth as honorable. The successful advisor pointed to the honorable course -- precisely that course which would be praised in retrospect.

The fundamental concern of deliberative oratory, according to Aristotle, is the expedient or the harmful.[34] At first this seems to present a contradiction with what has just been said with regard to the relationship between praise and counsel. Aristotle recognized, however, that people in making decisions about a course of action responded to several motives: "Motives of choice are the noble, beneficial, and pleasant (καλοῦ συμφέροντος ἡδέος); motives of avoidance are the shameful, harmful, and painful (αἰσχροῦ βλαβεροῦ λυπηροῦ: *Nic. Eth.* 2.3.7)."[35] The deliberative orator was always concerned to show that one course of action was better than another, and would bring greater benefit to the hearers. For Aristotle, the goal of the deliberative orator was to persuade the hearers that the recommended course would be conducive to the happiness of the hearers.[36] Happiness included considerations beyond considerations of honor:

> its component parts must necessarily be: noble birth, numerous friends, good friends, wealth, good children, numerous children, a good old age; further, bodily excellences, such as health, beauty, strength, stature, fitness for athletic contests, a good reputation, honour, good luck, virtue (*Rh.* 1.5.4).

Under certain circumstances, considerations of honor and expediency would be at odds with one another, and one would have to choose between the two.[37]

---

[34] *Rh.* 1.3.5 "The end (telos) of the deliberative speaker is the expedient or harmful; for he who exhorts recommends a course of action as better, and he who dissuades advises against it as worse; all other considerations, such as justice and injustice, honour and disgrace, are included as accessory in reference to this."

[35] These are reduced to two in *Nic. Eth.* 3.1.11: "Pleasure and nobility (τὰ ἡδέα καὶ τὰ καλά) between them supply the motives of all actions wnatsoever (τούτων γὰρ χάριν πάντες πάντα πράττουσιν)."

[36] *Rh.* 1.5.1-2: "This aim [common to people], briefly stated, is happiness and its component parts....All who exhort or dissuade discuss happiness and the things which conduce or are detrimental to it. For one should do the things which procure happiness or one of its parts, or increase instead of diminishing it, and avoid doing those things which destroy or hinder it or bring about what is contrary to it."

[37] For example, Achilles chose between an honorable course and the more expedient course when Patroclus was slain and unavenged. Although he knew the honorable course of action would be fatal, he nevertheless chose honor above expediency (*Rh.* 1.3.6): "To him such a death was more honourable, although life was more

The author of the *Rhetorica ad Herennium* speaks in similar terms of deliberative oratory, the aim of which is "advantage." Advantage, however, consists of two subcategories -- security and honor.[38] Again it is important to note that considerations of safety (or security) could prevail over considerations of honor, although the orator would never do well to admit that the course he proposes, though safe, is not honorable (3.5.8-9). While the value of safety might rise above that of honor, it is worth noting that the author sees the admission that a certain course lacks honor is self-defeating: "to be sure, no one will propose the abandonment of virtue" (3.3.5), but will rather redefine virtue so as to include the safe course. At least the illusion of honor had to be maintained for a course of action to meet with approval.

Quintilian, writing near the end of the first century CE, objects to the assignment of the "expedient" as the goal of deliberative oratory:

> I am surprised that deliberative oratory also has been restricted by some authorities to questions of expediency. If it should be necessary to assign one single aim to deliberative I should prefer Cicero's view [given in *de Oratore* 2.82.334] that this kind of oratory is primarily concerned with what is honourable (*Inst.* 3.8.1).

For Quintilian, the honorable course alone provides the advantageous course, and nothing dishonorable could be expedient. He acknowledges the fact that many do not share his conviction on this point:

> As we most often express our views before an ignorant audience, and more especially before popular assemblies, of which the majority is usually uneducated, we must distinguish between what is honourable and what is expedient and conform our utterances to suit ordinary understandings.... For there are many who do not admit that what they really believe to be the honourable course is sufficiently advantageous, and are misled by the prospect of advantage into approving courses of the dishonourable nature (*Inst.* 3.8.2-3).

Nevertheless, this same majority exhibits a certain sensitivity to honor -- if not out of devotion to the highest virtues, at least out of a desire to receive praise and rise in the estimation of public opinion (8.39).

---

expedient."

[38] *Rhet. Her.* 3.2.3: "The orator who gives counsel will throughout his speech properly set up Advantage (*utilitas*) as his aim (*finem*), so that the complete economy of his entire speech may be directed to it.... Advantage in political deliberation has two aspects: Security and Honour (*tutam, honestam*)."

The role of honor in deliberative rhetoric is thus quite clear. While other values might outweigh honor in certain decisions, an orator might expect that considerations of honor could provide the necessary motivation for an audience to respond as the orator urges. We learn also from the author of the *Rhetorica ad Herennium* that the discussion of the virtues of wisdom, justice, temperance, and courage all relate to honor, since the possession of these virtues is a component of honor.[39] He also provides definitions of the realms of discourse belonging to each of these virtues:

> We shall be using the topics of Wisdom in our discourse if we compare advantages and disadvantages (*commoda cum incommodis coferemus*), counselling the pursuit of the one and the avoidance of the other;...or if we recommend some policy in a matter whose history we can recall either from direct experience or hearsay -- in this instance we can easily persuade our hearers to the course we wish by adducing the precedent. (3.3.4)

> We shall be using the topics of Justice ...if we show that it is proper to repay the well-deserving with gratitude;...if we urge that faith (*fidem*) ought zealously to be kept;...if we contend that alliances and friendships should scrupulously be honored; if we make it clear that the duty imposed by nature towards parents, gods, and the fatherland (*in parentes, deos, patriam*) must be religiously observed; if we maintain that ties of hospitality, clientage, kinship, and relationship by marriage must inviolably be cherished; if we show that neither reward nor favour nor peril nor animosity ought to lead us astray from the right path. (3.3.4)

> When we invoke as motive for a course of action steadfastness in Courage, we shall make it clear that...from an honorable act no peril or toil, however great, should divert us; death ought to be preferred to disgrace; no pain should force abandonment of duty;...for country (*patria*), for parents, guest-friends, intimates, and for the things justice commands us to respect, it behooves us to brave any peril and endure any toil. (3.3.5)

> We shall be using the topics of Temperance if we censure the inordinate desire for office, money, or the like. (3.3.5)

---

[39] "The Honourable is divided into the Right and the Praiseworthy.... Subheads under the Right are Wisdom, Justice, Courage, and Temperance" (*Rhet. Her.* 3.2.3).

These virtues, fundamental for Greco-Roman civilization, were the subject and cause of praise;[40] those who displayed them were recognized by their peers as honorable people, and the thought of gaining honor made the pursuit of these virtues desirable. Hence the description of a course of action as just, courageous, or the like would be a strong sanction in favor of that course.

The other major component of honor for the author of the *Rhetorica ad Herennium* is the praiseworthy:

> The Praiseworthy (*laudabile*) is what produces an honourable remembrance, at the time of the event and afterwards. I have separated the Praiseworthy from the Right, not because the four categories which I list under the apellative Right usually fail to engender this honourable remembrance, but because, although the praiseworthy has its source in the right, we must nevertheless in speaking treat one apart from the other. Indeed we should pursue the right not alone for the sake of praise; but if praise accrues, the desire to strive after the right is doubled. When, therefore, a thing is shown to be right, we shall show that it is also praiseworthy, whether in the opinion of qualified persons (if, for example, something should please a more honourable class of men, and be disapproved by a lower class), or of certain allies, or all our fellow citizens, or foreign nations, or our descendants (3.4.7).

The author does not view the "Praiseworthy," therefore, as separate from the "Right," but distinguishes them for the sake of bringing out two aspects of motivating people to an honorable course of action. One follows the other as a natural consequence. The role of epideictic elements in this context is obvious. Figures of past or present history may be held up as exemplifying a particular virtue or praiseworthy accomplishment. Long lists of such people may be adduced to demonstrate that an honorable remembrance does indeed attach to a certain course of action or to the demonstration of a particular virtue. This would motivate the hearers to emulate the exemplar in an attempt to attain similar recognition for oneself.

The passage cited above also introduces a concept which will become increasingly more important for our discussion as it progresses, namely,

---

[40] Cf. Aristotle, *On Virtue and Vice*, 1.1-2 (LCL): "Fine things are the objects of praise, base things of blame; and at the head of the fine stand the virtues, at the head of the base the vices; consequently the virtues are objects of praise, and also the causes of the virtues are objects of praise, and the things that accompany the virtues and that result from them, and their works, while the opposite are the objects of blame." Aristotle's own expansion of the catalog of virtues to include gentleness, great-spiritedness, and liberality suggests that the four cardinal virtues were not an exclusive list of virtues which would confer honor on a person or course of action.

the establishment of the body of people in whose eyes something is held to be praiseworthy and honorable. From whom can one expect approval and honor for a particular action? From whom ought one to seek such approval and honor, and whose opinion ought one to disregard? What constitutes honor is group-specific; the definition of the body of "significant others" will also define the constellation of attitudes, behaviors, and commitments which come together under the larger heading of "honor."

Aristotle indicates that a speech persuades its hearers by three distinct means, and that a successful speech requires attention to be given to each:[41]

> Now the proofs furnished by the speech are of three kinds. The first depends upon the moral character of the speaker, the second upon putting the hearer into a certain frame of mind, the third upon the speech itself, in so far as it proves or seems to prove (*Rh.* 1.2.3).

Arguing that a certain course of action was honorable or dishonorable belongs to the third mode of proof (*logos*); showing oneself to be an honorable person, and hence a credible cousellor, belongs to the first mode (*ethos*).[42] The second mode of proof -- *pathos*, or the appeal to the emotions of the hearer[43] -- affords many opportunities for the orator to

---

[41] On the equal importance of appeals to *logos*, *pathos*, and *ethos*, see Kraftchick, "Ethos and Pathos," 62-66.

[42] *Rh.* 1.9.1: "We will next speak of virtue and vice, of the noble and the disgraceful, since they constitute the aim of one who praises and of one who blames; for, when speaking of these, we shall incidentally bring to light the means of making us appear of such and such a character, which, as we have said, is a second method of proof; for it is by the same means that we shall be able to inspire confidence in ourselves or others in regard to virtue." Cf. also Quintilian, *Inst. Orat.* 3.8.13: "But what really carries greatest weight in deliberative speeches is the authority of the speaker. For he, who would have all men trust his judgement as to what is expedient and honourable, should both possess and be regarded as possessing genuine wisdom and excellence of character."

[43] *Rh.* 1.2.5: "The orator persuades by means of his hearers, when they are roused to emotion by his speech; for the judgements we deliver are not the same when we are influenced by joy or sorrow, love or hate." Cf. also *Rh.* 2.1.8-9 "The emotions (*pathē*) are all those affections which cause men to change their opinion in regard to their judgements, and are accompanied by pleasure and pain; such are anger, pity, fear, and all similar emotions and their contraries. And each of them must be divided under three heads; for instance, in regard to anger, the disposition of mind which makes men angry, the persons with whom they are usually angry, and the occasions whichh give rise to anger. For if we knew one or even two of these heads, but not all three, it

use the hearers' sense of honor to create the desired moods and motivations in the hearers. In his discussion of how to arouse the various emotions required to motivate the hearers to arrive at the desired decision, Aristotle provides clues to how honor and dishonor function on the level of "pathetic" proof.

Anger may be provoked by a display of dishonor: "Let us then define anger (ὀργή) as a longing, accompanied by pain, for a real or apparent revenge (τιμωρία) for a real or apparent slight (ὀλιγωρία; *Rh.* 2.2.1)." An orator, to rouse his hearers to anger (in the service of causing them to decide on a certain course of action), would make them feel that they had been slighted or dishonored. Aristotle provides a helpful definition of slighting:

> Slighting (ὀλιγωρία) is an actualization of opinion (δόξα) in regard to something which appears valueless (μηδενὸς ἄξιον)....Now there are three kinds of slight: disdain (καταφρόνησις), spitefulness, and insult (ὕβρις)....He who disdains, slights, since men disdain those things which they consider valueless and slight what is of no account (ὅ τε γὰρ καταφρονῶν ὀλιγωρεῖ· ὅσα γὰρ οἴονται μηδενὸς ἄξια, τούτων καταφρονοῦσιν, τῶν δὲ μηδενὸς ἀξίων ὀλιγωροῦσιν; *Rh.* 2.2.3).

Anger may therefore be roused when an orator suggests that others have acted towards the addressees out of an inappropriately low opinion of their worth. Anger embodies the desire for satisfaction, the reassertion of worth by confronting and, if possible, inflicting some injury or penalty on the offending party. Under what circumstances, and toward whom, are people prone to feel anger when slighted? Aristotle suggests as one possibility that

> Men are angry at slights from those by whom they think they have a right to expect to be well treated; such are those on whom they have conferred or are conferring benefits (εὖ πεποίηκεν ἢ ποιεῖ)...and all those whom they desire, or did desire, to benefit (2.2.8).

Certain social relations (such as the benefactor-client relationship) create an expectation of honor; if the benefactor's gift if not reciprocated by a gift of enduring honor and esteem, the result will be anger.

---

would be impossible to arouse that emotion." Quintilian (*Inst. Orat.* 3.8.12) continues to stress the importance of this mode of proof: "As regards appeals to the emotions, these are especially necessary in deliberative oratory. Anger has frequently to be excited or assuaged and the minds of the audience have to be swayed to fear, ambition, hatred, reconciliation."

Fear presents a sort of reciprocal emotion to anger with reference to honor. While the experience of being slighted leads to anger, the act of slighting may lead to fear:

> Let fear ($\phi\acute{o}\beta o\varsigma$) be defined as a painful or troubled feeling caused by the impression of an imminent evil ($\kappa\alpha\kappa o\hat{v}$) that causes destruction or pain.... Such signs are the enmity and anger ($\dot{o}\rho\gamma\acute{\eta}$) of those able to injure us in any way...and outraged virtue ($\dot{\alpha}\rho\epsilon\tau\grave{\eta}$ $\dot{v}\beta\rho\iota\zeta o\mu\acute{\epsilon}\nu\eta$) when it has power, for it is evident that it always desires satisfaction (2.5.1, 3, 5).

The fear aroused in the hearers is proportionate to the honor and power of the one who has been slighted. Thus, augmenting the honor and virtue of a figure through encomiastic embellishment will proportionately augment the fear felt by those who have dishonored, or are in danger of dishonoring, such a figure.

Another emotion which the orator might arouse is shame ($\alpha\dot{\iota}\sigma\chi\acute{v}\nu\eta$), which Aristotle defines as

> a kind of pain or uneasiness in respect of misdeeds, past, present, or future, which seem to tend to bring dishonour; and shamelessness as contempt and indifference ($\dot{\eta}$ $\delta'\dot{\alpha}\nu\alpha\iota\sigma\chi\upsilon\nu\tau\acute{\iota}\alpha$ $\dot{o}\lambda\iota\gamma\omega\rho\acute{\iota}\alpha$ $\tau\iota\varsigma$ $\kappa\alpha\grave{\iota}$ $\dot{\alpha}\pi\acute{\alpha}\theta\epsilon\iota\alpha$) in regard to these same things (2.6.2).

The orator may move an audience to adopt or discontinue a certain course by causing them to feel that their reputation is at stake, or that their reputation has already been marred and must be repaired quickly. Similarly, shaming the audience may aim at motivating them to pursue some good which they ought to have attained but have for some reason or other failed to secure, for:

> It is also shameful not to have a share in the honourable things which all men, or all who resemble us, or the majority of them. have a share in. By those who resemble us I mean those of the same race, of the same city, of the same age, of the same family, and, generally speaking, those who are on an equality; for then it is disgraceful not to have a share, for instance, in education and other things, to the same extent (2.6.12).

The orator must also set the audience's actions or omissions of actions before the eyes, so to speak, of those whom the audience would respect, for people "are not ashamed...before those whose opinion in regard to truth they greatly despise -- for instance, no one feels shame before children or animals ($o\dot{v}\kappa$ $\alpha\dot{\iota}\sigma\chi\acute{v}\nu o\nu\tau\alpha\iota$ $\dot{\omega}\nu$ $\pi o\lambda\grave{v}$ $\kappa\alpha\tau\alpha\phi\rho o\nu o\hat{v}\sigma\iota$ $\tau\hat{\eta}\varsigma$ $\delta\acute{o}\xi\eta\varsigma$ $\tau o\hat{v}$ $\dot{\alpha}\lambda\eta\theta\epsilon\acute{v}\epsilon\iota\nu$, *Rh.* 2.6.23)." People only feel shame, in the sense especially of pressure to conform to a given set of standards of "excellence," before those "whose opinion they do not despise (μὴ καταφρονεῖ τῆς δόξης. *Rh.* 2.6.15)." Again we note that the approval or disapproval of a certain group or level of people often matters more than the opinion of the masses, and that considerations of honor and disgrace have their fullest meaning only with regard to that body of significant others.[44]

A positive correlate to "shame" appears in ζῆλος, or "emulation." Emuluation resembles ambition, particularly the ambition to maintain one's status among one's peers:

> Let us assume that emulation (ζῆλος) is a feeling of pain at the evident presence of highly valued goods, which are possible for us to attain, in the possession of those who naturally resemble us -- pain not due to the fact that another possesses them, but to the fact that we ourselves do not. Emulation therefore is virtuous and characteristic of virtuous men, whereas envy is base and characteristic of base men; for the one, owing to emulation, fits himself to obtain such goods, while the object of the other, owing to envy, is to prevent his neighbour possessing them (2.11.1).

Again, an orator might choose to bring in praiseworthy examples, or heighten the desirability of a good which others have attained, in order to stir up the hearers to desire that good themselves and take the course

---

[44] In several places, Dio Chrysostom argues that it is not the opinion of the masses that one should heed, but only the opinion of the wise: "Well then, do you believe that a good flautist takes pleasure in his skill and is proud when praised by unmusical and unskilled persons, and that, if youthful swineherds and shepherds crowding around him express their admiration and applaud him, he is elated over this thing itself and feels that praise from those persons is worth everything? Why, the Theban flautist made it plain that he did not pay very much attention either to the audience in the theatre or to the judges, inexperienced in flute-playing as they were -- and that, too, although he was contending for a prize and victory -- but for all that, he did not venture to depart even slightly from the proper rhythm, but he said that he was piping for himself and the Muses."

"Well, if as regards flute-playing and singing to the cithara and pre-eminence as a wrestler or a boxer the praise of experts above all others is sweetest to the ears of connoisseurs and worth the most serious attention, as regards wisdom and justice and virtue as a whole is the praise of fools and nobodies sufficient to cheer the heart of the man of sense and to satisfy his intelligence...? Evidently, then, if one is by nature really prudent, he would pay no heed at all to the talk of the masses, nor would he court their praise by any and every means, and consequently he will never regard this praise as important or valuable or, if I may say so, good. But not regarding it as a good, he will be incapable of viewing with malice on that account those who have it" (*Or.* 77/78.21, 25; LCL).

necessary to attain that good. Hearing others praised for the attainment of some goal which is within the grasp of the hearers could be expected to motivate the hearers to pursue that goal with zeal.[45]

The handbooks have shown that, in theoretical discussions of rhetoric, considerations of honor weigh heavily. A course shown to be the more honorable would more than likely be the course adopted; consideration of other values might prevail over questions of honor, but even so, an admission that a course was not honorable could jeopardize its acceptance. Honor consisted in acting in accordance with the virtues or values which upheld Greek life, a course which would make for a praiseworthy remembrance. People sensitive to their own honor and the honor of others could be moved to a variety of emotions because honor had been trampled, was endangered, or could be enhanced. They could thus be persuaded on several levels -- indeed on the levels of *logos*, *pathos*, and *ethos*[46] -- to adopt or discontinue a certain course of action by an orator's skillful use of language related to honor and shame.

3 Honor as Motivator in Greek Speeches

Speeches from the Classical and Greco-Roman period (whether written for delivery or as literary pieces) reveal that the theory of the rhetorical reflected actual practice. An analysis of several sample speeches allows for the further refinement and clarification of these observations, and provides several important parallels to the rhetorical moves discovered in the argumentation of Hebrews.

---

[45] Plutarch, for example, suggests that praise of self could be excused if the aim was "to exhort his hearers and inspire them with emulation and ambition (εἰ προτροπῆς ἕνεκα καὶ ζήλου καὶ φιλοτιμίας), as Nestor by recounting his own exploits and battles incited Patroclus and roused the nine champions to offer themselves for the single combat" (*On Inoffensive Self-Praise*, 15 [*Mor.* 544D]).

[46] While the foregoing discussion has focused on how an effective orator might appeal to the values of honor and shame in argument developed through *logos* (the appeal to rational argument) and *pathos* (the appeal to the hearers' emotions), *ethos* is also essential -- only the speaker who demonstrates within the speech that he is a person of honor will be regarded as a reliable counsellor.

PERICLES' FUNERAL ORATION

Thucydides (c. 455-400 BCE) came from a propertied and influential family in Thrace and served under Pericles in the first years of the Peloponnesian War. His history seeks to provide an accurate chronicle of the events of those years, and captures along the way the spirit of Athenian culture. In the second book of *The Peloponnesian War*, the author inserts a long epideictic oration, delivered on the occasion of the funeral services for those who had fallen in the first year of the war. While not providing a transcript of the actual oration given by Pericles, the speech at least represents what Thucydides thought "was called for by [the] situation" (*Hist.* 1.22; LCL). As such it affords a glimpse of the funeral oration, the chief occasion for using epideictic oratory independently of other genres. The placement of this speech on the lips of Pericles, whom we may suppose to have delivered the funeral oration in memory of his fallen soldiers, carries more than historical significance. Pericles was one of the greatest orators of his generation, whose policies and person embodied many values central to Athenian society. In Plutarch's biography of him, he explains that part of his purpose in dwelling on figures like Pericles is the rousing of his hearers' emulation, such that they will seek to imitate the virtues of such great men of the past (*Per.* 3). Pericles is therefore an appropriate speaker for the praise of Athens and the exhortation to those virtues which maintain and promulgate the Athenian way of life.

Pericles' speech opens somewhat apologetically by stating that honoring the fallen soldiers with deeds -- the acts of processing, lamenting, making offerings for the dead -- was a more fitting tribute than honoring them with the words of a speech (2.35.1). What follows provides important insights into how praise of an individual or group of individuals might stir the hearers:

> For the hearer who is cognizant of the facts and partial to the dead will perhaps think that scant justice has been done in comparison with his own wishes and his own knowledge, while he who is not so informed, whenever he hears of an exploit which goes beyond his own capacity, will be led by envy (διὰ φθόνον) to think there is some exaggeration. And indeed eulogies of other men are tolerable only in so far as each hearer thinks that he too has the ability to perform any of the exploits of which he hears; but whatever goes beyond that at once excites envy and unbelief (φθονοῦντες ἤδη καὶ ἀπιστοῦσις; 2.35.2).

Praise of others which puts their deeds and behaviors beyond the reach of the hearers' imitation runs the risk of exciting envy and unbelief. The other side of this shows that the hearers would be stirred to emulate the virtues and behaviors of those they heard praised -- at least to the point of affirming that, if called upon, they could exhibit the same virtues -- in the hope of preserving and increasing their own honor and sense of worth. As one proceeds to the end of this oration, moreover, one finds that this is precisely the speaker's aim.

The largest part of the oration praises not the soldiers who died defending their city, but rather the city itself, its founders, its preservers, its way of life and its values. The funeral oration becomes the occasion for restating the values and ideals for which the departed have died, in order to move the hearers to reaffirm their own commitment to the society's "way of life." Within the description of the life of the citizen, Pericles provides insight into an important function of honor and shame language:

> But while we thus avoid giving offense in our private intercourse, in our
> public life we are restrained from lawlessness chiefly through reverent
> fear (δέος), for we render obedience to those in authority and to the
> laws, and especially to those laws which are ordained for the succour of
> the oppressed and those which, though unwritten, bring upon the
> transgressor a disgrace which all men recognize.

The statement suggests how values attached to honor and shame restrain conduct where laws are not specific, and thus fill in a sort of gap in explicit conduct codes. "Noble" and "shameful" become powerful sanctions for and against types of behavior, every bit as powerful for the person of honor as the distinction between lawful and unlawful. The quality of shame, in its more positive sense of sensitivity to public opinion, becomes an important force in maintaining certain standards of conduct.[47]

Focusing on the civic virtues for which the soldiers fought and died has the double aim of honoring those who, recognizing the worth of these values, gave up their lives to preserve them, and of exhorting those who remain to exhibit a similar commitment to those values. The epideictic embellishments of the worth of the city, and the nobility of the way of life embodied in its ideal, lend force to this double aim:

---

[47] Sophocles' *Antigone* affords a view of a case where adherence to the human laws of the State and the unwritten laws conflict. Antigone considers the latter to carry greater weight: honor, particularly the honor due her kin, compels her to break Creon's decree. In an impassioned speech defending her decision, she appeals to the importance of showing justice and duty to the dead, which for her form a body of significant others the gravity of whose opinion surpasses that of the living.

> It is for this reason that I have dwelt upon the greatness of our city; for I have desired to show you that we are contending for a higher prize than those who do not enjoy such privileges in like degree, and at the same time to let the praise of these men in whose honour I am now speaking be made manifest by proofs (2.42.1).

Praise of the civic values and those who died for their preservation gives way to direct exhortation, although from what had been said at the beginning of the oration one expects that a sort of internal exhortation had already been occurring, as the hearers felt themselves stirred by the rhetorical display of the "greater prize" for which they were contending, and moved to emulation by the presence of such desirable goods.

> Nay rather you must daily fix your gaze (θεωμένους) upon the power of Athens and must become lovers of her, and when the vision of her greatness has inspired you, reflect that all this has been acquired by men of courage who knew their duty and in the hour of conflict were moved by a high sense of honour.... For they gave their lives for the common weal, and in so doing won for themselves the praise which grows not old and the most distinguished of sepulchres -- not that in which they lie buried, but that in which their glory survives in everlasting remembrance, celebrated on every occasion which gives rise to word of eulogy or deed of emulation.... Do you, therefore, now make these men your examples.... For the love of honour alone is untouched by age (2.43.1-4).

Public praise of figures such as these soldiers appealed to the hearers' own desire for honor, moving them to desire the same opportunity for praise. It encourages them to reaffirm their belief that adherence to the civic virtues leads to fulfillment of their desire for honor. Perhaps they will not attain it in battle, but within the constellation of Greek virtues they will have some opportunity. By this epideictic display they are aroused to avail themselves of that opportunity.[48] It is noteworthy that the author of

---

[48] A similar hortatory peroration appears in Dio's eulogy for the boxer, Melancomas (*Or.* 29.21): "Therefore, sirs, you should take these considerations into account and regard him as blessed, and should yourselves therefore be none the less eager for toil and the distinction it brings.... Come then, train zealously and toil hard, the younger men in the belief that this man's place has been left to them, the older in a way that befits their own achievements; yes, and take all the pride in these things that men should who live for praise and glory (πρὸς ἔπαινον καὶ δόξαν ἀγαθὴν βιοῦντας) and are devotees of virtue." 4 Maccabees, which refers to itself as a "demonstration" (ἐπίδειξις, 1:10), also closes with an exhortation, urging the same fidelity to Torah exhibited by the martyrs: "O Israelites, offspring of the seed of Abraham, obey this law and exercise piety in every way, knowing that pious reason is master of the passions,

Hebrews also explicitly directs the addressees' gaze toward the consideration of exemplars of faith, especially Jesus.[49]

Epideictic rhetoric does indeed relate closely to deliberative oratory. Public praise of a person or group of persons provides the opportunity for the reaffirmation of the values, commitments, and behaviors which rendered the subjects of the speech praiseworthy. This same act of honoring these subjects, of holding them up as examples of honorable behavior which leads to recognition, stirs the hearers to emulation, to renewed commitment to the values the subjects embodied, and motivates them to act in accordance with these values when occasion arises. This internal exhortation (the stirring of emulation) is often released by means of a hortatory peroration.

DIO'S POLITICAL ADDRESSES

The orations of Dio Chrysostom (c. 40-112 CE) reveal on the one hand the professional orator and politician, thoroughly imbued in the civic values of Greek society and able to stir people through appeal to honor and reputation to adopt or discontinue a course of action; on the other hand they reveal a philosopher who criticizes vigorously the quest for honor and repute in the eyes of the masses. Dio's own experience of exile, removal from the political scene, and adoption of the life of a philosopher accounts for the emergence of the more critical edge. When he was restored from exile, however, he appears to have lived out both dimensions fully, giving public addresses and writing more philosophical discourses. He represents the dominant culture's self-examining and reflective side.

His political discourses make much use of honor and shame language to motivate the addressees to adopt a certain course of action. The Forty-eighth Oration, for example, seeks to prepare the assembled citizens for the arrival of the new proconsul of Bithynia. Dio is concerned that certain citizens would take this opportunity to vent their frustrations and bring charges against their fellow-citizens. He considers the occasion of the proconsul's arrival to be unsuitable for such an outcry, and delivers a short speech urging silence on this matter until after the proconsul has been received in the province and has taken up his duties.

---

not only of suffering from within, but also of those from without" (18:1).

[49] Cf. 12:1-3: "let us run with perseverance the race that is set before us, looking to (ἀφορῶντες εἰς) Jesus the pioneer and perfecter of faith, who for the joy that was set before him endured the cross, despising the shame, and is seated at the right hand of the throne of God."

Dio's strategy for gaining assent rests heavily upon affirming civic unity as a source of honor and repute for a city and civil disturbances as a source of dishonor:

> If ever a quarrel [a civic quarrel representing division of the *polis*] arises and your adversaries taunt you with having wicked citizens, with dissension, are you not put to shame? (48.5).

> For truly it is a fine thing (καλὸν γὰρ) and profitable for one and all alike to have a city show itself of one mind, on terms of friendship with itself and one in feeling, united in conferring both censure and praise, bearing for both classes, the good and the bad, a testimony in which each can have confidence (48.6).

A common set of values, that is, a shared understanding of what is honorable and what disgraceful, is presented as an essential element of civic unity. Few cities could boast of such unanimity. Dio's view, however, shows how alternate definitions of the honorable and disgraceful held by minority groups could be seen as a source of disturbance, a threat to the peace and well-being of a community as well as to its values, eroding confidence in the civic ideals of what is honorable and shameful. As he had earlier used "noble" as a positive sanction in favor of a peaceful showing, Dio's peroration returns to the use of "disgraceful" as a sanction against displays of disunity:

> Is it not disgraceful (οὐκ αἰσχρόν ἐστιν) that bees are of one mind and no one has ever seen a swarm that is factious and fights against itself, but, on the contrary, they both work and live together.... Is it not disgraceful, then (οὔκουν αἰσχρὸν), as I was saying, that human beings should be more unintelligent than wild creatures which are so tiny and unintelligent? (48.15-16).

Dio thus constructed his deliberations in large measure upon the addressees' desire to act honorably, coupled with their reluctance to make a dishonorable display.

The power of these concepts for guiding and motivating behavior becomes even more apparent in the lengthy oration addressed to the citizens of Rhodes (*Oration* 31). This is an especially important text for our analysis of Hebrews in that it brings to light many expectations and inner dynamics belonging to the cultural script of patron-client relations, which we shall show to be the backbone, as it were, of Hebrews (see chapter five). The Rhodians were in the custom of honoring benefactors by ordering statues to be erected for them in the city. They had, however, fallen into the practice of simply striking out an old name on a statue and replacing it with the name of a benefactor recently voted honors. Dio seeks to move the assembly to do away with this practice and only vote the honors it intends to confer and preserve for all posterity. In order to gain the attention and concern of the audience, Dio appeals to the marred reputation of Rhodes. Fearing that they will pass over this issue as of trifling importance, Dio asserts that the honor of the city is at stake, thus ensuring that the matter will receive serious consideration:

> But if you find that my topic is really of the greatest possible importance, and, furthermore, that the situation of which I speak is very bad indeed, so that the state as such is in evil repute (διαβεβλῆσθαι) on that account, and that you yourselves, one and all, though you bear a good reputation (εὐδοκιμοῦντας) in everything else, in this one matter do not enjoy the general esteem (καθ᾿ ἓν τοῦτο δόξης οὐ προσηκούσης τυγχάνειν) to which you are entitled, you would have good reason to be grateful to me and to regard me as a true friend of yours (31.2).

Only after he has made the hearers think that they are somehow being deprived of the reputation they merit on other counts does he present the actual problem he seeks to redress, knowing that the assembly will view the practice as a threat rather than an expedient.

Throughout the argument that follows, Dio stresses that showing appropriate honor to benefactors is a mark of justice:[50]

> If we except the honours which we owe the gods, which we must regard as first in importance, of all other actions there is nothing nobler or more just than to show honour to our good men and to keep in remembrance those who have served us well.... For those who take seriously their obligations toward their benefactors and mete out just treatment to those who have loved them, all men regard as worthy of favour (πάντες ἡγοῦνται χάριτος ἀξίους), and without exception each would wish to benefit them to the best of his ability (31.7).

Such a course of action is a particular instance of living "justly and honourably (δικαίως καὶ καλῶς, 31.5)," in accordance with the highest of Greek values. However, the practice of removing the names of benefactors long dead for the sake of re-dedicating their statues to new benefactors outrages the former, ranking with the crime of impiety:[51]

---

[50] Cf. Aristotle, *Nic. Eth.* 5.2.12, in which the proper distribution of honor is considered a category of "particular justice (τῆς δὲ κατὰ μέρος δικαιοσύνης)."

[51] "But to commit an outrage against good men who have been the benefactors of the state (εὐεργέτας ὑβρίζειν), to annul the honours given them and to blot out their remembrance, I for my part do not see how that could be otherwise termed" (31.14).

> Noble men of former times who were zealous for your state, not alone
> those in private station, but also kings, and, in certain cases, peoples,
> are being insulted and robbed of the honours which they had received
> (ὑβριζομένων καὶ τὰς τιμὰς ἀποστερουμένων, 31.8).

Dio argues that it is shameful to treat benefactors as the laws direct one
should treat traitors -- revoking the honors that they had attained.[52]
Further, he argues that it is universally recognized as a shameful thing to
do what is ignoble for the sake of money.[53] Dio contrasts the present
policy with a policy adopted in the city's recent past:

> I wish, moreover, to mention a deed of yours which took place not very
> long ago, and yet is commended by everyone no less than are the deeds
> of the men of old, in order that you may know by making comparison
> whether on principle it is seemly for people like you to be guilty of such
> behaviour as this. After that continuous and protracted civil war among
> the Romans... all the provinces were granted a remission of their debts.
> Now the others accepted it gladly, and saw in the measure a welcome
> gift; but you Rhodians alone of all rejected it,... and while deferring to
> the Romans in everything else, you did not think it right to yield to them
> in this one respect -- of choosing a dishonourable course for the sake of
> gain (τὸ μηδὲν αἰσχρὸν αἱρεῖσθαι κέρδους ἕνεκα, 31.66-68).

This situation stands in stark contrast to the present, when there has been
no disaster to threaten the economy, but for the sake of conserving public
funds this disgrace is being perpetrated on the statues designated for the
honor of past benefactors. Dio anticipates that holding before the hearers
the memory of their former policy which won them fame and prestige

---

[52] "If, for instance, any man who formerly was thought respectable should
afterwards commit any unpardonable and grievous sin, such as plotting treason or a
tyranny, the practice is to revoke this man's honours, even if previously he had
received the honour of an inscription. Then is it not a disgrace (οὐκ αἰσχρὸν;) for you
to consider that men who are admittedly the noblest deserve the same treatment as that
which the laws command to be imposed on the impious and unholy, men who have not
even a claim to burial?" (31.28).

[53] "Again, since this practice is quite improper, or impious rather, it would be less
of an outrage (ἧττον ἂν δεινὸν ἦν) if it were done under the pretext which some offer
by way of excusing the city. For everybody considers it a greater disgrace to do for
money anything whatsoever that is in other respects disgraceful, than to do it for any
other reason. So when they put forward as a plea the cost and the necessity of going
to heavy expense if you shall ever undertake to make another lot of statues, and thus
seek to condone the practice, it is clear that they make the reproach (τὸ ὄνειδος) all the
worse, since men are going to think that you are doing a wrong thing for the sake of
money, and that too although you are rich (31.100)."

among the cities of the Mediterranean will move them to act out of the same commitment to honor (as opposed to considerations of conservation of funds) in the present situation.

In the Rhodian Oration, Dio appeals to the addressees' sense of honor in several ways. He plays upon their concern for their own prestige; he shames them by pointing to their past history, when, in worse conditions, they acted out of an unblemished concern for determining and pursuing the honorable course; he seeks to move them to fear at the indictment of having transgressed piety, having committed acts which dishonor those who ought to have been held in honor by them. He holds before them the fearful prospect that the damage done to their reputation for justice and honorable dealings will jeopardize future benefactions.[54] Throughout the speech he appeals to the powerful sanction of the αἰσχρόν, the "shameful," in order to turn them from a course of action towards its remedy.

THE SPEECHES IN JOSEPHUS' BELLUM JUDAICUM

Josephus (c. 37-96 CE) writes as a spokesperson for the Jewish people in the wake of the first Jewish revolt against Rome; he also writes as a spokesperson for the Flavian emperors, legitimating their accession to the imperial office and presenting them to his Jewish readership as sympathetic and benevolent conquerers. He seeks to present his people in a manner which would be understood and respected by members of the dominant Greco-Roman culture. The Jewish people demonstrate the same dedication to the same virtues as the best members of the Greco-Roman world: the difficulties brought about by unscrupulous governors and ill-disciplined Zealots who were all alien to these shared virtues should not alienate the Jewish people from the goodwill of the Greco-Roman world.

Josephus weaves numerous speeches into his narrative of the course of the Jewish War of 66-70 C.E. No doubt following Thucydides' practice of providing what would have been a speech proper to the occasion rather than an actual transcript, Josephus creates deliberative speeches before significant events of the narrative. These speeches rely heavily on the language of honor and shame to effect "persuasion" in the characters of the narrative.

After the people of Jerusalem had decided against paying the tribute, and had broken down the porticoes connecting the Temple to the governor's palace, King Agrippa addressed the city with an impassioned

---

[54] Cf. Aristotle, *Rh.* 2.6.24: "Men are likely to feel shame ... [before those] from whom they need some service, which they will not obtain if they lose their reputation."

plea to avoid war. He embarks upon a long enumeration of the states which have submitted to Rome, dwelling especially on those which had greater resources for resisting Rome than do the Judeans. In this, he appears to be using an argument which is the reverse of rousing emulation. That is, he points out that states equal to or greater than that of Judea have submitted to Rome, such that Judea's continued submission cannot be considered shameful. Revolution, however, would surely lead to disgrace, lowering Judea's prestige among these same nations:

> What is there, then, to prevent you from dispatching with your own hands your children and wives and from consigning this surpassingly beautiful home of yours to the flames? By such an act of madness you would at least spare yourselves the ignominy of defeat (τό γε ἥττης ὄνειδος κερδήσετε). It were well, my friends, it were well (καλόν...καλόν), while the vessel is still in port, to foresee the coming storm, and not to put out into the midst of the hurricane to meet your doom. For to victims of unforeseen disaster there is left at least the meed of pity; but he who rushes to manifest destruction incurs opprobrium (προσονειδίζεται) to boot.
>
> There may be some who imagine that the war will be fought under special terms, and that the Romans, when victorious, will treat you with consideration; on the contrary, to make you an example (εἰς ὑπόδειγμα) to the rest of the nations, they will burn the holy city to the ground and exterminate your race (2.395-397; LCL).

Agrippa rests his case, hoping that the fear of disgrace will turn the people of Judea away from revolting. The only course of action with a potential for a noble outcome would be to surrender.

The late stages of the siege of Jotapata provide the setting for an impassioned speech by Josephus himself. The soldiers under his command, having learned that Josephus was planning to surrender, confront him with the berating words:

> Ah! Well might the laws of our fathers groan aloud and God Himself hide His face for grief -- God who implanted in Jewish breasts souls that scorn death (θανάτου καταφρονούσας)! Is life so dear to you, Josephus, that you can endure to see the light in slavery? How soon you have forgotten yourself! How many have you persuaded to die for liberty! False, then, was that reputation for bravery (ψευδῆ μὲν ἄρα δόξαν ἀνδρείας), false that fame for sagacity (ψευδῆ δὲ καὶ συνέσεως), if you can hope for pardon from those whom you have fought so bitterly, or, supposing that they grant it, can deign to accept life at their hands (3.356-358).

Josephus' plan appears to the troops the epitome of cowardice. As a result, his former fame for courage and wisdom is in jeopardy and all but revoked. Taking upon themselves the "care for the country's honor," the troops prepare to dispatch their general before he can lead them into disgrace.

The stage is set for Josephus' defense and counter-deliberations. The fact that Jospehus cannot dismiss the question of honor but rather must answer their objections point for point demonstrates the power of this term of value:

> Another says, 'It is honourable (καλὸν) to die in war': yes, but according to the law of war, that is to say by the hand of the conqueror.... 'It is honourable (καλὸν) to die for liberty,' says another: I concur, but on the condition that one dies fighting, by the hands of those who would rob us of it.... 'It is noble (γενναῖον) to destroy oneself,' another will say. Not so, I retort, but most ignoble (ἀγενέστατον); in my opinion there could be no more arrant coward (δειλότατον) than the pilot who, for fear of a tempest, deliberately sinks his ship before the storm (3.363-369).

Josephus must first reestablish his own credibility as a person of honor by affirming the ideals of courage in war (thus arguing in the ethical mode of proof) while critiquing and reshaping the troops' definition of the honorable course of action. Having argued that the troops, rather, stand at the threshold of a dishonorable course, he proceeds to attempt an argument from *pathos*:

> And God -- think you not that He is indignant when man treats His gift with scorn (τὸν δὲ θεὸν οὐκ οἴεσθε ἀγανακτεῖν, ὅταν ἄνθρωπος αὐτοῦ τὸ δῶρον ὑβρίζῃ;)? For it is from Him that we have received our being, and it is to Him that we should leave the decision to take it away.... How can he who casts out from his own body the deposit which God has placed there, hope to elude Him whom he has thus wronged (ἀδικούμενον, 3.371-372)?

By portraying suicide as an affront to God that would provoke the indignation of the Almighty, Josephus seeks to move the troops to fear. An outrage to God will result in God's gaining satisfaction from the one who has not shown God the proper honor. The alternative to suicide, namely living out life faithfully until God recalls the breath of life results in a grant of great honor:

> Know you not that they who depart this life in accordance with the law of nature and repay the loan which they have received from God, when

He who lent is pleased to reclaim it, win eternal renown (κλέος αἰώνιον, 3.374)?

Josephus argues that it would be καλόν not to add to their calamities the crime of δυσσέβεια against God, by scorning God's gift of life (3.379). The only noble choice is to live, and to face with courage what the future holds:

> If our lives are offered us, let us live: there is nothing dishonourable (οὐκ ἄδοξος) in accepting this offer from those who have had so many proofs of our valour; if they think fit to kill us, death at the hands of our conquerors is honourable (καλόν, 3.380).

The importance of the value of honor appears in the concentration of appeals to this realm of discourse for the promotion of one course over another. The course which can lay claim to being the more honorable will be the course adopted.

A similar concentration of appeals to honor appears in Titus' address to his troops at a critical juncture in the siege of Jerusalem. Josephus relates Titus' rationale for such considerations on the threshold of battle:

> Titus, believing that the ardour of troops in warfare is best roused by hope and encouraging words, and that exhortations and promises often induce forgetfulness of danger and sometimes even contempt of death (τάς τε προτροπὰς καὶ τὰς ὑποσχέσεις πολλάκις μὲν λήθην ἐνεργάζεσθαι κινδύνων, ἔστι δ᾿ ὅτε καὶ θανάτου καταφρόνησιν), called his stalwarts together and put to the proof the mettle of his men (6.33).

As would befit a harangue to troops before battle, Titus' speech seeks to elevate considerations of honor above those of security. For the Roman army, defeat would result in disgrace:

> For shameful were it (αἰσχρὸν γὰρ) that Romans ... should be outdone, either in strength or courage, by Jews, and that when final victory is in sight and we are enjoying the co-operation of God (6.38).

> It would indeed be disgraceful (πῶς δ᾿ οὐκ αἰσχρὸν;) that Jews, to whom defeat brings no serious discredit (οὐ πολλὴν αἰσχύνην) since they have learnt to be slaves, should, in order to end their servitude, scorn death (θανάτου καταφρονεῖν) and constantly charge into our midst, not from any hope of victory, but for the sheer display of bravery (6.42).

To the Romans, "not to conquer is a disgrace (τὸ μὴ νικᾶν ὄνειδος, 6.43)." Alongside the attempt to stir the troops to defend against falling into disgrace, Titus also shames them into regarding the loss of life as a fitting and noble service due their country:

> But if men are doomed to an inevitable end and the sword is a gentler minister thereof than any disease, surely it were ignoble ($\pi\hat{\omega}\varsigma$ $o\dot{v}\kappa$ $\dot{\alpha}\gamma\epsilon\nu\nu\dot{\epsilon}\varsigma$;) to deny to the public service what we must surrender to fate (6.49).

At the head and peroration of the speech, however, Titus goads them on by the promise of their gaining honor and renown through courageous action on the battlefield:

> That the scaling of this wall is arduous I, therefore, myself grant you at the outset; but that to contend with difficulties best becomes those who aspire to heroism, that it is glorious to die with renown ($\kappa\alpha\lambda\dot{o}\nu$ $\dot{\epsilon}\nu$ $\epsilon\dot{v}\kappa\lambda\epsilon\dot{\iota}\alpha$ $\tau\epsilon\lambda\epsilon v\tau\dot{\eta}$), and that the gallantry of those who lead the way will not go unrewarded -- on those points I would now dwell (6.36).

> As for him who leads the assault, I should blush ($\alpha\dot{\iota}\sigma\chi v\nu o\dot{\iota}\mu\eta\nu$ $\ddot{\alpha}\nu$) were I not to make him an enviable man in the award of honours ($\zeta\eta\lambda\omega\tau\dot{o}\nu$ $\dot{\epsilon}\nu$ $\tau\alpha\hat{\iota}\varsigma$ $\dot{\epsilon}\pi\iota\kappa\alpha\rho\pi\dot{\iota}\alpha\iota\varsigma$); and while the survivor shall command those who are now his equals, the blessed meed of valour ($\mu\alpha\kappa\alpha\rho\iota\sigma\tau\dot{\alpha}$ ... $\tau\dot{\alpha}$ $\dot{\alpha}\rho\iota\sigma\tau\epsilon\hat{\iota}\alpha$) shall follow the fallen to the grave (6.53).

The prospect of honor in this life for the living and a praiseworthy remembrance for the dead is further enhanced by the promise of radiant afterlife for those who die in battle (6.47). In this straightforward military address, the prospects of honor and dishonor serve as spur and goad to instill in the hearers a certain determination to face the struggles ahead and fulfill the ideal of courage.

A final set of speeches appears near the conclusion of the *Jewish War*, as Eleazar addresses the last remaining forces of the Jewish resistance on Masada, anticipating its fall to the Roman army the next morning. Eleazar desires that the hearers steal the victory away from the Roman forces by dispatching their families and then one another. Throughout both speeches, considerations of the preservation of honor predominate. He opens by urging the inhabitants of the fortress to act in accordance with their former resolve not to live as servants of Rome:

> At this crisis let us not disgrace ourselves ($\mu\dot{\eta}$ $\kappa\alpha\tau\alpha\iota\sigma\chi\dot{v}\nu\omega\mu\epsilon\nu$); we who in the past refused to submit even to a slavery involving no peril, let us not now, along with slavery, deliberately accept the irreparable penalties awaiting us if we are to fall alive into Roman hands (7.324).

He interprets their opportunity to forestall the Roman victory as a gift from God, who has provided them with the opportunity to die nobly rather than live in shame:

> Moreover, I believe that it is God who has granted us this favour (χάρις), that we have it in our power to die nobly and in freedom (καλῶς καὶ ἐλευθέρως ἀποθανεῖν).... Our fate at break of day is certain capture, but there is still the free choice of a noble death (τοῦ γενναίου θανάτου ... αἵρεσις) with those we hold most dear (7.325-326).

The absolute value of honor comes to expression in the second speech, in which Eleazar posits ζῆν καλῶς ἢ τεθνάναι as the only two options for ἀνδρές ἀγαθοί (7.341).[55] Without the possibility of a noble life, a noble death was the next best choice.[56] He further urges the hearers on in this direction by citing the example of the Indian philosophers who choose the time of their deaths and set their own funeral pyres ablaze, thus employing the rhetorical strategy of *synkrisis*. This example of courage aims at stirring up emulation of the same virtue:

> Are we not, then, ashamed (οὐκ αἰδούμεθα) of being more mean-spirited than Indians, and of bringing, by our faint-heartednesss (διὰ τῆς αὐτῶν ἀτολμίας) shameful reproach (αἰσχρῶς ὑβρίζοντες) upon our country's laws (τοὺς πατρίους νόμους, 7.357)?

The example introduces the equally potent exhortation to avoid the outrages that would follow capture. This is expressed largely in connection with the mistreatment of the Jewish women ("reserved by the enemy for the basest outrage [πρὸς ὕβριν αἰσχίστην]," 7.377) and children, for whom the men

---

[55] That the ancients would view suicide under such circumstances as a noble rather than a cowardly act is well documented in A. J. Droge and J. D. Tabor, *A Noble Death: Suicide and Martyrdom among Christians and Jews in Antiquity* (San Francisco: Harper, 1992). What these authors write about the suicide of Saul is equally applicable to Eleazar at Masada: "He fears the dishonor and shame of falling into enemy hands and being humiliated" (*Noble Death*, 55). The persuasiveness of this line of reasoning is demonstrated by the mass suicide. The suicide of Razis in 2 Maccabees is also portrayed as a noble act, preserving the aged counsellor from outrage at the hands of the enemy: "Being surrounded, Razis fell upon his own sword, preferring to die nobly rather than to fall into the hands of sinners and suffer outrages unworthy of his noble birth" (2 Macc 14:41-42).

[56] Cf. 7.380: "But seeing that we have been beguiled by a not ignoble hope (οὐκ ἀγεννὴς ἐλπὶς), that we might perchance find means of avenging [Jerusalem] of her foes, and now that hope has vanished and left us alone in our distress, let us hasten to die honourably (σπεύσωμεν καλῶς ἀποθανεῖν)."

were responsible, although they too could look forward to outrages against their person:

> For we were born for death.... But outrage (ὕβρις) and servitude and the sight of our wives being led to shame (εἰς αἰσχύνην) with their children -- these are no necessary evils imposed by nature on mankind, but befall, through their own cowardice (διὰ ... δειλίαν) those who, having the chance of forestalling them by death, refuse to take it (7.382).

The fact that there would be no opportunity for satisfaction renders the outrages intolerable. Each of the two speeches concludes with an exhortation to execute the course of action which alone would preserve honor. Because mutual slaughter would keep the hearers from disgrace, mutual murder could be transformed into a "noble benefaction" or "noble service":

> Let our wives die undishonoured (ἀνύβριστοι), our children unacquainted with slavery; and, when they are gone, let us render a generous service (εὐγενῆ χάριν) to each other, preserving our liberty as a noble winding-sheet (καλὸν ἐντάφιον, 7.334).

> While those hands are free and grasp the sword, let them render an honourable service (καλὴ ὑπουργία, 7.386).

By such a course, Eleazar asserts that the end result would be honor and renown in the sight even of the enemy, when they see the result of their determination:

> Haste we then to leave them [the Romans], instead of their hoped-for enjoyment at securing us, amazement at our death and admiration of our fortitude (ἔκπλησιν τοῦ θανάτου καὶ θαῦμα τῆς τόλμης καταλιπεῖν, 7.388).

Summary

This brief survey of speeches found in a selection of Greek authors has shown that considerations of honor form an important part of evaluative and decision-making processes. Epideictic oratory, exemplified by Pericles' Funeral Oration, provides an opportunity for the hearers to renew their commitment to given values, based on the public ascription of honor upon those who have embodied these values. Thus we may affirm George Kennedy's observation that "funeral orations and panegyrics were intended to be persuasive and often imply some need for actions, though in a more general way than does deliberative oratory."[57]   Virtues and behaviors praised as honorable became desirable for the hearers of this praise. Indeed, the labels of "noble" and "shameful" were powerful sanctions for and against the deeds and commitments so described.

The deliberative speeches of Dio and Josephus show how an array of strategies which build on the audience's sense of honor -- their own honor and the honor of others -- are found both in the rhetorical handbooks and in rhetorical practice. A course might be adopted or abandoned based on its being shown to be honorable or dishonorable (Aristotle *Rh.* 1.9.35-36; Quintilian *Inst.* 3.8.1; cf. Dio *Or.* 48.6, 15-16; 31.5; Josephus *BJ* 2.395-97); hearers could be moved to act through appeal to their desire to restore, preserve, or enhance their honor or through their fear of treading upon the honor of another, as in Dio's Rhodian Discourse (*Or.* 31) or Josephus' speeches (cf. *BJ* 3.371-72); they could be moved to emulation by the judicious praise of others, as in Eleazar's praise of the courage of the Indians (*BJ* 7.357).

It is clear that honor and shame were important values in the ancient world, and that the appeal to these values would have an effect on the inhabitants of that world. The strategies for the use of this language in the rhetorical handbooks reflects and, to some extent, shapes the actual practice of oratory. By holding up a course as honorable or dishonorable, by appealing to the emotions of the hearers through their jealousy for their honor and fear of affronting another's honor, an orator could reasonably expect to exert a powerful influence upon his or her audience. Careful attention to what the orator describes as "noble" or resulting in "dishonor" leads the modern reader closer to the heart of what is at issue in the ancient text.

4 Honor, Shame, and the Inculcation of Values

We turn now to a third body of ancient witnesses, namely the ethical literature of the Classical and Hellenistic periods. This corpus reveals that language expressing honor and dishonor served to establish and affirm the values of society. In both ethical treatises and collections of wisdom sayings, values essential to social and political life were passed on from one generation to the next in large part through the recommendation of those values as the path to honor and a good reputation. "Honor" thus comes to embody the behaviors, commitments, and motivations essential

---

[57] G. Kennedy, *New Testament Interpretation*, 73-74.

to the preservation of social relationships, civic strength, and political survival. A sense of shame, then, in its positive meaning as a regard for the opinion of others and the worth of traditional values, is indispensable for becoming a properly socialized part of one's society. Notably, those labelled as "shameless" embody different values, often transgressing the values which are central for maintaining the social order (such as valuing pecuniary gain over the bond of friendship). That the authors of ethical compositions setting forth the components of proper conduct could appeal to the recipients' desire to live with honor bears witness to this orientation as a basic part of the societies of these periods.

The inculcation of values -- the promotion of virtues, ambitions, and commitments essential to society's orderly functioning and survival -- is thus often achieved by linking behaviors with honor and dishonor. Honor may be achieved (or dishonor suffered) as a result of certain activities, or honor may be enjoyed (or disgrace experienced) in the doing of certain activities. By linking honor with given behaviors, these authors also train their readers to attend to considerations of honor in their own evaluations and decisions. Will a certain course of action lead to distinction and honor, or to dishonor and a loss of reputation? By leading the readers to evaluate a course by these criteria, and by attaching the sanctions of "noble" and "disgraceful" to a variety of behaviors and commitments, the authors of these ethical works seek to impress upon the readers, or reaffirm for the readers, the constellation of values which support the society.

ARISTOTLE'S NICOMACHEAN ETHICS

Aristotle (384-322 BCE) devoted his life to investigation and reflection. While an influential member of the dominant culture (epitomized in his appointment to teach Alexander the Great), he nevertheless provides a reflective and self-examining look at that culture. Aristotle provides a comprehensive treatment of behavior in the treatise on ethics written for his son, Nicomachus. Treatment of the whole lies beyond the scope of this survey: we will limit our discussion to a number of observations sufficient to illustrate further the role of the values of honor and shame in the evaluation and promotion of behaviour. The *Ethics* differs from collections of advice or wise sayings about successful behavior in that Aristotle reflects "scientifically" on the values of his society. His work does not urge so much as observe and analyze, in order to arrive at the heart of what makes a life worthwhile and successful. In this way, and in a manner distinctive from his *Rhetoric*, his work provides an important window into the place of honor in his society.

Aristotle first provides a cautionary note to the modern view that honor is the be-all and end-all of Mediterranean culture. For him, it is one of a number of goods which "ordinary people" pursue.[58] Neither wealth nor pleasure nor honor, however, are identical with happiness, which is the true and "final" aim of life:[59]

> Men of refinement...and men of action think that the Good is honour -- for this may be said to be the end of the Life of Politics. But honour after all seems too superficial to be the Good for which we are seeking; since it appears to depend on those who confer it more than on him upon whom it is conferred, whereas we instinctively feel that the Good must be something proper to its possessor and not easy to be taken away from him. Moreover, men's motive in pursuing honour seems to be to assure themselves of their own merit (ἔτι δ' ἐοίκασι τὴν τιμὴν διώκειν ἵνα πιστεύωσιν ἑαυτοὺς ἀγαθοὺς εἶναι); at least they seek to be honoured by men of judgement and by people who know them, that is, they desire to be honoured on the ground of virtue. It is clear therefore that in the opinion at all events of men of action, virtue is a greater good than honour.... (1.5.4-5)

Aristotle anticipates the insight of cultural anthropologists that the pursuit of honor is intrinsically related to a person's self-evaluation. Praise of an individual by his or her significant others ("they seek to be honoured by men of judgement and by people who know them") indicates that that individual has lived up to or surpassed the expectations of his or her society. Such a mental process again indicates how an emphasis on honor as a measure of worth reinforces the commitment of a population to the values of the society, and thus directs the inhabitants to the activities and commitments which preserve their society.

Again, Aristotle directs our attention to an array of considerations which inform judgement, of which honor and disgrace are only one pair (2.3.7): motives of choice are the noble, beneficial, and pleasant (καλοῦ συμφέροντος ἡδέος); motives of avoidance are the shameful, harmful, and

---

[58] *Nic. Eth.* 1.4.3: "Ordinary people identify [happiness] with some obvious and visible good, such as pleasure or wealth or honour." Honor remains, however, "clearly the greatest of external goods," which is proved by the fact that honor is the gift offered to the gods (4.3.10).

[59] *Nic. Eth.* 1.7.5: "Now happiness above all else appears to be absolutely final in this sense [i.e., as the goal for which all other things are chosen], since we always choose it for its own sake and never as a means to something else; whereas honour, pleasure, intelligence, and excellence in its various forms, we choose indeed for their own sakes,... but we also choose them for the sake of happiness, in the belief that they will be a means to our securing it."

painful (αἰσχροῦ βλαβεροῦ λυπηροῦ).   Nevertheless, Aristotle presents a
picture of a society in which regard for social verdicts of praise and blame
play an important role in people's choices:

> Now the virtues and vices are not feelings, because we are not
> pronounced good or bad according to our feelings, but we are according
> to our virtues and vices; nor are we either praised or blamed for our
> feelings -- a man is not praised for being frightened or angry, nor is he
> blamed for being angry merely, but being angry in a certain way -- but
> we are praised and blamed for our virtues and vices (2.5.3).

The court of public opinion still provides powerful sanctions against
malice, shamelessness, envy, murder, theft, and adultery (2.6.18).   The
fear of disgrace marks the person of honor, who alone is capable of
achieving a life of virtue, and thus of experiencing happiness.   In his
discussion of the cardinal virtue of Fortitude, Aristotle writes:

> Now it is clear that the things which we fear are fearful things, which
> means, broadly speaking, evil things; so that fear is sometimes defined
> as the anticipation of evil.   It is true then that we fear all evil things, for
> example, disgrace, poverty, disease, lack of friends, death; but it is not
> thought that Courage is related to all these things, for there are some
> evils which it is right and noble to fear and base not to fear, for
> instance, disgrace (ἔνια γὰρ καὶ δεῖ φοβεῖσθαι καὶ καλόν, τὸ δὲ μὴ
> αἰσχρόν, οἷον ἀδοξίαν).   One who fears disgrace is an honourable man,
> with a due sense of shame; one who does not fear it is shameless (ὁ μὲν
> γὰρ φοβούμενος ἐπιεικὴς καὶ αἰδήμων, ὁ δὲ μὴ φοβούμενος
> ἀναίσχυντος; 3.6.2-3).

The shameless person appears consistently in this literature in a negative
light, for an obvious reason: lacking a sense of shame, the person cannot
be relied upon to devote himself or herself to the virtues which maintain
a society and its institutions.   Disgrace furnishes the society with a
powerful sanction to enforce behavior conducive to the life of the society.
When one ceases to fear this disgrace, social control becomes more
difficult.   An inferior motive by which to enforce behavior is fear, by
which, according to Aristotle, the majority of humankind is ruled: "For it
is the nature of the many to be amenable to fear but not to a sense of
honour (οὐ γὰρ πεφύκασιν αἰδοῖ πειθαρχεῖν ἀλλὰ φόβῳ), and to abstain
from evil not because of its baseness (διὰ τὸ αἰσχρόν) but because of the
penalties it entails" (10.9.4).

Aristotle contributes to our investigation of the question of the "court
of reputation," that body of significant others before whom one feels
shame, and thus that body to whose expectations one conforms and whose

approval and praise one seeks. Because the common herd do not, for Aristotle, share the convictions of the virtuous who are guided in all their conduct by a sense of shame, their standards do not apply, and their praise or censure are of no consequence:

> Children imagine that the things they themselves value are actually the best; it is not surprising therefore that, as children and grown men have different standards of value, so also should the worthless and the virtuous. Therefore...those things are actually valuable and pleasant which appear so to the good man; but each man thinks that activity most desirable which suits his particular disposition, and therefore the good man thinks virtuous activity most desirable (10.6.4-5).

Concerning ὸ μεγαλόψυχος, the "great-souled person," he writes:

> Honour rendered by common people and on trivial grounds he will utterly despise (ὸλιγωρήσει), for this is not what he merits. He will also despise dishonour, for no dishonour can justly attach to him (ὸμοίως δὲ καὶ ὰτιμίας· οὐ γὰρ ἔσται δικαίως περὶ αὐτόν; 4.3.17).

The person guided by a desire to live in accordance with virtue -- the four cardinal virtues of Greek society, but also the virtues of liberality, and, notably, friendship[60] --, and who has a high sense of honor, is in a position to despise both the honor and disgrace accorded from those who are not guided by the same considerations. This concept will become increasingly important as we turn our attention to minority groups who must redefine honor to serve the interests of the survival of the group and promotion of its culture over against a dominant society.

While Aristotle enumerates interests and concerns other than, and higher than, honor, sensitivity to matters of honor remain essential to him for the pursuit of a virtuous life and thus for the attainment of happiness, the chief end of humankind. The social sanctions of "honorable" and "disgraceful" still uphold the behaviors, orientations, and relationships essential to the functioning and preservation of Greek society; while the "mass of humankind" may be more responsive to fear than honor -- and at

---

[60] Cf. *Nic. Eth.* 8.1.5: "Friendship is not only indispensable as a means, it is also noble in itself. We praise those who love their friends, and it is counted a noble thing to have many friends; and some people think that a true friend must be a good men." Honor promotes self-sacrifice in the service of one's friends, providing assistance to them in their need (9.8.1): "A good man acts from a sense of what is noble, and the better he is the more he so acts, and considers his friend's interest, disregarding his own." This emphasis on gaining honor from serving the interests of one's friends is lacking in the strictly "agonistic" model advanced by Malina.

this point one wonders whether or not Aristotle was in touch with those masses -- Aristotle identifies a circle of people, located in the forefront of Greek society, that is sensitive to honor and responsive to considerations of honor.

ISOCRATES' ADVICE TO DEMONICUS

The collection of gnomic sayings in *Ad Demonicum* to the son of Isocrates' friend Hipponicus appears now in the light of research to be pseudonymous. The work was attributed by its author to the influential speech-writer and trainer of orators, Isocrates (436-338 BCE). Prominently situated in the dominant culture, Isocrates accompanied Timotheus on his campaigns, argued passionately for a pan-Hellenic league, and wrote letters to Philip urging a Persian campaign. His participation in the political life and destiny of Athens, moreover, was that of a reflective critic, so committed to the ideal of the honor of Athens that he starved himself to death in protest of the Peace of Demades (338 BCE). Attributing his collection of advice to such a figure, the author of the *Ad Demonicum* offered his *sententiae* as the way to live out fully the virtues most highly valued by the Greek world, and thus to enjoy success and a good reputation in that world.

Demonicus is presented as one of those who "strive for distinction (δόξης ὀρεγομένους)." The treatise does not profess to teach any particular skill, such as oratory, but rather how young persons "may win repute as men of sound character" (*Ad Dem.* 4; LCL). The goal of the work is to assist Demonicus to "attain virtue -- that possession which is the grandest and the most enduring thing in the world." Virtue, one will recall from the discussion of rhetorical treatises, appears as one of the subheadings under honor, and is itself the subject of and cause for praise and a praiseworthy remembrance.

The author seeks to cultivate in his young friend a concern for his own reputation, presenting reputation as something to be jealously guarded. He urges Demonicus to live his whole life as if every part were open to public scrutiny, portraying secret, shameful acts as hostages given to fortune.[61]

---

[61] *Ad Dem.* 17: "Guard yourself against accusations, even if they are false; for the multitude are ignorant of the truth (ἀλήθειαν) and look only to reputation (δόξαν). In all things resolve to act as though the whole world would see what you do; for even if you conceal your deeds for the moment, later you will be found out. But most of all will you have the respect of men, if you are seen to avoid doing things which you would blame others for doing." For Isocrates, it is enough that one should see one's

Honor is more to be cherished than safety.[62] Honor is to be prized above wealth.[63] Considerations of honor must rule over considerations of pleasure.[64] A person with a well-developed sense of shame will show proper honor to those to whom it is due:

> First of all, then, show devotion to the gods, not merely by doing sacrifice, but also by keeping your vows....Do honour to the divine power at all times, but especially on occasions of public worship; for thus you will have the reputation both of sacrificing to the gods and of abiding by the laws (*Ad Dem.* 13).

> Fear (φοβοῦ) the gods, honour (τίμα) your parents, respect (αἰσχύνου) your friends, obey (πείθου) the laws (*Ad Dem.* 16).

The most important social relationships are thus maintained by the value of honor -- the quest for honor leads to the preservation of a certain code of conduct, a care for the interests of the community (manifested in the reverence paid to the gods), the maintenance of the institution of the family and the role of parents as the heads of households, and the subjugation of one's own desires to the values of one's significant others. The desire to avoid disgrace -- in the view of others or in one's own eyes -- leads also to the checking of personal desires in the interest of the preservation of society and its institutions:

> Practise self-control in all the things by which it is shameful for the soul to be controlled, namely, gain, temper, pleasure, and pain. You will attain such self-control if you regard as gainful those things which will increase your reputation and not those which will increase your wealth (*Ad Dem.* 21).

---

own disgrace: "Never hope to conceal any shameful thing which you have done; for even if you do conceal it from others, your own heart will know" (*Ad Dem.* 16).

[62] *Ad Dem.* 43: "Guard more carefully against censure than danger (Μᾶλλον εὐλαβοῦ ψόγον ἢ κίνδυνον),...good men should dread ignominy during life."

"Strive by all means to live in security, but if ever it falls to your lot to face the dangers of battle, seek to preserve your life, but with honour and not with disgrace; for death is the sentence which fate has passed on all mankind, but to die nobly is the special honour which nature has reserved for the good."

[63] *Ad Dem.* 37: "the praise of a people is better than many possessions (πολλῶν γὰρ ξρημάτων κρείττων ὁ παρὰ τοῦ πλήθους ἔπαινος)."

[64] *Ad Dem.* 16: "Pursue the enjoyments which are of good repute; for pleasure attended by honour is the best thing in the world, but pleasure without honour is the worst."

Ps.-Isocrates connects honor with benefaction (as indeed honor was the reward of benefactors throughout the Greco-Roman world). Honor, however, demanded not just participation in conferring benefits, but distinction in this arena: "Consider it equally disgraceful to be outdone by your enemies in doing injury and to be surpassed by your friends in doing kindness (ταῖς εὐεργεσίας)" (*Ad Dem.* 26). Honor takes on a competitive edge, with regard to dealing both in gifts and in injuries. The value of honor, in Ps.-Isocrates' view, encourages industry in the expenditure of labor, most likely in public service, even as withdrawal from public service brings censure:

> [Virtue] considers sloth a disgrace and toil an honour (τὸν μὲν ὄκνον ψόγον, τὸν δὲ πόνον ἔπαινον ἡγουμένη). This it is easy to learn from the labours of Heracles and exploits of Theseus, whose excellence of character has impressed upon their exploits so clear a stamp of glory (εὐδοξίας χαρακτῆρα) that not even endless time can cast oblivion upon their achievements (*Ad Dem.* 7-8).[65]

This same sense of honor supports the interest of public trust, which are to be occasions not for the gaining of wealth (which would be to subject civic interests to personal interests) but for acquiring praise for noble service (subjecting personal to civic interests).[66] Demonicus is thus counselled to set honor as his aim, and to let the considerations of what is honorable guide his decisions in public and private. He is to live his life before the whole company of significant others who bestow honor and censure: the public (17), the network of his friends (16), the example of his father (whom he is to honor by emulating his example, 9-12), the verdict of his socially internalized conscience (16), and benefactors such as the implied author, Isocrates: "And I shall be most grateful to the gods if I am not disappointed in the opinion (εἰ μὴ διαμάρτοιμι τῆς δόξης) which I have of you" (*Ad Dem.* 45). Specific behaviors and activities are identified as honorable or disgraceful: in the framework of evaluation provided, namely choosing the honorable and avoiding disgrace, these sanctions become powerful guides for behavior.

---

[65] The expectation that the elite class should expend themselves in the governing and maintenance of the state is well attested. One may compare, for exmple, Thucydides *Hist.* 2.40.2: "For we alone regard the man who takes no part in public affairs, not as one who minds his own business, but as good for nothing."

[66] *Ad Dem.* 37: "Retire from your public trusts, not more wealthy, but more highly esteemed; for the praise of a people is better than many possessions (πολλῶν γὰρ χρημάτων κρείττων ὁ παρὰ τοῦ πλήθους ἔπαινος)."

PROVERBS

Language of honor and shame displays a similar prominence in Jewish literature of the post-exilic period. The Psalms are replete with expressions calling for deliverance from disgrace and calling down shame upon one's enemies (e.g., Ps 119:39; 132:18); the prophetic texts use the promise of honor and threat of disgrace extensively in exhorting the hearers (e.g., Is 54:4; Jer 23:40; Ez 16:52). Wisdom literature also employs honor and dishonor as important values by means of which to promote a particular code of conduct. The collection of aphorisms and longer instructions in Proverbs, for example, uses honor in many of the same ways as did Aristotle or Isocrates, promoting the behaviors and virtues central to the dominant culture of Israel.[67] The collection appears to have taken its present form by the fourth century BCE, thus predating the particular pressures of the Hellenizing crisis of the second century.[68] It reflects a situation of optimism rather than cultural warfare, such as one encounters in Sirach.

Proverbs stands as another warning against seeing honor and dishonor as the only concerns of Mediterranean people. Many of the proverbs rest on the contrast between wealth and want rather than renown and disgrace. While wealth is a means to honor (e.g, through private and public benefactions), it represents a potentially separate pursuit. The definitions of shameless persons as those who "despise a disgraceful reputation for the sake of gain"[69] coupled with the concern in ethical works such as Aristotle for the acquisition of wealth only through the right (i.e., honorable) means shows the tension between these axes of value.[70]

---

[67] In the discussion that follows, primary reference will be made to the LXX text of Proverbs, first for the sake of comparison with the other authors writing in the Greek language discussed throughout this chapter and the chapters which follow, and, second, as the form in which it would have exercised its influence on the author of Hebrews, who consistently follows the LXX over the MT in his citations of Israel's scriptures. Throughout, the relationship of the LXX to the Hebrew will be noted in the footnotes, especially where the LXX contains significant alterations of the Hebrew. See A. Barucq, S.D.B., *Le Livre de Proverbes* (Paris: Gabalda, 1964), 38-39 for an overview of explanations for the LXX's departures from the MT.

[68] Berhard W. Anderson, *Understanding the Old Testament* (4th ed.; Englewood Cliffs, NJ: Prentice-Hall, 1986), 575.

[69] Cf. Theophrastus, *Characters* 9.1: ʽΗ δὲ ἀναισχυντία ἐστι μέν, ὡς ὅρῳ λαβεῖν, καταφρόνησις δόξης αἰσχροῦ ἕνεκα κέρδους.

[70] See *Nic. Eth.* 4.1.43: "But the dicer and the footpad or brigand are to be classed as mean, as showing sordid greed, for both ply their trade and endure reproach for gain (κέρδους γὰρ ἕνεκα ... ὀνείδη ὑπομένουσιν), the robber risking his life for plunder,

Proverbs also places a heavy emphasis on the value of safety (or security) as opposed to danger, which, as the *Rhetorica ad Herennium* demonstrates, is the other aspect of Advantage, the aim of deliberative rhetoric.[71] The "fear of the Lord" is a stronghold and a sure hope for those who have regard for God, and is thus promoted on the basis of providing security.[72]

With this in mind, it may still be maintained that considerations of honor figure prominently in Proverbs and are expected to cultivate commitment in the hearers to those virtues and behaviors which lead to honor. The collection seeks to affirm the value of wisdom and the fear of the Lord, which are directly and genetically related.[73] The pursuit of Wisdom results in the attainment of honor, among other goods; the ways of Wisdom are themselves honorable:

---

and the dicer making gain out of his friends, to whom one ought to give; hence both are guilty of sordid greed, trying as they do to gain from wrong sources."

[71] Cf. Prov 3:21-26: "My child, do not let these escape from your sight: keep sound wisdom and prudence, and they will be life for your soul.... then you will walk on your way securely and your foot will not stumble. If you sit down, you will not be afraid; when you lie down, your sleep will be sweet. Do not be afraid of sudden panic, or of the storm that strikes the wicked; for the Lord will be your confidence and will keep your foot from being caught" (NRSV).

[72] Cf. 10:29: "The way of the Lord is a stronghold for the upright"; and 14:26: "in the fear of the Lord one has strong confidence" (NRSV).

[73] Cf. 1:7: "The fear of the Lord is the beginning of knowledge, and those practicing it have good understanding; piety toward God is the beginning of understanding, but fools despise wisdom and instruction" (ἀρχὴ σοφίας φόβος θεοῦ σύνεσις δὲ ἀγαθὴ πᾶσι τοῖς ποιοῦσιν αὐτήν εὐσέβεια δὲ εἰς θεὸν ἀρχὴ αἰσθήσεως σοφίαν δὲ καὶ παιδείαν ἀσεβεῖς ἐξουθενήσουσιν, au. trans.). Commentators regard this as "the motto of the whole book" (C. H. Toy, *The Book of Proverbs* [ICC; New York: Scribner's Sons, 1899], 10), or as the summarizing maxim of 1:7-9:10, the first section of Proverbs (R. B. Y. Scott, *Proverbs [and] Ecclesiastes* [Garden City, NY: Doubleday, 1965], 15). The phrase roots the internationally shared pursuit of wisdom or understanding in the particular values of the Jewish dominant culture. Cf. also 9:10: "The fear of the Lord is the beginning of wisdom, and the counsel of the saints is understanding. To know the Law belongs to good discernment (ἀρχὴ σοφίας φόβος κυρίου καὶ βουλὴ ἁγίων σύνεσις τὸ γὰρ γνῶναι νόμον διανοίας ἐστὶν ἀγαθῆς." The LXX of Prov 1:7 has added the two middle phrases of this 1:7, expanding the promise which attaches to fearing the Lord as well as introducing the value of "piety" (εὐσέβεια), which was a central virtue in the Mediterranean world, and intepreting it within the Jewish framework. In 9:10, also, the LXX has expanded the MT, adding the final clause. This indicates that the translators already held the perception that the Jewish values articulated in Proverbs required some expansion, clarification, and strengthening in the context of the interaction of Jewish and Greek culture (cf. Barucq, *Proverbes*, 49; Toy, *Proverbs*, 11 considers it plausible, thought not necessary, that the LXX may represent an original Hebrew version).

Length of life and years of living are in [Wisdom's] right hand, and in her left hand are riches and reputation (μῆκος γὰρ βίου καὶ ἔτη ζωῆς ἐν τῇ δεξιᾷ αὐτῆς ἐν δὲ τῇ ἀριστερᾷ αὐτῆς πλοῦτος καὶ δόξα).... Her ways are noble, and all her paths peaceful (αἱ ὁδοὶ αὐτῆς ὁδοὶ καλαί καὶ πάντες οἱ τρίβοι αὐτῆς ἐν εἰρήνῃ, 3:16-17).[74]

Wealth and honor belong to me, and many possessions and justice (πλοῦτος καὶ δόξα ἐμοὶ ὑπάρχει καὶ κτῆσις πολλῶν καὶ δικαιοσύνη, 8:18).[75]

Attention to or neglect of the fear of the Lord and pursuit of Wisdom divide the human population into the just and unjust, the pious and impious. The respective fates of these groups is calculated to affirm commitment to Wisdom and the conduct which embodies Wisdom and the fear of the Lord:

The wise shall inherit renown, but the impious have exalted dishonor (δόξαν σοφοὶ κληρονομήσουσιν οἱ δὲ ἀσεβεῖς ὕψωσαν ἀτιμίαν, 3:35).[76]

---

[74] While καλός is a suitable translational equivalent for Heb נעם, "beautiful," it also brings the discourse into the realm of the noble and honorable.

[75] Cf. also 24:14, where πλοῦτος καὶ δόξα are again among the fruits of pursuing Wisdom. Following Wisdom also leads to a noble end (καλὴ τελευτή), a thing highly prized in the Greek world: οὕτως αἰσθήσῃ σοφίαν τῇ σῇ ψυχῇ· ἐὰν γὰρ εὕρῃς ἔσται καλὴ ἡ τελευτή σου καὶ ἐλπίς σε οὐκ ἐγκαταλείψει (24:14). The LXX has here reinterpreted the Hebrew אחרית, "posterity" -- which meant the survival of one's life and honor, or name (so Barucq, *Proverbes*, 165), in the life of the offspring, and hence the capstone of a meaningful life -- with the corresponding Greek notion of the noble death (which meant survival in an honorable remembrance, and hence the capstone of a meaningful life).

[76] Toy (*Proverbs*, 82) notes that "the approbation of society is presented as a motive for right doing" and that this is a "powerful inducement," thus acknowledging the role of public opinion and concern for honor in social control. The LXX preserves one possible solution of the problematic Hebrew text (see Toy, *Proverbs*, 82-83); Barucq (*Proverbes*, 64) suggests "the impious have dishonor for their inheritance." It is noteworthy that the Hebrew כבוד, קלון, and בוש regularly stand behind the LXX δόξα, ἀτιμία, and αἰσχύνη, respectively. If a variety of Hebrew terms stood behind a single Greek term, it might be argued that the LXX translators brought the Hebrew text into a more codified framework of values. It appears, however, that both Hebrew and Greek had an equally well-codified set of terms within the honor/shame discourse, such that substitution was practiceable.

The just person hates an unjust account, but the impious is disgraced and will have not confidence (λόγον ἄδικον μισεῖ δίκαιος ἀσεβὴς δὲ αἰσχύνεται καὶ οὐχ ἕξει παρρησίαν, 13:5).[77]

Instruction removes disgrace and poverty, and the one who attends to reproofs will come into honor (πενίαν καὶ ἀτιμίαν ἀφαιρεῖται παιδεία ὁ δὲ φυλάσσων ἐλέγχους δοξασθήσεται, 13:18).[78]

Like snow in summer or rain in harvest, so no honor comes to the fool (ὥσπερ δρόσος ἐν ἀμήτῳ καὶ ὥσπερ ὑετὸς ἐν θέρει, οὕτως οὐκ ἔστιν ἄφρονι τιμή, 26:1).

The path to honor and away from disgrace is thus established as the path of wisdom, of walking in the fear of the Lord. This latter expression, so important for the book, sets before the eyes of the wise person at all times the honor which is due God; "to fear" in this phrase means to acknowledge the superior worth and power of the Lord, and thus to avoid provoking God's anger and desire for satisfaction through some deed which shows slight regard for God's requirements.

Proverbs makes frequent use of honor and dishonor as sanctions for and against certain types of behavior. The threat of dishonor could be presumed meaningful enough to cause one to reconsider transgressing certain boundaries, while the promise of honor made a course more appealing. Respect for parents and the marriage bond receive strong support through use of these sanctions. Dishonoring parents leads to one's own dishonor and reproach. The threat of disgrace here again reinforces the Torah: "the one who dishonors his father and drives away his mother shall be disgraced and reproached" (ὁ ἀτιμάζων πατέρα καὶ ἀπωθούμενος μητέρα αὐτοῦ καταισχυνθήσεται καὶ ἐπονείδιστος ἔσται, 19:26).[79]

---

[77] What was descriptive in the Hebrew ("the wicked act shamefully and disgracefully") has been transformed in the LXX into a sanction against behaviors contrary to piety and fear of the Lord. Again one sees traces of the LXX sharpening the content of the Hebrew in an increasingly pluralistic world where the Jewish definitions of values must be increasingly reinforced, not simply articulated. This variation also appears in the Targum of Proverbs (Toy, *Proverbs*, 263).

[78] The LXX simply makes a positive sanction (the promise of the removal of disgrace for those who attend to instruction) out of the negative sanction in the Hebrew (disgrace as fruit of neglecting instruction).

[79] The LXX translation of Hebrew מְשַׁדֶּד, "the one striking," with ὁ ἀτιμάζων provides another piece of evidence that attacks on the physical person were interpreted as attacks on that person's honor and dignity. Additionally, what in Hebrew was more descriptive ("the son who strikes his father...brings shame") is turned into a negative sanction in the LXX ("the son...will be disgraced"). Toy (*Proverbs*, 380) notes that

Similarly, scorn of aged parents will result in death without burial, the ultimate disgrace: "The eye that mocks a father or dishonors an aged mother (ὀφθαλμὸν καταγελῶντα πατρὸς καὶ ἀτιμάζοντα γῆρας μητρός) - - may the ravens of the valleys pluck it out, and may the young vultures devour it!" (30:17). Adultery brings in its wake pain, disgrace, and lasting reproach: "the adulterer through lack of good sense gains destruction for his soul: it brings grief and dishonor (ὀδύνας τε καὶ ἀτιμίας ὑποφέρει), and his reproach (τὸ δὲ ὄνειδος αὐτοῦ) shall never be erased" (6:32-33).

Similar sanctions undergird rules for relating to the socially and economically disadvantaged. Almsgiving and justice lead to renown: "the path of righteousness and almsgiving finds life and honor" (ὀδὸς δικαιοσύνης καὶ ἐλεημοσύνης εὑρήσει ζωὴν καὶ δόξαν, 21:21).[80] Justice towards others preserves one's own honor, whereas abuse of the honor of the weaker members of society brings disgrace upon one's head:

> As long as the blameless hold onto justice, they shall not be put to shame (οὐκ αἰσχυνθήσονται), but the foolish, being desirous of outrage (οἱ δὲ ἄφρονες τῆς ὕβρεως ὄντες ἐπιθυμηταί), having become impious (ἀσεβεῖς γενόμενοι), have hated understanding, and have become subject to reproaches (ὑπεύθυνοι ἐγένοντο ἐλέγχοις, 1:22).[81]

Oppression of the poor is recommended against as a provocation of (i.e., an expression of dishonor towards) the One who made the poor person. Honor of God must be reflected in one's relations to the poor and needy: "the one who informs against the needy provokes the One who made him, but whoever honors God shows mercy to the poor" (ὁ συκοφαντῶν πένητα παροξύνει τὸν ποιήσαντα αὐτόν, ὁ δὲ τιμῶν αὐτὸν ἐλεᾷ πτωχόν, 14:31).[82] Dishonoring the helpless calls forth the advocacy of God for

---

nothing is said concerning the punishment of the offending son, an omission thus corrected in the LXX.

[80] The LXX replaces the Hebrew חֶסֶד, "loyalty," with almsgiving, part of a trend within the LXX version to expand Proverbs in the direction of a greater interest in social justice issues. Cf. also the LXX transformation of 1:22.

[81] The LXX has completely altered the Hebrew, which reads: "How long, O simple ones, will you love being simple? How long will scoffers delight in their scoffing and fools hate knowledge." The LXX thus shows a heightening of interest in care for the honor of others, and develops the Greek concept of *nemesis*, by which those who unjustly provoke or dishonor one's fellow human beings provoke the gods to act against that unjust individual. MT Proverbs, however, is not devoid of this concept (cf. 22:22-23; 14:31).

[82] Two slight alterations have occurred in the process of translation. First, the nature of the offense against the poor has been particularized -- what was "oppress" or "extort" in the Hebrew is now "inform against" or "accuse falsely" in the Greek, thus

the injured. On account of the Divine Advocate, and the verdict of God's court, one may not count on mistreating the helpless in society with impunity (22:22-23).[83]

Proverbs shows a very high interest in cultivating an appreciation of the honor of others. The fear of the Lord is set in opposition to injury, affront, and arrogance: φόβος κυρίου μισεῖ ἀδικίαν ὕβριν τε καὶ ὑπερηφανίαν (8:13).[84] The one who acts humbly (i.e., does not tread upon the honor of the other) is promised honor, while the "arrogant" person who is bent on "outrage" or "affront" to the honor of others will come to a shameful end:

> Before destruction a man's heart is uplifted, and humble before honor (πρὸ συντριβῆς ὑψοῦται καρδία ἀνδρός καὶ πρὸ δόξης ταπεινοῦται, 18:12).[85]

> Pride degrades a person, but the Lord upholds the humble-minded with honor (ὕβρις ἄνδρα ταπεινοῖ τοὺς δὲ ταπεινόφρονας ἐρείδει δόξῃ κύριος, 29:23).[86]

> Where outrage enters, there is also dishonor (οὗ ἐὰν εἰσέλθῃ ὕβρις ἐκεῖ καὶ ἀτιμία, 11:2).[87]

---

envisioning the misuse of a legal system for financial gain. Second, the consequences have been sharpened. In the Hebrew, this oppression amounts to a "reproach" of the God who made the poor person. The LXX makes explicit what the Hebrew leaves implicit -- the oppressor now stands as one who has challenged God and awaits God's response, which will mean satisfaction against the oppressor.

[83] While the LXX alters the ending of this proverb, both MT and LXX agree that God will plead the case of the poor person against the one who oppresses and dishonors him or her.

[84] Commentators regard the first phrase, "the fear of the Lord hates injustice," as an addition to the text (in both LXX and MT) since it breaks the development of the discourse and breaks the meter (Barucq, *Proverbes*, 88; Toy, *Proverbs*, 164; Scott, *Proverbs*, 72). It possibly represents a marginal gloss which has been incorporated into the text. On the opposition of insolence to wisdom, or the fear of the Lord, see also 2:12; 6:12-19; 16:6.

[85] The LXX translates the Hebrew זדון with ὕβρις. Both refer to a human being acting with presumption, acting improperly with regard both to his or her own worth and the honor of others.

[86] The LXX adds an explicit reference to the Lord as the one who will vindicate the honor of the humble person, while the Hebrew leaves this unexpressed (and perhaps implicit in the passive verb).

[87] See also 13:10; 15:33; 16:18-19 (Toy, *Proverbs*, 514).

It is in this light that one should read the proverbs which speak of accepting rather than rejecting reproof and correction.[88] According to Malina's model, reproofs could be understood as a challenge to honor, calling for a counter-reproof or some other response calculated to restore honor in the public eye. In the collection of Proverbs, however, honor becomes obedience to the law and conducting oneself in the fear of God. A correction or reproof calucated to bring one into closer conformity with the law becomes an opportunity for honor, which is preserved not in despising instruction but rather in embracing it.

The value-forming power of honor manifests itself also in a number of proverbs in which a behavior is criticized as "not noble" (οὐ καλόν).[89] Several of these focus on establishing the integrity of the courts of law. Punishing the just person, for example, is censured as οὐ καλόν: ζημιοῦν ἄνδρα δίκαιον οὐ καλόν (17:26). Regarding the external qualities of an impious person -- a frequent impediment to justice -- belongs to the class of base acts: θαυμάσαι πρόσωπον ἀσεβοῦς οὐ καλόν, οὐδὲ ὅσιον ἐκκλίνειν τὸ δίκαιον ἐν κρίσει (18:5).[90] The same sanction is employed as a means of promoting the integrity of the market: "a double standard is an abomination to the Lord, and false scales are not noble in God's sight" (βδέλυγμα κυρίῳ δισσὸν στάθμιον καὶ ζυγὸς δόλιος οὐ καλὸν ἐνώπιον αὐτοῦ, 20:23).

The authors of Proverbs also recognized that the goals of prestige and wealth could be secured by other means. While encouraging the hearers and readers to pursue these by means of commitment to the law and the fear of God, they also bear witness to the fact that the success of "sinners" in terms of wealth and honor could provoke emulation of their ways. The impious, the transgressors, the sinners, are thus held up throughout Proverbs as unworthy objects of emulation:

> Do not acquire the reproaches due base men, nor be emulous of their ways (μὴ κτήσῃ κακῶν ἀνδρῶν ὀνείδη μηδὲ ζηλώσῃς τὰς ὁδοὺς αὐτῶν), for every transgressor is unclean before the Lord (ἀκάθαρτος γὰρ ἔναντι κυρίου πᾶς παράνομος), neither does he sit among the righteous

---

[88] Cf. 13:18: "Instruction removes disgrace and poverty, and the one who attends to reproofs will be honored (πενίαν καὶ ἀτιμίαν ἀφαιρεῖται παιδεία ὁ δὲ φυλάσσων ἐλέγχους δοξασθήσεται)."

[89] This phrase translates consistently the Hebrew לֹא-טוֹב, "not good." As such, it represents an equivalent negative assessment of the appropriateness of an act, and hence of the honor of the one who enacts such unfitting behavior.

[90] Cf. also 24:23: ταῦτα δὲ λέγω ὑμῖν τοῖς σοφοῖς ἐπιγινώσκειν αἰδεῖσθαι πρόσωπον ἐν κρίσει οὐ καλόν.

(ἐν δὲ δικαίοις οὐ συνεδριάζει). God's curse is in the houses of the impious, but the dwellings of the just are blessed (3:31-33).[91]

Let not your heart be emulous of wicked men, but be in the fear of the Lord all day long (μὴ ζηλούτω ἡ καρδία σου ἁμαρτωλούς ἀλλὰ ἐν φόβῳ κυρίου ἴσθι ὅλην τὴν ἡμέραν, 23:17).[92]

These may enjoy the goods of prestige and wealth for a time, but they live under God's curse and will come to a shameful end. The impious are not part of the just person's group of significant others, or "court of reputation."

The one who attends to Wisdom is called rather to regard the opinion of the "good" people, that is, the pious devotees of the law. These are the significant others before whom the just person will feel shame. "Whoever is not ashamed before good people is not a good person, and will sell a man for a loaf of bread (ὃς οὐκ αἰσχύνεται πρόσωπα δικαίων οὐκ ἀγαθός ὁ τοιοῦτος ψωμοῦ ἄρτου ἀποδώσεται ἄνδρα, 28:21)."[93] The ultimate significant other, before whose face all life is exposed, is God: "for the ways of a man are before the eyes of God, and God looks into all his paths" (5:21). This is reinforced throughout Proverbs, as in 15:3: "The eyes of the Lord are in every place, keeping watch on the evil and the good."[94] The so-called motto of the first part of Proverbs, namely that

---

[91] Once again the LXX sharpens the injunction found in the Hebrew by the addition of an explicit reference to "reproach" or "disgrace" befalling the wicked, and, by extension, those who emulate them. Both LXX and MT are concerned, however, to direct emulation away from such figures, whatever their apparent success. For details on the textual differences, which do not affect the sense, see Barucq, *Proverbes*, 64; Toy, *Proverbs*, 80.

[92] Twice more the sinful are held up as unfit models for emulation: "Child, do not emulate bad people, nor desire to be with them" (υἱέ μὴ ζηλώσῃς κακοὺς ἄνδρας μηδὲ ἐπιθυμήσῃς εἶναι μετ' αὐτῶν, 24:1); "Do not rejoice over evilders, nor emulate sinners" (μὴ χαῖρε ἐπὶ κακοποιοῖς μηδὲ ζήλου ἁμαρτωλούς, 24:19; the first verb in the LXX departs from the MT on account of mistaking a final consonant [Toy, *Proverbs*, 451]).

[93] The LXX differs substantially from the MT in this verse, which in the Heb reads "To show partiality is not good, yet for a piece of bread a person may do wrong." In both Hebrew and Greek versions, however, the opinion of the wise alone is held up as valuable, embodying the reproofs to be accepted. The opinion of the "fools" by that very name is set forward as of no value for the pious person's self-evaluation. In both versions, then, the significant others are delineated with the same broad strokes, to the exclusion of the approval or reproach of the impious.

[94] The authors of Proverbs direct the pupil's attention to God's all-seeing gaze also at 15:11; 24:12.

"the fear of the Lord is the beginning of knowledge" (1:7) also points in this direction. The wise person will have regard for God's decrees and opinion, taking care not to provoke God's anger through slighting or neglect. Toy suggests that this "fear" provides a "permanent and efficient moral guide," an apt comment given the power of one's significant others to determine one's choices and behaviors.[95]

Like the Greek authors of ethical texts, the authors and editors of Proverbs saw in the values of honor and dishonor a strong force to motivate and dissuade. These values function here, as before, as sanctions for and against a wide array of behaviors and seek to establish and reaffirm commitment to the central values of Jewish society, namely loyalty to God and God's law. Those who do not embody these values are not fit models for imitation or emulation; rather the "sinners" carry on in a sense outside the society (as the "shameless" do in Aristotle's construction of the social order). God and those committed to the law are the figures whose approval and disapproval, whose grants of honor and disgrace, are to guide one's conduct and ambitions.

5 Conclusions

The foregoing discussion confirms the thesis that honor and shame were prominent values for the Greco-Roman world of the first century. Rhetorical tractates, literary speeches, and ethical treatises all show that appeals to honor and dishonor were expected to persuade. That is to say, the people addressed by these works (or who were to be addressed by the speeches composed after the advice of the rhetoricians) sought to preserve or attain honor and to avoid dishonor. At several points the importance of other values has imposed itself on the discussion, values which could be opposed to honor, cautioning modern scholars against collapsing all values into the axis of honor and shame.

These documents have also provided a number of insights into the way values of honor and dishonor functioned in these societies, and in the texts produced by and speaking to these societies. The rhetorical handbooks and samples of speeches show the power of honor to motivate and dissuade, and display the many avenues by which orators might use this realm of discourse to achieve their ends. The addressees would be prone to adopt courses which led to the preservation or increase of their honor, and to avoid courses which led to disgrace; they would be moved to anger at the

---

[95] Toy, *Proverbs*, 10. Scott (*Proverbs*, 52) also notes that "the thought of the all-seeing eye of God" provides "a reason for doing what is right."

thought of their honor being disregarded and to fear at the thought of trampling the honor of a more powerful person or nation; they would be moved to emulation at the praise of others, seeking to gain such approval and honorable remembrance for themselves. The demonstration that a course of action both led to honor for the hearers and showed proper honor to those to whom it was due would stand a good chance of winning the hearers over to that course.

Honor and shame language have also been shown to be indispensable to the construction and reaffirmation of the values and expectations of a society. Orators and ethicists could capitalize on the widespread desire for honor and aversion toward dishonor to support the ethos and social networks of their culture. Since courage in war receives acclamation in commemorative speeches, people will give their lives for their city; since benefactors receive the honor they desire, they will be disposed to continue in beneficence, and others desirous of honor will be moved to give as well. Similarly the institution of marriage and the place of parents in their families are supported through the sanction of dishonor; the same promise of disgrace seeks to avert violation of the sanctity of gods or laws. Honor is an ideal which binds a society together in a common culture -- a shared constellation of values and commitment to those values. Because honor is granted by one's society, and because one desires honor, one will act in accordance with the norms and values of one's society, and often subordinate one's own interests to the interests of the larger society.

This investigation assists us in our task of analyzing the use of honor and shame in the rhetorical strategy of the author of Hebrews, a deliberative speech which makes extensive use of epideictic rhetoric. The rhetorical handbooks and the actual speeches open up several avenues of investigation.   What courses of action lead to the increase of the addressees' honor? What courses of action carry the threat of the loss of honor? How does the author use honor and shame language in his appeal to the emotions of the hearers (the essential argument from *pathos* prescribed by all teachers of rhetoric), especially their sense of shame, fear, emulation, and indignation? In what directions does the author's praise or censure of historical figures, or the community itself, seek to drive the hearers? The author's use of this realm of discourse is also connected with the construction and maintenance of cultural values. What, then, is the nature of the Christian culture promulgated by the author? What is the relation of this culture to the dominant cultures of the Greco-Roman world?   The foregoing discussion has not provided sufficient evidence from the ancient world for us to answer these latter questions. What has been lacking is an investigation of how honor and shame discourse functions in minority cultures (subcultures, ethnic subcultures, and countercultures). How do such groups in the ancient world use honor and shame language to preserve and inculcate their own group values over against the values of the dominant culture?

Honor remains an empty concept until given specific content within a particular culture. Honor may indeed serve as a means of reaffirming a minority group's commitment to its values and its boundaries. In this enterprise, the language of honor and shame functions largely in the same way as for a dominant cultural group. However, the definition of one's significant others who constitute the "court of reputation" becomes more important, as does the placement of this court on a higher level than that of the dominant culture, such that in the eyes of this court society's opinion of the minority group (and thus the powerful social pressure exerted upon the minority group to conform) is delegitimated. As we move through these minority groups and their use of honor and shame language to uphold group ideals, boundaries, and interests, we move closer to the world of the Epistle to the Hebrews.

CHAPTER THREE

Honor, Shame, and the Rhetoric of Minority Cultures

The foregoing discussion has explored the power of honor and shame language to affirm certain values, encourage certain actions, and establish a means of social control within a dominant culture. One's behavior is not merely defined by written laws, but by the socially transmitted sanctions of what is noble and what is shameful.[1] Since honor and esteem are socially granted, one who is sensitive to honor will conform to the norms of that society in order to gain recognition as a person of worth. Cultural anthropologists have noted, however, that the cultural situation is often more complex in that one regularly finds competing (or, at least, alternative) cultures within a society.[2] In the Mediterranean world, for example, there was not just a single dominant culture in a given area, but minority cultures set within dominant cultures. This could appear in many different forms, resulting in a cultural map akin in design to a Chinese puzzle box. An indigenous culture (e.g., Egyptian) might exist alongside a conquering culture (Greek) together with a transplanted minority culture (Judaism), such as was the case in Alexandria and its environs. A voluntary minority culture, such as a philosophical school or religious sect, could also exist within the dominant culture.

Within this matrix of alternative systems of values, beliefs, and commitments, the language of honor and shame became an important tool by which to encourage the maintenance of one's own minority culture. To

---

[1] Cf. Dio Chrysostom, *Or.* 14.14: "Well then, do you think that it is permitted to *you* to do all things, which, while they are not expressly forbidden by the laws, yet are regarded as base and unseemly (αἰσχρὰ δὲ ... καὶ ἄτοπα) by mankind?"

[2] Cf. Pitt-Rivers, "Honour," 22; Malina and Neyrey, "Honor and Shame," 26.

become (or remain) sensitive to one's reputation in the eyes of outsiders meant sacrificing one's commitment to the values of the minority group. Shame before outsiders -- concern for their approval of one's activities and aspirations -- continued the influence of dominant cultural values. The maintenance of a minority culture required that one's body of significant others be circumscribed to include primarily the constituency of that culture, and members of other cultures only incidentally.

The literary products of minority cultures therefore give considerable attention to the question of who constitutes the "court of opinion."[3] The authors undermine the reliability of public opinion concerning what is honorable or disgraceful, pointing the reader instead to those whose approval or disapproval reflect the counter-definitions of the group. The exclusion of the many and choice of the few for one's court of reputation is legitimated by means of an appeal to the divine or to some super-social force, often with the promise of future vindication. Such literary witnesses to minority cultures demonstrate how honor and shame retain their prescriptive and proscriptive force within the new definitions of the honorable and disgraceful established by each minority group. The use of honor and shame language enables the member to seek distinction in the eyes of the group, and to disregard the evaluation of outsiders.

1 Greco-Roman Philosophical Writings

Many philosophers and the devotees of certain schools enjoyed distinguished careers within the dominant culture. The degree of overlap between Stoic and statesman in Seneca or between philosopher and politician in Dio Chrysostom should not obscure the fact that, in their literary remains at least, such figures desired to maintain a distance between their values and the dictates of public opinion. Critical of the common herd and banded together by shared values, ethical standards, and a commitment to follow reason rather than reputation, devotees of philosophy formed a voluntary minority culture, and used the language of honor and shame to reinforce both distance and commitment.

---

[3] Cf. Pitt-Rivers, "Honour," 27.

PLATO

Born into an aristocratic family and having friends and relations among "The Thirty," Plato (c. 429-347 BCE) was well-placed in Athenian society.[4] He nurtured political ambitions in his youth, abandoning Athenian politics only after the condemnation and execution of Socrates.[5] After travelling for several years, he returned to Athens and founded the Academy, teaching many who would themselves become active in politics in Athens and abroad. Plato and his Academy were thus closely connected with the dominant culture. Nevertheless, Plato's writings demonstrate a certain distance from that culture -- at least a reflective and critical engagement with it. He taught his students to hold themselves answerable not to the opinion of the many, but only to the ideals of philosophy and the opinion of the wise person, and to engage in the activities of the dominant culture from this vantage point. In this way, Plato and his adherents form a sort of subculture within the dominant culture. His use of the language of honor and shame -- not just "shame" in the sense of dishonor, but "shame" in the sense of concern for opinion and reputation -- calls the reader away from the fulfillment of values as defined by representatives of the dominant culture to the fulfillment of those values according to the ethical ideals of Platonic philosophy. He calls his reader to be accountable to the opinion of the "wise person," rather than the "lay person" (the non-initiate of philosophy), measuring actions or aspirations by the standard of philosophy.

In the *Crito*, Plato develops a discussion concerning whose opinion one is to regard. Crito visits Socrates in prison in order to make preparations for his escape. He tells Socrates all the provisions that he and his friends have at their disposal to assist him, urging Socrates to consent to a plan not only in order to save himself but also the reputation of his friends:

> And yet what reputation could be more disgraceful than that of considering one's money of more importance than one's friends? For most people will not believe that we were eager to help you to go away from here, but you refused (44C; LCL).

Socrates objects to Crito's formulating an action with regard to the opinion of the majority. Crito's sense of shame before that court of reputation jeopardizes his esteem before the court of the "most reasonable men":

---

[4] Cf. Plato, *The Seventh Letter*, 324C-D.

[5] Cf. Plato, *The Seventh Letter*, 324D-325C.

But, my dear Crito, why do we care so much for what most people think (' Ἀλλὰ τί ἡμῖν ... οὕτω τῆς τῶν πολλῶν δόξης μέλει;)? For the most reasonable men, whose opinion is more worth considering (μᾶλλον ἄξιον), will think that things were done as they really ought to be (44C).

Crito should rather find encouragement to continue in the "just" course of action (refusing to do violence to Athenian law, even though it has done violence to Socrates), considering the opinion of the few who share the viewpoint of philosophy whether some course of action is honorable or disgraceful. Socrates' own predicament, however, imposes on Crito another lesson, which he seeks to teach his master: the power of the many to inflict evil should lead one to care for public opinion (τῆς τῶν πολλῶν δόξης μέλειν, 44D).[6]

Through his accustomed method of question and answer, Socrates tries to bring Crito back to their former way of thinking, namely that they ought to consider the opinions of the wise and disregard the opinions of the foolish (46C-47D):

S: Come then, what used we to say about this? If a man is an athlete and makes that his business, does he pay attention to every man's praise and blame and opinion or to those of one man only who is a physician or a trainer?

C: To those of one man only.

S: Then he ought to fear the blame and welcome the praise of that one man and not of the multitude.... Then in other matters, not to enumerate them all, in questions of right and wrong and disgraceful and noble and good and bad. which we are now considering, ought we to follow and fear the opinion of the many or that of the one, if there is anyone who knows about them, whom we ought to revere and fear more than all the others? And if we do not follow him, we shall injure and

---

[6] While creating a distinction between "the opinion of the masses" and the "truth" as embodied in the norms and values of those in power (i.e., the members of the dominant culture) is a common strategy for the self-legitimation of the dominant culture, here the distinction clearly functions in the service of subcultural values. Socrates, the spokesperson for the philosophical subculture, has been victimized by the members of the dominant culture on account of his devotion to philosophy, a devotion which often led him to question the definitions and values of the dominant culture. In effect, Plato has turned the dominant cultural technique against the dominant culture, placing the opinion of those in power alongside the opinion of the masses as equally unreliable as guides to "truth." Plato speaks for a philosophical subculture, rather than a counterculture, in that the actual values are not in dispute. Rather, the devotee of philosophy fulfills the values of justice or piety (valued also by the dominant culture) better than the member of the dominant culture who does not pursue philosophy.

cripple that which we used to say is benefitted by the right and ruined
by the wrong.

    S: Then, most excellent friend, we must not consider at all what the
many will say of us, but what he who knows about right and wrong, the
one man, and truth herself will say.

Disregard of the praise or blame of the "lay persons" is required for those
who would act in accordance with the highest ideals of philosophy. One
chooses a course of action with regard solely for the praise and blame of
the wise person, that is, one's like-minded philosophers and one's own
internalized ideal.

    Indeed, a chasm exists between those who are committed to "Truth"
and those who follow the opinion of the many, who are not committed to
philosophy. This comes to expression, for example, in Socrates'
discussion of one of the first principles of philosophical ethics, namely that
"we ought neither to requite wrong with wrong nor to do evil to anyone,
no matter what he may have done to us":

> And be careful, Crito, that you do not, in agreeing to this, agree to
> something you do not believe; for I know that there are few who believe
> or ever will believe this. Now those who believe this, and those who do
> not, have no common ground for discussion, but they must necessarily,
> in view of their opinions, despise one another (τούτοις οὐκ ἔστι κοινὴ
> βουλή, ἀλλὰ ἀνάγκη τούτους ἀλλήλων καταφρονεῖν, ὁρῶντας τὰ
> ἀλλήλων βουλεύματα, 49D).

In saying that the philosopher and the lay person, as it were, "despise one
another," Socrates distinguishes the groups which constitute the court of
opinion. Within the philosopher's court of reputation the sanctions of
"noble" and "disgraceful" (καλόν, αἰσχρόν) can now be used to reinforce
the actions which reflect commitment to philosophical ideals. Socrates will
not consider the reproaches of the public, whether the opinion of the
majority or the opinion of those representatives of the dominant culture
who, like Anytus and Meletus, are not devotees of philosophy. Only the
laws of Athens can justly accuse Socrates of attempting to do them harm
(50A-52A). Similarly, one is to feel ashamed not at the verdict of the
many, but at discovering that one has not lived up to one's ideals and
professions (52C).

    The redefinition of the honorable and the shameful, as well as the court
of opinion before which one is to feel shame, occupies a prominent place
in the *Gorgias* as well. Socrates engages first Polus and then Callicles on
the question of whether or not doing wrong is more disgraceful than
suffering wrong. Socrates agrees that, "as is the greatness of the evil so
is the honour of being able to avert them in their several degrees, and the

disgrace of not being able to avert them" (509C; Jowett translation), but uses this to support his thesis that doing wrong is the more disgraceful. For him, honor consists in living in accordance with this rule and disgrace befalls the one who transgresses it. Thus for him, even though he may be disgraced in a human court, he holds that no dishonor truly clings to him:

> Let us proceed in the next place to consider whether you are right in throwing in my teeth (ἃ σὺ ἐμοὶ ὀνειδίζεις) that I am unable to help myself or any of my friends or kinsmen, or to save them in the extremity of danger, and that I am in the power of another like an outlaw to whom any one may do what he likes [by reason of Socrates' lack of rhetorical training and experience in the courts] -- he may box my ears, which was a brave saying of yours; or take away my goods or banish me, or even do his worst and kill me; a condition which, as you say, is the height of disgrace (αἴσχιστον).... I tell you, Callicles, that to be boxed on the ears wrongfully is not the worst evil to befall a man, nor to have my purse or my body cut open, but that to smite and slay me and mine wrongfully is far more disgraceful (αἴσχιον) and far more evil; aye, and to despoil and enslave and pillage, or in any way at all to wrong me and mine, is far more disgraceful and evil to the doer of the wrong than to me who am the sufferer (508C-D).

The verdict of a human court, whether the court of law or court of opinion, is not a matter of concern to Socrates, such that he should shape his life and mold his actions with a view to gaining its approval. Rather, he sets before Callicles a portrait of the court with a view to whose verdict and opinion he does live his life -- the court of God. Indeed, the only disgrace which counts for him is the threat of disgrace before that court of reputation, and those who live with a view to human courts may find themselves in great danger before the divine court:

> Now I, Callicles, am persuaded of the truth of these things, and I consider how I shall present my soul whole and undefiled before the judge in that day. Renouncing the honours at which the world aims, I desire only to know the truth, and to live as well as I can, and, when I die, to die as well as I can. And, to the utmost of my power, I exhort all other men to do the same. And, in return for your exhortation of me, I exhort you also to take part in the great combat (ἀγών), which is the combat of life, and greater than every other earthly conflict. And I retort (ὀνειδίζω σοι) your reproach of me, and say, that you will not be able to help yourself when the day of trial and judgement, of which I was speaking, comes upon you; you will go before the judge, the son of Aegina, and, when he has got you in his grip and is carrying you off, you will gape and your head will swim around, just as mine would in the courts of this world, and very likely someone will shamefully box you on the ears, and put upon you any sort of insult (526D-527A).

Disgrace before that court has eternal value, and so counts infinitely more than disgrace in the eyes of those who do not live with a view to God's court. The prize of honor and a favorable opinion before God's court is well worth the endurance of insult and contempt in this life:

> Follow me then, and I will lead you where you will be happy in life and after death, as the argument shows. And never mind if someone despises you as a fool, and insults you, if he has a mind; let him strike you, by Zeus, and do you be of good cheer, and do not mind the insulting blow, for you will never come to any harm in the practise of virtue, if you are a really good and true man (527C-D).

While Plato aimed at making better citizens, he did so by bracketing the unreflecting acceptance of dominant cultural definitions of values and the opinion of its unreflective members. The subcultural mode of his rhetoric is clearly shown from the fact that those who follow philosophy will fulfill the commonly valued virtues better than those members of the dominant culture (and those among the masses) who do not. The *Crito* and *Gorgias* contain elements which are developed more fully among minority groups whose members remove themselves even further from the dominant culture in order to preserve the values and pursue the goals of their alternative cultures. First, the language of honor and shame is used to maintain distance from the opinion of those who do not subscribe to philosophy (as defined by Plato and the Academy). The judgements and evaluations of such "lay persons" are relativized and rejected in order to preserve commitment to the ideals taught by philosophy. Only before "truth herself" and those who seek her is one to feel a sense of shame, such that the sanctions of "noble" and "disgraceful" are now applied to acting in accordance with or departing from these ideals. One's life is set before the court of God, which will ascribe honor or disgrace according to whether or not one's life has been lived in accordance with the truth taught by philosophy.

SENECA

Like Plato and his students, Seneca (d. 65 CE) and his correspondents were well placed in the dominant culture. Seneca was himself born into an equestrian family of some distinction: his brother, Gallio, became the

Achaean proconsul, and his aunt was wife to the governor of Egypt.[7] He attained distinction himself in the courts of Rome -- at least enough to attract the attention of Caligula. After an eight-year period of exile, he returned to Rome as tutor to Nero and as virtual co-regent of the empire during Nero's minority. Nevertheless, his writings also exhibit a desire to set aside the opinion of others (again, both the opinion of the masses and the opinion of members of the dominant culture who do not subscribe to philosophy, now as defined by the Stoa) as a guide to actions and commitments in order to establish a higher guide -- the Stoic virtues and the conscience. While neither he nor his correspondents withdrew from engaging the dominant culture, his writings reflect a strategy for preserving adherence to virtue and attaining particularly Stoic goals (unconcern, freedom) through carefully delineating the court of opinion before whom one is to feel shame and providing the means for disregarding the opinion of all others as impediments to virtue and the fulfillment of one's goals. Once more, the language of honor and shame create and maintain an alternative culture within the dominant culture.

The wise person does not choose his actions in order to gain the approval of public opinion. "Rumour and reputation," he advises, are "matters that must, not guide, but follow our actions" (*De beneficiis* 6.43.3; LCL). Only "those who are not perfected ... still conduct themselves in accordance with public opinion" (*De constantia sapientis*. 19.3; LCL). The wise person, however, esteems neither the honor nor disgrace ascribed by the majority of people, since he regards them as children:[8]

> In the same spirit in which he sets no value (*nihilo aestimat*) on the honours they have, he sets no value on the lack of honour they show. Just as he will not be flattered if a beggar shows him respect, nor count it an insult if a man from the dregs of the people, on being greeted, fails to return his greeting, so, too, will he not even look up if many rich men look upon him. For he knows that they differ not a whit from beggars.... For men may all differ one from another, yet the wise man

---

[7] Everett Ferguson, *Backgrounds of Early Christianity* (Grand Rapids, MI: Eerdmans, 1987), 289; *Seneca ad Lucilium Epistulae Morales*, vol 1 (3 vols; tr. Richard M. Gummere; London: Heinemann, and New York: Putnam's Sons, 1917), vii-viii.

[8] In *Constant.* 11.2-12.1, Seneca notes that one does not take a child's actions as insulting, because children are inferior, and that "the same attitude...the wise man has toward all men whose childhood endures even beyond middle age and the period of grey hairs."

> regards them as all alike because they are all equally foolish (*Constant.*
> 13.2, 5).

The approval and contempt alike of the majority are removed from the consideration of the wise person. That this "majority" refers not only to the masses who are removed from power but also to those in power (i.e., the dominant culture) is seen in Seneca's response to the opinion of the "rich," that is, to those who have wealth, belong to the propertied class, and therefore exercise a share in power. The wise person, however, is called to look away from the opinion both of the "majority culture" and dominant culture to the reputation one will have among future generations for holding to a virtuous course of action:

> Virtue is never lost to view; and yet to have been lost to view is no loss.
> There will come a day which will reveal her, though hidden away or
> suppressed by the spite of her contemporaries. That man is born merely
> for the few, who thinks only of the people of his own generation. Many
> thousands of years and thousands of peoples will come after you; it is to
> these that you should have regard (*Epistulae* 79.17; LCL).

Thus while a person may experience disgrace in the opinion of contemporaries for choosing virtue, Seneca promises that the virtuous person will be vindicated at a future time. While this expresses the expectation for a reversal of opinion in this-worldly terms (although after the death of the virtuous person), it is comparable to the place of the divine court of opinion in Plato's construction of an alternative court of reputation. Ultimately, the court of opinion one is called to respect is that of the conscience, which is the spark of the divine in the human being: "No one...rates virtue higher or is more consecrated to virtue than he who has lost his reputation for being a good man in order to keep from losing the approval of his conscience" (*Ep.* 81.20).

The wise person is thus set free from public opinion's sanctions with regard to the noble and the shameful, able to set aside the goals of external things in favor of goals which lead to imperturbability ($\dot{\alpha}\tau\alpha\rho\alpha\xi\dot{\iota}\alpha$). Riches, titles, and power "are not praised because they ought to be desired, but they are desired because they have been praised; and when the error of individuals has once created error on the part of the public, then the public error goes on creating error on the part of individuals" (*Ep.* 81.29). The false opinion that these external things themselves make for a happy life perpetuates itself upon succeeding generations, as individuals see the wealthy, the powerful, and the eminent receive the rewards of high esteem and honor. The wise person knows, however, that this is error, and that true happiness consists of living in accordance with nature and preserving one's virtue, withdrawing one's hope and fear from external things (*Constant.* 9.2): "The wise man can lose nothing. He has everything invested in himself, he trusts nothing to fortune, his own goods are secure, since he is content with virtue....If his virtue is safe, his possessions are safe" (*Constant.* 5.4).[9]

For the Stoic, freedom from concern for the opinion of the masses leads to the freedom to value and pursue goals other than those sought by the majority of people. Only by setting as one's goal living in accordance with virtue can one gain freedom from injury and insult:

> Unconcern (*securitas*), however, is the peculiar blessing of the wise man, and he will never allow himself to pay to the one who has offered him an insult the compliment of admitting that it was offered. For, necessarily, whoever is troubled by another's scorn, is pleased by his admiration (*Constant.* 13.5).

Injury and insult do not harm the wise person's honor or self-respect. Rather, they provide the opportunity for the wise person to put his virtue to the test and prove its genuineness: that is, the slanders and slights of the lay person are transformed into an opportunity to gain honor in one's own estimation and in the eyes of the wise and of God (*Constant.* 9.3; 3.4). The wise person is able to despise insults and injuries, and thus these have no power as negative sanctions to shape behavior:

> Both schools [i.e., Stoic and Epicurean] urge you to scorn injuries (*contemnere iniurias*) and, what I may call the shadows and suggestions of injuries, insults (*contumelias*). And one does not need to be a wise man to despise these (*quas despiciendas*), but merely a man of sense -- one who can say to himself: "Do I, or do I not, deserve that these things befall me? If I do deserve them, there is no insult -- it is justice; if I do not deserve them, he who does the injustice is the one to blush" (*Constant.* 16.3).

The wise person's disregard for the opinion of the many provides not only freedom from the experience of dishonor as something externally ascribed; it also provides freedom for right action, as determined by the consideration of how to enact the Stoic virtues in a given situation. Again, the Stoic's rejection of public opinion's positive and negative sanctions is in view:

---

[9] The thesis of Seneca's *De Constantia* is that "no wise man can receive either injury or insult" (2.1).

> Otherwise, from the fear of insults or from weariness of them, we shall
> fall short in the doing of many needful things, and, suffering from a
> womanish distaste for hearing anything not to our mind, we shall refuse
> to face both public and private duties.... Liberty is having a mind that
> rises superior to injury, that makes itself the only source from which its
> pleasures spring, that separates itself from all external things in order
> that man may not have to live his life in disquietude, fearing everybody's
> laughter, everybody's tongue (*Constant.* 19.2-3).

Ultimately, the wise person's distance from public opinion enables the
execution of "both public and private duties," that is, permits the
fulfillment of life within the dominant culture. The execution of those
duties, however, may be guided internally by one's commitment to virtue,
rather than externally by the sanctions of public opinion. Indeed, despite
one's engagement with the dominant culture, one finally forms one's own
court of reputation, seeking self-respect from conscience on the basis of
adherence to the life of virtue.[10]

In Seneca one finds a person deeply engaged with the dominant culture
who nevertheless rejects the claim of the opinion of the representatives of
that culture to shape the actions and aspirations of the wise. Rather, the
wise person disregards both honor and dishonor as ascribed or defined by
public opinion, and is free both from the painful experience of falling into
disgrace (*securitas*) and from the proscriptive power of the threat of
disgrace (*libertas*). This makes possible an engagement with the dominant
culture which is guided by a commitment to the values of an alternative
culture -- the Stoic philosophy -- and which seeks honor or avoids disgrace
strictly in terms of what accords with the Stoic ethical principles.

EPICTETUS

The writings of Epictetus (c. 55-135 CE), the one-time slave, pupil of
Musonius Rufus, and teacher of Stoic philosophy, afford ample evidence
concerning how the language of honor and shame fosters alternative
cultures and sets of goals, while setting aside the opinions and evaluations
of the dominant culture. The first principle of Epictetus' Stoicism makes

---

[10] This passage challenges the notion of the dyadic personality as described by
Malina (*New Testament World*, 67-73), according to which a person's perception of the
self is based on the opinion others hold of that person. Seneca's restructuring of the
body of significant others (the court of reputation) provides the possibility of great
freedom from the social constraints of public opinion and outlines a personal basis for
self-respect.

a distinction between that which is under the control of the individual person and that which is not:

> Some things are under our control, while others are not under our control. Under our control are conception, choice, desire, aversion, and, in a word, everything that is our own doing; not under our control are our body, our property, reputation, office, and, in a word, everything that is not our own doing. Furthermore, the things under our control are by nature free, unhindered, and unimpeded; while the things not under our control are weak, servile, subject to hindrance, and not our own (*Encheiridion* 1.1-2; LCL).

The former things belong to the province of the "moral purpose" (ἡ προαίρεσις); the latter are classified as "externals." Epictetus considers what belongs to the moral purpose as superior to external things. "Reputation" appears here (and consistently throughout Epictetus) as an external thing, and as something which the Stoic will regard with detachment and as a thing far removed from the area of his concern.

Stoicism presents a new definition of what constitutes the good and the bad, that is, the things which shapes one's goals and evaluations:

> Of things that be, some are good, others evil, and others indifferent; Good things are virtues and everything that partakes in the virtues; evil are the opposite; while indifferent are wealth, health, repute (ἀγαθὰ μὲν οὖν ἀρεταὶ καὶ τὰ μετέχοντα τῶν ἀρετῶν· κακὰ τὰ δ' ἐναντία· ἀδιάφορα δὲ πλοῦτος, ὑγεία, δόξα, *Dissertations* 2.9.15; LCL).

The good is confined to virtue and living according to one's moral purpose (*Ench.* 13). All external things are ἀδιάφορα -- "indifferent things" -- aspects of life of which the Stoic may say "it is nothing to me" (*Ench.* 1.5). This new, or alternative, definition of values (even on the most basic level of "good" and "bad") shows that Epictetus is engaging in countercultural rhetoric. That is, he is presenting an alternative way of life, and an alternative system of norms for evaluation, to the life and norms of the dominant and majority cultures. The Stoic is motivated neither positively nor negatively by external impressions,[11] and is therefore challenged continually to choose the moral purpose and not be

---

[11] Cf. *Diss.* 2.8.1: "God is helpful; but the good is also helpful. It would seem, therefore, that the true nature of the good will be found to be where we find that of God to be. What, then, is the true nature of God? Flesh? Far from it! Land? Far from it! Fame? Far from it! It is intelligence, knowledge, right reason. Here, therefore, and only here, shall you seek the true nature of the good."

distracted by seeking to improve external things. Progress in one arena excludes the quest for progress in the other:

> You cannot be continually giving attention to both externals and your own governing principle (τὸ ἡγεμονικόν, *Diss.* 4.10.25).

> For be assured that it is no easy matter to keep your moral purpose (προαίρεσις) in a state of conformity with nature (κατὰ φύσιν), and, at the same time, to keep externals; but the man who devotes his attention to one of these two things must inevitably neglect the other (*Ench.* 13).

The goal sought by the one who tends the moral purpose and remains detached from external things is the enjoyment of the full constellation of Stoic values. These include the maintenance of "tranquility, freedom, and calm (ἀπάθειαν, ἐλευθερίαν, ἀταραξίαν, *Ench.* 29.6)," as well as the formation of a virtuous character, one which is "faithful, reverent, noble, unperturbed (πιστόν, αἰδήμονα, γενναῖον, ἀτάραχον, *Diss.* 2.8.27)."[12]

Epictetus argues that the Stoic conception of human existence alone gives one the ability to determine what constitutes the noble, the honorable, the disgraceful, the just, and so forth. All people agree that justice, piety, and honor are to be maintained, but just as Agamemnon and Achilles could agree that the noble thing must be done yet differed over what constituted noble action, so different people came into conflict over applying their ideals of the noble, or the pious, or the just to particular cases (*Diss.* 1.22.1-8). The certain basis for arriving at correct judgements in particulars is the Stoic distinction between things under one's control and not under one's control, together with the consideration of the law of nature (*Diss.* 1.22.9-10). Those who do not observe these principles, but rather retain concern over externals, are rendered incapable of attaining to true piety, justice, or nobility. Those who do not exercise their reason with regard to distinguishing what belongs to the moral purpose and what belongs to the realm of the external live in error and cannot form correct opinions:

---

[12] The attainment of these goals is impeded, indeed, rendered impossible, if one attaches desire or aversion to any external conditions. Cf. *Diss.* 2.17.24-25: "Give to poverty and to wealth your aversion and your desire: you will fail to get what you wish, and you will fall into what you would avoid. Give them to health; you will come to grief; so also if you give them to offices, honours, country, friends, children, in short to anything that lies outside the domain of moral purpose. But give them to Zeus and the other gods; entrust them to their keeping, let them exercise the control; let your desire and aversion be ranged on their side -- and how can you be troubled any longer?"

> The man who does not know who he is, and what he is born for, and
> what sort of a world this is that he exists in, and whom he shares it
> with; and does not know what the good things are and what are the evil,
> what the noble and what the base; and is unable to follow either reason
> or demonstration, or what is true and what is false, and cannot
> distinguish one from the other; and will manifest neither desire, nor
> aversion, nor choice, nor purpose in accordance with nature; will not
> assent, will not dissent, will not withhold judgement -- such a man, to
> sum it all up, will go about deaf and blind, thinking that he is somebody,
> when he really is nobody (δοκῶν μέν τις εἶναι, ὢν δ' οὐδείς, *Diss.*
> 2.24.19).

Lacking a knowledge of the noble and the base, the good and the bad, the
"lay person" forms a false estimation of self based on attainment of
external things, and so forms false evaluations of other based on the same
mistaken criteria. The conversion from lay person to philosopher is often
portrayed as a transition from shamelessness to a true sense of shame (ἐξ
ἀναισχύντου αἰδήμων ἔσῃ, *Diss.* 4.9.17; cf. 2.10.29), which places the
Stoic in a class apart from the many whose shamelessness makes them unfit
to pass judgement on the philosopher.

For the one desirous of being a Stoic, however, Epictetus opens up an
alternative arena for ambition. The philosopher removes himself from the
popular arenas in which people seek to fulfill ambition and gain esteem, in
favor of seeking to attain honor in the province proper to the self:

> Let not these reflections oppress you: 'I shall live without honour, and
> be nobody anywhere'. For, if lack of honour is an evil, you cannot be
> in evil through the instrumentality of another, any more than you can be
> in shame. It is not your business, is it, to get office, or to be invited to
> a dinner-party? Certainly not. How, then, can this be any longer a lack
> of honour? And how is it that you will be 'nobody anywhere', when
> you ought to be somebody only in those things which are under your
> control, wherein you are privileged to be a man of the very greatest
> honour (ἐν οἷς ἔξεστί σοι εἶναι πλείστου ἀξίῳ, *Ench.* 24.1).

Epictetus seeks to reassure the would-be philosopher that the pursuit does
not result in the deprivation of honor. The novice is depicted as
considering the honors enjoyed by those who pursue external goods, and
which he might enjoy if he devotes similar attention to those ambitions.
Epictetus seeks, in effect, to check any swelling of emulation, the "feeling
of pain at the evident presence of highly valued goods, which are possible
for us to attain, in the possession of those who naturally resemble us"
(Aristotle *Rh.* 2.11.1). While the failure to attain "a share in the
honourable things which all men, or all who resemble us, or a majority of
them, have a share in" would be considered "shameful" (Aristotle *Rh.*

2.6.12) by the members of the dominant culture, Epictetus' Stoicism overturns that verdict by its counter-evaluation of external things and its elevation of the realm of the moral purpose. It is in this arena that the philosopher seeks to make "progress" (προκοπή) toward securing the virtues and fruits of Stoicism.[13]   One gains distinction not through advancement in external things but through the right use of external impressions and maintenance of one's moral purpose in the face of what comes to pass (*Diss.* 1.6.37).

The Stoic's source of honor and self-respect is the claim to kinship with God.   While all human beings share this common heritage, the majority are unaware both of the fact of this kinship and of the consequences which follow:

> If a man could only subscribe heart and soul, as he ought, to this doctrine, that we are all primarily begotten of God, and that God is the father of men as well as of gods, I think that he will entertain no ignoble or mean thought about himself.... Since, then, it is inevitable that every man, whoever he be, should deal with each thing according to the opinion which he forms about it, these few, who think that by their birth they are called to fidelity, to self-respect, and to unerring judgement in the use of external impressions (πρὸς πίστιν... καὶ πρὸς αἰδῶ καὶ πρὸς ἀσφαλείαν τῆς χρήσεως τῶν φαντασιῶν), cherish no mean or ignoble thoughts about themselves, whereas the multitude do quite the opposite (*Diss.* 1.3.1, 4).

The distinction between externals and moral purpose, and the vocation of the Stoic, are grounded in this claim to kinship with Zeus. The Stoic also has a grant of honor from God in that God calls the philosopher to a life of bearing witness to the nature of God and the justice of God. Tending one's moral purpose and withdrawing one's desire and aversion from external matters gives one a claim to honor, which is accorded recognition by God in calling forth the philosopher's testimony:

> "'Take a governorship'. I take it and having done so I show how an educated man comports himself. 'Lay aside the laticlave, and having put on rags come forward in a character to correspond'. What then? Has it not been given me to display a fine voice? 'In what role, then, do you mount the stage now?' As a witness summoned by God. God says, 'Go

---

[13] Cf. *Diss.* 1.4.18, 21: "Where, then, is progress? If any man among you, withdrawing from external things, has turned his attention to the question of his own moral purpose (ἡ προαίρεσις), cultivating and perfecting it so as to make it finally harmonious with nature, elevated, free, unhindered, untrammelled, faithful, and honourable... this is the man who in all truth is making progress."

you and bear witness for Me; for you are worthy to be produced by me as a witness. Is any of those things which lie outside the range of the moral purpose either good or evil? Do I injure any man? Have I put each man's advantage under the control of any but himself?' What kind of witness do you bear for God? 'I am in sore straits, O Lord, and in misfortune; no one regards me, no one gives me anything, all blame me and speak ill of me'. Is this the witness that you are going to bear, and is this the way in which you are going to disgrace the summons (καταισχύνειν τὴν κλῆσιν ἣν κέκληκεν) which He gave you, in that He bestowed this honour upon you and deemed you worthy to be brought forward in order to bear testimony so important (ὅτι σε ἐτίμησεν ταύτην τὴν τιμὴν καὶ ἄξιον ἡγήσατο προσαγαγεῖν εἰς μαρτυρίαν τηλικαύτην; *Diss*. 1.29.44-49)?"

The Stoic is called to act in accordance with virtue and nature both in the role of governor and that of beggar. Indeed, loss of external things affords the opportunity to bear witness to the freedom that God grants to those who take on the Stoic estimation of human existence, and that Stoic re-evaluation makes it possible to turn loss and dishonor into an honorable commission.

The fulfillment of this divine commission requires that the philosopher not be carried away by external impressions of what is honorable and disgraceful. Epictetus warns against falling back into the view of the majority that advancement in public opinion or power makes one happy:

Beware lest, when you see some person preferred to you in honor (προτιμώμενον); or possessing great power, or otherwise enjoying high repute, you are ever carried away by the external impression, and deem him happy (*Ench*. 19.2).

Such external matters, Epictetus asserts, are of no value to the mature person, that is, the philosopher. Lay people may scurry about to secure such trifles, but not the Stoic:

But when I hear someone called blessed (μακαριζόμενον), because he is being honoured by Caesar, I say, 'What is his portion? Does he, then, get also a judgement such as he ought to have for governing a province? Does he, then, also get the ability to administer a procuratorship? Why should I any longer push my way in? Somebody is scattering dried figs and nuts; the children snatch them up and fight with one another, the men do not, for they count this a small matter (μικρὸν γὰρ αὐτὸ ἡγοῦνται, *Diss*. 4.7.21-22).

Setting value on externals jeopardizes the entire Stoic enterprise -- "In a word, then, remember this -- that if you are going to honour anything at all outside the sphere of the moral purpose, you have destroyed your moral purpose" (*Diss.* 4.4.23). All external things -- all aspects of life that are "indifferent" -- have to be despised if progress is to be made and the moral purpose kept in conformity with nature:

> For if the true nature of the good is one of the things that are under our control, there is no place for either envy or jealousy (οὔτε φθόνος οὔτε ζελοτυπία); and you yourself will not wish to be a praetor, or a senator, or a consul, but a free man. Now there is but one way that leads to this, and that is to despise the things that are not under our control (καταφρόνησις τῶν οὐκ ἐφ᾽ ἡμῖν, *Ench.* 19.2).

Concern for reputation and fear of dishonor (in the eyes of lay persons) are among the things the philosopher is to cast behind him in order to attain the victory (*Diss.* 1.18.21; cf. 1.30.2). The lay person could ascribe to the philosopher neither honor nor disgrace, at least, not in a way as would be accepted as such. Praise and insult from such sources were alike rejected (cf. *Diss.* 2.1.36).

The only honor and disgrace which could justly attach themselves to the Stoic, according to Epictetus, were those which resulted from making the right use of externals and preserving the moral purpose or allowing oneself to be impeded in these pursuits:

> It is a disgrace and a reproach (αἰσχρόν ἐστι καὶ ἐπονείδιστον) to have lost one's sense of shame, one's dignity, and one's gentleness, which are lost through our own fault, being things under our control; loss of externals not disgraceful, just as their possession is not noble (ἐκεῖνα μὲν οὔτ᾽ ἔχειν καλόν ἐστιν οὔτ᾽ ἀπολλύειν αἰσχρόν ἐστιν, *Diss.* 2.10.15-16).

Within the arena of Stoic ambition, Epictetus can use the negative sanction αἰσχρόν δε with great frequency in order to strengthen commitment to perseverance in philosophy (*Diss.* 2.2.13; *Ench.* 29.1-3), to urge the right use of external impressions (*Diss.* 1.6.18-20), to motivate conformity with the divine will (*Diss.* 1.12.12), and so forth. No external thing can rightly bring disgrace upon a person who knows "what the disgraceful things are (τίνα τὰ αἰσχρά ἐστιν)," namely, that only what is one's own doing can lead to honor or disgrace (*Diss.* 3.26.7-9).

The philosopher's court of reputation again excludes the members of the dominant culture as well as the "masses." We have seen already how, according to Epictetus, the majority of people do not take as their starting point their kinship with God (*Diss.* 1.3.4) and are unable to correctly determine what things are noble, shameful, just, or pious (1.22.1-10).

Unaware of these things, they are, by and large, "shameless" until they become philosophers, who alone exchange shamelessness for a true sense of shame (*Diss*. 4.9.17). Comparing people who place high value on external things to children, and philosophers to the mature (*Diss*. 4.7.22), carries significance as well for the question of who constitutes the court of reputation for the philosopher. Aristotle noted that one did not feel shame before children, that is, did not consider the estimation of a child as a factor in deciding upon a course of action (*Rh*. 2.6.23). The labelling of lay persons as "children" or comparable to children (cf. Seneca, *Constant*. 11.2-12.1) removes them from the philosopher's court of reputation, since their powers of reasoning and evaluating were deemed faulty.

Reputation is itself an external thing, and concern for public opinion is everywhere branded as incompatible with the pursuit of philosophy.[14] The negative evaluation of the philosopher by the lay person is turned back upon the one evaluating:

> But the one who has authority over you declares, 'I pronounce you impious and profane'. What has happened to you? 'I have been pronounced impious and profane'. Nothing else? 'Nothing'. But if he had passed judgement upon some hypothetical syllogism and had made a declaration, 'I judge the statement, "If it is day, there is light," to be false', what has happened to the hypothetical syllogism? Who is being judged in this case, who has been condemned? The hypothetical syllogism, or the man who has been deceived in his judgement about it? ...But shall the truly educated man pay attention to an uninstructed person when he passes judgement on what is holy and unholy, and on what is just and unjust? (*Diss*. 1.29.50-54)

Insults, reviling, and rebuke from such people can be disregarded. The Stoic may defeat being reviled (λοιδορεῖσθαι) and outrage (ὕβρις) by not accepting it as a real challenge to one's honor (*Diss*. 1.25.28-30). Indeed, these experiences are transformed into a sort of training exercise for the philosopher in the virtues of patience, detachment, and gentleness (*Diss*. 3.20.9). Only the judgement of those who are similarly concerned about virtue and the moral purpose carries any weight, and these will approve the one pursuing Stoicism:

---

[14] Cf. *Diss*. 3.2.9: "Wretch, even while you are studying these very topics you tremble and are worried for fear someone despises you, and you ask whether anybody is saying anything about you (μή τίς σου καταφρονήσῃ, καὶ ... μή τίς τι περὶ σοῦ λέγει)."

What then? Do you want me to be despised? -- By whom? By men of
understanding? And how will men of understanding despise the gentle
and the self-respecting person (καὶ πῶς καταφρονήσουσιν εἰδότες τοῦ
πρᾴου, τοῦ αἰδήμονος)? No, but by men without understanding? What
difference is that to you? Neither you nor any other craftsman cares
about those who are not skilled in his art (*Diss.* 4.5.22).

While distancing the Stoic from concern for the opinion of the
representatives of the dominant culture, and thus freeing such a one from
the dominant culture's definitions of the honorable and shameful, Epictetus
sets before his students the court of reputation whose approval they are to
seek. The primary constituent of this alternate court is God, before whom
a person lives out every aspect of life:

It is within yourself that you bear Him, and do not perceive that you are
defiling Him with impure thoughts and filthy actions. Yet in the
presence of even an image of God you would not dare to do anything of
the things you are now doing. But when God Himself is present within
you, seeing and hearing everything, are you not ashamed to be thinking
and doing such things as these, O insensible of your own nature, and
object of God's wrath (*Diss.* 2.8.13-14)!

In this passage he castigates the lay person for failing to live according to
one's nature which is kin to the divine, which is for Epictetus the mark of
shamelessness. The philosopher is, however, always aware of whom one
must seek to please: "When you come into the presence of some prominent
man, remember that Another looks from above on what is taking place,
and that you must please Him rather than this man" (*Diss.* 1.30.1). In
calling the philosopher to live so as to gain God's approval, however,
Epictetus calls that one to live in accordance with the "governing principle"
(τὸ ἡγεμονικόν), which is the seat of the divine in the human being (*Diss.*
1.15.3-4). Keeping the governing principle in conformity with nature --
that is, rightly using desire and aversion -- correlates with honoring God
and gaining divine approval. In such honoring of God is the Stoic's claim
to honor and security. Epictetus hopes that he will die while occupied with
tending his moral faculty, so that he may claim before God: "the faculties
which I received from Thee to enable me to understand Thy governance
and to follow it, these I have not neglected (τούτων οὐκ ἠμέλησα); I have
not dishonoured Thee (οὐ κατῄσχυνά σε) as far as in me lay" (*Diss.*
4.10.14). In maintaining a faithful witness to God's governance and justice
(cf. *Diss.* 1.29.44-49) and in keeping one's character and moral purpose
in conformity with nature (*Diss.* 2.8.21), the Stoic displays his concern to
show God the proper honor. It is before this court -- God and the

governing principle -- that the Stoic feels a sense of shame and maintains self-respect.

In Epictetus one finds again that honor and shame play an important role in the establishment of values and goals. According to the Stoic view of existence, however, all external things were irrelevant for attaining the good or falling into the bad. Progress in externals gained nothing of value -- only progress in virtue and keeping one's moral purpose in conformity with nature produced worthwhile fruit (tranquility, freedom, unconcern). These definitions and goals were supported by a use of the language of honor and shame similar to the use seen in Plato and Seneca. Those who do not hold to philosophy (as the Stoics defined it) were excluded from one's company of significant others from whom one sought approval and esteem. Lacking knowledge of the true nature of things (external *vs.* the moral purpose), lacking knowledge of the truly noble and shameful, lay persons were not equipped to evaluate (and thereby motivate) the philosopher's commitments and behaviors. The opinion of the majority of the members of the dominant culture was thus reduced to one of the external things which the philosopher was called to despise. One's honor and worth came from the fulfillment of the Stoic's vocation as a child and witness of God's governance as revealed in nature, and not from advancement in the public arenas wherein recognition, honor, and affirmation were generally sought.

Epictetus provides an alternate arena for the fulfillment of φιλοτιμία, within which the first principles of Stoic philosophy determine what is honorable or shameful. Within that arena, he may extend the promise of honor and the warning of disgrace in order to motivate his students to maintain their commitment to that alternative culture, its values, and its measures of worth. Desire for honor is satisfied through progress (προκοπή) in bringing the moral purpose in line with the rule of nature, and not through advancement in external, indifferent things. Whether they become governors or beggars, they are called to conceive of honor solely in terms of the standards of their philosophy, and not lapse into being "carried away by external impressions." To do so -- to have regard for the opinion of the many -- would be to compromise one's allegiance to the ideals of the minority culture, and to allow one's choice or refusal to be influenced from outside.

2 Jewish Writers

Adherence to a philosophical school and the values and goals it promoted was a strictly voluntary matter. Stoics or Platonists were separated from other inhabitants of the Greco-Roman world by their commitment to the alternative definitions and evaluation of experience, not by ethnic or socio-economic barriers. When one turns to consider the place of Jews in the Hellenistic world, however, one encounters a minority culture bound together by ethnic ties as well as by adherence to a particular set of ideals and customs (i.e., Torah).[15] Resistance to assimilation with another culture was part of the Jewish heritage. Thus when they moved from being a dominant culture to being a subjugated nation and minority culture within a larger dominant culture, it was natural that discussions should arise as to whether and how to maintain their heritage in a new socio-historical situation. While many found it preferable to renounce ethnic and traditional ties by "Hellenizing," others staunchly opposed the dissolution of their culture. Honor and shame language played an essential part in their effort to reaffirm Jewish values in the face of the cultural imperialism of Hellenistic monarchs.

THE WISDOM OF BEN SIRA

We turn first to a discussion of the date and setting of Ben Sira's work and writing in order to gain an appreciation for the peculiar cultural and social tensions which provide the context for his instruction, and in light of which he shapes his reformulations of wisdom traditions. The date and socio-historical setting of this collection of wisdom sayings and instructions can be determined with some certainty. Ben Sira's grandson, who translated the Hebrew original into Greek, migrated to Egypt in the thirty-eighth year of Ptolemy VII Euergetes II, or 132 BCE.[16] This would place his grandfather's period of flourishing in the first decades of that century. As the hymn in praise of the ancestors concludes with an encomium on the high priest Simon II, but contains no references to the deposition of Onias III or the Hellenization crisis of 175-164 BCE, the date of composition is

---

[15] Vernon Robbins ("Rhetoric and Culture: Exploring Types of Cultural Rhetoric in a Text," *Rhetoric and the New Testament* [ed. S. E. Porter and T. H. Olbricht; JSNTSS 90; Sheffield: JSOT, 1993], 447) observes that this ethnic background creates a special type of subculture, which "has its origins in a language different from the languages in the dominant culture," and which "attempts to preserve and perpetuate an 'old system' in a dominant cultural system in which it now exists, either because a significant number of people from this ethnic culture have moved into a new cultural environment or because a new cultural system is now imposing itself on it."

[16] Martin Hengel, *Judaism and Hellenism* (tr. John Bowden. 2 vols.; Philadelphia: Fortress, 1974), 131; Alexander A. DiLella, "Wisdom of Ben-Sira," pp. 931-45 in *The Anchor Bible Dictionary*, vol. 6 (6 vols.; New York: Doubleday, 1992), 932.

generally placed between 190 and 175 BCE.[17] In an epilogue, Ben Sira identifies his residence as Jerusalem (50:27), where it is believed the sage had a school (the "house of instruction," 51:23).[18]

The date and location place Ben Sira in a time of cultural tension, in which some Jews are being attracted to the Greek way of life while others are concerned to preserve the Jewish way of life or discover some viable synthesis between the two. It is now widely recognized that the Hellenization crisis under Antiochus IV did not occur solely at his own initiative, but rather in collusion with Jews who favored the adoption of a fully Hellenized way of life. 1 Macc 1:11-12, for example, describes the action of certain Jews -- "renegades" -- who, shortly after Antiochus IV's accession "came out from Israel and misled many, saying, 'Let us go and make a covenant with the Gentiles around us, for since we have separated from them many disasters have come upon us'" (NRSV). Even in this anti-Hellenist's history it is remembered that "the proposal pleased them." The author of 2 Maccabees focuses this initiative in the person of Jason (2 Macc 4:7-13), but notes that much of the priesthood was enthusiastic for these reforms (2 Macc 4:14-15). For Hellenization to have had the success that it did in Jerusalem (according to the author of 2 Maccabees), one would have to posit the necessity of a significant period of pro-Hellenizing sentiments. While Sirach lived and wrote before Hellenization had reached this pitch, it is reasonable to conclude that there were already growing leanings in that direction.[19]

---

[17] Hengel, *Judaism*, 131; DiLella, "Wisdom," 932; G. W. E. Nickelsburg, *Jewish Literature Between the Bible and the Mishnah* (Philadelphia: Fortress, 1981) 64; J. L. Crenshaw, *Old Testament Wisdom* (Atlanta: John Knox, 1981) 158. Cf. H. Duesberg, O.S.B. and P. Auvray, *Le Livre de L'Ecclésiastique* (Paris: Cerf, 1958), 8: "This date is confirmed by certain internal clues, particularly by the passage devoted to Simon, the high priest and son of Onias (ch. 50), whom the author appears to have known personally."

[18] DiLella, "Wisdom," 933; Crenshaw, *Wisdom*, 158; Hengel, *Judaism*, 132.

[19] So Duesberg and Auvray, *L'Ecclésiastique*, 8-9: "In this period Greek civilization exercised a strong pressure upon Judaism.... For more than a century, Greek civilization, introduced by Alexander, was spreading through the Orient, adorned with the prestide of victory and maintained by the extraordinary allurement of beauty and opportunity. The Jews, enclosed within their rigorous legalities, appear to have resisted at first. But around the turn of the century, aided by external pressure, the seductiveness became stronger. The setting of completely Hellenized cities, the frequent contacts with Egypt and Syria, in the end led to spectacular apostasies." Cf. also R. Smend, *Die Weisheit des Jesus Sirach erklärt* (Berlin: Reimer, 1907) xx-xxi; A. A. Di Lella, "Conservative and Progressive Theology: Sirach and Wisdom," *CBQ* 28 (1966) 140; R. T. Siebeneck C. P P. S., "May Their Bones Return to Life! -- Sirach's Praise of the Fathers," *CBQ* 21 (1959) 411.

It has become something of a scholarly commonplace to speak of Sirach as an anti-Hellenistic work, identifying the author's chief concern as the preservation of the Jewish way of life amidst Hellenizing propaganda:

> Both Ptolemies and Seleucids vigorously promoted the policies of Hellenization instigated by Alexander the Great.... At home as well as in his travels abroad, Ben Sira must have witnessed the baneful effects of Hellenization on the faith and practices of the Jews. He must have encountered many Jews whose faith was rocked by the questions and doubts that arose from Greek philosophy, religion, and lifestyle. To strengthen the faith and confidence of his fellow Jews Ben Sira published his book. His purpose was not to condemn Hellenism as such, but rather to demonstrate to Jews and even gentiles of good will that true wisdom is to be found primarily in Jerusalem and not in Athens.[20]

A number of indications in the text support the claim that Sirach is particularly concerned with combatting the influence of Hellenism. Of special interest have been passages which focus on the young and their relationship to their parents and their parents' traditions. Crenshaw, for example, suggests that "Sirach's admonition to honor parents rather than making fun of old people signals a decisive shift in values resulting from the conflict between the generations brought on by Hellenism."[21] Hengel also attributes Sirach's frequent admonitions addressed to young men to the "especial danger from the attractions of Hellenistic civilization."[22] By themselves these observations would be unconvincing, since Wisdom literature as a genre is frequently concerned with instructing the young. Combined, however, with the complete identification of wisdom with Torah (19:20; 1:26)[23] and the criticism of circles which have forsaken the

---

[20] DiLella, "Wisdom," 933.

[21] Crenshaw, *Wisdom*, 162.

[22] Hengel, *Judaism*, 132 (cf. the "zeal of neophytes in favor of Hellenism" noted by Duesberg and Auvray [*L'Ecclésiastique*, 9]). He further reads 3:21-24, an appeal to the young for intellectual modesty, as an attempt to bring them back from criticism of their traditions from the perspective of Greek speculation to modest acceptance of what God has given them as their portion (*Judaism*, 138-39).

[23] Hengel, *Judaism*, 139; DiLella ("Wisdom," 940) states that Ben Sira's "fundamental thesis is this: wisdom, which is identified with the Law, can be acquired only by one who fears God and keeps the commandments." Duesberg and Auvray (*L'Ecclésiastique*, 14) note this as a development original to Ben Sira, and therefore, one may conclude, an essential part of his program: "The development concerning the relationship between wisdom and law (24:23-34) is more recent and gives expression to conceptions unknown to the ancient sages." C. Spicq ("L'Ecclésiastique," *La Sainte*

law of Moses (41:8-9),[24] there arises a substantial case to be made for Ben Sira's alleged "controversy with Hellenistic liberalism."[25]

Our investigation of the setting of the Wisdom of Ben Sira yields a dynamic picture of the cultural climate in which the wisdom sayings and instructions were formed and within which they spoke. After nearly one-and-a-half centuries of Hellenization (from the campaigns of Alexander the Great to the reign of Ptolemy VII), Jews, like other groups which had held onto their native culture, found themselves at the frontier of an emerging world-culture, superior in power and, for some, superior in promise for personal achievement and enjoyment of life's pleasures. Internal desires to join with this dominant culture and Antiochus' ambitions to fulfill Alexander's dream of a single world united by a common culture would soon precipitate a severe crisis for Judaism. Sirach lives at a time when certain age groups and classes no longer took it as given that, being born Jewish, they would adhere to Jewish law and custom. The world was changing, and Israel was a small place in a corner of that world, continually passed back and forth from Ptolemaic to Seleucid control. It was thus a minority culture in a world of competing powers which

---

Bible [ed. L. Pirot and A. Clamer. 12 vols; Paris: Letouzey et Ané, 1946], 6.553) extends "wisdom" to include for Ben Sira the whole of Israel's religion, that is, both Law and cult.

[24] Hengel, *Judaism*, 151; Spicq ("L'Ecclésiastique," 553) and Di Lella ("Theology," 141) likewise find evidence that Ben Sira aims his work at those who have turned away from Torah-obedience and those who are wavering in their commitment.

[25] Hengel, *Judaism*, 138. Nickelsburg (*Jewish Literature*, 64) calls attention to the "lack of specific, pointed, and explicit polemics against Hellenism," the more general applicability of statements read as anti-Hellenistic polemics, and the fact that Ben Sira's "thought is sometimes couched in language that was at home in Hellenistic philosophy" in order to present a strong caveat with regard to the majority view. Hengel (*Judaism*, 147-150), of course, did not fail to notice the Stoic elements in Ben Sira's thought. He attributes this, however, to the perceived need "to adapt himself to the learned arguments of his time, if only to be heard and understood by his pupils and his opponents in the youth of the aristocracy" (*Judaism*, 148). Crenshaw (*Wisdom*, 173; cf. also DiLella, "Wisdom," 933-34) attributes the presence of Hellenistic elements and influences to Ben Sira's "willingness to enrich his own teachings from the scholarly tradition within Hellenism" with the result that he "strengthened his appeal to those who longed for intellectual respectability in the Greek world." These authors all see, therefore, a strategic use of elements of Hellenistic thought rather than the signs of Ben Sira's complete openness to Hellenism. He may embrace aspects of Greek thought, such as the identification of virtue and knowledge (G. H. Box and W. O. E. Oesterly, "Sirach," *APOT* 1.481), while still seeking to preserve an essential commitment to Jewish particularism and unqualified obedience to Torah.

nevertheless shared a dominant culture -- Hellenism. Within such a setting, Ben Sira's use of the language of honor and shame becomes most illuminating as a means of preserving or promoting adherence to the values and customs of the minority ethnic group, combatting strong tendencies to assimilate and become "like the Gentiles."[26]

Proverbs and Ben Sira

Ben Sira's use of honor and shame language bears many similarities to the use of this realm of discourse in other wisdom literature, notably the earlier collection of wisdom material called Proverbs.[27] "Being a wisdom teacher himself, Ben Sira chose to reflect and comment especially on the sacred literature most like his own, the Book of Proverbs."[28] He did not merely reiterate a saying, "but explained it and developed its implications for his own day and his own society." As the influence of Proverbs on Ben Sira is pervasive, Ben Sira's distinctiveness, and the conservative direction of his program, become clearer through a comparison with this collection. Such a comparison brings into sharper relief his intensification of claims for Torah as the heart and sum of Wisdom, and hence as the surest path to attain honor and approval.

Ben Sira shares with the authors of Proverbs the expectation that pursuing Wisdom leads to honor and a good reputation:

> The fear of the Lord is glory and exultation, and gladness and a crown of rejoicing (φόβος κυρίου δόξα καὶ καύχημα καὶ εὐφροσύνη καὶ στέφανος ἀγαλλιάματος). The fear of the Lord delights the heart, and gives gladness and joy and long life. For those who fear the Lord it will go well at the end (εὖ ἔσται ἐπ' ἐσχάτων); on the day of their death they will be blessed (ἐν ἡμέρᾳ τελευτῆς αὐτοῦ εὐλογηθήσεται). To fear the

---

[26] The following discussion is based on the LXX text, the form in which Ben Sira's thought penetrated Diaspora Judaism and which translates Hebrew values into Greek cultural perceptions. This will allow for more direct comparisons with Wisdom of Solomon and 4 Maccabees, as well as with Hebrews itself. Where the LXX departs significantly from the Hebrew original, these discrepancies will be noted and the discussion modified accordingly.

[27] The date of the collection is placed in the early fifth century B.C. by P. W. Skehan (*Studies in Israelite Poetry and Wisdom* [CBQMS 1; Washington, DC: Catholic Biblical Association, 1971], 15-26).

[28] P. W. Skehan and A. A. Di Lella, *The Wisdom of Ben Sira* (AB 39; New York: Doubleday, 1987), 43.

Lord is the beginning of wisdom (ἀρχὴ σοφίας φοβεῖσθαι τὸν κύριον, 1:11-14; NRSV, with adaptations).[29]

The fear of the Lord is the crown of wisdom, making peace and perfect health to flourish. He saw her and apportioned her; he rained down knowledge and discerning comprehension, and he exalted the glory of those who held her fast (δόξαν κρατούντων αὐτῆς ἀνύψωσεν, 1:16-17; au. trans.).

Whoever holds her [Wisdom] fast will obtain glory (ὁ κρατῶν αὐτῆς κληρονομήσει δόξαν), and the Lord will bless the place she enters (4:13).

Wisdom gives a person his or her καύχημα, his or her "claim to honor."[30] Wisdom clothes a person in the trappings of honor (6:29-31), and is presented metaphorically as a tree whose branches are "glory and favor" and whose fruits are "prestige and wealth" (24:16-17).[31] Wisdom still preserves one from dishonor: "Whoever obeys me will not be disgraced" (24:22).[32]

The promise of honor and threat of disgrace function here, as in Proverbs, as sanctions for and against certain behaviors, reinforcing social expectations, rules of conduct, and postures required for successful life and social relationships. One's own honor is still inextricably bound to the honor of one's parents:

Do not seek to augment your honor through your father's disgrace, for your father's disgrace is no source of renown for you (μὴ δοξάζου ἐν ἀτιμίᾳ πατρός σου οὐ γάρ ἐστίν σοι δόξα πατρὸς ἀτιμία). For a man's honor comes from his father's prestige, and a mother in disgrace is a

---

[29] Skehan and Di Lella (*Ben Sira*, 143) comment that "fear of the Lord is the source of the best things that life can offer." Ben Sira's embellishment of that traditional "offer" may reflect his awareness of the strong "counter-offer" Hellenism was making, and which would eventually triumph in the prelude to the Antiochene crisis of 167 B.C.

[30] Spicq ("L'Ecclésiastique," 564) recognized the meaning of this word as an indicator of one's basis for and claim to receiving honor.

[31] Skehan's translation obscures Ben Sira's identification of honor and wealth as the fruits which follow devotion to Wisdom, although Di Lella restores this sense in his commentary (Skehan and Di Lella, *Ben Sira*, 335 (cf. p. 328).

[32] As is typical for commentaries written before the rediscovery of honor and dishonor as prominent values in the Mediterranean world, lost with the decline of Classical Humanism (especially the attention given to classical rhetoric), Skehan and Di Lella (*Ben Sira*, 335-36) note the presence of these promises of freedom from disgrace without developing the rhetorical significance or persuasive force such declarations would bear for the hearer.

reproach to her children (ἡ γὰρ δόξα ἀνθρώπου ἐκ τιμῆς πατρὸς αὐτοῦ, καὶ ὄνειδος τέκνοις μήτηρ ἐν ἀδοξίᾳ, 3:10-11).[33]

The sanctity of marital relationships is still protected by the sanction of lasting dishonor as the reward of adultery. Since Ben Sira appears not to have held to a belief in life after death, a person's "only hope for survival lay in continuance of family and good reputation."[34] The destruction of one's reputation, leaving only a disgraceful memory, becomes the worst possible fate:

> [The adulteress] will leave her memory for a curse, and her dishonor will not be erased (καταλείψει εἰς κατάραν τὸ μνημόσυνον αὐτῆς καὶ τὸ ὄνειδος αὐτῆς οὐκ ἐξαλειφθήσεται). Those who remain will recognize that nothing is better than the fear of the Lord, and nothing sweeter than to keep the Lord's commands (23:26-27).

Similarly, false speech and infidelity in friendships carry with them the promise of disgrace:

> Glory and dishonor (δόξα καὶ ἀτιμία) come from speaking, and a man's tongue is his downfall (5:13).

> In great and small matters do not act amiss, and do not become an enemy instead of a friend; for a bad name incurs shame and reproach

---

[33] The NRSV (as the RSV) renders these verses as a sanction against dishonoring one's parents: "Do not glorify yourself by dishonoring your father, for your father's dishonor is no glory to you. The glory of one's father is one's own glory, and it is a disgrace for children not to respect their mother." In so doing, it departs from the LXX at both 3:10a and 3:11b. While it follows the Hebrew fragment of Sirach commonly designated MS A for the latter colon (cf. Skehan and Di Lella [*Ben Sira*, 153-154]), there is no justification in the Hebrew manuscripts for its rendering of 3:10a (which Skehan and Di Lella translate as "glory not in your father's disgrace," although Box and Oesterley ["Sirach," 324] interpret the meaning of this phrase in a manner which supports the NRSV translation). Skehan and Di Lella (*Ben Sira*, 156) acknowledge that Sir 3:10-11a reflects a cultural milieu in which "the glory of one's parents is also one's own glory," an observation which they support with a reference to Sophocles *Ant.* 703-704 (cf. also Prov 17:6, noted in Skehan and Di Lella, *Ben Sira*, 42). The LXX translation of 3:11b extends this argument to the mother, whose disgrace would reflect on the children's honor just as the father's would. The LXX thus offers a more complete synonymous parallelism in 3:11 than MS A, and allows the reflection upon the children of the esteem in which the parents are held to govern the couplet, developing the thought as a motivator to honor one's parents without reiterating the command.

[34] Snaith, *Ecclesiasticus* (Cambridge: Cambridge University, 1974), 118.

(ὄνομα γὰρ πονηρὸν αἰσχύνην καὶ ὄνειδος κληρονομήσει): so fares the double-tongued sinner (5:15-6:1).

The disposition of a liar brings disgrace, and his shame is ever with him (ἦθος ἀνθρώπου ψευδοῦς ἀτιμία καὶ ἡ αἰσχύνη αὐτοῦ μετ' αὐτοῦ ἐνδελεχῶς, 20:26).

Indolence is condemned as making one an object of disgrace (22:1), while the promise of honor and good reputation is still used to motivate the pupils of wisdom to pursue justice in their dealings and relationships (27:8). Finally, Ben Sira also cautions his pupils against emulation of sinners, urging them not to be stirred up by the apparent success of the ungodly:

> Do not envy the honors of a sinner, for you do not know what his end will be (μὴ ζηλώσῃς δόξαν ἁμαρτωλοῦ οὐ γὰρ οἶδας τί ἔσται ἡ καταστροφὴ αὐτοῦ). Do not delight in what pleases the ungodly; remember that they will not be held guiltless as long as they live (9:11-12).[35]

In the end, they will not enjoy blessing but rather will come to misery; only those who refrain from sin (i.e., the transgression of Torah) remain confident in the Lord.[36]

One sees in Ben Sira, however, an intensification of the claims made in Proverbs. These intensifications reveal the fact that Ben Sira was conscious of cultural alternatives to Judaism, indeed that Judaism constituted an ethnic subculture, a minority viewpoint within the broader international scene. The very need for a translation of a Jewish writing into Greek demonstrates how far the dominant culture of Hellenism had encroached upon Jewish life. The promises of honor and wealth attached to wisdom are more extravagant and placed more prominently near the beginning (1:11-19). Moreover, "fear of the Lord," that is, caution with regard to provoking God by showing disregard for God, is no longer simply the beginning of wisdom (Prov 1:7; Sir 1:14), but also its fullness

---

[35] The injuction, "envy not" (9:11), refers not to a prohibition against wishing the ungodly to be dispossessed of their goods and prestige, but rather to a prohibition against desiring to be like them (cf. Box and Oesterley, "Sirach," 347).

[36] Skehan and Di Lella (*Ben Sira*, 220) refer one to the graphic depiction of this reversal in Ps 73:2-16, which deals at greater length with the temptation to envy the sinner's temporary success (and thus be led to emulate his or her ways), and with the remedy for that temptation.

(1:16) and its crown (1:18).[37]   Indeed, "the whole of wisdom is the fear
of the Lord, and in all wisdom there is the doing of the Law" (19:20).[38]
There can be no doubt that Ben Sira specifically has in mind the Torah, the
law of Moses, as that which constitutes wisdom. The way to acquire the
wisdom which promises honor, prestige, wealth, and a noble end (1:9-19)
is straightforward: "If you desire wisdom, keep the commandments" (1:26,
NRSV).[39] As Skehan and Di Lella observe, "Wisdom, which is identified
with the Law, can be achieved only by one who fears God and keeps the
commandments."[40]   The inclusion of the qualifier "only" is central to
Sirach.   It is a defensive strategy, serving Ben Sira's program of
maintaining ethnic cultural values and customs in the face of the Hellenistic
dominant culture.

---

[37] M. Gilbert, "Wisdom Literature," *Jewish Writings of the Second Temple Period*
(ed. M. E. Stone; Assen: Van Gorcum, and Philadelphia: Fortress, 1984) 294. Skehan
and Di Lella (*Ben Sira*, 144) insightfully comment on the three meanings of
"beginning" in the phrase "beginning of wisdom": "(1)point of departure or starting
point, as in 15:14; (2) the most important part of the thing, as in 29:21 and 39:26; (3)
the best part or essence of a thing, as in 11:3. In v 14a, all three meanings are
present." J. G. Snaith (*Ecclesiasticus* [Cambridge: Cambridge University, 1974], 12)
concurs with this interpretation.

[38] Hengel, *Judaism*, 139; Crenshaw, *Wisdom*, 154. Hengel (*Judaism*, 138) affirms
the delineation of the "decisive tendency of the work" as stated by R. Smend (*Weisheit*,
xxxiii): "Sirach heightens the statement in Prov I.7, 9, 10, that the fear of the Lord is
the beginning of wisdom ... by asserting that all wisdom comes from the Lord and that
it has been with him from eternity. In these words, which he sets at the head of his
work, he formulates a Jewish declaration of war against Hellenism."   A similar
observation is made by Skehan and Di Lella (*Ben Sira*, 77): "True wisdom has her
domain 'in Jerusalem' (24:11b), and not in Athens or Alexandria. All of which is to
say that Israelite wisdom is incomparably superior to Hellenistic wisdom and culture."
Cf. also Box and Oesterley, "Sirach," 269; Siebeneck, "Fathers," 412.   Siebeneck
("Fathers," 413) argues that Ben Sira's praise of the great figures of Israel's past in
chapters 44 through 50 affords the proof through examples of Israel's superiority: "This
wisdom as lived within the assembly of the people of God has really produced men of
gigantic stature. Hellenism may boast of its men of renown; Israel also had her heroes
and of these Sirach would sing. The illustrious men of the past were the concrete
expression of Israel's exclusive possession of true wisdom."

[39] Hengel, *Judaism*, 139; Crenshaw (*Wisdom*, 155) points the reader also to Sir
15:1: "whoever holds to the Law will attain wisdom." Smend (*Weisheit*, xxiii; cited
in Skehan and Di Lella, *Ben Sira*, 74) notes the close connections established by Ben
Sira between wisdom, Torah, and fear of the Lord: "Subjectively, wisdom is fear of
God; objectively, it is the law book of Moses (chap. 24)."

[40] Skehan and Di Lella, *Ben Sira*, 76.

Honor, Shame, and the Program of Ben Sira

1. Torah-Obedience as the Definitive Claim to Honor

Within the context of cultural conflict between adoption of the dominant culture's way of life and preserving the ancestral (and now minority) culture, Sirach affirms that the latter course remains the way to secure honor. Indeed, for Ben Sira fear of the Lord and obedience to the commandments become the decisive criteria for the evaluation of honor:

> What race is worthy of honor? The human race. What race is worthy of honor? Those who fear the Lord. (σπέρμα ἔντιμον ποῖον; οἱ φοβούμενοι τὸν κύριον.) What race is unworthy of honor? The human race. What race is unworthy of honor? Those who transgress the commandments. (σπέρμα ἄτιμον ποῖον; οἱ παραβαίνοντες ἐντολάς.) Among brothers their leader is worthy of honor, and those who fear the Lord are worthy of honor in his eyes. The rich, and the eminent, and the poor -- their glory is the fear of the Lord (πλούσιος καὶ ἔνδοξος καὶ πτωχός τὸ καύχημα αὐτῶν φόβος κυρίου). It is not right to despise an intelligent poor man, nor is it proper to honor a sinful man. The nobleman, and the judge, and the ruler will be honored, but none of them is greater than the man who fears the Lord (μεγιστὰν καὶ κριτὴς καὶ δυνάστης δοξασθήσεται καὶ οὐκ ἔστιν αὐτῶν τις μείζων τοῦ φοβουμένου τὸν κύριον, 10:19-24; RSV).[41]

---

[41] The Hebrew original differs from the LXX in several important respects, although the point of the passage is essentially the same in both. In 10:22, the Hebrew reads "Resident alien, stranger, foreigner, and pauper -- their glory is the fear of Yahweh" (A. Di Lella, "Sirach 10:19-11:6: Textual Criticism, Poetic Analysis, and Exegesis," *The Word of the Lord Shall Go Forth: Essays in Honor of David Noel Freedman in Celebration of His Sixtieth Birthday* (ed. C. L. Meyers and M. O'Connor; Winona Lake, IN: ASOR-Eisenbrauns, 1982), 159). The point of the verse in the Hebrew is to provide the socially disadvantaged with a basis for honor and self-respect. Nevertheless, Ben Sira's desire to detach evaluations of honor from ambiguous, external criteria, is attested elsewhere in the book (e.g., 10:24; 10:22-23). Di Lella ("Sirach 10:19-11:6," 160) reconstructs 10:20b (the Hebrew MS witness is lacking) as "he who fears God (is honored) among his [God's] people," replacing God as the significant other here with the visible court of reputation formed by the congregation of the faithful. Still, the governing sense is preserved, namely that "fear of the Lord" provides the surest basis for honor. Thus Di Lella's comment on the Hebrew text ("Sirach 10:19-11:6," 160) is still relevant: "The point of v 20 is that the one who fears God has among God's own people equal to that which earthly leaders receive because of their office. B and Syriac go even further: the God-fearing person receives more honor than the earthly leader (cf. 25:10)."

According to this instructional period, fear of the Lord alone gives one a claim to honor, while transgression of the law (which corresponds to disregarding the Lord) alone makes one worthy of disgrace. Indeed the fear of God is here equated with obedience to Torah, with the result that "people are honorable only when they fear the Lord."[42] External criteria -- wealth, poverty, eminence (10:22)[43] -- do not give one a claim to honor nor make one liable to dishonor. For the evaluation of honor, obedience to Torah counts more than poverty (10:23), and without obedience to the law one has no claim to honor. Moreover, fear of the Lord gives one a claim to honor which cannot be surpassed:

> How great is he who has gained wisdom (ὡς μέγας ὁ εὑρὼν σοφίαν)!
> But there is no one superior to him who fears the Lord (ἀλλ' οὐκ ἔστιν
> ὑπὲρ τὸν φοβούμενον τὸν κύριον). The fear of the Lord surpasses
> everything; to whom shall be likened the one who holds it fast (φόβος
> κυρίου ὑπὲρ πᾶν ὑπερέβαλεν, ὁ κρατῶν αὐτοῦ τίνι ὁμοιωθήσεται; 25:10-
> 11)?

External criteria are unreliable. Riches and reputation gained apart from the Lord may not last long -- a reversal of fortunes may occur at any time (11:4-6). The value of wealth depends on whether or not that wealth was acquired in accordance with obedience to Torah; similarly, the lack of wealth carries no intrinsic disgrace: "Riches are good if they are free from sin, and poverty is evil in the opinion of the ungodly" (13:24).[44]

If riches could only be acquired through assimilation to the Hellenic culture and transgression of Torah, then for Ben Sira poverty would be more honorable. The decisive criterion was adherence to Torah, and fear of the Lord one's only claim to honor (one's καύχημα, "boast" -- 9:16; 10:22). Nevertheless, Ben Sira also promises that those who adhere to the Law, that is, pursue wisdom, will not suffer any loss of status, but rather will enjoy prestige and elevation above those who have not committed themselves wholly to the Lord:

---

[42] Di Lella, "Sirach 10:19-11:6," 160. Cf. also Snaith, *Ecclesiasticus*, 56-57; Box and Oesterley, "Sirach," 350.

[43] Cf. 40:26-27: "Riches and strength lift up the heart, but the fear of the Lord is better than both. There is no loss in the fear of the Lord, and with it there is no need to seek for help. The fear of the Lord is like a garden of blessing, and covers a man better than any glory (φόβος κυρίου ὡς παράδεισος εὐλογίας, καὶ ὑπὲρ πᾶσαν δόξαν ἐκάλυψεν αὐτόν)."

[44] Crenshaw, *Wisdom*, 157.

The one who believes the law heeds the commandments, and the one who trusts the Lord will not be brought low (ὁ πιστεύων νόμῳ προσέχει ἐντολαῖς καὶ ὁ πεποιθὼς κυρίῳ οὐκ ἐλαττωθήσεται, 32:24).

The one who fears the Lord will do this, and he who keeps hold of the law will obtain wisdom. He will stand firm upon her and will not bend, and he will rely on her and will not be disgraced (οὐ μὴ καταισχυνθῇ). And she will lift him up above his neighbours, and open his mouth in the midst of the assembly (καὶ ὑψώσει αὐτὸν παρὰ τοὺς πλησίον αὐτοῦ καὶ ἐν μέσῳ ἐκκλησίας ἀνοίξει τὸ στόμα αὐτοῦ, 15:1, 4-5; au. trans.).[45]

Rather, it is those who forsake the Law that will come to disgrace, a shame which will cover their memory and their offspring: "The inheritance of the children of sinners will perish, and on their posterity will be a perpetual reproach (ἐνδελεχιεῖ ὄνειδος). Children will blame an ungodly father, for they suffer reproach because of him. Woe to you, ungodly men, who have forsaken the law of the Most High God!" (41:6-8; RSV). Thus Ben Sira threatens the apostates (and potential apostates) with the deprivation of one of the greatest blessings -- to live on in an honorable remembrance.[46]

In keeping with the growing danger of abandoning the Jewish ways and customs, Ben Sira augments earlier warnings found among the sages with regard to arrogance and outrage. Arrogance remains a harmful trait with regard to the bonds between members of human society: "Do not get angry with your neighbour for every injury, and do no acts of insolence. Arrogance is a hated thing before the Lord and before human beings, and injustice is offensive to both" (10:6-7; au. trans.). The root of arrogance, however, is apostasy: "The beginning of a person's arrogance is the forsaking of the Lord, and the turning of the heart away from the One who made it. The beginning of arrogance is sin, and the one who clings to it rains forth abominations. On account of this, the Lord confounds them with assaults, and overturns them completely" (10:12-13). Transgression of the law (sin) stems from the refusal to honor God as God merits, a course of action which leads to God's satisfaction of God's honor in the annihilation of the transgressor.[47]

---

[45] According to Skehan and Di Lella (*Ben Sira*, 265), opening one's mouth in the assembly was the privilege, and hence honor, of the wise; fools were to remain silent (Prov 24:7).

[46] Cf. Crenshaw, *Wisdom*, 153: "Accordingly, persons deserving contempt were those who failed to keep commandments, rather than foolish sluggards who had provoked earlier sages' ire."

[47] Spicq ("L'Ecclésiastique," 621) suggests that the quest for honor which entails transgression of God's Law leads only to pride, or a false claim to honor, which stands opposed to the "true honor of a person" which comes from the "fear of God."

2. Sirach's Construction of the "Court of Reputation"

Fear of the Lord brings the promise of honor; transgression of God's Law carries the threat of disgrace and punishment. But in whose eyes does obedience bring honor and transgression shame? In cities of the diaspora, assimilation to Greek culture no doubt offered access to prestige heretofore denied Jews; those who remained exclusively committed to Jewish ways found themselves cut off from many avenues of advancement and honor. In the land of Israel, too, taking up the Greek way of life may have become a symbol of status and prestige among the aristocracy, and certainly opened the door to gaining distinction abroad. How could Ben Sira sustain the promise of honor and threat of disgrace, or, rather, direct these to uphold specific values and courses of action? Like Plato in the *Crito*, he directs the readers' attention to an alternative court of reputation, whose verdict will differ from that of the majority, yet nevertheless has greater value.

Before whom, then, is one to feel shame -- that is, before whose eyes does one live out one's life and from whom is one to hope for a positive evaluation of one's worth? In answer to this question, Ben Sira points frequently to God. In an extended discourse on proper and improper shame or modesty (41:16-42:5), he tells his readers to "Be ashamed before the truth of God and his covenant" (41:19). This injunction stands out from the rest in the sequence, which instruct the readers to be ashamed of some specific act or class of transgression before a specific audience. It is likely that the LXX, followed here, departs from the Hebrew original.[48] Indeed, the translator may have been influenced by 42:2: "Do not be ashamed of the law and covenant of the Most High" (NEB). Just as this verse excludes those who are not followers of Torah from the body of one's significant others (those people whose approval one is to seek and from whom honor is granted),[49] the Greek translator refashioned 41:19 to point back to God and Torah as the ultimate significant others, whose

---

[48] Snaith (*Ecclesiasticus*, 205) suggests: "The Greek translation reminds the reader of the religious background of all the author's thought. But the Hebrew probably read '(be ashamed) of changing your oath and agreement'; the Greek translator mistook the Hebrew *'ālāh* ('oath') for *'elōah* ('God'), the consonantal text probably being the same, and then tried to make sense of the misreading."

[49] Thus Skehan and Di Lella (*Ben Sira*, 482): "the colon serves as a reminder to the Jews who are tempted to compromise their faith for the blandishments of the Greek way of life." So also Snaith (*Ecclesiasticus*, 206): "Ben Sira now turns to a list of things one should not be ashamed of when ridiculed or criticized in public.... Gentile ridicule of Jewish observances had led many Jews to be lax and remain popular." Cf. also Spicq, "L'Ecclésiastique," 787.

approval is of sole importance. The LXX, however, merely introduces into the text at this point a leading idea of other verses throughout Ben Sira.

The entirety of a person's life is lived before the court of God and in light of God's covenant (whether for blessing or curse):

> A man who breaks his marriage vows says to himself, "Who sees me? Darkness surrounds me, and the walls hide me, and no one sees me. Why should I fear? The Most High will not take notice of my sins." His fear is confined to the eyes of men, and he does not realize that the eyes of the Lord are ten thousand times brighter than the sun; they look upon all the ways of men, and perceive even the hidden places (23:18-19; RSV).[50]

> Their ways are always before him, they will not be hid from his eyes (17:15).[51]

Seeking what pleases God -- living according to God's requirements (i.e., Torah) -- is therefore the wise course of action:

> The greater you are, the more you must humble yourself; so you will find favor in the sight of the Lord (ὅσῳ μέγας εἶ τοσούτῳ ταπείνου σεαυτόν καὶ ἔναντι κυρίου εὑρήσεις χάριν). For great is the might of the Lord; he is glorified by the humble (3:18, 20).

> Those who fear the Lord will not disobey (οὐκ ἀπειθήσουσιν) his words, and those who love him will keep his ways. Those who fear the Lord will seek his approval, and those who love him will be filled with the law. Those who fear the Lord will prepare their hearts, and will humble themselves before him (2:15-17).

> For the fear of the Lord is wisdom and instruction, and he delights in fidelity and meekness (σοφία γὰρ καὶ παιδεία φόβος κυρίου καὶ ἡ εὐδοκία αὐτοῦ πίστις καὶ πραότης, 1:27).

---

[50] Skehan and Di Lella (*Ben Sira*, 324) point out that, while the adulterer takes precautions to avoid discovery and the public dishonor which discovery would bring, and even though only God's eyes see his adultery, the result is still loss of honor before both God and the community (23:21).

[51] Cf. Prov 5:21, where, again, the ultimate significant other, before whose face all life is exposed, is God: "for the ways of a man are before the eyes of God, and God looks into all his paths (ἐνώπιον γὰρ εἰσιν τῶν τοῦ θεοῦ ὀφθαλμῶν ὁδοὶ ἀνδρός εἰς δὲ πάσας τὰς τροχιὰς αὐτοῦ σκοπεύει, au. trans.)."

In these verses again one sees the connection between fearing (and loving) God and obedience to the Law of Moses. Indeed, one could say that, since God is known primarily as revealed in the Law, Ben Sira in effect holds up the Torah itself as the court of reputation before which the readers live out their lives.

The social counterpart to God as "significant other" is the "congregation," the ἐκκλησία. It is before the congregation that one will be disgraced:

> Do not exalt yourself lest you fall, and thus bring dishonor upon yourself (μὴ ἐξύψου σεαυτόν ἵνα μὴ πέσῃς καὶ ἐπαγάγῃς τῇ ψυχῇ σου ἀτιμίαν). The Lord will reveal your secrets and cast you down in the midst of the congregation, because you did not come in the fear of the Lord, and your heart was full of deceit (1:30).

In the same way, it is the congregation -- the assembly of Israel -- which, Ben Sira posits, will attest to the honor which the Lord grants to the obedient:

> He will lean on [Wisdom] and will not fall, and he will rely on her and will not be put to shame (οὐ μὴ καταισχυνθῇ). And she will raise him up above his neighbours, and open his mouth in the midst of the assembly (καὶ ὑψώσει αὐτὸν παρὰ τοὺς πλησίον αὐτοῦ καὶ ἐν μέσῳ ἐκκλησίας ἀνοίξει τὸ στόμα αὐτοῦ, 15:4-5; RSV, with alterations).

Significantly, there can no recognition of such honoring by God apart from the community which shares the same commitment to the Torah and honors the God of Israel. While Ben Sira sets God as the ultimate "other" before whom one is to feel shame, the congregation forms an essential reinforcement:

> Be ashamed (αἰσχύνεσθε) of immorality, before your father or mother;
> and of a lie, before a prince or a ruler;
> of a transgression, before a judge or magistrate;
> and of iniquity, before the congregation and the people (41:18;
> RSV, with alterations).

In contrast, Ben Sira seeks to distance his readers from concern for the opinion of those who do not fear the Lord, whose judgement is therefore often mistaken and certainly unreliable: "Riches are good for one who is free from sin, and poverty is evil in the mouths of the ungodly" (13:24). In shifting criteria of evaluation of worth and honor away from external signs of success (which may have been gained at the cost of one's total commitment to God and God's Law), Ben Sira also directs his pupils' sensitivity to the opinion of others away from those who still evaluate by those criteria, leading them to ask only how they might gain honor and favor in the sight of God and those faithful to God's covenant.[52]

3. The Encomium on Illustrious Ancestors

The last major section of Ben Sira's work is the famous hymn in praise of illustrious ancestors. More than simply a celebration of Israel's heritage, this encomium serves to enforce the values and motivations promoted throughout the work as discussed above. The hymn begins with an invitation to praise the distinguished men of Israel's past:

> Let us praise persons of renown, and our fathers by race (αἰνέσωμεν δὴ ἄνδρας ἐνδόξους καὶ τοὺς πατέρας ἡμῶν τῇ γενέσει). The Lord apportioned to them great honor, his majesty from eternity (πολλὴν δόξαν ἔκτισεν ὁ κύριος τὴν μεγαλωσύνην αὐτοῦ ἀπ᾽ αἰῶνος, 44:1-2; au. trans.).

In so doing, Ben Sira will set forth what behavior and commitments are worthy of praise and an honorable remembrance. We should note that here at the outset Ben Sira claims that it is the Lord who "created honor" for such figures, who gives them a share in God's own honor. At the conclusion of the prologue Ben Sira points to the other, social element of the court of reputation:

> Their line will continue for ever, and their reputation will not be erased. Their bodies were buried in peace, and their name lives for generations (τὸ ὄνομα αὐτῶν ζῇ εἰς γενεάς). Peoples will tell of their wisdom, and the congregation proclaims their praise (σοφίαν αὐτῶν διηγήσονται λαοί, καὶ τὸν ἔπαινον ἐξαγγέλλει ἐκκλησία, 44:13-15).

---

[52] Hengel (*Judaism*, 152) interprets 11:24 ("Receive a stranger into your house and he will alienate your way of living and estrange your family from you") as a caution against close contact between Jews and their non-Jewish friends, "by which the confines of Jewish morality and religion which separated Israel from the non-Jewish world were shattered." According to such a reading, Ben Sira urges a degree of separation (and thus insulation) from the carriers of non-Jewish values who might influence their Jewish associates to accommodate themselves to Greek values and, by their presence in Jewish lives, continue to form a part of the "court of opinion" in whose eyes Jews would seek to be esteemed. For Ben Sira, the universalism of earlier wisdom literature has given way to Jewish particularism (cf. 36:6-12). The Gentile nations are again entirely outsiders from whom one seeks to be delivered, not to be honored according to their standards.

116   *Despising Shame*

Again one finds the people of Israel (λαοί) and the congregation of the
faithful (ἐκκλησία) posited as those who perpetuate the honorable
remembrance of those who have held to the values and laws of the Jewish
people.[53]

Ben Sira praises the ancestors partly because such remembrance is their
due, partly because such memorial is required by the socio-historical
situation. Ben Sira's choice of examples, and the aspects of the ancestors'
lives he chooses to hold up as praiseworthy, are calculated to have an
effect upon the hearers as well. Remembering that encomia were expected
to rouse the hearers to emulation,[54] indeed that successful encomia limited
themselves to praising in those figures to be honored what was possible for
the hearers to imitate,[55] one can see in Ben Sira's hymn the continuation

---

[53] The prologue contains one striking problem, namely the identity of those who
"have no memorial, who have perished as though they had not lived; they have become
as though they had not been born, and so have their children after them" (εἰσὶν ὧν οὐκ
ἔστιν μνημόσυνον, καὶ ἀπώλοντο ὡς οὐχ ὑπάρξαντες, καὶ ἐγένοντο ὡς οὐ γεγονότε,ς
καὶ τὰ τέκνα αὐτῶν μετ᾽ αὐτούς, 44:9; RSV). Who has passed away into oblivion and
been deprived of a lasting, honorable remembrance? Smend (*Weisheit*, 419), as well
as G. H. Box and W. O. E. Oesterley ("Sirach," 480-81), see this as a reference to the
fate of the ungodly. Sirach, however, prefers to depict their fate as lasting
remembrance of a dishonorable sort, a perpetuating of their disgrace as the greatest
possible punishment. Further, the shift of subject is not made explicit and is made
more difficult to maintain in the face of syntactic considerations, namely that verses 8
and 9 provide two subcategories ("some...others....") of the "all" mentioned in verse
7. But would Ben Sira want to leave his readers with the impression that fidelity to
God could go unrewarded? The verses which follow seem to assure the readers that
the righteous deeds of these people have not been forgotten (even though they have left
no memorial), and that their name lives forever (44:14). Are the readers to understand
that their fame lives on in the memory of God, or that the congregation can somehow
attest to their righteousness even though there is no specific memory of these people?
Are the nameless individuals somehow still included in the praise of the congregation?
This is a possible solution, given the corporate notion of election and of honor. Skehan
and Di Lella (*Ben Sira*, 501) suggest that the author refers to the faithful "who for
whatever reason are no longer remembered by later generations of Israelites" whose
fidelity will nevertheless not be forgotten by God.

[54] Cf. Thucydides *Hist.* 2.43.1-4: "Their glory survives in everlasting
remembrance, celebrated on every occasion which gives rise to word of eulogy or deed
of emulation.... Do you, therefore, now make these men your examples, and judging
freedom to be happiness and courage to be freedom, be not too anxious about the
dangers of war."

[55] Cf. Thucydides *Hist.* 2.35.2: "Eulogies of other men are tolerable only in so far
as each hearer thinks that he too has the ability to perform any of the exploits of which
he hears; but whatever goes beyond that at once excites envy and unbelief (φθονοῦντες
ἤδη καὶ ἀπιστοῦσις)."

of the inculcation of the minority culture's values which he began in 1:11. The subjects of his encomium receive praise on account of their loyalty to the covenant.[56] The discussion of the expectations of encomia generally leads one to affirm that the purpose of this praise is to motivate the hearers to imitation of the ancestors' faithfulness and commitment to God through obedience to Torah.[57]

What makes one worthy of praise? Abraham, who is lauded as being of incomparable honor (οὐχ εὑρέθη ὅμοιος ἐν τῇ δόξῃ), attained it thus: "he kept the law of the Most High, and was taken into covenant with him; he established the covenant in his flesh, and when he was tested he was found faithful" (44:20; RSV). Fidelity to God (cf. 2:10) and perseverance in the covenant (cf. 41:19) lead to a praiseworthy remembrance. Phineas is ranked third in honor on account of his zeal "in the fear of the Lord" (καὶ Φινεες υἱὸς Ελεαζαρ τρίτος εἰς δόξαν ἐν τῷ ζηλῶσαι αὐτὸν ἐν φόβῳ κυρίου, 45:23). Phineas' zeal, it will be remembered, manifested itself in the public, spontaneous slaughter of an Israelite and his non-Israelite wife, in the wake of a crisis of idolatry (Num 25:1-9). His honor derives from a concern for the strict worship of the God of Israel and the strict maintenance of boundaries between the congregation and the Gentiles. Caleb, who held fast to God's command and encouraged Israel to follow God's way, enjoyed the distinction (shared with Joshua) of being the only two people from their generation to see the promised land. He shows that "it is good to follow the Lord (ὅτι καλὸν τὸ πορεύεσθαι ὀπίσω κυρίου, 46:10)." Ben Sira interjects into his encomium a wish: "May their bones revive from where they lie, and may the name of those who have been honored live again in their sons (46:12)!" This makes certain the paraenetic purpose of this hymn, indeed of the whole collection of sayings and instructions, namely that Ben Sira's pupils and contemporaries, the children of such committed ancestors, should continue in their ancestral ways -- should embody the values, behaviors, and commitments which marked the distinguished people of Israel's past.

Part of this rehearsal of glorious figures is a presentation of some who have fallen short -- what makes the many worthy of praise is clarified by

---

[56] Indeed, the Hebrew original makes this quite plain in the introduction to the hymn, where the subjects of the author's praise are not "famous men" (so the LXX) but "men of *hesed*" (MacKenzie, *Sirach*, 168), or "people of covenant loyalty." This is "the essential quality that makes them worthy of note and praise and imitation" (Skehan and Di Lella, *Sirach*, 500); cf. also Siebeneck, "Fathers," 417.

[57] Cf. MacKenzie (*Sirach*, 168): Sirach praises the ancestors "with the very practical aim of motivating his young hearers to similar loyalty."

noting what mars or precludes praise. After describing Solomon's fine achievements, Ben Sira continues:

> You put stain upon your honor, and defiled your posterity, so that you brought wrath upon your children (ἔδωκας μῶμον ἐν τῇ δόξῃ σου καὶ ἐβεβήλωσας τὸ σπέρμα σου ἐπαγαγεῖν ὀργὴν ἐπὶ τὰ τέκνα σου) and they were grieved at your folly, so that the sovereignty was divided and a disobedient kingdom arose out of Ephraim (47:20-21).

Solomon's own honor as well as the soundness of the kingdom was irreparably harmed by the indiscretions of the king's old age -- again (as in the case of Phineas) centering on the transgression of boundaries between the chosen people and the Gentiles and the failure to observe God's exclusive claim to worship. Among the kings of Judah and Israel, only David, Hezekiah, and Josiah receive high praise.   Solomon, of course, receives blemished praise; all the others are passed over in this brief note of censure: "Except David and Hezekiah and Josiah they all sinned greatly, for they forsook the law of the Most High; the kings of Judah came to an end; for they gave their power to others, and their glory to a foreign nation" (49:4-5).   These all receive lasting disrepute, in striking contrast to the other figures lauded in the hymn, on account of "forsaking the Law of the Most High."   In so doing, they relinquished their only claim to honor.

Conclusion

The program of Alexander, carried on by his generals and their successors, presented both opportunity and crisis: for some, Hellenization brought the prospects of enjoying advancement in a world community; for others, Hellenization was a current form of apostasy, of becoming "like the nations" and forsaking the covenant with God. Ben Sira, while indeed influenced by popular Hellenistic thought, nevertheless belonged to the latter group. Being subject to the rule of Hellenistic and Hellenizing monarchs, Israel's inhabitants no longer lived in a dominant culture, but rather in a minority culture which was called into question by the availability of Hellenization and the attractions attached to the Greek way of life in an increasingly Greek world.

Ben Sira constructs a strong response to this socio-cultural situation. While adopting certain Hellenistic modes of thought, he nevertheless seeks to establish "the fear of the Lord" as the best canopy under which to live one's life. Through his school, teachings, and dissemination of thought through writing, he seeks to maintain the centrality of the "fear of the

Lord" and fidelity to Torah (the covenant) for the lives of the Jewish people. Language of honor and dishonor play a large role in this program. Wisdom remains the path to honor and a distinguished life, but is now wholly identified with obedience to Torah and the fear of the Lord. Moreover, Ben Sira seeks to promote a standard of evaluation of honor which takes as its first and definitive criterion loyalty to God and the covenant; conversely, transgression of the law and apostasy from the covenant must cancel out any other claims to honor and meet with disgrace.

While Jewish people have had their gaze directed toward their Hellenic rulers and a larger community of people, and while some have begun to seek distinction in Hellenic manners and honor from non-Jews, Ben Sira calls their focus back to the all-seeing eyes of God. If one is to have shame, that is, be sensitive to the opinion of another, that other must be God first. Effectively this points to Torah, the revelation of God's standards and criteria for honor before God, as the court of reputation before which one lives and on the basis of which one claims honor. The social expression of this criterion is the congregation of the faithful, who attest to one's honor or bear witness to one's disgrace, and who are charged with perpetuating the honorable remembrance of those who have been faithful in all times. Thus the models -- the *exempla* -- which Ben Sira holds up for emulation are not Gentiles but the figures of Israel's past noted for fidelity to God, the covenant, and the boundaries of God's people.

In a period of cultural crisis, Ben Sira has made effective and wide use of the language of honor and dishonor in order to promote loyalty to the values of the ethnic culture, and to provide insulation from the non-Jewish world -- and from the growing tendency of Jews to desire recognition from that world. He employs ethnic subcultural rhetoric in order to call them back to the "old ways" of Torah obedience rather than the new way of assimilation with the dominant Hellenistic culture. They are called back to pursue honor before God and God's people, to estimate their own honor according to the criteria internal and exclusive to Judaism. Ben Sira provides strong assurance from the wisdom tradition that they would in fact receive the honor they desire.

WISDOM OF SOLOMON

Scholars debate the precise date and socio-historical setting of Wisdom of Solomon, for which there are fewer internal clues than for Ben Sira with its helpful prologue. The early boundary may be set from the author's use

of the Septuagint version of Isaiah.[58]   Most scholars argue for Egyptian
provenance, on the basis of the hostility towards Egyptian idolatry as "the
height of pagan folly"[59] and towards Egyptians generally as more
blameworthy than the Sodomites.[60]   Winston argues that the description
of the development of the ruler cult in 14:16-20 best describes not the
centrally promoted cult of the Ptolemies, but the spontaneous, decentralized
development of the cult under Augustus, under whom Egypt's ruler was
first "remote."   Linguistic evidence -- the use of some 35 terms or
constructions which do not appear in secular Greek before the first century
CE -- supports the argument for a date in the Roman period.[61]   An
intriguing hypothesis is that the work comes from the period of Gaius,
perhaps responding to the "desperate historical situation" of the Jews under
Flaccus.   Such a situation of open persecution would easily motivate the
"ferocious passion" with which the author narrates "the annihilation of the
wicked" in 5:16-23 as well as the particularly intense anti-Egyptian
sentiments of the work.[62]

Such an exact socio-historical hypothesis may exceed the evidence, but
the arguments for an Egyptian provenance and a Roman date nevertheless
remain the most plausible.   Further details must come from an investigation
of the text itself.   With regard to the purpose of the book, scholars agree
that the author sought to provide comfort and encouragement to fellow-
Jews who were "perplexed and disheartened by disappointment, ridicule,
and persecution (2:10-12, 17-20)."[63]   The author seeks to provide a sort
of theodicy, placing the present experiences of these Jews in the light of
the eternal destiny of the faithful.[64]   Some argue that the author also
hoped to convince non-Jews of the folly of idolatry, and to convert them
to the worship of the One God;[65] similarly, the book addresses pagan
rulers, who "have abandoned the principles of divine justice" and are

[58]   E. G. Clarke, *The Wisdom of Solomon* (Cambridge: Cambridge University,
1973), 1-2; David Winston, "Solomon, Wisdom of," vol. 6, pp. 120-27 in David N.
Freedman (ed.), *The Anchor Bible Dictionary* (6 vols.; New York: Doubleday, 1992),
122.

[59]   Nicklesburg, *Jewish Literature*, 184.

[60]   Winston, "Wisdom," 123, citing Wisd 19:13-17.

[61]   Winston, "Wisdom," 122. Cf. David Winston, *The Wisdom of Solomon* (AB;
New York: Doubleday, 1979), 22-23.

[62]   Winston, "Wisdom," 123; Nicklesburg, *Jewish Literature*, 184.

[63]   Clarke, *Wisdom*, 5; Nicklesburg, *Jewish Literature*, 184; Winston, "Wisdom,"
126.

[64]   Winston, "Wisdom," 123; M. Gilbert, "Wisdom Literature," 309.

[65]   Clarke, *Wisdom*, 5; Nicklesburg, *Jewish Literature*, 184.

called to return to the ideals of kingship.[66]   Clarke also mentions apostate
Jews as a target of the author, who seeks to motivate them to return to
their ancestral faith by demonstrating that "Judaism need not take second
place to anything in Hellenism."[67]   Such proposed purposes of the
composition are formed partly on internal evidence and partly upon
hypotheses concerning date and situation.   They provide an adequate
starting point for our investigation of how the author uses the language of
honor and shame, and how his usage sharpens perception of the purpose
of the book.

Sub Specie Aeternitatis

1. The righteous and the ungodly

The first five chapters of Wisdom of Solomon are of special interest
to a study of the use of honor language both in this book and in literature
from minority cultures generally.   When Nicklesburg points to "the
repeated contrast between right and wrong perception" as the "most
striking feature in these chapters," he draws the reader's attention to a
point of great importance.[68]   At issue is not just the perception -- or,
opinion ($\delta\delta\xi\alpha$!) -- of the true nature of life in this world, but also the
"ungodly" person's perception, or opinion, of the righteous person and the
righteous person's opinion of the ungodly and of himself or herself.   From
this it becomes clear that the author seeks to address issues concerning the
evaluation of honor, on what criteria honor is to be evaluated, and whose
evaluation is to be regarded or disregarded.
The opening section (1:16-5:23) presents two distinct groups -- the
"righteous" and the "ungodly." The righteous consist of those who remain
faithful to their training in the law (2:12), who "boast" that they stand in
special relationship to God as children to a father (2:13, 16). They base
their claim to honor (their $\kappa\alpha\dot{\upsilon}\chi\eta\mu\alpha$) in their allegiance to God and hope
in God.   The ungodly include the idolatrous Gentiles, as the polemic

---

[66] Winston, "Wisdom," 126.

[67] Clarke, *Wisdom*, 4. This supposition is strengthened by Crenshaw's observation
(*Old Testament Wisdom*, 177-78) that "according to 7:17-22, Wisdom was thought to
have provided instruction in the fundamental subjects comprising the curriculum in a
Greek school: philosophy, physics, history, astronomy, zoology, religion, botany,
medicine." Thus training in Jewish Wisdom would afford one all the benefits of Greek
education.

[68] Nicklesburg, *Jewish Literature*, 178.

against idolatry in chapters 12 through 19 indicates. The devotees of idols are called "the ungodly" (ἀσεβεῖς) throughout his censorious narration of the Egyptians who suffered the plagues and judgements of God for their "folly."[69]   Not only idolatrous Gentiles are charged with ἀσεβεία: in chapters 1 through 5 the ungodly include those Jews who have betrayed their upbringing -- forsaken their allegiance to the Torah (2:12), who have turned away from the Lord (3:10).[70]   Scholars have not wished to read in the description of the "ungodly" the actual acts of former Jews.   Both Clarke and Gilbert indicate that the author addresses "ungodly Jews who live only for the moment," who have "abandoned the Jewish tradition...to opt for a world view of the Epicurean type,"[71] but neither attributes the persecution of the righteous person to these agents.[72]   It may well be the case that the author addresses a community which has experienced insult and persecution (in some form) from their former co-religionists.   After having fully joined themselves to the Hellenistic world, they would be especially sensitive to the sort of implicit or explicit criticism which would come from Jews who remained steadfast.   The author is thus concerned with the elevation of fidelity to Jewish tradition (as seen, for example, in

---

[69] In 10:6, the author distinguishes the righteous Lot who was sojourning among the ungodly inhabitants of the five cities; in 10:20, the righteous Hebrews plunder the ungodly Egyptians; in 11:9, God's provisions for the Hebrews' thirst teaches them how God tormented the ungodly by depriving them of their water, referring to the plague of turning the Nile into blood; in 12:9, the Canaanites are described as the ungodly on account of their "detestable" worship practices (12:4-6); in 14.16, ruler cults are described as an ungodly custom, one common to many Gentile groups; 16:16, 18 return to the plagues visited upon the "ungodly" Egyptians, and 19:1 to God's judgement upon those "ungodly" ones at the Red Sea.

[70] The apposition in 2:12 indicates that the ungodly whom the author has in mind are, in the first instance, apostate Jews: "Let us lie in wait for the righteous man, because he is inconvenient to us and opposes our actions; he reproaches us for sins against the law (ἁμαρτήματα νόμου), and accuses us of sins against our training (ἁμαρτήματα παιδείας ἡμῶν, RSV)."   Again, the phrase in 3:10, τοῦ κυρίου ἀποστάντες, seems to indicate a prior relationship with the God of Israel which has been abandoned.   The identification of these "ungodly" ones as former Jews is strengthened by the author's description of them as having made a "covenant with death" (1:16), which takes up a motif used by Isaiah to describe the activity and lifestyle of the apostate rulers of Jerusalem, who had abandoned their ancestral ways and religion (Is 28:15).

[71] Clarke, *Wisdom*, 2; Gilbert, "Wisdom Literature," 309.

[72] Clarke (*Wisdom*, 26) attributes this to the "ungodly in general," while Gilbert ("Wisdom Literature," 309) treats the passage as a sort of fantasy: "But since the believer is a burden by the very fact that he is true to his faith, the apostates go so far as to envisage persecuting and killing him."

Torah-obedience) as the decisive factor of remaining among the "righteous," who enjoy God's care and promise of vindication. Dedication to these values supersedes ethnic ties. The apostate Jews, who may indeed be primarily responsible for increasing pressures on their former co-religionists and for heaping abuse on them for their parochial manner of life, are placed "outside" of the author's body of significant others, together with the Gentiles. Both groups are misled in their thinking and have incorrect opinions about the true nature of life.

2. The Opinion of the Ungodly

The author describes the world view of the "ungodly" as limited in every respect to life this side of death (2:1-3, 5). The supposition that existence ends at death leads them to indulge fully in the pleasures of this life (2:6-9), even though these pleasures be purchased at the cost of oppressing the helpless (2:10). There is no "fear of God in their eyes," which might prevent them from committing acts of injustice. The "righteous man" of 2:12 presents a challenge to their understanding of the world and their way of life (2:12-15). Indeed, the ungodly feel that their own honor is attacked by this witness to the Law, who leaves the impression that he considers the ungodly "base" and their ways "unclean" (2:16). It is therefore partly out of a desire for satisfaction that they seek to test the "righteous" person, to determine the validity of his claims (2:17). They deliberately assault his honor -- first through insult and abuse, then through inflicting a shameful death (ὕβρει καὶ βασάνῳ ἐτάσωμεν αὐτόν... θανάτῳ ἀσχήμονι καταδικάσωμεν αὐτόν, 2:19-20) -- in an attempt to prove whether or not God will uphold the honor of the righteous through deliverance. According to their perspective, vindication of the righteous will have to occur this side of death. If they succeed, however, in stripping the righteous person of his honor and leaving him with no means of satisfaction (since he is dead), then they conclude that the righteous person's opinion was false, and are confirmed both in their view of reality and estimation of the righteous. Indeed, as the discourse progresses it becomes clear that the author speaks as though the ungodly were successful in their assault.

The author breaks off the discourse of the ungodly at this point and interposes an evaluation of their line of reasoning. "They were led astray, for their wickedness blinded them" (2:21). The ungodly's opinion is fundamentally unsound because they have not taken account of the full picture -- they have not sought out the purposes of God behind the events of this life, nor the purpose of God to cause God's faithful ones, who have kept themselves "holy" (2:22), to attain the prize of immortality, the very purpose latent in the creation of humanity (2:23). All their reasonings have been based on a flawed premise, namely the finality of death. Seen by those who hold to the view that personal existence continues after the death of the body, the opinion of the ungodly -- both with regard to the world and to the righteous person -- cannot be taken as a serious evaluation. While the righteous person may die in disgrace at their hands, the ungodly have not witnessed the final verdict. Therefore, the "court of opinion" formed by them has, as it were, no jurisdiction.

3. The Broader Perspective

The author affirms that beyond death stands the judgement of God, at which those who live faithful to God's law will receive the reward of immortality and honor in the shelter of God (3:1; 5:16), while those who have disregarded God and the law will receive punishment and disgrace (3:10; 4:17-20). Against this cosmic backdrop, the verdict given by the ungodly at the death of the righteous in disgrace must be reversed. The disgrace, insult, and suffering which the righteous experience in this life are reinterpreted in the light of their new standing before the court of God:

> Having been disciplined a little, they will receive great good, because God tested them and found them worthy of himself (καὶ ὀλίγα παιδευθέντες μεγάλα εὐεργετηθήσονται, ὅτι ὁ θεὸς ἐπείρασεν αὐτοὺς καὶ εὗρεν αὐτοὺς ἀξίους ἑαυτοῦ); like gold in the furnace he tried them, and like a sacrificial burnt offering he accepted them (3:5-6).

The dishonoring experiences are recast as the means by which the righteous were trained, in effect, and by which their worth (i.e., the validity of their claim to honor) was proved. Far from resulting ultimately in dishonor, their experiences at the hands of the ungodly became for them a road to honor.

In the vivid depiction of this overturning of norms, the ungodly themselves are made to see their error in their assessment of the righteous person. The author places them, shuddering, before the righteous whom they oppressed: "When they see him, they will be shaken with dreadful fear, and they will be amazed at his unexpected salvation (ἰδόντες ταραχθήσονται φόβῳ δεινῷ καὶ ἐκστήσονται ἐπὶ τῷ παραδόξῳ τῆς σωτηρίας, 5:2)." The Greek word παραδόξῳ in this sentence indicates that the ungodly are challenged by the sight to reverse their former opinion. Here at last the righteous are vindicated, as the impious now come to realize that they had everything upside down:

This is the man whom we once held in derision and made a byword of reproach (εἰς γέλωτα καὶ εἰς παραβολὴν ὀνειδισμοῦ) -- we fools! We thought that his life was madness and that his end was without honor (τὸν βίον αὐτοῦ ἐλογισάμεθα μανίαν καὶ τὴν τελευτὴν αὐτοῦ ἄτιμον). Why has he been numbered among the sons of God? And why is his lot among the saints? So it was we who strayed from the way of truth (ἄρα ἐπλανήθημεν ἀπὸ ὁδοῦ ἀληθείας), and the light of righteousness did not shine on us, and the sun did not rise upon us (5:4-6).

The righteous will thus be declared correct in their opinion, and their disgrace removed. They will take a place of honor before God, who acts as their benefactor (cf. 3:5, where εὐεργετηθήσονται, in the divine passive, indicates this relationship):

Therefore they will receive a glorious crown and a beautiful diadem from the hand of the Lord (διὰ τοῦτο λήμψονται τὸ βασίλειον τῆς εὐπρεπείας καὶ τὸ διάδημα τοῦ κάλλους ἐκ χειρὸς κυρίου), because with his right hand he will cover them, and with his arm he will shield them (5:16).

The ungodly, however much they may prosper in their pursuits in their life before God's judgement, will come to a dishonorable end. While they may deride the death of the righteous person, they can only look forward to an old age without honor (3:17) and a death without burial -- an image of the utmost horror and disgrace in the ancient world (cf. Sophocles' *Antigone*):

For they will see the end of the wise man, and will not understand what the Lord purposed for him, and for what he kept him safe. They will see, and will have contempt for him, but the Lord will laugh them to scorn (ὄψονται καὶ ἐξουθενήσουσιν, αὐτοὺς δὲ ὁ κύριος ἐκγελάσεται). After this they will become dishonored corpses, and an outrage among the dead for ever (καὶ ἔσονται μετὰ τοῦτο εἰς πτῶμα ἄτιμον, καὶ εἰς ὕβριν ἐν νεκροῖς δι' αἰῶνος); because he will dash them speechless to the ground, and shake them from the foundations; they will be left utterly dry and barren, and they will suffer anguish, and the memory of them will perish (4:17-20).

Thus for the author of Wisdom of Solomon, as for Ben Sira, the path to honor is dedication to Wisdom, which is the knowledge revealed by the God of Israel in Torah. Wisdom leads to repute and honor in this life (8:10); Wisdom teaches what pleases God, the final awarder of honor and disgrace (9:10); Wisdom teaches the knowledge of what things are noble (τὰ καλά, 10:8); Wisdom vindicates the righteous person from slander and gives such a one eternal renown (10:13-14).

God's Throne as the "Court of Reputation"

Within this construction of a world beyond the visible world, the "secular" court of reputation is relativized and displaced by the affirmation of existence beyond the confines of this life and the prospect of judgement at the close of this life. Evaluations made by the ungodly, who value and form opinions solely on the basis of what is observable within this life, are of no account, for they have not taken into consideration the whole picture. The ungodly themselves will come to understand this as they stand in the presence of God and see the vindication of the righteous. A. W. Adkins writes that the "belief in a 'real' future existence would make possible a use of the most powerful terms of value in a sense which did not entail success *in this life*."[73] This is precisely what has enabled the author of Wisdom of Solomon to enable the Jews that received his teaching to hold onto their claim to honor in the face of low status in Hellenistic society. It allowed them to face disgrace and shameful treatment boldly, knowing that such experiences were not in fact dishonoring, but rather were a means of proving their worthiness of the honor to which God had called them.

The author reminds them that they live before the eyes of God, and that God will render a final verdict in a judgement after death. All verdicts prior to and apart from that court carry no weight. Those who do not share (any longer) in the Jewish world view may well hold the faithful in contempt, may well seek to bring them into disrepute, may well even put them to a shameful execution without any hope of regaining honor in this life. The opinion of such people is less to be regarded than the opinion of children; their own opinion will be overruled and they will be forced to confess, contrary to their opinion (παράδοξος), that the righteous were correct; they will bear witness to God's vindication of the righteous. The author of Wisdom thus comes very close to the alternative courts juxtaposed in Plato's *Gorgias*, where Socrates displays his lack of concern regarding his vulnerability before human law courts and urges Callicles to have a care so to live as not to be vulnerable to disgrace and shameful treatment before the court of Zeus.

In seeking to relativize and defuse the power of the honor rating of those who are not loyal followers of Torah, the author hopes to free his audience from concern over whether they are regarded highly or basely by those who do not share their commitment to the Jewish way of life. In so doing, he sets their eyes on God's court of reputation and seeks to motivate them to pursue a favorable opinion in God's eyes, whatever the cost during

---

[73] A. W. Adkins, *Merit and Responsibility*, 179.

this life. They are thus empowered to adhere to their particularly Jewish values and commitments even in the face of dishonor on account of those commitments. In a time of potentially great social tension -- at least from former Jews now fully Hellenized, at most from the anti-Jewish program of Flaccus and those who pulled his strings -- the author offers an argument carefully constructed to undermine the dominant society's use of promises of honor and sanctions of dishonor in order to preserve the boundaries of the ethnic counterculture and its values.[74] The boundaries of the group coincide with the boundaries of the court of reputation -- the social counterpart of the court of God -- in whose eyes alone one seeks esteem, and before whom one feels shame. Those outside the group have been shown to hold a flawed opinion of reality, and thus their evaluation of the honorable and disgraceful cannot prove reliable. The way to attain lasting honor is contained in fidelity to the Torah and fidelity to the One God; any compromise of these commitments may gain for one the adulation and approval of the ungodly, but will also secure a share in their disgrace before God's judgement seat.

FOURTH MACCABEES

The Setting and Purpose of 4 Maccabees

4 Maccabees presents itself as a piece of epideictic oratory.[75] It speaks of itself as a demonstration (ἐπιδείκνυσθαι, 1.1; ἀπόδειξις, 3.19; ἀπέδειξα, 16.2) of a philosophical proposition, which has led certain scholars to view the work as an example of diatribe.[76] It also presents itself as an encomium upon the Maccabean martyrs: it offers an ἔπαινος (1.2), "praise," of virtue; it seeks to praise (ἐπαινεῖν, 1.10) the

---

[74] Wisdom of Solomon appears to use countercultural rhetoric insofar as it stresses the difference and incompatibility between what the "righteous" and "ungodly" value and looks forward to a reversal of the dominant culture's evaluation of the appropriateness of these norms.

[75] Cf. Hans-Josef Klauck, *4 Makkabäerbuch* (Jüdische Schriften aus hellenistisch-römischer Zeit 3.6 [Gütersloh: Gerd Mohn, 1989], 659, who claims that the generic designation of "epideictic speech" is the most secure.

[76] Cf. Moses Hadas, *The Third and Fourth Books of Maccabees* (New York: Harper, 1953), 101; Hugh Anderson, "4 Maccabees (First Century A.D.). A New Translation and Introduction," (pp. 531-564 in J. H. Charlesworth [ed.], *The Old Testament Pseudepigrapha*, vol. 2 [Garden City, NY: Doubleday, 1985], 531.

Maccabean martyrs as exemplars of virtue.[77] 4 Maccabees has elements
of a commemorative speech, written for a specific occasion: "On this
anniversary it is fitting for me to praise for their virtues those who, with
their mother, died for the sake of nobility and goodness" (1.10; NRSV).

Such encomia, we will recall from the discussion of Pericles' Funeral
Oration, often took on a "subtle deliberative purpose," seeking to persuade
the hearers to strengthen their adherence to some value "as the basis for a
general policy of action."[78] Praise in the ancient Mediterranean world
was thus closely linked with emulation.[79] It is this subtly deliberative
function of epideictic which leads scholars to see the demonstration of a
thesis as merely the formal function of 4 Maccabees, and not its crucial
one. The author appears rather to seek "to inculcate and preserve national
and religious loyalty" and "to advocate fidelity to the Law."[80]

The protreptic purpose of the whole work becomes clearer as one
considers the numerous deliberative elements embedded in the larger
encomium, directing the modern readers to the nature of the impact which
the author hopes to make on his audience. The author addresses several
exhortations to the audience. The initial *captatio benevolentiae* in 1.1, a
call to the hearers to pay earnest attention to philosophy, is transformed
into the concluding exhortation of 18.1-2: "O Israelite children, offspring
of the seed of Abraham, obey this law and exercise piety in every way."
Other funeral orations conclude with similar exhortations to the audience
to live out the virtues which the deceased have embodied. For the author
of 4 Maccabees, this entails absolute loyalty to Torah as the "policy" upon
which all other actions are based.

Through the expansion of the narrative of 2 Maccabees 6 and 7, the
author creates a deliberative world within his epideictic discourse. This is

---

[77] J. C. H. Lebram ("Die literarische Form des vierten Makkabäerbuches," [*VC*
28 (1974) 81-96] 83) favors this description. Based on internal indications of oral
delivery at a specific occasion and the suggestion of an epitaph for the martyrs in 17.8,
he further classifies it as a funeral oration, particularly the Athenian *Epitaphios*
("Form," 96). Cf. also M. Gilbert, "4 Maccabees," (pp. 316-19 in Michael Stone
(ed.), *Jewish Writings of the Second Temple Period* [CRI II/2; Assen: Van Gorcum &
Philadelphia: Fortress, 1984], 317).

[78] G. Kennedy, *New Testament Interpretation*, 73-74.

[79] In Thucydides' *History* (2.35, 43, 44), Pericles closes his reflection on the virtue
of the fallen soldiers by seeking to foster the auditors' feeling of emulation, even by
direct exhortation and application. Similarly, the author of 4 Maccabees aims at
inspiring the feeling of emulation among his auditors, and seeks to lead them into the
resolve to "keep the same daring spirit," drawing them in by the hope of honor and
praiseworthy remembrance and by their own sense of honor.

[80] Hadas, *Maccabees*, 93; Anderson, "Fourth Maccabees," 532.

seen first from the explicit presence of two opposing "counselors" in the martyrs' arena, juxtaposed in 9.2-3: "We are obviously putting our forebears to shame unless we should practice ready obedience to the Law and to Moses our counselor" (σύμβούλου Μωυσεῖ); they reject the advice of the "tyrant and counselor of lawlessness" (σύμβουλε τύραννε παρανομίας).[81]   Antiochus seeks to persuade the martyrs to adopt a certain course of action: "I would advise you (συμβουλεύσαιμ' ἄν) to save yourself by eating pork" (5.6); "not only do I advise you not to display the same madness as that of the old man...but I also exhort you to yield to me and enjoy my friendship" (συμβουλεύω ... παρακαλῶ, 8.5).   Antiochus' attempts to move the martyrs toward capitulation and away from persistence in obedience to Torah are countered by the martyrs' rejoinders, which are strengthened further by the exhortations which the martyrs address to one another (6.22; 9.23-24; 13.9-18). The mother's exhortation captures the essence of the larger deliberative argument: "My sons, noble is the contest to which you are called to bear witness for the nation. Fight zealously for our ancestral law.... Remember that it is through God that you have had a share in the world and have enjoyed life, and therefore you ought to endure any suffering for the sake of God" (16.16-19). As the implied hearers have been led at every point to identify with the martyrs, these deliberations and exhortations are also addressed to them.[82] These auditors would no doubt have had to consider the applicability of such advise to their own situations. The "hortatory" potential of epideictic rhetoric is thus intensified.

---

[81]   Hadas (*Maccabees*, 193) points this out as an intentional contrast.

[82]   David Seeley (*The Noble Death: Graeco-Roman Martyrology and Paul's Concept of Salvation* [Sheffield: JSOT Press, 1990], 93-94) has argued that it is in fact the mimetic process which led to the martyrs' victory over Antiochus: "the martyrs become the 'cause of the downfall of tyranny' precisely because 'all people' marvel at their 'courage and endurance'. By inspiring others to re-enact their resistance they create an implacable barrier to Antiochus's efforts, sending him finally on his way....1.11 and 18.5 make clear that the critical factor is the mimetic process by which others follow the martyrs' example." Furthermore, the author intends for his audience to be affected by the narrative so as to find the heart to imitate the martyrs as well: "It is clear that the vicarious effect of the martyrs' deaths can be appropriated mimetically even without having to re-enact literally their grisly end....Through describing the details, [the author] seeks to inspire obedience in his audience the way (he says) the martyrs' deaths inspired their contemporaries. This purpose accounts for the lingering, detailed description. By means of such mental re-enactment, the audience will benefit from the deaths. It will put itself in the martyrs' place, come to understand that it, too, could endure torment, and thus gain courage to live, or, if necessary, to die obediently (cf. 18.1, the first direct exhortation to the audience, which is told to 'obey this law')."

4 Maccabees seeks to hold up a pattern of how to act honorably, and thus how to assure an honorable remembrance. Just as the martyrs are considered "blessed for the honor in which they are held" (1.10), so also those who embody their values will enjoy esteem both during life and after death. The composition employs the values of the dominant Greco-Roman culture (e.g., the four cardinal virtues) as well as the values of the ethnic subculture for which it is written. Indeed, only those who adhere to Torah, the central value of the ethnic subculture, can truly and perfectly embody the virtues valued by the dominant culture.

While scholars have advanced several hypotheses concerning the date of the book,[83] it appears to be safer and more useful to eschew the attempts to locate the book and its intended effects too narrowly, and seek rather to examine how the book might have effect a more general audience of Jews living in the Hellenized world.[84] Klauck correctly indicates that 4 Maccabees is an "inner-directed apology"[85] presented to Jews who have lost their certainty with regard to the Torah as the surest path to the exhibition and attainment of true honor. The situation of Diaspora Jews may best be described as one of "profound tension,"[86] which may be expressed as a fluctuation "between the ambition to assimilate arising from the Jew's desire to exist among strangers by his individual powers, and the adherence to tradition, induced in the struggle for existence by the need of support from the strong collective organization represented by the community."[87]

Jews were faced with the tension between remaining faithful to the ancestral Law, which alienated them in many ways from Gentile society, and attaining a place of distinction, acceptance, and honor in Gentile society. For some, the stakes may have seemed nearly as high as for the Maccabean martyrs -- if not torture and death, at least economic and social

---

[83]   Hadas (*Maccabees*, 95-99), Elias J. Bickermann ("The Date of Fourth Maccabees," pp. 275-81 in *Studies in Jewish and Christian History*, vol. 1. [Leiden: E. J. Brill, 1976]), and Townshend ("Maccabees," 654) favor a date under Caligula, reading it in the context of the calamities suffered by the Alexandrian Jews. Urs Breitenstein (*Beobachtungen zu Sprache, Stil und Gedankengut des Vierten Makkabäerbuchs* [Basel/Stuttgart: Schwabe, 1978] 173-75) advances a date between the Jewish Wars under Trajan and Hadrian's persecution.

[84]   Anderson, "Fourth Maccabees," 453.

[85]   Klauck, *4 Makkabäerbuch*, 665.

[86]   P. D. Redditt, "The Concept of *Nomos* in Fourth Maccabees" (*CBQ* 45 [1983] 249-70) 264.

[87]   Victor Tcherikover, *Hellenistic Civilization and the Jews* (New York: Atheneum, 1977), 346.

deprivation. For Jews committed to Torah, the author presents material to reinforce their commitment and fuel the heart to endure whatever form of tension with the larger society they must face. For wavering or confused Jews, the author presents material to exhort them to take a stand for Torah and piety, calling them back to commitment to Jewish particularism as the means of achieving highest honor and reputation.[88]

The Attainment of Honor in 4 Maccabees

4 Maccabees connects the attainment of honor with the cultivation of the εὐσεβὴς λογισμός, the "devout reason" (1.1). This faculty restrains the impulses which hinder rational judgement, justice, temperance, and courage (1.2-4), which are the classical four cardinal virtues seen as essential components and sources of honor (cf. *Rhet. Her.* 3.2.3). Furthermore, those who have displayed the sovereignty of the εὐσεβὴς λογισμός are held up as exemplars of virtue (ἀρετή, 1.8) and are, as such, praiseworthy (1.10), the other component of honor according to the author of the *ad Herennium* (3.3.7). The true honor attained through the cultivation of εὐσεβὴς λογισμός stands in direct opposition to other forms of claiming and pursuing honor, which the author calls "the malevolent tendency" (ἡ κακοήθης διάθεσις, 1.26) of the soul. Apart from "devout reason," all attempts to satisfy the "thirst for honor" are but "empty reputation," "arrogance," and "boastfulness" (1.26; 2.15).

The epithet given to "reason" in the phrase εὐσεβὴς λογισμός points more precisely to the focus of the author's demonstration,[89] namely the qualification of the nature of the reason that is able to hold sovereignty over τὰ παθή.[90] 4 Macc 1.15-18 brings the reader from Hellenistic ideology squarely into the heart of Jewish particularity:

---

[88] Cf. Hadas, *Maccabees*, 133: the author's goal is "to furnish guidance to readers perplexed by real alternatives."

[89] S. Lauer ("*Eusebes Logismos* in IV Macc." [*JJS* 6 (1955) 170-71] 170) sees this expression as oxymoronic or paradoxical, while Hadas (*Maccabees*, 144) comments that the use of "devout" as a qualifier of reason "is a logical solecism only if we equate 'reason' with 'rationalism'. In the Stoic view it is nearer tautology, for all reason is God-directed."

[90] Redditt ("*Nomos*," 249) is correct in saying that "the dominance of reason over emotion is, however, only the formal and not the crucial focus of 4 Maccabees," but only insofar as the author is concerned rather to demonstrate the nature of the reason which is so dominant, and in so doing advance his program for the promotion of obedience to Torah among Diasporic Jews who are constantly attracted to the advantages of some measure of assimilation to Hellenistic society.

> Reason is the mind that with sound logic prefers the life of wisdom.
> Wisdom, next, is the knowledge of divine and human matters and the
> causes of these. This in turn, is education in the law, by which we learn
> divine matters reverently and human affairs to our advantage. Now the
> kinds of wisdom are rational judgment, justice, courage, and
> self-control.

The Reason that leads to the life of virtue and praiseworthy remembrance
chooses the life which accords with wisdom. While this wisdom is further
defined by the author in the exact terms of Stoic philosophy: *rerum
divinarum et humanarum scientiam cognitionemque quae cuiusque rei
causa sit* (cf. Cicero, *Tusculan Disputations* 4.26.57), the manner of
wisdom's acquisition is "education in the Law" (ἡ τοῦ νόμου παιδεία,
1.17). The author has in mind not the Stoic law of nature, at least not as
presented by Antiochus in 5.8-9, but rather the Jewish Torah, as the
examples in 1.30-3.18 of particular commands taken from the Torah
indicate.[91] Torah educates reason and leads to the mastery of feelings and
the expression of virtue which is the heart of honor and honorable
remembrance.[92]

4 Maccabees further promotes Torah-obedience, and thus adherence to
the Jewish subculture's central values, as the path to honor through the
choice of the martyrs as exemplars of the perfection of reason. It is
precisely in Eleazar, the seven brothers, and their mother that one may see
most clearly the mastery of devout reason over feelings (1.7-8) -- hence the
recurring reference back to the thesis after each one's death (6.31-33; 7.10;
13.1, 5; 16.1-2). Their suffering and death on behalf of "virtue" (1.8) or
"piety" (6.22; 7.16; 9.6, 7, 30; 11.20; 16.17; 17.7) or "reverence for
God" (7.22) were clearly also deaths on account of fidelity to Torah. The

---

[91]   Lebram ("Form," 81) captures the essence of this shift in focus: "faithful
obedience to the Jewish Law is presented as the equivalent of mastery of the παθή.
This obedience is ... εὐσεβὴς λογισμός" (*au. trans.*). Cf. also Emil Schürer, *The
History of the Jewish People in the Age of Jesus Christ (175 B.C. - A.D. 135). A new
English version* (ed. Geza Vermes, Fergus Millar, and Martin Goodman; III, 1;
Edinburgh: T. & T. Clark, 1986), 589-90.

[92]   Cf. Eleazar's reply to Antiochus in 5.23-24: "It teaches us self-control, so that
we master all pleasures and desires, and it also trains us in courage, so that we endure
any suffering willingly; it instructs us in justice,so that in all our dealings we act
impartially, and it teaches us piety, so that with proper reverence we worship the only
living God." The appearance of piety here in place of wisdom is less a real than an
apparent substitution. Wisdom consists, after all, of knowledge of and proper response
to human and divine matters, and so embraces justice and piety (cf. Plato, *Gorgias*,
507: "In relation to other men [the temperate man] will do what is just; and in his
relation to the gods he will do what is holy").

matter at issue in each one's trial was whether or not to transgress the Law (5.19-21, 29; 9.1-2, 4; 13.15). 4 Maccabees' examples for the reason which conquers emotions, therefore, are examples of unwavering fidelity to Torah. The author thus stresses that obedience to Torah is what makes virtue (honor) and honorable remembrance possible.[93]   The phrase εὐσεβὴς λογισμός becomes a leitmotif for firm obedience to Torah.[94]

The author does not promote Torah as one means among others of attaining virtue and the honor which attends virtue, but rather as the superior and exclusive means to that end. He begins by stating that victory over the emotions which hinder the practice of justice comes "as soon as one adopts a way of life in accordance with the law" (2.8); in unfolding God's provisions in the creation of humanity for a life of virtue, the author states that "to the mind he gave the Law; and one who lives subject to this will rule a kingdom that is temperate, just, good, and courageous (2.23)."[95] As the demonstration progresses and the audience is caught up more and more by the noble examples of fidelity to Torah, the author becomes more exclusive in his claims. "As many as attend to religion with a whole heart, these *alone* are able to control the passions of the flesh" (7.18; emphasis mine). Lest the reader think that the author speaks of religion in general terms, he adds an explanation for his claim which anchors it in Jewish religion: "since they believe that they, like our patriarchs Abraham and Isaac and Jacob, do not die to God but live to God" (7:19). Finally, the author places upon the lips of the eldest brother the thesis which their deaths demonstrate: "I will convince you that children of the Hebrews *alone* are invincible where virtue is concerned" (9.18). Since the author seeks to demonstrate obedience to Torah as the exclusive means to attain and practice virtue, the work takes on a clearly protreptic character, advancing the maintenance of Jewish subcultural values within a world dominated by Hellenism.

---

[93] Cf. H. Anderson, "Maccabees, Books of: Fourth Maccabees" (*ABD* 4:452-54; New York: Doubleday, 1992), 452.

[94] Cf. J. J. Collins, *Between Athens and Jerusalem* (New York: Crossroad, 1983), 189: "'reason' in 4 Maccabees is virtually equated with obedience to the law," specifically, "the Jewish law in all its particularity."

[95] Hadas (*Maccabees*, 157) notes that the Stoic ideal of the wise person as king here is attained through the agency of Torah. One may also compare with this the Platonic ideal of the temperate person, who rules over his or her pleasures and passions (*Gorg.* 491C-D).

The Conflict of Cultures in 4 Maccabees

4 Maccabees depicts a conflict of value systems between the dominant culture represented by Antiochus IV and the ethnic subculture represented by the martyrs.   As a deliberative speaker and counselor, Antiochus is given the opportunity to make a case for the course he urges. This results in the appearance of what Klauck fittingly called *Rededuelle*,[96] "speech-duels" in which Antiochus offers his counsel (5.5-13; 8.5-11; 12.3-5) which is repudiated by the martyr (5.16-38; 9.1-9; 12.11-18).   These speeches are important not only as means of heightening the drama, but also as a means of engaging the arguments against the thesis that Torah is the way to virtue and that uncompromising obedience to Torah is the path to perfecting virtue.[97]   The arguments considered may well reflect tensions experienced by the implied readers as they sought to live as a Jewish community in a Greco-Roman world which did not universally respect Judaism.[98]

In Antiochus' address to Eleazar, the following issues are raised: Is following Judaism on a parity with pursuing the noble task of philosophy? (5.7); does not Jewish law conflict with the law of nature, to which the wise person must conform himself or herself? (5.8); is it not unjust to treat nature's gifts with contempt? (5.9); does adherence to the Jewish law not amount to holding an empty opinion with regard to the truth? (5.10); would it not be better to adopt a more philosophical guide, such as reasoning according to the truth of what is beneficial (5.11)? Finally, Antiochus bids Eleazar consider that no divinity would blame him for transgressing under compulsion (5.13), an argument which appears again in connection with the seven brothers (8.14).   Eleazar, however, presents a counter-proposal answering these objections and defending the course of resistance as

---

[96]   Klauck, *4 Makkabäerbuch*, 652.

[97]   Hadas (*Maccabees*, 169) believes these speeches to be important as a means of conveying doctrine, but the deliberative setting leads me to view them rather as a means of dealing with the arguments which certain members of the audience might raise in objection to the author's program and in advocacy of a greater assimilation to Hellenistic ways of life.

[98]   Cf., for example, the calumnies against Judaism recorded and refuted by Josephus in *Contra Apionem* 2.1-14, §1-144, as well as the anti-Semitic presentation of Jews in Tacitus, *Histories* 5.3-5. Even Quintilian manages to give evidence of this attitude in the midst of his discussion of epideictic rhetoric (*Inst.* 2.7.21): "founders of cities are detested for concentrating a race which is a curse to others, as for example the founder of the Jewish superstition." *Superstitio* was itself a derogatory term for a foreign religion among Romans.

reasonable and honorable.[99]   Since Torah enables living in accordance with the cardinal virtues (5.22-24) and results in a reputation for piety (5.18), it would be shameful indeed for him to abandon his course of obedience.

The second *Rededuell*, between Antiochus and the seven brothers, raises issues of patronage and advancement in Hellenistic society. Antiochus offers the brothers a place of honor: "I encourage you, after yielding me, to enjoy my friendship (παρακαλῶ συνείξαντάς μοι τῆς ἐμῆς ἀπολαύειν φιλίας)" (8:5), the king's "friend" being an influential position.   He proposes a new patron-client relationship between himself and the seven brothers, replacing that between God and the brothers. "I can be a benefactor to those who obey me (δυναίμην δ'ἂν ... εὐεργετεῖν τοὺς εὐπειθοῦντάς μοι)" (8:6). He promises to raise them to positions of authority (ἀρχαί, 8:7).   The only requirement is that they conform to the Hellenistic way of life, which is presented as a life of enjoyment: "Enjoy your youth by adopting the Greek way of life and by changing your manner of living" (8.8).[100]   The only alternative to this is their protracted degradation and death -- a meaningless death in the eyes of the dominant culture, which ascribes the motive for resistance to "folly" (μανία, 8.5) and "stupidity" or "senselessness" (ἀπονοία, 12.3).

Such deliberations reveal the possibility that the author sought to address the peculiar tension which would be felt by Jews living in the centers of Greek civilization, who had themselves accepted Greek as their language and many aspects of Greek thought as their thought as well. Perhaps some felt, as did the innovators mentioned in 1 Macc 1.11, that separation from the Gentiles only meant disaster and decline for themselves, that one was indeed faced with a choice of becoming Greek in ever deeper ways so as to strengthen one's place in the network of patronage and clientage which held together the Greco-Roman world or to be subject to the tensions, deprivations, and marginalization of an ethnic and religious minority group. The importance of these considerations for the author's audience is emphasized by the repetition of the offer and alternatives by Antiochus to the last surviving brother in 12.3-5.

The martyrs choose honor above dishonorable advantage and compulsion. The highest compulsion, their spokesperson Eleazar declares,

---

[99] Redditt ("*Nomos*," 250) rightly notes this apologetic aspect of 4 Maccabees. He further stresses that, for the author, Torah is in fact in deepest accord with the law of nature, since both Torah and nature have their origin in the one God ("*Nomos*," 257).

[100] Significantly, this exhortation recalls the negative example of Jason, who "changed the nation's way of life and altered its form of government in complete violation of the law" (4.19).

is obedience to the law (5.16), which translates roughly into piety or reverence for God (cf. 7.22: θεοσέβεια). The martyrs are highly sensitive to God's honor, even as Apollonius and Jason were insensitive to God's honor and provoked God's wrath (4.7-12; 4.21). The concern for showing respect for God's law guides their choices (5.19-21, 27-28; 9.4; 13.13) and is superior to the concern for honoring the demands of Antiochus where these hinder observance of God's law (4.24, 26; 5.10).

This obedience to God is linked with the martyrs' experience of God as Benefactor and their hope for the continued experience of God's benefits. The mother urges her sons on to death in obedience to God's law based on God's beneficence: "Remember that it is through God that you have had a share in the world and have enjoyed life, and therefore you ought to endure any suffering for the sake of God" (16.18-19; cf. 13.13). The martyrs hope thus to gain future benefits from their Benefactor, both for the nation in the form of deliverance from political oppression (6.27-28) and for themselves as individuals in the form of eternal life in the presence of God (7.19; 9.8; 15.2-3, 13; 16.25; 17.18-19). As honorable clients, therefore, they set their hope in this Benefactor (16.25; 17.4) and demonstrate πίστις with regard to God (7.19; 15.24; 16.21-22; 17.2, 3). πίστις here retains the sense of "firmness" or "loyalty," and thus expresses the proper stance of a client toward a benefactor, the proper return for benefits conferred.

The brothers refuse the offered relationship, holding to their relationship with God. Antiochus' promise (benefaction) can only effect temporary safety (15.3) and advancement; God's promise (benefaction) of eternal life is infinitely to be preferred (15.2). Their willingness to provoke Antiochus, who now regards them as ungrateful as well as disobedient (9.10), reflects their proper evaluation of the danger of God's outraged virtue as greater (13.14-15; cf. Matt 10.28). The ultimate tribunal is the court of God's judgement. The martyrs' conviction of this fact enables them to disregard the verdicts of the lower court. The only benefaction they accept from Antiochus is an ironic gift -- that of martyrdom: "Tyrant, they are splendid favors that you grant us (καλάς ... χάριτας ἡμῖν χαρίζη) against your will, because through these noble sufferings you give us an opportunity to show our endurance for the law" (11.12).

The Transformation of Disgrace

The martyrs' commitment to Torah does not lead immediately to a place of honor in the eyes of the dominant culture. While the author extends the perhaps unrealistic hope that those who are faithful to the end will be recognized at least for their courage and endurance (1.11; 17.23),[101] he depicts the opinion of the martyrs in the eyes of the dominant culture's representatives as primarily negative. Antiochus and the torturers speak of the martyrs' position as "madness" ($\mu\alpha\nu\iota\alpha$, 8.5; 10.13) and "folly" ($\alpha\pi o\nu o\iota\alpha$, 12.3), rather than piety and courage. The martyrs were carelessly throwing away the gift of life not for religion but for "vain opinion" ($\kappa\epsilon\nu o\delta o\xi\iota\alpha$, 5.10). Their deaths were the just (and therefore all the more shameful) punishment ($\tau\iota\mu\omega\rho\iota\alpha$) of the foolish, disobedient, and the ungrateful. There was nothing to mitigate their disgrace in the eyes of the Gentile world as they were subjected to complete degradation through the physical violation of their bodies.[102]

For the author of 4 Maccabees, however, the martyrs' experience resulted in the perfection of their honor. The tortures and physical outrages to the martyr's bodies do not challenge their honor, but rather confirm it. The author solves this problem in terms that express the convictions of Greco-Roman philosophy, especially Stoicism: the tortures are a test of virtue (10.10; 11.2, 12, 20);[103] the treatment is undeserved and therefore not an insult or injury (9.15, 31; 10.10; 11.2; 12.11);[104] the despising of injuries is the sign of a wise and courageous person (1.9; 5.27; 6.9; 9.6; 13.1; 14.1, 11). Even if the body is stripped (exposed, shamed) or made to fall, the martyr remains clothed with virtue and his mind unconquered (6.2, 7).[105]

The author also solves this problem metaphorically through the use of "contest" and "conquest" imagery. He transforms ignominious death into a victory over a foreign invader: "By their endurance they conquered the

---

[101] Collins (*From Athens*, 190) rightly calls this a blatant fiction.

[102] Cf. The discussion in Malina and Neyrey ("Honor and Shame," 34-36 and 55-58) on the replication of honor in the treatment of the physical body.

[103] Cf. Seneca *Constant.* 9.3: the wise man "counts even injury profitable, for through it he finds a means of putting himself to the proof and makes trial of his virtue."

[104] Cf. Seneca *Constant.* 16.3: "Both [Stoics and Epicureans] urge you to scorn injuries and, what I may call the shadows and suggestions of injuries, insults. And one does not need to be a wise man to despise these, but merely a man of sense -- on who can say to himself: "Do I, or do I not, deserve that these things befall me? If I do deserve them, there is no insult -- it is justice; if I do not deserve them, he who does the injustice is the one to blush."

[105] Cf. Plato *Gorg.* 523-26. Socrates recounts the tale of the divinely appointed judgement of people at their deaths; judging them while alive and clothed led to bad judgements, so they are now judged after death and naked. The goodness of the soul, not how the body fared in life, is what is judged and what determines eternal destiny.

tyrant" (1.11). Indeed, the same virtues of courage and endurance (ἀνδρεία καὶ ὑπομονή, 1.8, 11) which are highlighted in praises of fallen warriors (cf. Pericles' Funeral Oration) are prominent features of the author's encomium on the martyrs. Similarly, the martyrs' experience of temptation and torture are throughout the oration likened to a contest (5.10; 7.3; 9.30; 11.20; 12.14; 15.29).[106]   Indeed, it is a competition held in high regard by God and the faithful: "My sons, noble is the contest (γενναῖος ὁ ἀγών) to which you are called to bear witness for the nation. Fight zealously for our ancestral law" (16.16). The author reflects that the contest was indeed divine, in an extended athletic metaphor:

> Truly the contest in which they were engaged was divine (ἦν ἀγὼν θεῖος), for on that day virtue gave the awards and tested them for their endurance. The prize (τὸ νῖκος) was immortality in endless life. Eleazar was the first contestant (προηγωνίζετο), the mother of the seven sons entered the competition (ἐνήθλει), and the brothers contended (ἠγωνίζοντο). The tyrant was the antagonist (ἀντηγωνίζετο), and the world and the human race were the spectators. Reverence for God was victor (θεοσέβεια δὲ ἐνίκα) and gave the crown to its own athletes (τοὺς ἑαυτῆς ἀθλητὰς στεφανοῦσα). Who did not admire the athletes (ἀθλητάς) of the divine legislation? (17.11-16)

What would have been regarded as complete degradation is thus transformed into an honorable victory and an exhibition of courage (ἀνδρεία) and endurance (ὑπομονή), two paired and primary values of the Greco-Roman world. In the eyes of the representatives of the ethnic subculture, accepting Antiochus' offers, with their promises of advancement in power and prestige, would have brought dishonor rather than honor. The rejection of compromise of Torah-obedience as "cowardly and unmanful" (8.16) can be seen in the author's treatment of the martyrs' hypothetical alternative responses to Antiochus (8.16-26; 16.5-11). 4 Maccabees thus continues to connect fidelity to Torah with the embodiment of Greek values. The Greek ideal of virtue, and hence the strongest claim to honor within the dominant culture, can be achieved for the Jew only by commitment to the Law and customs of the minority culture.

The author identifies the martyrs as those who care about their honor. The are associated in various ways with the virtue of καλοκἀγαθία, a word used in the LXX only in this book. According to Danker, this is "an alternate expression for *anēr tēs aretēs* (man of arete) and other terms used

---

[106] Cf. Victor C. Pfitzner, *Paul and the Agon Motif: Traditional Athletic Imagery in the Pauline Literature* (Leiden: E. J. Brill, 1967), 23-48, for the use of this imagery in Greco-Roman and Hellenistic Jewish literature.

to describe high achievers or benefactors."[107]   The martyrs died "on account of καλοκάγαθία" (1.10); they die "equipped with καλοκάγαθία," their deaths attesting to their character (11.22; 15.9), and lived with "a common zeal for καλοκάγαθία" (13.25).   This same term of distinction is applied to all who give religious reason dominion over their passions, this is, who emulate the martyrs' choices (3.18).   The martyrs act out of a commitment to ἀρετή, "excellence" or "virtue," as well as the reputation for being of such a character.   The brothers' deaths "for the sake of ἀρετή" (1.8; 10.10; 11.2) assures them also of receiving the "prize of ἀρετή" (9.8).

In particular, the martyrs are credited with the virtue of εὐσέβεια, "piety."   This is not properly one of the four cardinal virtues of Stoicism or Platonism, but often appears as a replacement for one of those virtues (cf. Philo, *De specialibus legibus* 4.147; Xenophon, *Memorabilia* 4.6), or as a subheading of justice, "giving to each thing what it is entitled in proportion to its worth" (*Rhet. Her.* 3.2.3) where what is due Deity is considered.[108]   Piety and dutifulness are closely related values, as one sees in the frequent use of the epithet *pius* to describe the hero of the *Aeneid*, who is dependable, faithful, and dutiful with regard to the requirements of family, country, and divinities.   As such, it is an important social virtue.   The martyrs in 4 Maccabees highly value this virtue, in that they suffer and die "on account of εὐσέβεια," of which the auditors are reminded throughout the oration (5.31; 7.16; 9.29; 15.12; 16.13, 17, 19).   Their choices are determined by their refusal to violate their life of εὐσέβεια and their reputation for this virtue (9.6, 25; 13.8, 10; 15.1, 3); as such, their deaths become a demonstration of piety (13.10).   Their refusal to violate the bond of loyalty which binds clients to benefactors is expressed in their commitment to God and rejection of Antiochus as a new patron, replacing God in that role.

The author may therefore rightly commend them as καλός and γενναῖος ("noble") frequently throughout the oration (6.10; 7.8; 8.3; 9.13; 10.3; 15.24, 30).   This nobility is manifested in remaining steadfast to God and Torah in their encounter with the demands of Gentile society (cf. 9.27,

---

[107]   F. W. Danker, *Benefactor: Epigraphic Study of a Greco-Roman and New Testament Semantic Field* (St. Louis, MO: Clayton Publishing House, 1982), 319.

[108]   Cf. also Socrates' definition of the temperate person in Plato *Gorg.* 507A: "And will not the temperate man do what is proper, both in relation to the gods and to men; -- for he would not be temperate if he did not?   Certainly he will do what is proper.   In his relation to other men he will do what is just; and in his relation to the gods he will do what is holy; and he who does what is just and holy must be just and holy?   Very true."

where the second brother's choice is simply referred to as τὴν εὐγενῆ γνώμην). The outcome of their lives secures their honor, even as Pericles looks to the soldiers' deaths as the seal of their virtue: "To me it seems that the consummation which has overtaken these men shows us the meaning of manliness in its first revelation and in its final proof" (Thucydides *Hist*. 2.42). Concern for his reputation leads Eleazar to resist Antiochus' offers, lest he become an "example of ἀσέβεια" (5.18, 6.19) in his old age.

As the consummation of piety and courage, therefore, the martyrs' suffering and dying is lauded as done "nobly" or "blessedly" (καλῶς, μακαρίως: 6.30; 9.24; 10.1, 15; 11.12; 12.1, 14; 15.32; 16.16). They are credited with having purged their πατρίς ("homeland") of a great evil (1.11: cf. Pericles' praise of the soldiers for the preservation of their country's freedom) through having achieved a victory over the tyrant and his forces (1.11; 6.10; 7.4; 8.2, 15; 9.6, 30; 11.20, 24-27; 16.14; 17.2). The results and rewards of their firmness clearly include a honorable remembrance (amplified by the oration itself, with its *encomia* of the martyrs in 7.1-15; 13.6-14.10; 14.11-17.6); they endured εἰς δόξαν, "unto a glorious reputation" (7.9), and enjoy the distinction of being honored by God (17.5), the patriarchs (who still "live" as a court of public opinion able to ascribe honor, 13.17), and their nation as its saviors (1.11; 17.20). They now enjoy the reward of standing in the presence of God (9.8; 17.5, 17-19; 18.23).

From within the court of opinion formed by those who adhere to the values of the ethnic subculture and award honor or censure on the basis of those values, those outside are shown to be truly without honor. Antiochus IV is presented as ὑπερήφανος, "arrogant" (5.15; cf. 9.15), not honorable. He lacks respect for what is due God, and so is described as ἀσεβής, "impious" (9.32; 10.11; 12.11). Opposing the martyrs' commitment to Torah, Antiochus shows himself to be a "hater of virtue" (μισάρετε, 11.4). In the voices of the martyrs, the author engages in a critique of the dominant culture which does not make a place for Torah-abiding Jews, but rather which lives itself contrary to the law of God and despises Jews for living by this law. Antiochus' punishment of the brothers shows his ignorance of what is just and what is honorable (11.4-6). From the perspective of the court of God, Antiochus himself may be evaluated as shameless, lacking justice -- the essential element of honor which regards the honor due God and other human beings (12.11-13). Antiochus is thus censured as a dishonorable client -- he does not acknowledge God's benefits and even sets himself against God's faithful clients; he also lacks that important element of αἰδώς which regards the honor of other human beings within the context of reverent fear of God. He is thus possessed of a ὑπερήφανος λογισμός ("arrogant reason," 9.30) rather than a εὐσεβὴς λογισμός, and so alienated from the attainment of virtue and honor.[109] No alliance with such a person (or like persons) is possible for honorable people.

4 Maccabees presents, however, a number of persons who did seek such an alliance, who were willing to compromise the maintenance of the Jewish subcultural values and assimilate to the dominant culture. Simon, who sought the approval of the Gentile leaders (4.2-4) is a betrayer of his πατρίς and described as κατάρατος, "accursed" (4.5). Jason, who "changed the nation's way of life and altered its form of government in complete violation of the law" (4.19), Hellenizing the city and suspending the temple service, more especially attracts the author's censure. Jason represents the course that Antiochus hopes the brothers will adopt: seeking advancement in Gentile society at the cost of obedience to Torah and honor toward God, however, only provokes the wrath of God and brings judgement upon the nation (4.21) and eternal torment upon individuals (9.9, 31; 10.21; 11.23; 12.12, 14, 18; 13.15; 18.5).

The path of the martyrs, therefore, is presented as the path of virtue and honorable remembrance: those who seek to answer the demands of pagan society through loosening of observation of Torah act dishonorably and irreverently, gaining a shameful reputation, in the author's estimation of honor, and earning the wrath of the Deity whom they despised through disregarding the Law. The martyrs receive honor from God and the patriarchs (13.3, 17; 17.5), and since this court of reputation delivers an eternal verdict its opinion is of the highest importance. The author suggests, however, that the only way to receive honor from the Gentiles is through obedience to the Jewish Law. Eleazar suggests, for example, that, at a deeper level, Antiochus would really despise the same capitulation he would seem to praise (6.21), and that transgression of the Law would lead not to honorable assimilation into Gentile society but would rather be an occasion for mockery and derision (5.27-28). To reinforce this, the author states that the martyrs' endurance provoked the admiration of their torturers (1.1; 6.11; 9.26; 17.16), and that Antiochus himself proclaimed them as an example of courage and manliness (17.23).

---

[109] He is thus a foil to David, as presented in 3.15-16. David refuses to drink the water stolen from the enemy camp at the jeopardy of two human lives. To cross the line and satisfy one's own desires with such disregard for other human beings' worth would be to act arrogantly in God's sight. He therefore reverently offers it as a drink offering.

Conclusion

4 Maccabees defines honor in terms of preserving ethnic subcultural values and commitments, and disgrace as the transgression of the same. It demonstrates that the path to honor through achieving the ideal of virtue is "pious reason" -- reason choosing wisdom as taught in God's law, the Jewish Torah. It thus exhibits a subcultural relationship to the dominant Hellenistic culture, insofar as it claims to fulfill the virtues and values central to that culture (e.g., courage, piety) better than the members of that dominant culture. Indeed, it lays an exclusive claim to fulfilling these virtues for those who adhere strictly to the Torah, the embodiment of the Jewish cultural norms. The Maccabean martyrs provide the model for honorable and praiseworthy response to the demands and tensions of the encounter with the Greco-Roman world. 4 Maccabees thus challenges those wavering in their commitment to Judaism as a result of the encounter with Greco-Roman society.

Similarly, the author is concerned to establish that honoring God and remaining firm in commitment to God (showing faith) is the only reasonable and honorable course. God will thus be known still and continually as Benefactor. Dishonoring God for the sake of acceptance by and assimilation into Greek culture and release from tension (whether the physical tension of the rack or the social tension of identification with a minority group and a suspect people) and becoming clients of the dominant culture leads to the experience of God as avenger of God's outraged honor and violated beneficence (cf. God's response to Jason, 4.21). The auditors are called also to preserve the collective honor of the Jewish people by not violating their "reputation for piety" (6:18). Indeed, the only dishonor which may justly attach itself to them is the disgrace which would result from their transgression of Torah for the sake of accommodating to the demands of Hellenistic society (5:27, 28; 6:20-21).

Delineation of the "court of reputation" again forms an essential component of the maintenance of the minority culture's values and norms. Those hostile to Judaism, who persist in a wrong opinion (cf. 5:22-24) of what is just and true, are excluded from consideration. The martyrs act consistently with a view to receiving approbation from God, the ancestors of the faith (13:17), one another, and future generations of Jews through leaving examples of fidelity to the Law. If the Jew is to attain honor in the eyes of non-Jews (cf. 17:17, 23-24), it must be through Torah-obedience, not through transgression of Torah (cf. 2 Macc 4:10, 14-15).

3 Synthesis

"What might be deviant and shameful for one group in one locality may be worthy and honorable for another. Yet all groups are concerned about their honor."[110] There is no consensus in the Mediterranean world of the first century as to what constitutes honor or disgrace. Rather, one finds competing definitions of the noble and shameful calculated to uphold each group's distinctive values, beliefs, and practices. A minority culture might be held in low esteem by the members of a dominant culture. The latter may exert a strong influence on members of the minority culture with its negative sanctions and offer of greater honor for those who adopt the standards of the dominant culture and seek recognition in its court of reputation. Such a pressure no doubt inspired the internally motivated Hellenizing program of Jason and other apostate Jews; such pressure no doubt weighed heavily on those addressed by Sirach; such pressure may well have been felt by Stoics as they sought to remind themselves that a life lived in conformity with nature was better than public advancement gained through compromise of that ideal.

For a minority culture to survive in a situation of cultural pluralism, it had to develop an alternate arena for the fulfilling of its members' desire for honor, their φιλοτιμία. Honor is now defined in terms of the minority culture's traditions and values; those who do not share these definitions are set aside as shameless, or as errant. The negative opinion which such people might have of the group and its members carries no weight -- it rests on error, and the representative of the minority culture can look forward to his or her vindication when the extent of that error is revealed. Rather, the group members are called to have concern for the opinion of a higher court, whether it be of nature, of the governing principle, of Zeus, or of the God of Israel. The members of the minority culture form a social counterpart to this higher court, and it is in their eyes that a member is challenged to seek honor and eschew falling into disgrace. Honor and Shame become powerful tools for social engineering, for maintaining group boundaries, values, and commitments in a world of competing cultures and arenas in which to gain recognition. Indeed, in the transvaluation of dominant cultural norms and the rejection of the applicability of society's standards, the use of the language of honor and shame in minority groups often leads to an escalation of tension between the group and society.

---

[110] Malina and Neyrey, "Honor," 26.

When we turn to the Letter to the Hebrews, we find all of these elements of minority cultural use of honor and shame language. The author seeks to dislodge the sting of the community's experience of dishonor in the eyes of the dominant culture, affirming the difference in standards between what the inhabitants of the world commonly consider honorable and what leads to the attainment of honor before God. It is not before the court of the world, but the court of God and of the Son that the Christian stands, and from which the Christian will receive an eternal grant of honor or dishonor. Commitment to the values of the minority group (e.g., faith) carries with it the promise of greater honor than the dominant culture could offer. Transgression of those values and of the patron-client bond between people and God, however, carries with it the sanction of greater disgrace. The author offers his readers a basis for self-respect grounded in the values and beliefs of the group, securing them against the insults of their neighbors, calling them to live so as to preserve the honor they have been given by God and not to lose it by accommodating to the pressures of the dominant culture.

CHAPTER FOUR

"Despising Shame": Counter-Definitions of the Honorable and Disgraceful in Hebrews

An important step in the strategy of the author of Hebrews is the dissociation of the recipients of the letter from any sense of accountability to the value judgements of the dominant culture. The author reveals little about the past history of the community he addresses, so that what he does mention appears all the more to serve an essential rhetorical function rather than to be a casual reminiscence. One of these windows into the community's past occurs in 10:32-34, a passage that sketches an intense experience of dishonor and rejection at the hands of the society. They had endured a "contest of sufferings," including being made a public spectacle -- θεατριζόμενοι -- through reproaches and trials, imprisonments, and the seizure of their property (10:32-34). Faith and faithful action may lead to the attainment of the honor of the children of God (cf. 2:10) before the throne of God, but they have already led the community into dishonor in the eyes of the society.

Within the concluding hortatory section, 10:19-13:17, the author holds up as exemplary a number of figures or groups whose choices reflect a disregard for the values of society and the opinion of those who embody those values. These exemplars embody the central value for the minority group, namely "faith" (πίστις), a value in which the addressees are called to persevere.[1] The exemplars of faith often move into a lower status in the eyes of society in order to attain what God has promised. They embrace disgrace before people in order to receive the attestation of God

---

[1] Faith (πίστις) appears throughout 10:32-12:2 with impressive frequency: cf. 10:38, 39; 11:1, 3, 6, 7, 13, 33, 39; 12:2. The refrain-like use of the dative form appears in 11:3, 4, 5, 7, 8, 9, 11, 17, 20, 21, 22, 23, 24, 27, 28, 29, 30, 31.

and a share in the honorable destiny of the people of God. The author argues, in effect, that faith implies a disregard for one's estimation in society's eyes, and an exclusive concern for one's honor in the eyes of God and Christ. The community's history, which continues the history of the people of God, shows that worldly honor and eternal honor are mutually exclusive. In light of the greater reward for the faithful, therefore, he calls his readers to maintain their former distance from society's estimation of their worth and continue to live out the values and commitments which result in God's approval and the attainment of the promises.

1 The Community's Experience of Dishonor

Commitment to Christianity, like commitment to its parent religion, Judaism, itself placed restrictions on its members' access to honor in the Greco-Roman world. Indeed, Christianity's commitment to the One God and rejection of all other deities led serious Christians to withdraw from participation in the cultic ceremonies which were a part of most political, business, and social enterprises in the Greco-Roman world.[2] As a result, Christianity inherited much of the suspicion and prejudice which had fallen to Judaism in a world where loyalty to the gods was intimately connected with loyalty to ruler, city, authorities, friends, family, and associates. Along with this suspicion came reproach, rumor, and slander, which together made it not only disgraceful but also dangerous to be associated with the name of "Christian."

THE DOMINANT CULTURE'S EVALUATION OF CHRISTIANS

What access could the Christian have to honor and a good reputation? One demonstrated one's honor through "piety" and benefaction. The latter trait -- the use of one's goods, influence, and the like to benefit others, thus establishing patron-client relationships, or to benefit one's city or

---

[2] The pervasiveness of cultic activity throughout all aspects of life in Greco-Roman society has been demonstrated in such works as Ramsay MacMullen, *Paganism in the Roman Empire* (New Haven: Yale, 1981), 38-39, 47. Wendell L. Willis (*Idol Meat in Corinth: The Pauline Argument in 1 Corinthians 8 and 10* [SBLDS 68; Chico, CA: Scholars Press, 1985], 7-64) collects an impressive array of evidence for the pervasiveness of cultic rituals in Greco-Roman social and civic life. Such insights have been used and expanded by such New Testament scholars as R. H. Mounce (*The Book of Revelation* [Grand Rapids: Wm. B. Eerdmans, 1977], 102-4).

country -- was such an important path to honor that φιλοτιμία, "love of honor," came to be used almost as a synonym for "generosity."[3] The former characteristic, εὐσέβεια, often translated "piety," might be better translated "dutifulness." One who is εὐσεβής acts out of his or her commitment to the gods, the state, the city, and family. Such a one fulfills one's obligations to all these claimants freely, and in return wins the approval of those benefitted, and hence honor and a good reputation. Religion was, for the Greco-Roman world, not divorced from familial, social, and civic duty -- it was not a separate sphere of life as it is for much of modern society.[4] Rather, it was woven into and upheld all aspects of life. For example, trade guilds were devoted to a particular deity (sometimes to a divinized emperor). Faithful service in one's duties within the guild was spoken of as faithful service to the patron deity.[5] Conversely, the inhabitants of the Greco-Roman world could be suspicious of those who did not honor the gods, and hostile to those who denied that those gods deserved honors (for example, the Jews who insisted on the existence and worship of the Lord alone).

Such suspicion and hostility arose not because of what we would understand as religious zeal, but because honor of the gods encapsulated one's honor of the state, the city, the family, the traditional values of the society. A religious statement such as "Christ is Lord," therefore, contained also a political message.[6] Greco-Roman religion was by its polytheistic nature tolerant of foreign divinities. Attempts were made to correlate Egyptian, Greek, and Roman deities. One could call on whatever god one wished, as long as one made a place for the other gods. The pinnacle of this correlation appears in Apuleius' *The Golden Ass* (11.2, 4), where Isis reveals herself to the novel's hero by listing a long string of

---

[3] Danker, *Benefactor*, 328.

[4] As Robert Wilken (*The Christians as the Romans Saw Them* [New Haven: Yale University, 1984] 56) observes, "originally the word *piety* was used to designate the honor and respect one showed to members of one's family.... The term came to be used in a wider sense, designating loyalty and obedience to the customs and traditions of Rome, to inherited laws, to those who lived in previous generations -- in short, to the 'fatherland'. As time went on, the term acquired a more specifically religious sense,... but the older sense of the word was never lost."

[5] Danker, *Benefactor*, 343.

[6] Wilken (*Christians*, 58) underscored the role of piety as the cement of social and political unions: "Piety toward the gods was thought to insure the well-being of the city, to promote a spirit of kinship and mutual responsibility, indeed, to bind together the citizenry. 'In all probability,' wrote Cicero, 'disappearance of piety towards the gods will entail the disappearance of loyalty and social union among men as well, and of justice itself, the queen of all virtues' (*Nat. D.* 1.4)."

different names by which the different cultures in the Hellenistic world called on her. To deny the gods, however, whether in favor of none or in favor of one's own ancestral/tribal divinity was to deny the order of society, or to assert that society's order was somehow perverse (e.g. in the charge that it goes after false gods). Such an attitude towards the traditional deities was labelled ἀθεότης, "atheism." So seriously did the society view this as a dangerous attitude that it was often punishable with death. The emperor Domitian, near the end of his reign in 95 AD, executed several high ranking Roman citizens on this charge. Dio Cassius connects their fate to their taking up of Jewish practices and beliefs (*Roman History* 67.14.2).

Those Christians who claimed that the God of Israel is the one true Deity therefore entered into a precarious relationship with society. Christian leaders such as Paul give clear evidence for the demand to withdraw from public associations with the traditional divinities of Greco-Roman religion and therefore from the economic, social, and civic activities which included worship of the gods as part of their festivities or ceremonies (cf. 1 Cor 10:14-22; 2 Cor 6:14-7:1; 1 Thess 1:9). What response did such strategies engender among the sect's pagan neighbors, and what was the reputation of this group? Our only sources for the Christians' reputation as a whole are the few remarks made by the pagan authors Tacitus, Pliny, Lucian, and Celsus, together with the Christian apologists' attempts to refute the church's detractors. We cannot draw a complete picture, but only derive some hints concerning the "honor" or lack thereof which might have adhered to Christian groups of the mid-first century.

Tacitus mentions the Christian movement only in his narration of the aftermath of the great fire near the end of Nero's reign (*Annals* 15.44), and it is thanks to him that we have the picture of the vindictive persecution of Christians as Nero's scapegoats:

> To suppress this rumour, Nero fabricated scapegoats -- and punished with every refinement the notoriously depraved Christians (as they were popularly called). Their originator, Christ, had been executed in Tiberius' reign by the governor of Judaea, Pontius Pilatus. But in spite of this temporary setback the deadly superstition had broken out afresh, not only in Judaea (where the mischief had started) but even in Rome. All degraded and shameful practices collect and flourish in the capital.... Large numbers were condemned -- not so much for incendiarism as for their anti-social tendencies.[7]

---

[7] Tacitus, *The Annals of Imperial Rome* (tr. Michael Grant; New York: Penguin, 1956).

If the honor of a group is defined by the honor of its head, the Christian community was stigmatized from its inception, as Tacitus notes that the leader of the movement was executed by the Roman governor.[8] Tacitus speaks of the Christians as a class of people "loathed for their vices" (*flagitia*). While he does not give specific examples, he indicates that they were reputed to be morally debased, engaging in shameful activities. Furthermore, the religion of these people is called a "pernicious superstition." Tacitus uses the derogatory term *superstitio* rather than the respectful term *religio*, reserved largely for the dutiful practice of traditional Roman religious observances.[9] The term "superstition" often referred to a cult of foreign origin, which was perceived not to support traditional values and social bonds, promoting rather the decay of society. The emergence of the group in Rome is regarded as one more example of "things horrible or shameful" from around the world breaking out in the imperial capital. Finally he attributes the cause for which the Christians were hounded out and brought to punishment to be not the genuine suspicion of arson but *odium humani generis*, "the hatred of the human race." The celebrated Latin phrase contains an ambiguity as to whether or not a subjective or objective genitive is intended (or perhaps the ambiguity is deliberate, meaning to suggest both).[10] Nevertheless, whether the Christians were thought to hate humanity generally or to have alienated the rest of the population and thus incurred the hatred of the larger society, it is clear that Tacitus casts the relationship of the Christians to the larger society as one of high tension and mutual rejection.

It is likely, indeed, that the Christians felt the need to withdraw from many public, economic, and civic associations and made themselves visibly absent during festivals in order to avoid idolatry.[11] They may well have

---

[8] Spicq (*Hébreux*, 2.388), commenting on Hebrews 12:2, sees a connection between Christ's response to the disgrace of crucifixion and the response called for by those who confess themselves to be the disciples of one condemned to death as a criminal.

[9] Suetonius uses the same term to describe the Christian group (*Nero* 16), as does Pliny (discussed below). Judaism was also considered a *superstitio* by Tacitus (*Hist.* 5.3-5) as well as by Plutarch (*De Superstitione* 8 [*Mor.* 169 C]).

[10] Ramsey MacMullen (*Paganism*, 40) appears to favor the objective genitive when he writes: "There existed ... no formal social life in the world of the Apologists that was entirely secular. Small wonder, then, that Jews and Christians, holding themselves aloof from anything the gods touched, suffered under the reputation of misanthropy!"

[11] Minucius Felix cites such criticism from his pagan neighbors: "You do not go to our shows, you take no part in our processions, you are not present at our public banquets, you shrink in horror from our sacred games" (*Octavius* 12, cited in Wilken, 66).

been seen as people who kept to themselves and excluded their former associates. Such behavior would be regarded as anti-social in the extreme, and would have also made the non-Christians look with disfavor upon the Christian counter-society.[12] Rather than this state of affairs resulting in a sort of reverence for the Christians as an austere and devout group, it earned them the reputation of anti-benefactors of the society, of people wholly unsupportive of the social endeavor. The Christians were further stigmatized (censured) as practicers of immorality, even barbarous atrocities.

Participation in traditional religious activities was a source of an honorable reputation in both the Greco-Roman and Jewish socities. Pseudo-Isocrates speaks for the former when he advises Demonicus (*Ad Dem.* 13):

> First of all, then, show devotion to the gods, not merely by doing sacrifice, but also by keeping your vows....Do honour to the divine power at all times, but especially on occasions of public worship; for thus you will have the reputation both of sacrificing to the gods and of abiding by the laws.

Matthew 6:1, 5 provides an interesting reflection of the latter:

> Beware of practicing your piety before others in order to be seen by them; for then you have no reward from your Father in heaven.... And whenever you pray, do not be like the hypocrites; for they love to stand and pray in the synagogues and at the street corners, so that they may be seen by others. Truly I tell you, they have received their reward (RSV).

What is of importance here is not the censure of the "hypocrites" but the fruit of public piety. Their reward is the attainment of a reputation for being pious, and therefore honorable, people. Christians, withdrawing from the traditional forms of piety and religion, deprive themselves of this means of gaining honor and approval, and indeed, incur disgrace and hostility. Plutarch demonstrates that piety and preservation of the state were inextricably linked -- belief in the gods was the bedrock of a stable society. Refusal of the worship of the gods, and removal of fear of the gods, meant political anarchy and the subversion of the state:

---

[12]   In effect, the Christians were placed in the same category as Jews and Epicureans, although the latter group apparently attempted to avoid censure by participating in the traditional religious festivals (cf. Plutarch, *A Pleasant Life Impossible* 21 [*Mor.* 1102 B-C]).

Again, the very legislation that Colotes praises provides first and foremost for our belief in the gods, a faith whereby Lycurgus made the Spartans a dedicated people, Numa the Romans, Ion of old the Athenians, and Deucalion well-nigh the whole Greek nation.... In your travels you may come upon cities without walls, writing, king, houses, or property, doing without currency, having no notion of a theatre or a gymnasium; but a city without holy places and gods, without any observance of prayers, oaths, oracles, sacrifices for blessings received or rites to avert evil, no traveller has ever seen or will ever see. No, I think a city might rather be formed without the ground it stands on than without a government, once you remove all religion from it, get itself established or once established survive. Now it is this belief, the underpinning and base that holds all society and legislation together, that the Epicureans ... proceed directly to demolish (*Reply to Colotes* 31 [*Mor.* 1125D-E]; LCL).

Withdrawal from, or criticism of, the traditional religion of Greco-Roman world made one a potential source of chaos and disorder, and therefore an enemy of the well-being of the people. That public disapproval and potential hostility would follow upon such withdrawal or criticism of traditional religion is made explicit by Plutarch, again in a discussion of the Epicureans (*A Pleasant Life Impossible* 21 [*Mor.* 1102 C-D]; LCL):

For out of fear of public opinion (διὰ φόβον τῶν πολλῶν) he goes through a mummery of prayers and obeisances that he has no use for and pronounces words that run counter to his philosophy; when he sacrifices, the priest at his side who immolates the victim is to him a butcher; and when it is over he goes away with Menander's words on his lips:
 I sacrifice to gods who heed me not.
For this is the comedy that Epicurus thinks we should play, and not spoil the pleasure of the multitude or make ourselves unpopular with them by showing dislike ourselves for what others delight in doing.

Regard for the many, and fear lest the many be incensed at the Epicureans' irreligion, led the followers of this school to participate in the traditional cultic activities. Conversely, one should expect that the Christians who did in fact withdraw from these cultic participations should excite the displeasure, even the indignation, of the many. While there is evidence that some Christians played the part of Epicureans, compromising for the sake of maintaining their place and status within the non-Christian society, many Christians followed Paul's directives in 1 Cor 10:14-22, namely that they should avoid all contact with ceremonies involving worship of idols and gods who are "no gods."

Such an ill reputation as attested by Tacitus clearly preceded the Christians to the tribunal of Pliny the Younger, imperial legate to Bithynia and Pontus in 110 AD. Faced with the denunciation of a large number of Christians in his province, he wrote to the emperor Trajan seeking his advice. His letter reveals a lack of clarity with regard to the position of Christians. Was it illegal in itself to be a Christian? Or was one only to punish the crimes associated with that name? Pliny truly expected to extract the confession of punishable crimes committed by the Christians when he interrogated two deaconnesses under torture. Nevertheless, for both Pliny and Trajan, confession of the name of "Christian" was enough to deserve execution. The name itself (remembering that "name" relates to reputation) was enough of an affront to the Greco-Roman society to merit extermination. Pliny, like Tacitus, refers to the movement as a "depraved superstition" (*superstitionem pravam et immodicam*), regarding it as a "wretched infection" (*Epistulae*, 10.96). Renunciation of the name of Christian (effected through imprecating the name of Christ, *male dicere Christo*) and return to traditional cultic observances was viewed as the means of redemption (*turba hominum emendari possit*), of redirecting the religious impulses of the Christians to honorable ends.

A mirror view of Pliny and Tacitus' expectation that the name of "Christian" carries with it accompanying vices or crimes appears in 1 Pet 4:14-16: "If you are reviled for the name of Christ, you are blessed (εἰ ὀνειδίζεσθε ἐν ὀνόματι Χριστοῦ, μακάριοι), because the Spirit of glory and of God (τὸ τῆς δόξης...πνεῦμα) rests upon you. By no means let any of you suffer as a murderer, or thief, or evildoer, or a troublesome meddler; but if as a Christian, let him not feel ashamed (μὴ αἰσχυνέσθω), but in that name let him glorify God (δοξαζέτο τὸν θεὸν ἐν τῷ ὀνόματι τούτῳ, NASB)." While 1 Pet 4:15 probably does not refer to specific crimes Christians were thought to practice (which appear to have focused more on incest, cannibalism, and infanticide),[13] the passage suggests that there was occasion to suffer simply for confessing to the name of "Christian," and that believers had the responsibility to make clear to their accusers by virtuous living that the whole *stasis* or controversy lay in the nature of the name itself and not in any morally reprehensible acts. It also establishes that, despite exemplary moral conduct, the very name of "Christian," that is, association with the name of Christ, would invite reproach (εἰ ὀνειδίζεσθε ἐν ὀνόματι Χριστοῦ) and the experience of humiliation (in light of which the author must urge the addressees, μὴ αἰσχυνέσθω).

The second-century critic Celsus, known only from Origen's non-sympathetic presentation of his censure of Christianity, attacked the reputation of the movement from another angle. He claims that

---

[13] Cf. Origen, *Contra Celsum* 6.27.

Christianity appeals only to the ignorant and unlearned, indeed that it specifically seeks such converts and turns away the wise or learned.[14] St. Paul's statement in 1 Cor 1:26-27 that "not many of you were wise according to the flesh" and that "God chose the foolish" appear to lend credence to the impression of outsiders like Celsus that Christianity was primarily a cult for the unlettered masses. Celsus also provides specific calumnies brought against the movement. They were slanderously accused of violating habitually the most basic taboos: human sacrifice, cannibalism, incest and orgiastic gatherings.

Celsus also criticizes Christians for not taking on the responsibilities of public offices, a criticism which Robin Lane Fox finds somewhat surprising in light of Celsus' portrayal of the Christians as coming from the lowest echelons of society.[15] As Origen reports the charge, "Celsus also urges us to 'take office in the government of the country, if that is required for the maintenance of the laws and the support of religion'."[16] To this charge Origen in effect pleads guilty, presenting it to be the common practice that Christians in fact decline public duties ("that they may reserve themselves for a diviner and more necessary service in the Church of God -- for the salvation of men"). Plutarch, again castigating the Epicurean school, connects the holding of such offices with the enjoyment of honor and increase of reputation (*Pleas. Life.* 19 [*Mor.* 1100B-D]):

> But surely men so enamoured of praise and celebrity confess their want of ability or resolution when they let slip such pleasures, shunning office and political activity and the friendship of kings, things that Democritus said are the fount of all that is heroic and glorious in our life.

Moreover, the avoidance of public duties brought with it a negative value judgement:

> But if celebrity is pleasant, the want of it is painful; and nothing is more inglorious than want of friends, absence of activity, irreligion, sensuality and indifference -- and such is the reputation of their sect among all mankind except themselves. 'Unfairly,' you say. But we are considering reputation, not truth.... If oracles and divination and divine providence and the affection and love of parent for child and political activity and leadership and holding office are honourable and of good report, so surely those who say that there is no need to save Greece, but

---

[14] Origen, *c. Cels.* 3.44 (*ANF* 4:481-82).

[15] Robin Lane Fox, *Pagans and Christians* (New York: Alfred A. Knopf, Inc., 1989), 302.

[16] Orgien, *c. Cels.* 8.75 (*ANF* 4:668).

> rather to eat and drink so as to gratify the belly without harming it, are
> bound to suffer in repute and to be regarded as bad men.

Participating in public life was essential to achieving honor. Christians who refrained from taking offices because of the increased exposure to idolatry were unable to develop "friends" (in the sense of *amicitia*, the alternating patron-client relationship between social equals) as well as form vertical patron-client relationships, which would have afforded protection in times of active hostilty against the Christian community. The Christians could be subject to the same critique as the Epicureans, and, as far as Plutarch would be concerned, to the same lack of esteem, indeed to ill repute.

Other voices were more moderate in their appraisal of the early Christians.[17] Lucian, for example, presents them as credulous and naive because they were taken in by the charlatan Peregrinus (*De morte Peregrinus* 12-13), but this is not a damning indictment. Indeed, there is even a note of admiration of their contempt for death and belongings as they boldly minister to the needs of their imprisoned leader. Nevertheless, there is clear evidence for much hostility directed towards the Christian group and a growing arsenal of weapons with which to assault the honor of the group. Bearing the name of "Christian" itself set one in the margins of Greco-Roman society. To be a Christian was in itself a mark against one's attainment of honor and a good reputation.

THE ENDANGERED HONOR OF THE COMMUNITY

While the authors and witnesses cited above come from a period later than Hebrews,[18] Tacitus records that the negative evaluation, and hence reputation, of Christians goes back to a period before the fire of 64 CE,

---

[17] Galen, the mid-second century physician, offers a remarkably generous depiction of the Christian group as a philosophical school, and thus differs from the other pagan authors here reviewed which more or less regarded the group as a *superstitio*, a "foreign cult whose origin and practices stood outside the accepted religious standards of the Greco-Roman world" (Wilken, *Christians*, 79). While Galen criticizes the Christian and Jewish philosophy as irrational, he is impressed with the "school's" ability to cultivate virtues in its adherents, such as discipline, self-control, justice, and courage (Wilken, *Christians*, 82). Thus, while pursuing their own beliefs, the early Christians nevertheless did manifest virtues which were valued by the dominant culture, and which might be recognized as such by the open observer.

[18] If one accepts a later dating for Hebrews, e.g. 95 CE, Tacitus, Suetonius, Pliny, and 1 Peter may be viewed as roughly contemporaneous with the letter.

when already Christians were "loathed for their vices" and their "hatred of the human race." The recipients of Hebrews undoubtedly inherited some part of this general stigma when they came to be associated with the "pernicious superstition." This inheritance need not be assumed. It is rather demonstrated in the society's actions against the community as described by the author of Hebrews. In the experience of the recipients one can see how public hostility has already been excited against Christians, and thus again how association with the group (and bearing the name) was damaging to -- indeed, destructive of -- a person's honor and reputation in the Greco-Roman society.

The author provides little detail concerning the addressees' history and current circumstances. In 10:32-34, however, he highlights one phase of their life as a community:

> But remember the former days in which, having been enlightened, you endured a hard contest with sufferings (πολλὴν ἄθλησιν ὑπεμείνατε παθημάτων), in part being publicly exposed to reproaches and afflictions, in part having become partners of those being thus treated (τοῦτο μὲν ὀνειδισμοῖς τε καὶ θλίψεσιν θεατριζόμενοι, τοῦτο δὲ κοινωνοὶ τῶν οὕτως ἀναστρεφομένων γενηθέντες). For you both showed sympathy to the imprisoned and accepted the seizure of your property with joy, knowing that you possessed better and lasting possessions (καὶ γὰρ τοῖς δεσμίοις συνεπαθήσατε καὶ τὴν ἁρπαγὴν τῶν ὑπαρχόντων ὑμῶν μετὰ χαρᾶς προσεδέξασθε γινώσκοντες ἔχειν ἑαυτοὺς κρείττονα ὕπαρξιν καὶ μένουσαν, au. trans.).

These experiences of loss and suffering clearly belong to the past of the community. it was a storm which they had weathered successfully. Commentators differ in their estimation of how much time has passed between this "contest" and the writing of Hebrews, the answer often being based on subjective opinions as to how much time must pass before events may be said to belong to "former days" or require the exhortation to remember. Lane, because he accepts the destination as Rome and the date as pre-70 CE, identifies this "contest" with the expulsion of the Jews from Rome under Claudius in 49 CE.[19] The Edict of Claudius, in fact, links the exile to certain riots among the Jewish inhabitants of the city "at the instigation of Chrestus." The point of view of the authorities would have been that some slave named Chrestus (a common slave name) had been stirring up trouble among the Jews. Lane argues that the authorities have simply misunderstood the nature of the quarrel. The dispute concerned the *Christus*, or Messiah, and this figure was not himself instigating riots but

---

[19] Lane, *Hebrews 1-8*, lxv-lxvi.

rather was their indirect cause.   According to Lane's hypothesis, the community now faces the Neronic persecution of 64 CE, so that the events of "the former days" occurred fifteen years before the writing of Hebrews.

Lane provides a thorough picture of the setting of Hebrews, satisfying the reader's desire for a detailed picture of the community to which the letter is addressed.   With the scarce data within Hebrews, and the impossibility of settling for certain the question of destination and date, however, all such reconstructions must remain highly tentative, and sound interpretations cannot depend upon the details of such reconstructions.   All that can be said for certain is that this period of disenfranchisement and persecution occurred at some point in the community's past, and that the author considers the remembrance of this time as somehow necessary for the addressees' response in the present -- that their activity then captures the image of what they lack now.   An examination of the author's description of their past experience reveals that their honor collectively and individually was attacked, degraded, and exposed to further degradation at every stage.

The experience is described first as a public spectacle.   The participle θεατριζόμενοι refers to being made a show of, to being held up to ridicule or shame.[20]   It is related specifically to the θέατρον where games, contests, and public punishments were held.[21]   Philo recounts a vivid example of the public nature of punishment in his depiction of the brutal pogroms against the Jews in *Against Flaccus* 74-75, 84-85, and 95.   In these Alexandrian riots, the suffering and crucifixion of Jews was arranged as a spectacle and show (ἡ θέα, τὰ πρῶτα τῶν θεαμάτων).   Similarly, the record of Nero's execution of Christians in Tacitus' *Annals* 15.44 show that derision was as crucial an element as pain in dealing with that marginal group.   The spectacle was designed to discourage the afflicted

---

[20]   *LSJ*, 313.   Commentators have consistently recognized this aspect of the addressees' experience. Cf. Attridge, *Hebrews*, 299: "the image...does indicate that there was at least an element of public humiliation in the persecution mentioned." Likewise Delitzsch, *Hebrews*, 192-193: "The proper signification [of θεατρίζεσθαι] is to be exposed in the theatre for shameful punishment, or to be made a spectacle of shame to the world, having to endure both scornful taunts (ὀνειδισμοί) and active persecution (θλίψεις)"; Héring, *Hebrews*, 96: "'*Theatrizomenoi*' (v.33) can be compared with '*theatron egenēthēmen*' in 1 Corinthians 4[9], 'to be made a public spectacle', but this does not necassarily imply an allusion to a violent death in the arena. At all events the victims must have felt as though they were being pilloried"; Spicq, *Hébreux*, 329: "The choice of this verb (θεατριζόμενοι) underscores the offical character, the public disgrace, of these reproaches."

[21]   Cf. G. Kittel, "θεάομαι," *TDNT* 3.43: "The θέατρον is by human standards, not a proud [spectacle], but a sorry and contemptible."

from continuing and others from participating in the sect.[22] The enaction of society's disapproval and imposition of the stigma of disgrace was a calculated attempt to bring deviants back into line with society's norms.

Such public exposure, indeed the deliberately crafted public spectacle in the use of the theatre as a site of punishment, torture, and execution, made for the natural and painful linking of "reproach" and "affliction" of which our author speaks (τοῦτο μὲν ὀνειδισμοῖς τε καὶ θλίψεσιν). Together, these depict two aspects of the public humiliation suffered by the addressees. The sense of the first term includes "disgrace," "shame," "scandal," and, secondarily, "abuse" and "objuration."[23] It involves verbal attacks on honor and character, and appears to have been the common property of Christians in a number of social settings.[24] The assigning of disgrace and censure to the name of "Christian" indicates widespread rejection of this group by the society. Refusing to accomodate itself to full participation in Greco-Roman life, the society responded with negative sanctions -- shame -- against the community's behavior and withdrawal.

Moffatt notes that the most bitter element of the community's experience was its exposure to public shaming: "All this had been, the writer knew, a real ordeal, particularly because the stinging contempt and insults had had to be borne in the open....They had been exposed to...taunts and scorn that tempted one to feel shame (an experience which our author evidently felt keenly), as well as to wider hardships."[25]

---

[22] Plato expresses this exemplary function of public punishments in the *Gorgias* (525 C). The gods, he declares, have "hung up as examples there in the infernal dungeon" those worst of malefactors as "a spectacle and a lesson (θεάματα καὶ νουθετήματα) to such of the wrongdoers as arrive there from time to time."

[23] J. Schneider, "Ονειδισμός" (*TDNT* 5:238). See Spicq, *Hébreux*, 328: " ' Ονειδισμός ... possesses a wide range of nuances from simple reproach to malediction, passing through affront, mockery, injury, and outrage. It is associated with sarcastic comments and very frequently with mockery accompanied by railings and degrading comments.... All these nuances suit this passage, especially the last which is particularly attested: the ignominy inflicted by the persecutors is borne on account of the cause of God, notably the disgrace which attaches to a crime, or which results from a public condemnation."

[24] Most notably 1 Pet 4:14-16 (see above) and Matt 5:11: "Blessed are you when people revile you and persecute you and utter all kinds of evil against you falsely on my account" (NRSV). Cf. Luke 6:22: "Blessed are you when people hate you, and when they exclude you, revile you, and defame you on account of the Son of Man." In all these cases the verbal assaults and insults are linked directly with association with Christ.

[25] Moffatt, *Hebrews*, 153.

Interesting is Moffatt's observation that the experience "tempted one to feel shame." While this remains undeveloped, it appears to contain *in nuce* the essence of what was at work in the society's reproaches of the Christians. As explored earlier, dishonor provided a means of social control. The burning experience of disgrace, the stinging disapproval of society, was meant to lead the Christians back to a proper sense of shame, that is, to respect once more the values, relations, and traditions of the society.[26] Their resistance to these attempts at social control in their past makes them, for the author, their own best examples for the present.

Verbal abuse was joined with physical attacks (θλίψεσιν).[27] Assaults on a person's body was more than the inflicting of physical pain. It was an attack on personal honor. Pitt-Rivers writes concerning Medieval and modern Mediterranean societies: "We should start by noting the intimate relation between honour and the physical person.... Any form of physical affront implies an affront to honour since the 'ideal sphere' surrounding a person's honour...is defiled."[28] Public punishment is viewed everywhere as disgraceful, all the more as satisfaction, or the regaining of honor, is impossible. That we should extend the modern Mediterranean view of physical abuse as dishonoring to the first-century world is demonstrated, for example, by Philo.

In his account of the sufferings of the Jews under Flaccus Philo repeatedly uses words denoting "disgrace" or "insult" when speaking of attacks on the body. He notes that some "were arrested, scourged, tortured and after all these outrages (μετὰ πάσας τὰς αἰκίας), which were all their bodies could make room for, the final punishment kept in reserve was the cross" (*In Flacc.* 72; LCL). Philo sums up the physical suffering of the Senators who had been hauled into the arena as "the

---

[26] Chrysostom, commenting on 10:32, notes the power of such disapproval and grants of dishonor to affect judgement: "Reproach is a great thing, and calculated to pervert the soul, and to darken the judgement....Since the human race is exceeding vainglorious, therefore it is easily overcome by this" (*NPNF¹* 14:461; Migne, *PG* 63.149).

[27] Cf. Lane, *Hebrews 9-13*, 299: "The complementary term ... appears to indicate that acts of violence had accompanied verbal abuse." Also Lünemann, *Hebrews*, 654: "ὀνειδισμοί has reference to the assaults upon honor and good name; θλίψεις to assaults upon the person (the life) and outward possessions."

[28] J. Pitt-Rivers, "Honour and Social Status," 25. This concept is taken up by Malina and Neyrey, "Honor and Shame in Luke Acts," 35: "A physical affront is a challenge to one's honor; unanswered it becomes a dishonor in the judgement of the people who witness the affront. A physical affront symbolizes the breaking of required social and personal boundaries, the entering of a person's bodily space without permission."

outrage to their persons" (τὴν ἐν τοῖς σώμασιν ὕβριν, *In Flacc.* 77). Ἀικία is translated in *LSJ* as "injurious treatment, an outrage, insult, affront"; ὕβρις includes among its meanings "despiteful treatment, an outrage, gross insult, assault and battery." Both terms combine physical maltreatment with an attack on the honor of the victim.

Because the author explicitly states that the addressees have not yet "resisted to the point of blood" (12:4), that is, because there had been no deaths as a result of the trials endured, the pogrom against the addressees was clearly less complete and brutal than that suffered by the Jews under Flaccus or Christians under Nero. Their commitment to Christ nevertheless exposed them to censure, defamation, and jeering (all falling under the heading of ὀνειδιμοί) as well as physical abuse (θλίψεις). Public disgrace and the physical violation of their person constituted a comprehensive assault on their honor. Malina and Neyrey have termed this sort of public shaming a "status-degradation ritual"[29] by which deviants (and thus the threat deviance poses for the social and political order) are neutralized and the order which they threatened reinforced as primary and ultimate.

Hebrews notes that another component of the readers' experience was the willingness of those presumably not singled out for this public punishment to display solidarity with those who were so treated, and thus who become "partners with those thus treated" (τοῦτο δὲ κοινωνοὶ τῶν οὕτως ἀναστρεφομένων γενηθέντες). Further, the addressees expressed a "fellow-feeling" with those who were confined in prison (καὶ γὰρ τοῖς δεσμίοις συνεπαθήσατε). This involved far more than mere "sympathy," as the term is used today. Rather, prison conditions being what they were, prisoners needed to be provided for by family or friends from the outside. Lucian provides a moving description of the sort of support a Christian group in the early second century could mobilize for one of its own (*Peregr.* 12-13), which included the provision of food and clothing as well as human company and fellowship throughout the day and night. The journey to Rome of the prisoner Ignatius of Antioch demonstrates also the willingness of the Christian groups to visit and send support to their own (*Eph.* 1, 2; *Magn.* 2; *Trall.* 1; *Phil.* 11). Paul himself, frequently in prison, received encouragement and support from his churches (for example, in the person of Epaphroditus, Phil 2:25).

Such activity showed a willingness to identify oneself with those afflicted with imprisonment, thus acknowledging their bond with them and

---

[29] Malina and Neyrey, "Conflict in Luke-Acts: Labelling and Deviance Theory," in *The Social World of Luke-Acts* (ed. J. H. Neyrey; Peabody: Hendrickson, 1991), 107.

sharing their disgrace. Ignatius appears to have been aware of this when he praises the Smyrnaeans: "My life is a humble offering for you; and so are these chains of mine, for which you never showed the least contempt or shame. Neither will Jesus Christ in his perfect loyalty show Himself ashamed of you" (οὐδὲ ὑμᾶς ἐπαισχυνθήσεται ἡ τελεία πίστις, ˙ Ἰησοῦς Χριστός, *Smyrn.* 10).[30] That "bonds" were considered to be an outrage to people of honor and a sign of disgrace is further demonstrated in Josephus, *BJ* 4.169 and 4.259, as well as in 2 Tim 1:16: "May the Lord grant mercy to the household of Onesiphorus, because he often refreshed me and was not ashamed of my chains." This last text also shows how association with those whom society had set aside by imprisonment or chains, the tokens of imprisonment, could be a source of disgrace. The reward promised is that Jesus, who has attained the place of highest honor in the Christian cosmos, will display the same loyalty to the Smyrnaeans as they displayed toward Ignatius. The displays of solidarity of both Jesus and the Smyrnaeans, however, appear to be credited as acts of "grace" precisely because they reach down to those of lower dignity and, in the latter case, are potentially damaging to the intact dignity of the Smyrnaeans who have not been singled out for punishment.[31]

That the expression of such sympathy and support for those who have been marked as deviants could be dangerous for the sympathizer is amply demonstrated by Philo (*In Flacc.* 72): "The friends and kinsmen of the true sufferers, simply because they grieved over the misfortunes of their relations, were arrested, scourged, tortured and after all these outrages, which were all their bodies could make room for, the final punishment kept in reserve was the cross." The addressees, however, showed no fear of the possible reprisals and chose rather to identify with their fellow-Christians, "sharing their perils by the active avowal of sympathy."[32]

The last aspect of this experience of persecution and marginalization which the author notes is the seizure (ἁρπαγή) of the believers' property. Was this an official confiscation? The term itself generally refers to popular plundering, such as befell Peregrinus' possessions in Parium while he himself was in exile elsewhere (Lucian *Peregr.* 14) or such as befell the

---

[30] *Early Christian Writings* (tr. Maxwell Staniforth; London: Penguin, 1968), 122.

[31] Cf. Aristotle *Rh.* 2.6.25: "Men also feel shame when they are connected with actions or things which entail disgrace, for which either they themselves, or their ancestors, or any others with whom they are closely connected are responsible." Association with those who had brought disgrace upon themselves (i.e., whom the society held in dishonor) was a cause of shame, and such associations might well be avoided out of a sense of shame.

[32] Westcott, *Hebrews*, 336; cf. Héring, *Hebrews*, 95.

propertied people of Jerusalem during the long siege of 69-70 CE (Josephus *BJ* 4.168) or such as befell the Jews in Alexandria after Flaccus had deprived them of their citizenship rights (Philo *In Flacc.* 5, 53-57). An official act of confiscation, however, could also be appropriately called "plundering" by those suffering confiscation.[33] It is also difficult to know exactly what sort of property was taken. An official act, or the decision of a court, could mean the loss of land and house or simply a fine; simple plundering would involve the loss of a house's contents, one's personal possessions, but which might nevertheless represent a substantial loss of wealth. Plundering could also include driving people from their homes, again such as befell the Alexandrian Jews under Flaccus, or such as is envisioned by the author of 2 Esdras 15-16 as part of the persecution of the righteous in the third century C.E.[34]

In either case, the loss of wealth (particularly as part of an assault on a person's honor and person) would entail also the loss of status. Wealth and possessions were not generally accumulated for their own sake in the ancient world. Rather wealth was bartered for prestige and honor through the system of private or public benefactions -- the giving of land or property to needy suitors or the provision of public buildings, roads, or games. A loss of wealth entailed a loss of potential prestige. In a recent study, Neyrey argues that honor in the ancient world was intimately bound to the display of wealth -- even the small wealth of a peasant in a village.[35] "Whatever wealth a peasant had, it was his 'treasure' and an important indicator of his status and honor in the village.[36] Loss of wealth would thus entail a proportionate loss of honor, and would provoke

---

[33] Indeed, the line between official decree and unofficial rapine might not have been clearly drawn. Melito of Sardis, in his "Petition to the Emperor Marcus Aurelius" (cited in Eusebius, *Ecclesiastical History* [tr. G. A. Williamson; London: Penguin, 1965] 4.26.5), gives evidence for a sort of open policy for the pillaging of those denounced as Christians: "Religious people as a body are being harried and persecuted by new edicts all over Asia. Shameless informers out to fill their own pockets are taking advantage of the decrees to pillage openly, plundering inoffensive citizens night and day."

[34] "For in many places and in neighboring cities there shall be a great insurrection against those who fear the Lord. They shall be like mad men, sparing no one, but plundering and destroying those who continue to fear the Lord. For they shall destroy and plunder their goods, and drive them out of their houses. Then the tested quality of my elect shall be manifest, as gold that is tested by fire" (2 Esd 16:70-73; RSV).

[35] J. Neyrey, "Poverty and Loss of Honor in Matthew's Beatitudes: Poverty as Cultural, Not Merely Economic Phenomenon" (an unpublished paper delivered at the CJA Seminar in October 1992), 4.

[36] Neyrey, "Poverty," 15.

contempt from others if the loss were judged to have been brought about by the victim's own fault.[37] From the situation of reproach and rejection already described in Heb 10:32-34, the Christians would have been thought to have brought their misfortune on themselves through their refusal to fulfill their obligations according to Greco-Roman standards.

The loss of their property, connected with their degradation as Christians (whether officially or unofficially), would entail additional disgrace.[38] It could also place them in a most difficult economic position. Philo (*In Flacc.* 57) records that the pillaging of the Alexandrian Jews and the seizure of their houses and workshops resulted in their fall into a penury from which they could not easily recover: "Thus poverty ($\pi\epsilon\nu\prime\alpha\nu$) was established in two ways: first, the pillaging, by which in the course of a single day they had become penniless, completely stripped of what they had, and secondly, their inability to make a living from their regular employments." If the recipients of Hebrews were subjected to a similar depredation, they too would find themselves forced into and fixed within a lower status with no easy means of regaining their economic position.

The overall effect of the experience of which the author reminds the addressees, therefore, was one of social marginalization, rejection, and degradation. The Christians' place in society was fundamentally challenged, and the individuals involved lost their status as solid and reliable citizens. Those who came to the aid of those directly pilloried bore witness themselves that they preferred the community of their fellow-believers to that of the dominant culture. They boldly stepped forward to the aid of their brothers and sisters in the face of a society's hatred. The result of these combined assaults on the honor of the Christians was loss of status within the society. The author suggests that, while they had met these challenges boldly in the faith (i.e., with $\pi\alpha\rho\rho\eta\sigma\prime\alpha$, 10:35), with the passage of time the situation has changed.

With the passage of time, they have begun to feel the desire to regain their place in society, to recover their honor in the sight of unbelievers. As they continued to live their lives they were confronted by the sight of those who were aware of their degradation, who may well have reminded

---

[37] Neyrey, "Poverty," 7.

[38] Even if the property were lost in lawsuits against Christians, the Christians' inability to defend themselves successfully, and thus suffer the loss of their goods, would have been regarded as disgraceful (cf. Plato *Gorg.* 508 C-D). Their lack of influential friends and advocates would also signal their marginal status and lack of honor.

the Christians of their new status in the society.[39] In effect, they have begun to feel shame (that is, concern for their reputation) before the representative of the society -- the machinery of social control, though resisted at the outset, is achieving its desired effect in the long run. It was perhaps easier, in the fire of persecution, in the fervor of religious solidarity, to set aside the opinion of outsiders. Living with their loss, however, has proven more difficult.[40]

Apostasy is presented as a lively danger in Hebrews: "How can we escape if we neglect so great a salvation?" (2:3; NRSV); "Take care, brothers and sisters, that none of you may have an evil, unbelieving heart that turns away (ἀποστῆναι) from the living God!" (3:12); "For it is impossible to restore those who...have fallen away" (6:4-6); "How much worse punishment...will be deserved by those who have trampled upon the Son of God, regarded as profane the blood of the covenant,... and outraged the Spirit of grace?" (10:29). Commentators have viewed this potential apostasy as motivated by fear of a forthcoming persecution or by a renewal of interest in Judaism. It is quite possible that apostasy would have been motivated by the more pedestrian inability to live within the lower status that Christian associations had forced upon them, the less-than-dramatic (yet potent) desire once more to enjoy the goods and esteem of their society. Since their confession brought about their degradation and deprivation, and since the society used shame and disgrace as means of recalling the deviant to an acceptable manner of life in accordance with the norms and values of that society, apostasy would indeed provide a step towards "recovery."[41]

---

[39] Aristotle (*Rh.* 2.6.27) indicates that people "are more likely to be ashamed when they have to be seen and to associate openly with those who are aware of their disgrace." That inhabitants of the Mediterranean world (as any society) were not above taunting their undesirables is shown from such complaints as Psalm 108:25: "I am an object of scorn to my accusers; when they see me, they wag their heads (καὶ ἐγὼ ἐγενήθην ὄνειδος αὐτοῖς· εἴδοσάν με, ἐσάλευσαν κεφαλὰς αὐτῶν)."

[40] With regard to their loss, one might again consult Aristotle (*Rh.* 2.6.12): "It is also shameful not to have a share in the honourable things which all men, or all who resemble us, or the majority of them. have a share in. By those who resemble us I mean those of the same race, of the same city, of the same age, of the same family, and, generally speaking, those who are on an equality; for then it is disgraceful not to have a share, for instance, in education and other things, to the same extent." Their deprivation of the esteem of the society and the enjoyment of property, their loss of place in society, now seems to them onerous, a malady to be cured.

[41] It will be part of the task of the further examination of Hebrews throughout this study to determine whether or not this is indeed the situation to which Hebrews provides a strategic response.

The author meets them at this critical juncture. The real danger, he asserts, lies in jeopardizing their honor in God's sight through "shrinking back" in the face of society's pressure to conform:

> Do not throw away your confidence, which has a great reward (μὴ ἀποβάλητε οὖν τὴν παρρησίαν ὑμῶν, ἥτις ἔχει μεγάλην μισθαποδοσίαν). For you have need of endurance in order that, having done the will of God, you may receive the promise (κομίσησθε τὴν ἐπαγγελίαν). For yet "but a little while" and "the one who is coming will come and not delay: and my righteous one will live by faith (ὁ δὲ δίκαιός μου ἐκ πίστεως ζήσεται), and if he or she shrinks back (ἐὰν ὑποστείληται), my soul has no pleasure in that one." But we are not characterized by shrinking back unto destruction but by faith unto the attainment of life (ἡμεῖς δὲ οὐκ ἐσμὲν ὑποστολῆς εἰς ἀπώλειαν ἀλλὰ πίστεως εἰς περιποίησιν ψυχῆς, 10:35-39; au. trans.).

The Christians' honor before God has not been harmed but only enhanced by their commitment to Christ through times of heavy social pressure. Their endurance of the former experiences may be seen as performing God's will. He urges them not to throw away their "confidence," as if such were their claim ticket to their receiving of the promised "greater and lasting possessions" (10:34) and "glory" (2:10). "Confidence" is, of course, an inadequate translation for παρρησία, which carries the meaning of boldness, candor, and openness. Significantly, it is also frequently opposed to αἰσχύνη, or shame.[42] The author points them to the great reward which they have already earned and which they will receive if they simply remain firm in their commitment. That is, he calls them to exhibit πίστις rather than execute a ὑποστολή, a turning back with regard to their commitment to Christ. The author therefore turns to the celebrated exemplars of commitment, πίστις, in order to stir up their flagging zeal for honor before God and to reinforce the detachment of Christians from society's honor rating.

---

[42] In both 1 Jn 2:28 and *1 Enoch* 97.1, 6; 98.10, these words are placed within the context of standing before the divine judge at the Parousia or the Last Day. The reward of those who have remained in Christ (or who have continued steadfast in the Law) is "confidence" or "open freedom" before God or Christ, which is contrasted to the shame of the wicked, who are unable to exercise any boldness or openness due to their disgrace before God.

2 The Example of Jesus

The author places the example of Jesus in 12:1-3 as the climax and capstone of the litany of the exemplars of faith. These heroes of πίστις form the body of spectators for the race set before the addressees, who are explicitly called to look to Jesus, the pioneer and perfecter of πίστις.[43] As such, Jesus encapsulates the most salient features of faith demonstrated in the exemplars of chapter 11. As the pioneer and perfecter of faith, Jesus shows most clearly what faith entails and thus how the recipients are to manifest faith in their situation.

Jesus' enactment of faith is documented simply in 12:2b: ἀντὶ τῆς προκειμένης αὐτῷ χαρᾶς ὑπέμεινεν σταυρὸν αἰσχύνης καταφρονήσας. To this is appended the declaration of the result of Jesus' faith, ἐν δεξιᾷ τε τοῦ θρόνου τοῦ θεοῦ κεκάθικεν. Jesus' attainment of the honor of session at God's right hand springs from enduring a cross and despising shame. With this latter phrase, attention to the language of honor and shame brings the reader to consider anew the nature of faith itself. We cannot yet assume that "despising shame" means "accepting humiliation," yet we may may ask what humiliation Jesus had to accept in order to accomplish God's will (cf. 10:5-9). The community endured the loss of status and honor in its quest to maintain commitment to God: they would surely be sensitive to the loss of status and honor which Jesus would have endured on their behalf to bring them the promised benefits.

After developing the extent of the exaltation of Jesus in chapter 1 and presenting a brief admonition in 2:1-4, the author performs a Christological exegesis of Psalm 8:4-6. At the heart of this application lie the phrases ἠλάττωσας αὐτὸν βραχύ τι παρ' ἀγγέλους, δόξῃ καὶ τιμῇ ἐστεφάνωσας αὐτόν (2:7). The latter phrase, "you crowned him with glory and honor," is taken to follow chronologically on the former phrase, "you made him a little less than the angels." When the author applies this to Jesus, however, he takes the βραχύ τι as an expression of time, thus giving a sense of a period of abasement followed by an exaltation. The author's exegesis of the psalm is thus similar to the Christ-hymn in Phil 2:6-11, in which, again, a voluntary loss of status is followed by a greater

---

[43] Lane (*Hebrews 9-13*, 399) insightfully recognizes that "faith" must be taken as absolute here, and the temptation to translate this phrase as "the pioneer and perfecter of *our* faith" avoided. The RSV, JB, NEB, TEV, NIV, and the NSRV insist on relating Jesus' work to "our faith," thereby disguising the function Jesus serves for the author of Hebrews as the greatest example of what faith entails.

exaltation.[44] Jesus' sharing in flesh and blood (a descent into the limited, material realm, 2:14) represented an abasement, embraced for the sake of doing the will of God ("a body you have prepared for me," 10:5, quoting Ps 40:6).

Christ's humiliation began with the incarnation, but clearly climaxes with the crucifixion. The suffering of Jesus mentioned in 2:10, 18; 5:8 takes the specific shape of a cross in 12:2, a death which occurs moreover in a place of dishonor and uncleanness ("outside the camp," 13:11). This death was preceded and accompanied by ἀντιλογία, "opposition, resistance" (*LSJ*), from the very "sinners" whom Christ had sought to benefit. The author may indeed have had in mind the insults and mocking which Jesus had to bear between trial and death,[45] the specific inclusion of which will provide a special connection with the experience of the addressees who have not yet "resisted sin to the point of shedding blood" (12:4), but have endured reproach and insult.[46]

Such a death was, by Greco-Roman standards, far from exemplary. For those steeped in the Jewish or Christian tradition, who are heirs to the ideal of the martyr's noble endurance and the transformation of the "noble death," it is difficult indeed to imagine the horror of the disgrace attached to the cross (or, for the Maccabean martyrs, death on the rack). There was indeed a strong tradition of the noble death in the ancient world. Such an end was an occasion to display the perfection of courage, one of the cardinal virtues.[47] A noble death, notably in battle or in some other form

---

[44] So Calvin, *Hebrews*, 91 (commenting on Heb 8:1): "Now, because Christ suffered in the lowliness of the flesh, and, taking the form even of a servant, was made of no reputation in the world, (Phil. 2,7) the Apostle calls us back to his ascension; whereby not only was the ignominy of the cross swallowed up, but also that mean estate, which he had put on together with our flesh, was thrown off." The taking on of human form was an integral part of Christ's humiliation.

[45] So Chrysostom (*NPNF¹* 14:494; Migne, *PG* 63.196): "The blows upon the cheek, the laughter, the insults, the reproaches, the mockeries, all these he indicated by 'contradiction'."

[46] As noted by Attridge, *Hebrews*, 358: "The term may allude to various instances of hostility expressed toward Jesus in his passion, but the image is shaped primarily by the situation of the addresees who need to bear with hostile reproach." Cf. also Peterson, *Perfection*, 170.

[47] Cf. Aristotle, *Eth. Nic.* 3.6.10: "The courageous man, therefore, in the proper sense of the term, will be he who fearlessly confronts a noble death." Circumstances had to be right for one to achieve a noble death (as opposed to an ordinary or shameful one). Again from *Eth. Nic.* (3.6.12), "courage is shown in dangers where a man can defend himself by valour or die nobly, but neither is possible in disasters like shipwreck."

of service to one's country, was viewed as a "special honour which nature has reserved for the good" (Ps.-Isocrates *Ad Dem.* 43).[48] A shameful death, however, which left one no chance to recover honor and a good name but rather bequeathed to one a lasting remembrance in disgrace, was the most feared of all evils. As expressed by the unknown poet quoted by Epictetus (*Diss.* 2.1.13), "It is not a fearful thing to die, but to die shamefully" (οὐ κατθανεῖν γὰρ δεινόν, ἀλλ' αἰσχρῶς θανεῖν, au. trans.). Similarly, as Adkins observes (from Euripides *Hercules Furens* 281ff.), "Megara says significantly that death is a terrible thing, but that to die in a manner which would give her enemies the opportunity to mock would be a greater evil than death."[49]

Death on a cross has long been recognized as a supremely shameful death. This form of execution was associated with "the lower classes, i.e. slaves, violent criminals and the unruly elements in rebellious provinces."[50] Liability to the sentence of crucifixion was already indicative of low status. Further, as crucifixion was the punishment for enemies and disturbers of the peace of the Roman order, "the crucified victim was defamed both socially and ethically in popular awareness."[51] Crucifixion was always a public affair -- the victim was hung up as an example (a παράδειγμα in the most negative sense)[52] to others not to transgress Roman order and rule. "By the public display of a naked victim at a prominent place...crucifixion also represented his uttermost humiliation."[53] Jesus' death on the cross was thus an experience of

---

[48] Indeed, a noble death could be regarded as a favor or gift from God, as in Eleazar's striking exhortation to suicide in Josephus, *BJ* 7.323-336 (especially 7.325-26).

[49] *Merit and Responsibility,* 155. One may also note Wisd 2:19-20, in·which the climactic assault of the godless on the righteous person is the infliction of a specifically shameful death: "Let us test him with insult (ὕβρει) and torture, that we may find out how gentle he is, and make trial of his forbearance. Let us condemn him to a shameful death (θανάτῳ ἀσχήμονι καταδικάσωμεν αὐτόν), for, according to what he says, he will be protected."

[50] M. Hengel, *Crucifixion in the Anceint World* (Philadelphia: Fortress, 1977), 87. Hengel's volume contains a wealth of primary materials documenting the nature, associations of, and reactions to crucifixion in the Greco-Roman and Jewish world.

[51] Hengel, *Crucifixion,* 88.

[52] Cf. Plato, *Gorg.* 525C, where Socrates speaks of those criminals hung up for display in Tartarus for the benefit not of themselves but of those who may contemplate their punishments and so avoid the crimes.

[53] Hengel, *Crucifixion,* 87. Cf. also Philo's description of the crucifixion of the Alexandrian Jewish senators as a spectacle and show (ἡ θέα, τὰ πρῶτα τῶν θεαμάτων), as well as the account in Tacitus (*Ann.* 15.44-45) of Nero's crucifixion of the Christians

complete humiliation, marking the complete stripping of his honor and place in society and social memory.[54] Nevertheless, it is this death which exemplifies the perfection of faith -- a death which involved not only the endurance of pain (which would be recognized as honorable, a mark of courage), but also the despising of shame.

Αἰσχύνης Καταφρονήσας

In what sense, then, did Jesus "despise shame," such that he has become the chief exemplar of faith for the community? The proper interpretation of this phrase must determine what exactly is meant by αἰσχύνη here as well as the force of the verb καταφρονέω. In the history of interpretation, some have favored the understanding that Jesus "braved" or "faced up to" the experience of humiliation which the cross entailed,[55] while others have seen in this phrase a Stoic disregard for the experience.[56] Moffatt offers an interpretation which goes slightly but helpfully beyond those offered by most other scholars:

> The special αἰσχύνη here is that of crucifixion. This, says the writer, Jesus did not allow to stand between him and loyalty to the will of God. It is one thing to be sensitive to disgrace and disparagement, another thing to let these hinder us from doing our duty. Jesus was sensitive to such emotions; he felt disgrace keenly. But instead of allowing these

---

in the circus amidst other "entertaining" and mocking forms of execution.

[54] Commentators across the centuries have recognized that humiliation was an essential component of crucifixion. Hughes, *Hebrews*, 525, reminds the reader that "it is important to recognise that the shame of the cross...is something infinitely more intense than the pain of the cross." Bengel, also commenting on Heb 12:2, had noted that the shame connected with the cross was of the greatest order (*maximam, cum cruce conjunctam*).

[55] So Delitzsch, *Hebrews*, 306: "He vouchsafed to undergo the most painful and ignominious of deaths, such a death as that of the cross, -- αἰσχύνης καταφρονήσας, despising, disdaining to shrink from any kind of shame." Lane (*Hebrews 9-13*, 414) follows this line of interpretation as well: "As a matter of fact, the attitude denoted by καταφρονεῖν, 'to scorn,' acquires in this context a positive nuance: 'to brave,' or 'to be unafraid' of an experience in spite of its painful character."

[56] Thus Michel (*Hebräerbrief*, 294) equates αἰσχύνης καταφρονήσας with "consider as nothing, be unconcerned about (für nichts achten, sich nicht kümmern um)." Attridge (*Hebrews*, 358 n.72) only hints at an interpretation in a footnote: "the heroic martyr, like a good Stoic, will disregard or despise suffering and death."

feelings to cling to his mind, he rose above them. This is the force of καταφρονήσας here.[57]

In Moffatt's mention of "sensitivity to disgrace and disparagement," and his connection of this sensitivity with perseverance in a course of action ("to let these things hinder us from doing our duty"), one finds a reminiscence of αἰσχύνη as "modesty," or a sense of shame such as "makes one sensitive to the honor rating and respectful of social boundaries."[58] The discussion in chapter two concerning how honor and shame language was used to motivate people to fulfill social obligations and embody the virtues valued by the society might lead one to suspect that when Jesus is said to "despise shame" (and is held up as exemplary at least in part for this reason), the author has in mind the overturning of society's evaluation of his actions in answer to a higher court of opinion.

In an attempt to provide parallels by means of which this phrase might best be interpreted, J. J. Wettstein[59] points the student first to the sole lexical parallel in the Greek literature (apart from works clearly dependent on Heb 12:2), namely, Dio *Or.* 7.139:

> Now at this point we must assuredly remember that this adultery committed with outcasts, so evident in our midst and becoming so brazen and unchecked, is to a very great extent paving the way to hidden and secret assaults (ὕβρεων) upon the chastity of women and boys of good family, such crimes being only too boldly committed when modesty is trampled upon (τῆς αἰσχύνης ἐς κοινῷ καταφρονουμένης).

Dio uses the term αἰσχύνη to denote "modesty," particularly connected in this passage with respect for the sexual ethics of the Greco-Roman society. As such, it is a fitting parallel. The sense of shame (the respect for the opinion and honor-rating of society), which should prevent certain behaviors for fear of disgrace, has somehow been neutralized. The author of Hebrews, of course, would never recommend "despising shame" in this sense, as he, too, is concerned about the preservation of chastity and the sanctity of the marriage bed (13:4). Nevertheless, the parallel is quite instructive for considering αἰσχύνη in a wider sense than the experience of dishonor.

Wettstein can provide no more exact lexical parallels, yet he insightfully and helpfully directs the reader to Diogenes Laertius,

---

[57] *Hebrews*, 236.

[58] Corrigan, "Paul's Shame for the Gospel" (*BTB* 16 [1986] 23-27) 24.

[59] *He Kaine Diatheke: Novum Testamentum graece* (Amsterdam: Dommer, 1751-52), 2.434.

Democritus 9.36: "It would also seem that he also went to Athens and was anxious not to be recognized, because he despised fame (δόξης καταφρονῶν; LCL)." The phrase δόξης καταφρονῶν here refers to the strange posture of "despising fame," or shrinking back from gaining popularity and repute. It was the mark of the true philosopher to act with detachment from public opinion, for the philosopher measured the honorable and disgraceful by different standards than the mass of people. Cato Minor, Seneca's "exemplar of the wise man" (*Constant.* 2.1), is remembered by Plutarch (*Cato Minor* 6.6.3) for his purposeful avoidance of conforming to fashion and popular signs of status:

> He was not hunting for notoriety by this strange practice, but accustoming himself to be ashamed only of what was really shameful, and to ignore men's low opinion of other things (οὐ δόξαν ἐκ ταύτης τῆς καινότητος θηρώμενος, ἀλλ᾽ ἐθίζων ἑαυτὸν ἐπὶ τοῖς αἰσχροῖς αἰσχύνεσθαι μόνοις, τῶν δ᾽ ἄλλως ἀδόξων καταφρονεῖν; LCL).

Such a stance indicates independence from the sanctioning power of honor and shame language. One may recall, however, that people within the ancient Mediterranean did not feel a sense of shame with regard to all other people, but only with regard to their significant others. These would generally include family, business associates, friends, those in authority, in short, the people whose respect was important to one's self-respect and the maintenance of a position of respect within the society. There were people whose opinion simply did not count, before whom one did not feel shame.

As Aristotle noted in *Rh.* 2.6.14-15, one only feels shame before those "whose opinion they do not despise (μὴ καταφρονεῖ τῆς δόξης)." For this reason, "no one feels shame before children or animals" (οὐκ αἰσχύνονται ὧν πολὺ καταφρονοῦσι τῆς δόξης τοῦ ἀληθεύειν, *Rh.* 2.6.23). Those who were dedicated to different ideals, moreover, could find themselves in separate "courts of opinion" which exercised no influence on each other's values or decisions. People like Aristotle who were devoted to the pursuit of virtue did not respect the opinion -- positive or negative -- which the common person might have entertained of them. Neither honor nor disgrace carried any weight, and both were regarded as nothing.[60]

---

[60] Aristotle *Eth. Nic.* 4.3.17: "Honour rendered by common people and on trivial grounds he will utterly despise (ὀλιγωρήσει), for this is not what he merits. He will also despise dishonour, for no dishonour can justly attach to him (ὁμοίως δὲ καὶ ἀτιμίας· οὐ γὰρ ἔσται δικαίως περὶ αὐτόν)." SImilarly, cf. Dio *Or.* 24.4: "For the truth is that, for and of itself, receiving the approbation of senseless persons (ἐπαινεῖσθαι ... ὑπὸ ἀνθρώπων ἀνοήτων), which is just what the majority are, or

Philosophers would frequently separate themselves from the evaluation of the lay persons who did not share their convictions about what constituted an honorable life by thinking of them as children, whose opinion and evaluation were therefore unreliable.[61]   The philosopher would thus remain unmoved by both the honor and dishonor showed him or her by the uninitiated:

> In the same spirit in which he sets no value (*nihilo aestimat*) on the honours they have, he sets no value on the lack of honour they show. Just as he will not be flattered if a beggar shows him respect, nor count it an insult if a man from the dregs of the people, on being greeted, fails to return his greeting, so, too, will he not even look up if many rich men look upon him. For he knows that they differ not a whit from beggars....(Seneca *Constant.* 13.2)

Epictetus places reputation, that is, one's worth in the eyes of other people, among the things "not under our control," which are all to be despised if one is to maintain one's moral purpose intact and achieve the freedom of nature.[62]

In light of this conceptual background, the phrase αἰσχύνη καταφρονήσας begins to look rather different from what has been suggested by most commentators. The survey lends considerable support to Bultmann's observation that "αἰσχύνη is fear of the αἰσχρόν and

---

having influence with men of that kind, or leading a pleasant life, will not, so far as happiness (πρὸς εὐδαιμονίαν) is concerned, be one whit better than being censured by them (οὐδὲν ἂν διαφέροι ... τοῦ ψέγεσθαι)."

[61]   Cf. Seneca *Constant.* 11.2-12.1, in which Seneca notes concerning the reproaches and insults offered the wise person that one does not take a child's actions as insulting, because children are inferior, and that "the same attitude...the wise man has toward all men whose childhood endures even beyond middle age and the period of grey hairs." Cf. also Aristotle *Eth. Nic.* 10.6.4.

[62]   Epictetus *Ench.* 19.2: "Beware lest, when you see some person preferred to you in honor (προτιμώμενον), or possessing great power, or otherwise enjoying high repute, you are ever carried away by the external impression, and deem him happy. For if the true nature of the good is one of the things that are under our control, there is no place for either envy or jealousy (οὔτε φθόνος οὔτε ζηλοτυπία); and you yourself will not wish to be a praetor, or a senator, or a consul, but a free man. Now there is but one way that leads to this, and that is to despise the things that are not under our control (καταφρόνησις τῶν οὐκ ἐφ' ἡμῖν)." Cf. *Ench.* 1.1: "Some things are under our control, while other are not under our control. Under our control are conception, choice, desire, aversion, and, in a word, everything that is our own doing; not under our control are our body, our property, reputation, office, and, in a word, eveything that is not our own doing.

therefore of one's δόξα."[63] Αἰσχύνη καταφρονήσας would then indicate
a rejection of regard for one's reputation, and would include a
corresponding negative counter-evaluation of those who would seek to
judge one's actions as disgraceful. The phrase would appear to indicate
Jesus' awareness of distance and difference between the world's evaluation
of the honorable and shameful and the standards which would apply to
him.[64] This was indeed the interpretation of the early church fathers.
Their proximity in both time and place to the culture of the New Testament
world makes them in many respects our most reliable guides in
interpretation.   Origen (*Fragmenta in Psalmos* 37.12.4-5) expands the
phrase thus to indicate specifically the source of the negative evaluation
and standard being despised: καταφρονήσας γὰρ τῆς παρ᾽ ἀνθρώποις
αἰσχύνης, "having despised disgrace from human beings." Gregory of
Nyssa expands this further to indicate Jesus' station above these worldly
values and definitions of what deserves honor or dishonor: οὗτος ὁ τῆς ἐν
ἀνθρώποις αἰσχύνης καταφρονήσας διὰ τὸ εἶναι τῆς δόξης κύριος, "this
one despised a disgraceful reputation among human beings on account of
his being the lord of glory."[65]

Moreover, these early interpreters fasten onto this aspect of Hebrews'
description of Christ's faith as an explicit model for the believers.[66] In
his exhortation to martyrdom in the period of the Decian persecution,
Origen (*Exhortatio ad Marytrium* 37.11-14) encourages the Christians to
withstand the pressures -- physical and social -- to abandon the faith by
holding up Jesus as a pattern for imitation, using the formula of Heb 12:2:

---

[63]   R. Bultmann, "Αἰδώς," *TDNT* 1.170. Strangely, in his article on αἰσχύνη
Bultmann wishes to distance the meaning of this word in the LXX and NT from its
meaning in extra-biblical literature.

[64]   In this respect, Hebrews 12:2 is akin to Jn 5:41: "I do not accept glory from
human beings." The different arenas for seeking honor appear shortly thereafter in Jn
5:44: "How can you believe when you accept glory form one another and do not seek
the glory that comes from the one who alone is God?" In these verses it is also
apparent that "honor" would frequently better serve as a translation for δόξα than
"glory."

[65]   *Contra Eunomium* 3.5 (Migne, *PG* 45.708 B 4-6). Among modern
commentators the connection of this phrase with the notion of the inapplicability of
human standards to the honor of Jesus was noticed especially by Westcott, *Hebrews*,
396: "But what men count shame was seen by Christ in another light. From His
position, raised infinitely above them, He could disregard their judgement."

[66]   This is, of course, not ignored by modern commentators. Weiß (*Hebräer*, 639)
believes this phrase to hold "a parenetic potential" for the addressees, and Attridge
(*Hebrews*, 357-58) notes that Christ's "despising shame" serves a "paradigmatic
function."

"Jesus then endured a cross, having despised shame, and on account of this sat down at God's right hand: and those who imitate him, despising shame, will sit with him and reign with him in the heavens."[67] John Chrysostom, commenting on Heb 12:2, also understands Jesus' stance as a rejection of the opinion of unbelievers, and, as such, a model for Chrysostom's hearers:

> What does "despising shame" signify (Τί δέ ἐστιν, Αἰσχύνης καταφρονήσας;)? It says that he chose a disgraceful (ἐπονείδιστον) death. Granted that he died: why also disgracefully? On account of nothing other than to teach us to count as nothing the opinion of human beings (Δι' οὐδὲν ἕτερον, ἀλλ' ἡμᾶς διδάσκων μηδὲν ἡγεῖσθαι τὴν παρ' ἀνθρώπων δόξαν).[68]

The addressees of Hebrews, in whom loss of honor and continued living with disgrace has begun to work the desire to adapt to society's norms and regain its approval, are thus strategically brought before the example of Jesus, in whom faith is perfected, that is, brought to its most complete expression. This perfection of faith (the virtue which leads to the approval of God, 10:38-39) embodies the rejection of the opinion of those who do not share the hope of the Christian. Jesus considered valueless society's evaluation of those acts which obedience to God required and the resultant honor-rating society would impose upon him; the believers are called to do likewise, in order that they may attain the promised reward and continue in their commitment to one another and to the God who called them in Christ. This rhetoric reflects a countercultural relationship between the Christian community and the Greco-Roman society, stressing the incommensurability of their standards.

Ἀντὶ τῆς προκειμένης αὐτῷ χαρᾶς

Jesus' choice of a course of action which a proper sense of "shame" (from the standpoint of society) would have caused one to avoid at all costs is presented as a choice made in light of another aspect of faith central to Hebrews, namely the consideration of the reward one will enjoy before

---

[67] Rowan A. Greer (tr.), *Origen* (New York: Paulist, 1979), 68. The Greek (from *TLG*) clearly shows the literary dependency on Heb 12:2: ὁ ˊ Ἰησοῦς δέ ποτε ὑπέμεινε σταυρὸν αἰσχύνης καταφρονήσας καὶ διὰ τοῦτο ἐκάθισεν ἐν δεξιᾷ τοῦ θεοῦ· καὶ οἱ μιμηταὶ δὲ αὐτοῦ αἰσχύνης καταφρονοῦντες συγκαθεδοῦνται αὐτῷ καὶ συμβασιλεύσουσιν ἐν τοῖς οὐρανοῖς.

[68] *NPNF¹* 14:493; Migne, *PG* 63.194.

God's court if one perseveres in faith. It is, indeed, this aspect which transforms the experiences of dishonor at the hands of unbelievers into a noble contest with an honorable prize.   How the phrase ἀντὶ τῆς προκειμένης αὐτῷ χαρᾶς is to be understood in its context is a matter of some debate. Calvin identifies this problem as a grammatical ambiguity caused by the multiple meanings of the preposition ἀντί.[69] One reading would yield "in place of the joy set before him," signifying that Jesus, who was able "to rid himself of all annoyance and live a life of happiness and abundance of all good things, yet did he of his own free will undergo a death painful and replete with ignominy."[70] The other reading translates the preposition as "for the sake of," that is, "in order to obtain."[71]

Several considerations strongly favor the latter reading. First, this preposition appears again in 12:16, where Esau's poor and godless choice is briefly depicted: "[Beware] lest anyone be immoral or impious like Esau, who for a single meal sold away his inheritance as firstborn" (μή τις πόρνος ἢ βέβηλος ὡς ῾Ησαῦ, ὃς ἀντὶ βρώσεως μιᾶς ἀπέδετο τὰ πρωτοτόκια ἑαυτοῦ; au. trans.). Esau chooses temporary safety and relief at the cost of his inheritance as the firstborn, which for him would have eternal significance. He thus appears as a sort of foil for those who make the correct evaluations of worth and act accordingly, like Moses or Christ. This paring of examples (Jesus vs. Esau) appears to be intended through the similar phrasing, and hence indicates that the preposition ought to be translated in the same way. As Attridge points out, Moses and Jesus would still be parallel examples, as Moses chose ill-treatment with the people of God with a view to the reward, i.e., in order to obtain the reward (11:26). A second consideration is an informative parallel from Aristotle, *Eth. Nic.* 3.1.7:

> "Sometimes indeed men are actually praised for deeds of this 'mixed' class, namely when they submit to some disgrace or pain as the price of some great and noble object (ἐπαινοῦνται, ὅταν αἰσχρόν τι ἢ λυπηρὸν ὑπομένωσιν ἀντὶ μεγάλων καὶ καλῶν); though if they do so without any such motive they are blamed, since it is contemptible to submit to a great disgrace with no advantage or only a trifling one in view."

---

[69] Calvin, *Hebrews*, 169.

[70] Calvin, *Hebrews*, 169-170. Such a reading is also preferred by Mary Rose D'Angelo (*Moses in the Letter to the Hebrews* [SBLDS 42; Missoula, MN: Scholars Press, 1976] 53), in light of a perceived parallelism with Moses' refusal of a life of ease in Pharaoh's court (11:24-26).

[71] This reading is preferred by Delitzsch (*Hebrews*, 306) and Attridge (*Hebrews*, 357).

While examples may be found in Aristotle where ἀντὶ requires the meaning of "in place of" or "instead of,"[72] this particular passage shares a number of components with Heb 12:2 which may suggest a pattern. In both there is mention of an experience marked by endurance of disgrace and the attainment of some noble goal (in Heb 12:2, the "joy" of session at God's right hand). Aristotle also suggests that the endurance of disgrace for some base end leads to blame, not praise, whereas a lofty end can, in effect, redeem the one who has submitted to disgrace as worthy of praise. The author of Hebrews may be playing on such a pattern, giving it the added twist that the disgrace endured at the penultimate level of the world and its society resulted in the attainment of honor at the ultimate level of God.

While unbelievers would continue to regard Jesus as a disgraced criminal, before the court of God Jesus may be shown to hold the highest honor, and by virtue of his attainment of that honor be shown to have remained at all times above reproach, to have acted in accordance with what is truly honorable. Aristotle (*Eth. Nic.* 3.6.3) posits that "one who fears disgrace is an honourable man, with a due sense of shame; one who does not fear it is shameless (ὁ μὲν γὰρ φοβούμενος ἐπιεικὴς καὶ αἰδήμων, ὁ δὲ μὴ φοβούμενος ἀν αἴσχυντος)." Disregarding disgrace for the sake of trivial gain, such as material wealth, was the mark of the shameless person, who was therefore not regarded as a reliable and worthy part of the social fabric.[73] Nevertheless, the end can justify (or render honorable) the means, as Aristotle shows above. One can honorably submit to disgrace if the goal is sufficiently noble. Within the community of those who share a common heritage in the Christian teaching, and who have once set their hearts on the attainment of the rewards God promises, Jesus' disregard for reputation (before the human court) would not have rendered him shameless. Rather, the nobility of Jesus' goal guarantees his honor.

The author of *Rhetorica ad Herennium* (3.7.14) includes in his discussion of the composition of encomia for people considerations such as the following: "if he is dead, what sort of death did he die, and what sort of consequences followed upon it?" A death which brought benefit to others was considered a most honorable death, such as a death in battle to

---

[72] E.g., *Eth. Nic.* 9.8.10: "[The good man] is naturally therefore thought to be virtuous, as he chooses moral nobility in preference to all other things (ἀντὶ πάντων αἱρούμενος τὸ καλόν)."

[73] So Theophrastus (*Char.* 9.1) defines "shamelessness": ʽ Η δὲ ἀναισχυντία ἐστι μέν, ὡς ὅρῳ λαβεῖν, καταφρόνησις δόξης αἰσχροῦ ἕνεκα κέρδους. Cf. also Aristotle *Eth. Nic.* 4.1.43.

preserve a country's liberty (cf. the praise of the fallen soldiers in Thucydides *Hist.* 2.35.1-46.2). The author of Hebrews is far from silent about the consequences of the death of Jesus, shameful in the eyes of the world but most honored and precious in the eyes of the believers. He refers throughout his argument to the benefits which Christ gained for his followers through his death.

Jesus' suffering of death is no sooner mentioned than it is described as a source of benefit: ὅπως χάριτι θεοῦ ὑπὲρ παντὸς γεύσηται θανάτου (2:9). Jesus tasted death on behalf of all, a benefit procured by the favor or gift (χάρις) of God. Jesus' death procures for his followers freedom from slavery to the fear of death (2:14-15) through breaking the power of the devil. Since people in the ancient world held that "freedom is the greatest of blessings, while slavery is the most shameful and wretched (αἴσχιστον καὶ δυστυχέστατον) of states" (Dio *Or.* 14.1), liberation from slavery would be considered a great benefit.[74] Through the consummation of suffering, that is, his death, Jesus became the "cause of eternal salvation for all who obey him" (ἐγένετο πᾶσιν τοῖς ὑπακούουσιν αὐτῷ αἴτιος σωτηρίας αἰωνίου, 5:9). As such, the author of Hebrews accords to Jesus a claim to honor, and particularly attaches this honor to his suffering of death, as Aristotle explains (*Eth. Nic.* 1.12.8): "that which is the first principle and cause of things good we agree to be something honourable and divine (τὴν ἀρχὴν δὲ καὶ τὸ αἴτιον τῶν ἀγαθῶν τίμιόν τι καὶ θεῖον τίθεμεν)." Again, Jesus' suffering and ignominious death constitute part of God's plan for bringing the many sons and daughters to "glory" (πολλοὺς υἱοὺς εἰς δόξαν ἀγαγόντα, 2:10). The future honor of the children of God, therefore, depends on Jesus' acceptance of the cross.[75] For the author, the most valuable benefit gained for Christ's

---

[74] Socrates' death was remembered as an attempt to liberate humankind from the fear of death, cf. Seneca *Ep.* 24.4: "Socrates in prison...declined to flee when certain persons gave him the opportunity... in order to free mankind from the fear of two most grievous things, death and imprisonment." Similarly Peregrinus attempts to pass off his self-immolation as a similar act of philosophical heroism (Lucian *Peregr.* 23): "He [Peregrinus] alleges that he is doing it [i.e., his self-immolation] ... that he may teach them to despise death (θανάτου καταφρονεῖν) and endure what is fearsome."

[75] Thus Calvin (*Hebrews*, 20, commenting on 2:10) could write concerning the author's intent: "His point is to make Christ's humiliation glorious in the eyes of the godly; for when he is said to have put on our flesh, he seems to be ranked with the common herd of men; but the cross debases him below all men. Therefore we must beware lest Christ be less esteemed because he humbled himself for us....For the Apostle shows that this very things ought to be glorious to the Son of God, because he was thus consecrated captain of our salvation. For who would lightly esteem that which is sacred, yea, which god sanctifieth? who would regard that as ignominious, whereby

followers -- read, his clients -- through his death appears to be the cleansing of the conscience of the worshipers and the securing of access to the throne of God as a throne of grace (χάρις). Jesus' high priesthood (4:15), and the sacrifice offered once for all upon the cross, allows Christ's followers to draw near to God in confidence and expectation (4:16): "Let us therefore approach the throne of grace (χάρις) with boldness, so that we may receive mercy and find grace (χάρις) to help in time of need."[76]

Jesus' death was likewise of benefit to himself, and brought Jesus greater honor before God than the cross brought him disgrace before human society. As the cross was the consummation of his sufferings, so it was also the perfection of his faith and obedience: "Although he was a Son, he learned obedience through what he suffered; and having been made perfect (τελειωθείς), became a source of eternal salvation...." (5:8-9). Perfection in Hebrews has been the subject of many investigations.[77] Attridge suggests succinctly that

> Christ's perfecting, as developed in the text, may be understood as a vocational process by which he is made complete or fit for his office. This process involves, not a moral dimension, but an existential one. Through his suffering, Christ becomes the perfect model, who has learned obedience (5:8), and the perfect intercessor, merciful and faithful (2:17).[78]

One may also compare Wisd 4:10-13, where τελειωθείς (4:13) appears to be functionally equivalent to, and defined by, εὐάρεστος θεῷ γενόμενος (4:10), which is also the goal of faith in Hebrews (cf. 11:6: χωρὶς δὲ πίστεως ἀδύνατον εὐαρεστῆσαι). The shameful death on the cross was for Jesus the final stage in his receiving the complete approval of God, as well as his preparation and qualification for his minstry as high priest. It is also the prerequisite to his exaltation to the place of highest honor, a seat at God's right hand (ἐν δεξιᾷ τε τοῦ θρόνου τοῦ θεοῦ κεκάθικεν, 12:2).[79]

---

we are fitted for glory?"

[76] Cf. also Heb 10:19-22.

[77] Most notably, David Peterson, *Hebrews and Perfection: An Examination of the Concept of Perfection in the "Epistle to the Hebrews"* (Cambridge: Cambridge University Press, 1982).

[78] Attridge, *Hebrews*, 87.

[79] Cf. Spicq, *Hébreux*, 29: "The preceding exhortation orients the reader's thought toward the saving ministry of Christ, and, consequently, evokes his humiliations and his death. Might this not, from certain perspectives, destroy the thesis established in chapter 1 concerning the absolute superiority of Christ over the angels? Certainly not. The role which Christ plays in the new economy assures him a place of distinction

The cross was the "pivotal event where humiliation ends and exaltation begins."[80] In the confession of God's vindication of Jesus' honor lies also the hope that God will similarly vindicate the honor of all who have committed themselves to seek God's approval at the cost of society's, who have said with the Psalmist, "On God rests my deliverance and my honor (ἡ δόξα μου); my hope is in God, the God of my help" (61:8).

Christ provides the model of choosing the course of action which fulfills obedience to God without regard for the approval or disapproval of society -- that is, of "despising shame." The mind of faith considers only what would result in God's approval, that is, in honor before God's court.[81] It looks to God's promise of honor, and remains steadfast in the face of the attempts of society to shame the follower of God into conforming to the norms and values of the society which has set itself apart from God. Christ also provides the proof that even the greatest disgrace which one could suffer at the hands of human beings may result in the greatest honor before God and the court of opinion formed by the people of faith.[82] The path of faith, though it entail disgrace, remains the way of honor. The author of Hebrews shares the expectation of vindication before the eyes of the unbelieving world, when God shall "put all things under [Christ's] feet" (2:8; cf. 1:13; 10:13). On that Last Day, there will no longer be two competing courts of opinion, but rather the court of God shall finally overturn the court of human opinion and all its former verdicts.

3 The Exemplars of Faith in Hebrews 11

As mentioned above, the example of Jesus is placed within the argument as the capstone of a great edifice of exemplary figures, the

---

among all.... The temporary abasement of the Son through the incarnation and Passion is the prerequisite and, at the same time, the providential cause of his exaltation."

[80] Attridge, *Hebrews*, 73. One may again compare the thought of Hebrews with the Gospel of John, where the hour of crucifixion is even more closely united with the hour of exaltation (12:23; 13:31-32; 17:1).

[81] Cf. H. Moxnes on Paul ("Honour and Righteousness, 68): "It is before God's court that the final decision on honour or shame is made. Thus, the ultimate 'significant other' is God."

[82] Thus one sees something here of Pitt-Rivers' observation that, in a complex society, "the individual's worth is not the same in the view of one group as in that of another, while the political authorities may view him in a different light again" ("Honour and Social Status," 22).

"perfecter" of πίστις. Between the author's depiction of the community's former struggle and the example of Jesus falls the well-known litany of the heroes of faith. There have been many attempts to find a common thread which unites these exemplars and the faith they demonstrate: to the many suggestions already made this study adds the observation that each of the major examples -- Abraham and the Patriarchs, Moses, and the miscellany of the martyrs and marginalized -- embrace a lower status in the world's eyes for the sake of the heavenly reward. They, like Jesus, "despise shame."

This chapter forms an integral part of the exhortation begun in 10:19. It helps demonstrate the nature of the faith (πίστις) in which the author summons the addressees to persevere. It has been prepared for, in effect, by 6:11-12, in which faith is presented as the means to avoid becoming "sluggish" (νωθροί) and to attain the reception of the promises:

> And we want each one of you to show the same diligence so as to realize the full assurance of hope to the very end, so that you may not become sluggish, but imitators of those who through faith and patience inherit the promises (μιμηταὶ δὲ τῶν διὰ πίστεως καὶ μακροθυμίας κληρονομούντων τὰς ἐπαγγελίας; NRSV).

Chapter 11 provides a litany of examples of "those who through faith and patience inherit the promises," thus filling out the details of the earlier exhortation. The author further prepares for this chapter through adducing the quotation from Hab 2:4, and contrasting πίστις with ὑποστολή. The former leads to life, to the attainment of the reward which God has prepared (10:35-36); the latter to God's disapproval and to destruction:

> "My righteous one will live by faith (ἐκ πίστεως). My soul takes no pleasure in anyone who shrinks back (ἐὰν ὑποστείληται, οὐκ εὐδοκεῖ ἡ ψυχή μου ἐν αὐτῷ)." But we are not among those who shrink back and so are lost, but among those who have faith and so are saved (ἡμεῖς δὲ οὐκ ἐσμὲν ὑποστολῆς εἰς ἀπώλειαν ἀλλὰ πίστεως εἰς περιποίησιν ψυχῆς).

The author first motivates the addressees to identify themselves with "faith" and stirs up the desire in them to make this their distinguishing characteristic, then proceeds to develop by example what faith entails.[83]

---

[83]   Cf. *Rhet. Her.* 4.3.5 (cited in Cosby, *Rhetorical Composition*, 100): "by example we clarify the nature of our statement." The examples cited in chapter 11 clarify the meaning of faith, particularly the definition given in 11:1-2. "After exhorting his audience to faith in 10:19-38 and affirming the existence of their faith in 10:39, in Hebrews 11 the author provides an extended series of examples to illustrate the

In so doing, he is developing rhetoric which reveals a subcultural relationship with the Jewish ethnic culture -- the author focuses on a value which is central to Judaism, namely loyalty to and trust in God, and proceeds to show how Christians may fulfill that virtue more fully than those Jews outside the Christian subculture.

Chapter two (above) has explored the intimate relationship of the epideictic and deliberative rhetorical genres.   One need only recall Aristotle's comment that "praise and counsels have a common aspect; for what you might suggest in counselling becomes encomium by a change in the phrase....Accordingly, if you desire to praise, look what you would suggest; if you desire to suggest, look what you would praise" (*Rh.* 1.9.35-36). What is praised (i.e., praiseworthy) may readily become the desired course of action for the hearers. The praise of the exemplars of faith is calculated to stir up emulation in the hearers. The use of examples here, as elsewhere in Hebrews, is part of the appeal to the emotions which makes an argument successful.[84] Aristotle (*Rh.* 2.1.8; cf. 1.2.5) informs the would-be orator that "the emotions (πάθη) are all those affections which cause men to change their opinion in regard to their judgements, and are accompanied by pleasure and pain; such are anger, pity, fear, and all similar emotions and their contraries."   Thus the rousing of certain emotions in the hearers must be part of an overall strategy of persuasion, of bringing the hearers to choose the course the orator recommends.

The feeling of emulation may be roused by the orator's speaking of "highly valued goods" which have been attained by others and which it is possible for the hearers to attain.   Under the sway of emulation, the virtuous person "fits himself to obtain such goods" (*Rh.* 2.11.1).[85] The rhetorical effect is heightened by means of closing the section with a hortatory peroration in 12:1-3, where the addressees are explicitly called again to conduct themselves in accordance with the perfect example of faith, Jesus, supplemented by the images of faithful decisions and activities from chapter 11.[86]   Through the praise of the ancients for their

---

characteristics of faith that please God" (Cosby, *Rhetorical Composition*, 89).

[84] Cosby (*Rhetorical Composition*, 101) notes that Cicero uses examples "to persuade the audience by affecting their emotions, not their intellect."

[85] Recall also Thucydides *Hist.* 2.35.2: "eulogies of other men are tolerable only in so far as each hearer thinks that he too has the ability to perform any of the exploits of which he hears." Plutarch also gives ample evidence that hearing the praise of others leads the hearer to desire similar distinction (cf. *On Inoffensive Self-Praise* 18 [*Mor.* 546C] and 20 [*Mor.* 546F-547A]).

[86] One may compare with this the hortatory perorations typical of epideictic orations, which exmplicitly hold up the subject of praise for imitation, such as occur

embodiment of this virtue, and their attainment of God's approval (11:2), the author seeks to motivate the hearers to choose for themselves in their own situation the course of action which embodies faith, commitment, and trust, so that they too may have a share in what God has promised for those who persevere -- indeed, a greater share (κρεῖττόν τι, 11:40).

Several aspects of the faith described in chapter 11 are of general interest to this investigation, as a background for the examination of individual exemplars and as a recognition of the author's presuppositions (which he makes explicit for his readers) concerning faith. The first element is that faith seeks God as a Benefactor. In 11:6, the author writes that "without faith it is impossible to please God, for whoever would approach him must believe [that is, trust] that he exists and that he rewards those who seek him (τοῖς ἐκζητοῦσιν αὐτὸν μισθαποδότης γίνεται)." Faith seeks a benefit from God (the "reward" referred to by the novel term μισθαποδοσία in its positive sense, 10:35; 11:26), in some cases to the exclusion of other potential benefactors (cf. Moses in 11:24, who rejects Pharaoh as patron and father). This involves the creation of a patron-client relationship with the most powerful patron possible, and as such has in view the honor of both patron and clients. Specifically, clients may call upon their patron as the vindicator of their honor. This is a frequent theme of the Hebrew Scriptures, which were written in the context of the covenant which establishes this patron-client relationship between God and the people of Israel: "On God rests my deliverance and my honor (ἡ δόξα μου); my hope is in God, the God of my help" (Psalm 61:8 LXX; au. trans.). The client's loyalty to the patron provides a claim for assistance: "Take away from me their scorn and contempt (ὄνειδος καὶ ἐξουδένωσιν), for I have kept thy testimonies.... Turn away the reproach (τὸν ὀνειδισμόν μου) which I dread; for thy ordinances are good" (Psalm 118: 22, 39 LXX; RSV). Faithful performance of one's duties to God, as to one's patron, affords one the confidence that the patron will assist in time of need and will not allow the client to fall into disgrace.

Second, faith takes into consideration the unseen and future realities in charting its course of action. This is a repeated theme of chapter 11 (11:3, 7, 10, 16, 20, 22, 26b, 27b, 35b), in which the heroes of faith make the proper evaluations and choices only because they are able to see past the visible, material world. Reference to the unseen and future realities relativizes the importance of the visible and present -- at the very least sets

---

in Dio *Or.* 29:21; Thucydides *Hist.* 2.43.4; 4 Macc 18.1.

it within a different perspective.[87] Because unbelievers do not share this perspective and the commitment that ultimate reality consists not in the present world but in the eternal kingdom of God, their opinion and evaluation are unreliable. Indeed, this criterion appears to function in a manner similar to that posed in the *Crito* (49C-D):

> Then we ought neither to requite wrong with wrong nor to do evil to anyone, no matter what he may have done to us. And be careful, Crito, that you do not, in agreeing to this, agree to something you do not believe; for I know that there are few who believe or ever will believe this. Now those who believe this, and those who do not, have no common ground for discussion, but they must necessarily, in view of their opinions, despise one another (τούτοις οὐκ ἔστι κοινὴ βουλή, ἀλλὰ ἀνάγκη τούτους ἀλλήλων καταφρονεῖν, ὁρῶντας τὰ ἀλλήλων βουλεύματα).

Indeed, it is by regarding the unseen as visible that the figures of Noah, Abraham, Moses, and the martyrs can endure the loss of status and prestige which the actions of faith bring in the eyes of unbelievers, and so attain life and honor before God and in the memory of the community of believers.

Third, faith is the way to gaining μαρτυρία, "attestation." Appended to the famous definition of faith in 11:1 is the phrase "for by this [i.e., faith] the elders received approval (ἐν ταύτῃ γὰρ ἐμαρτυρήθησαν οἱ πρεσβύτεροι; au. trans.)." While defined in *LSJ* primarily as a forensic term, the verb acquired a sense of "give recognition to" and the noun a sense of "favorable recognition" or even "praise." F. Danker's study of inscriptions to benefactors reveals the frequent use of these terms when speaking of the endorsement by Roman authorities of a person whom a local assembly wished to honor. It represented the approval of the authorities that the candidate was worthy of receiving honors (and was politically reliable).[88] Danker then adduces numerous NT examples of the use of this word carrying the sense of "bearing favorable testimony" and thus "spreading a good reputation."[89] Noteworthy among these is 1 Tim

---

[87] Cf. 2 Cor 4:16-18: "So we do not lose heart. Even though our outer nature is wasting away, our inner nature is being renewed day by day. For this slight momentary affliction is preparing us for an eternal weight of glory beyond all measure, because we look not at what can be seen but at what cannot be seen; for what can be seen is temporary, but what cannot be seen is eternal" (NRSV).

[88] Danker, *Benefactor*, 442-443.

[89] Danker, *Benefactor*, 443-447. Rather surprisingly, he does not cite any of the occurrences of this term in Hebrews, although he opened this section speaking of the

3:7, in which one of the qualifications for the bishop is given as a good reputation (δεῖ...μαρτυρίαν καλὴν ἔχειν) among outsiders. The concentrated use of μαρτυρεῖσθαι in the opening verses of the litany of faith (11:2, 4, 5) and the re-occurrence of this term at the transition from encomium to hortatory peroration (11:39) suggest that the author wishes to emphasize that perseverance in faith will result in a similar recognition of the addressees before God's court, a testimony to their worth and a grant of honor.

ABRAHAM AND THE PATRIARCHS

We may now approach a closer examination of several discrete exemplars. Not all the exemplars of chapter 11, by any means, are held up for their "despising shame." Nevertheless this element appears prominently in the author's portrayal of Abraham's faith (11:8-19), the faith of Moses (11:24-26), and the faith of the martyrs and marginalized (11:35-38), as well as, of course, the faith of Jesus (12:2-3).

The faith of Abraham and his family is portrayed by calling attention to a number of aspects of their familial history:

> By faith Abraham obeyed when he was called to go out to a place which he was to receive as an inheritance; and he went out, not knowing where he was to go. By faith he sojourned in the land of promise, as in a foreign land, living in tents with Isaac and Jacob, heirs with him of the same promise. For he looked forward to the city which has foundations, whose builder and maker is God. By faith Sarah herself received power to conceive, even when she was past the age, since she considered him faithful who had promised. Therefore from one man, and him as good as dead, were born descendants as many as the stars of heaven and as the innumerable grains of sand by the seashore.
>
> These all died in faith, not having received what was promised, but having seen it and greeted it from afar, and having acknowledged that they were strangers and exiles on the earth. For people who speak thus make it clear that they are seeking a homeland. If they had been thinking of that land from which they had gone out, they would have had opportunity to return. But as it is, they desire a better country, that is, a heavenly one. Therefore God is not ashamed to be called their God, for he has prepared for them a city.
>
> By faith Abraham, when he was tested, offered up Isaac, and he who had received the promises was ready to offer up his only son, of whom it was said, "Through Isaac shall your descendants be named." He

---

importance of enjoying the favorable testimony of the gods.

considered that God was able to raise men even from the dead; hence,
figuratively speaking, he did receive him back (11:8-19; RSV).

What dominates the author of Hebrews' portrayal of Abraham's faith is
not, as in Paul, the firm conviction that God would fulfill his promise to
give Abraham offspring (cf. Gal 3:15-18; Rom 4:13-21), which is here
allocated more to Sarah than Abraham. The aspect of Abraham's faith
which receives comment, and is thus emphasized, is his departure from his
native land in obedience to God's call (11:8-10). It is this element of faith
which the author highlights disproportionately in 11:13-16, wherein their
confession to be "strangers and exiles on the earth" bears witness to the
city of God and wins them association with God (11:16).

Greco-Roman and Jewish literature attest both to the importance of
one's native land to one's sense of identity and to the trials that attended
the foreigner and sojourner. Dio indicates in an address to his native city
of Prusa that one's native land held a special place in the heart of its
citizens:

> Fellow citizens, no sight is more delightful to me than your faces, no
> voice dearer than yours, no honours greater than those you bestow, no
> praise more splendid than praise from you. Even if the whole Greek
> world, and the Roman people too, were to admire and praise me, that
> would not so cheer my heart. For though, in truth, Homer has spoken
> many wise and divine words, he never spoke a wiser of a truer word
> than this: "For naught is sweeter than one's native land" (*Or.* 44.1).

The fellow inhabitants of one's native country or city formed one's group
of significant others, one's primary reference group. Hence Dio may say
that he would regard honor (praise) from his fellow Prusans as greater and
more meaningful than honor from the people of other cities or countries.
Therefore, to lose their respect would be of correspondingly greater pain.

Living away from one's native land, however, exposed one to a loss
of status and to limited access to acquiring honor in the foreign land.
While philosophers consoling those sent into exile might argue that it was
ridiculous to suppose that one could not gain fame in a foreign land to
make up for the loss felt by being denied a place at home, it was
nevertheless so supposed. Lucian, for example, records that

> Those who get on well [in a foreign land], however successful they may
> be in all else, think that they lack one thing at least, a thing of the
> greatest importance, in that they do not live in their own country but
> sojourn in a strange land; for thus to sojourn is a reproach (ὄνειδος γὰρ
> τὸ τῆς ξενιτείας, *My Native Land* 8).

Plutarch (*De exil.* 17 [*Mor.* 607 A]) likewise gives evidence that to live away from one's native land exposed one to reproach and dishonor on that very basis. Plutarch's imaginary interlocutor interjects into his discussion of endurance of exile the objection: "But 'exile' is a term of reproach (ἐπονείδιστον)." Plutarch responds: "Yes, among fools, who make terms of abuse out of 'pauper', 'bald', 'short', and indeed 'foreigner' and 'immigrant' (τὸν ξένον καὶ τὸν μέτοικον)." What is important here is not Plutarch's objection to the use of these terms as insults, but the fact that such a use is current. Sirach provides a similarly dismal picture of the life of the stranger (29:24-28).

Living as a stranger in a foreign land implies that the foreigner has not been enfranchised in the new location -- possesses no citizenship and the rights which accompany such status. Lack of citizenship in the ancient world exposed one to further experiences of disgrace and loss. Dio (*Or.* 66.15) paints this picture of those who have lost their citizenship, which one may suspect will also hold for those who never possessed it: "To the disenfranchised (ἀτίμοις) life seems with good reason not worth living, and many choose death rather than life after losing their citizenship, for whoever so desires is free to strike them and there exists no private means of punishing him who treats them with contumely." Rescinding the citizenship of the Alexandrian Jews was a prelude to the disasters which stripped them of honor, property, and life, as Philo (*In Flacc.* 53-55) describes:

> When then his attack against our laws by seizing the meeting-houses without even leaving them their name appeared to be successful, he proceeded to another scheme, namely, the destruction of our citizenship (τῆς ἡμετέρας πολιτείας), so that when our ancestral customs and our participation in political rights, the sole mooring on which our life was secured, had been cut away, we might undergo the worst misfortunes with no cable to cling to for safety. For a few days afterward he issued a proclamation in which he denounced us as foreigners and aliens (ξένους καὶ ἐπήλυδας) and gave us no right of pleading our case but condemned us unjudged.... And then to the first two wrongs he added a third by permitting those who wished to pillage the Jews as at the sacking of a city....

Citizenship brought security, some "mooring" within a society: lack of citizenship left one adrift, a prey to abuse and insult.

When the faith of Abraham and his family, then, motivates them to embrace the life of "ξένοι καὶ παρεπίδημοί" (11:13), this would be heard as a choice of a lower status liable to dishonor and danger. Whether or not Abraham suffered any of these ills in his sojourning, the cultural context of the hearers suggests that both author and addressees of Hebrews would have understood Abraham's choice as an embracing of a loss of status for the sake of obedience to God's call.[90]   In light of the addressees' experiences detailed in 10:32-34 it would be appropriate to consider that the author of Hebrews has fastened onto this aspect of Abraham's faith because it answers most nearly the condition of the letter's recipients.   There is no clear indication that they had physically moved from their native land (although Lane suggests strongly that they were),[91] but at the very least they were socially removed from their native land through the open degradation they suffered at the hands of their neighbors. One might even have cause to re-evaluate Elliott's claim that the political terms "ξένοι καὶ παρεπίδημοί" are purely metaphorical in Hebrews whereas they are to be literally and legally applied to the addressees in 1 Peter.[92]   The author of Hebrews also mentions explicitly that the patriarchs rejected the option of returning to their native land, that is, to enfranchisement and the protection from dishonor and danger which that brings (11:15), in order to persevere in the quest for a "better homeland, that is, a heavenly one" (11:16). This gloss may provide another window into the addressees' situation, where apostasy would provide the surest route back to favor within the unbelieving society.

Philosophers in the Greco-Roman world had long confronted the pain of exile with considerations of claiming citizenship in the city of God or in the world-city;[93] the author of Hebrews depicts Abraham as one who chooses exile in order to attain the "better, heavenly" city which God has prepared (11:16). Just as Pericles argues that the fallen soldiers whom he

---

[90]   The element of choice is important, as D. Worley ("God's Faithfulness," 72-73) has underscored: "The depiction in verse 9 of Abraham living in tents, behaving like a person in a foreign land is not the picture of a man victimized by circumstances, living the life of an alien unable to possess the promised land. Rather, his life style is one of his choosing because of his expectations for a city of God. He lives in tents because he believes his inheritance to be elsewhere, in a city with permanent foundations designed and built by God."

[91]   Lane, *Hebrews 1-8*, lxiv-lxvi.

[92]   J. H. Elliott, *A Home for the Homeless: A Sociological Exegesis of 1 Peter* (Philadelphia: Fortress, 1981), p.55 n.75. Attridge (*Hebrews*, 330, n. 26) similarly takes exception to this statement: "The 'alienation' involved here may not, however, be purely spiritual. Similarly, the alienation involved in 1 Peter may well be a social one occasioned by the addressees' Christian confession, without being strictly legal."

[93]   Cf. Musonius Rufus, who asserts that a virtuous person regards himself or herself as a πολίτης τῆς τοῦ Διὸς πόλεως (A. C. van Geytenbeek, *Musonius Rufus and Greek Diatribe* [Assen: Van Gorcum & Co., 1963], 145). Cf. Epictetus *Diss.* 1.9.1; Plutarch *De exil.* 5 (*Mor.* 600 F), 17 (*Mor.* 607C-D); Seneca *Ep.* 24.17.

praises were contending for a greater prize than those fighting for other cities,[94] so the author of Hebrews adds a number of details by which he points to the greatness of the prize to be won by those contending for the city of God. In praising a city, Quintilian (*Inst.* 3.7.26) prescribes,

> Cities are praised after the same fashion as men. The founder takes the place of the parent, and antiquity carries great authority....The advantages arising from site or fortifications are however, peculiar to cities. their citizens enhance their fame just as children bring honour to their parents.

The author of Hebrews describes the city for which Abraham embraced the foreigner's status and dishonor as designed and built by God (11:10), a city "with foundations" (11:10), that is, strong, lasting, and able to withstand assault, situated in a "better, heavenly" country (11:16).

The author's description of the patriarchs' quest as κρείττονος ὀρέγονται ... τοῦτ᾽ ἔστιν ἐπουρανίου [πατρίδος] demonstrates a Jewish-Christian revision of Platonic dualism. Platonism divided reality into the "phenomenal" world and the "noumenal" world, the former being "characterized by movement, change, and corruption -- and, therefore, only partial knowledge," and the latter "by changelessness and incorruptibility because it is not material but spiritual."[95] The noumenal world is more real than the phenomenal, is of greater value, and allows for a truer perception of reality.[96] Platonic dualism could readily be modified into the spatial dualism of the Jewish cosmos: heaven and earth.[97] Heaven, the abode of the eternal God, was a realm superior to that of earth

---

[94]   Thucydides *Hist.* 2.42.1: "It is for this reason that I have dwelt upon the greatness of our city; for I have desired to show you that we are contending for a higher prize than those who do not enjoy such privileges in like degree, and at the same time to let the praise of these men in whose honour I am now speaking be made manifest by proofs."

[95]   L. T. Johnson, *The Writings of the New Testament: An Interpretation* (Philadelphia: Fortress, 1986), 420.

[96]   Johnson, *Writings*, 420: "The distinction is metaphysical: one realm of being is denser and more 'real' than the other. It is epistemological: the world of change allows only approximate perceptions, therefore, 'opinions'; but ideas can truly be 'known'. The distinction is also axiological" the noumenal world is 'better' than the phenomenal."

[97]   Johnson (*Writings*, 421) adduces several examples from Philo to show how Platonic dualism could be approproated in scriptural exegesis. Noteworthy is Philo's exegesis of Exod 25:40, which is cited by our author in Heb 8:5 with much the same result.

-- it possessed a greater value and, within the temporal framework of Jewish eschatology, a permanence not shared by earthly realities.[98]

Therefore, the heavenly city founded by God carries greater value than earthly cities founded by human beings, and so confers on its citizens greater prestige than the citizens of earthly cities. It is for honor within such a homeland that the people of faith strive, with no less vigor than those who are ambitious to gain honor in earthly cities.[99] Abraham and his family kept this higher prize before them at all times (11:10, 14), and so evaluated with the eyes of faith that they would profitably endure temporary disgrace as a means to attaining the goal. They are commended for persevering in faith (11:13), although they never saw the realization of the promise, which they will attain only together with the addressees of Hebrews (11:39-40). The addressees are implicitly encouraged to take up the same stance. The author's appeal to the heritage of Judaism (subcultural rhetoric) serves his program of maintaining the community's alternative culture (the Christian counterculture). They are to embrace the status of "foreigner" with regard to the dominant Greco-Roman society in order to become citizens of God's city.

How, then, did Abraham, and the decendants who followed Abraham into voluntary exile, despise shame? In leaving their native land in obedience to God, they embraced the lower status of foreigner, sojourner, and stranger and the exposure to reproach and dishonor which attended this change of status. They confessed this status and persevered in it (11:13, 16), despite the fact that the option to return to their former status in their native land remained a possibility (11:15). In all this they are portrayed

---

[98] While several apocalypses do anticipate the removal of both heaven and earth at the end of time in favor a the "new heavens and the new earth" (Isaiah 66; Revelation 21), the author of Hebrews does not share this expectation. On the contrary, for him there is a realm of reality which will be shaken and removed, and a realm which will abide and survive the eschatological "shaking" (12:26-28). The believers are given the promise of an inheritance in the latter, better realm. After the important studies of C. K. Barrett ("The Eschatology in the Epistle to the Hebrews," *The Background of the New Testament and Its Eschatology* [Ed. W. D. Davies andD. Daube; Cambridge: Cambridge University, 1954], 363-93) and R. Williamson ("Platonism and Hebrews," *SJT* 16 [1963] 415-24), it is impossible to claim that the author was a true Platonist, but rather only to explore how Platonic categories are reinterpreted by or give expression to aspects of the Jewish/Christian world view.

[99] Cf. Dio *Or.* 44.8: "I rejoice to see [so many] aiming without envy and jealousy to vie with one another, and with all other men as well, concerning character and good repute (εὐδοξία) both their own and that of their country too, and also striving that each may gain first rank in his fatherland for being just and patriotic (δίκαιός τε εἶναι καὶ φιλόπολις) and not incapable of promoting his country's welfare."

as being unaffected by any sense of shame before the worldly court of opinion, such that they are not moved to return from their marginal relationship with society to a place of honor in society's eyes. Rather, they seek only the honor of a better citizenship before God and God's approval, which they receive in the form of association with God's name (11:16).[100] Their refusal of "at-homeness" within the world manifests their loyalty to God and their commitment to God's call. In this regard, Dio's claim (*Or.* 44.6) before his native city is informative:

> I have given practical demonstration of this [civic loyalty] too. For although many people in many lands have invited me both to make my home with them and to take charge of their public affairs, not merely at the present time, but even earlier, as the time when I was an exile -- and some went so far as to send the Emperor resolutions thanking him for the honour he had done me -- yet I never accepted such a proposal by so much as a single word, but I did not even acquire a house or a plot of ground else, so that I might have nothing to suggest a homeland (πατρίς) anywhere but here.

Dio's refusal to accept enfranchisement in any other city, and thus his perseverance in the status of exile and foreigner, serves as proof of his devotion to his native land, which he expects will win him greater approval and honor there where he most desires it. Similarly, the confession of the patriarchs results in a grant of honor and approval before God, who, on the basis of their confession and persistence in faith, "is not ashamed (οὐκ ἐπαισχύνεται) to be called their God" (11:16).

The phrase appears earlier in Heb 2:11, and reminds one of Mark 8:38: "Those who are ashamed (ὃς γὰρ ἐὰν ἐπαισχυνθῇ) of me and of my words in this adulterous and sinful generation, of them the Son of man will also be ashamed (ἐπαισχυνθήσεται) when he comes in the glory of his Father with the holy angels." The verb is thus used in contexts where boldly owning one's association with Christ (or God) is in view: the negative evaluation of such associations in the eyes of the Greco-Roman society is not to induce one, out of a sense of shame before that court of opinion, to deny that association. The cost of such care for one's reputation before human beings would be one's eternal reputation before God and the holy angels. In sharing God's name with the patriarchs, God grants honor and bears witness to the virtue and worth of those who have

---

[100] D. Worley ("God's Faithfulness," 74) demonstrates an awareness of this dual status of the people of faith: "the heirs are foreigners in the land, this land in which they dwell in tents, but they are not foreigners in another place."

lived by faith.[101]   Associating God's own name with them, God undertakes to preserve their honor as an extension of God's own honor.[102]

Abraham and the patriarchs "despise shame" in that they allow the command of God to define what constitutes honorable and dishonorable behavior, disregarding the opinion of the ungodly. When faced with the experience of his own exile, Dio Chrysostom (*Or.* 13.6-8) appeals to the opinon that Apollo would have of exile rather than the opinion of people. Since Apollo urged Croesus, the Lydian king, to "go voluntarily into exile, and not to feel himself disgraced ($\mu\eta\delta\grave{\epsilon}\nu$ $\alpha\grave{\iota}\sigma\chi\acute{\upsilon}\nu\epsilon\sigma\theta\alpha\iota$) if he should be looked upon by men as a coward," Dio reasoned that exile could not be "altogether injurious or unprofitable, nor staying at home a good and praiseworthy thing." While exile is regarded by people as a great disgrace, Dio drew the conclusion that the opinion of the many must be mistaken, "for Apollo would not have urged and advised exile" were this course truly disgraceful.

As Dio allows the Delphic god to determine what constitutes true honor and disgrace, so the people of faith in chapter 11 look to God's call as the path to honor and the means to attain God's promises as honorable, despite contrary opinions among unbelievers. Obedience to God leads to honor, never disgrace; it also leads to good repute and attestation in the community of the faithful (witness the praise of these exemplars here in Hebrews, or the praise of the martyrs in 4 Maccabees). By faith, Abraham sets God's evaluation over the evaluation of people, and thus despises shame (that is, a sense of accountability to society's norms of the honorable and disgraceful) before the human court.

---

[101] Cf. Michel, *Hebräerbrief*, 266: "$\dot{\epsilon}\pi\alpha\iota\sigma\chi\acute{\upsilon}\nu\epsilon\sigma\theta\alpha\iota$ in the context of an act of confession answers the $\dot{\alpha}\rho\nu\epsilon\hat{\iota}\sigma\theta\alpha\iota$ of Mt 10:33. $o\dot{\upsilon}\kappa$ $\dot{\epsilon}\pi\alpha\iota\sigma\chi\acute{\upsilon}\nu\epsilon\tau\alpha\iota$ is thus an old circumlocution for confession, for a bold and open declaration, and not a psychological feeling. God thus becomes a witness (= $\mu\alpha\rho\tau\upsilon\rho\epsilon\hat{\iota}$) for the patriarchs, in that God calls himself by their names (Gen 28:13; Exod 3:6)."

[102] Cf. Daniel's prayer for the deliverance and vindication of Israel and Jerusalem in Dan 9:18-19: "O my God, incline thy ear and hear; open thy eyes and behold our desolations, and the city which is called by thy name; for we do not present our supplications before thee on the ground of our righteousness, but on the ground of thy great mercy. O Lord, hear; O Lord, forgive; O Lord, give heed and act; delay not, for thy own sake, O my God, because thy city and thy people are called by thy name" (RSV).

MOSES

A second prominent exemplar of πίστις in Hebrews 11 is Moses, whose praiseworthy choices and actions are depicted in 11:24-29:

> By faith Moses, when he was grown up, refused to be called the son of Pharaoh's daughter, choosing rather to share ill-treatment with the people of God than to enjoy the fleeting pleasures of sin. He considered abuse suffered for the Christ greater wealth than the treasures of Egypt, for he looked to the reward. By faith he left Egypt, not being afraid of the anger of the king; for he endured as seeing him who is invisible. By faith he kept the Passover and sprinkled the blood, so that the Destroyer of the first-born might not touch them. By faith the people crossed the Red Sea as if on dry land; but the Egyptians, when they attempted to do the same, were drowned (RSV).

Again the author appears to formulate his description of Moses' faith to answer the needs of the situation of his addressees. Moses' fame as the giver of the Law and mediator of the Covenant is nowhere mentioned, as would of course be expected in a Christian document which stresses the supercession of the nomistic covenant.[103] What is central to the author's depiction of Moses' faith is his renunciation of a place of honor in the world's eyes and choice of the status of slave in solidarity with the people of God -- a pattern which has been replicated in the community's past (10:33-34) and is called for in the community's present (13:3).

After mentioning the faith of Moses' parents in 11:23, the author presents Moses' first enactment of faith as his refusal "to be called a son of a daughter of Pharaoh" (11:24). Presented as a member of the royal family of Egypt, and possibly regarded by the author, as by Philo and Josephus, as the heir of Egypt's throne,[104] Moses occupied a place of

---

[103] Moses is not, however, denigrated by the author of Hebrews, who uses him as a positive model here and as an esteemed figure in comparison with whom he may establish Christ's greater dignity in 3:1-6 (see chapter 5 below).

[104] Philo *De vita Mosis* 1.13: "The king of the country had but one cherished daughter, who, we are told, had been married for a considerable time but had never conceived a child, though she naturally desired one, particularly of the male sex, to succeed to the magnificent inheritance of her father's kingdom (τὸν εὐδαίμονα κλῆρον τῆς πατρῴας ἡγεμονίας), which threatened to go to strangers if his daughter gave him no grandson." Cf. also Josephus, *Antiquities* 2.9.7, §232-234: "Thermutis...carried Moses to her father... and said to him, 'I have brought up a child who is of divine form, and of a generous mind; and as I have received him from the bounty of the river, in a wonderful manner, I thought proper to adopt to adopt him for my son and the heir of thy kingdom.' And when she had said this, she put the infant into her father's

exceptionally high status and honor. Remaining Pharaoh's grandson, and thus looking to Pharaoh not only as *paterfamilias* but also as patron and benefactor, would have afforded Moses the power and status of a ruler of a great kingdom, and access to the "treasures of Egypt" (a storehouse of honor as potential benefaction). Nevertheless, led by faith Moses renounces these highest of worldly honors and promises of honor and rejects Pharaoh as a source of honor and benefits. He exchanges his adoptive inheritance for the inheritance of the faithful. Several commentators see in Moses' refusal a note of disdain or contempt for the honor offered by human courts of reputation.[105]

Moses renounces, even spurns, these honors in favor of "maltreatment together with the people of God (συγκακουχεῖσθαι τῷ λαῷ τοῦ θεοῦ)." He left behind the honors of the throne of Egypt in order to join himself to slaves, people of the lowest status and subject to insult and physical outrage (expressed in the single word, συγκακουχεῖσθαι). The pleasure of the Egyptian court, however, is qualified by two terms. First, it is πρόσκαιρος, "temporary," a term which stands in stark contrast to μένων, "abiding," which is used frequently in this section to describe the inheritance of the faithful (10:34; 12:27; 13:14). Here again, the influence of Platonic categories may be seen, although these are thoroughly translated into the framework of Jewish/Christian eschatology. Thus, the honor or ease this temporary enjoyment of worldly status and wealth bestows has no lasting value and is subject to being transformed into disgrace and pain at God's visitation.[106] This result is made all the more certain by the second qualification, namely the identification of such pleasure as ἁμαρτία, "sin." Several scholars have argued cogently that

---

hands; so he took him, and hugged him close to his breast."

[105] So Lünemann, *Hebrews*, 684; Spicq, *Hébreux*, 357: "Moses had been raised by the daughter of Pharaoh, who treated him as a son. He could have claimed all the honors and advantages of his royal station and insisted upon his offical title. What glorious prospects for an adopted child! But when he came to adulthood, Moses rejected and disowned these advantages of which he was beneficiary;... the personal decision, it seems, contains a nuance of scorn or disdain." Josephus (*AJ.* 2.9.7 §233) also attributes to Moses contempt for the offer of Egypt's honors: "on his daughter's account, in a pleasant way, (Pharaoh) put his diadem upon [Moses'] head; but Moses threw it down to the ground, and, in a puerile mood he wreathed it round, and trod upon it with his feet."

[106] So Delitzsch, *Hebrews*, 261: "One of Moses' reasons for refusing the enjoyments and the splendours of a courtly life in Egypt is hinted at in the word πρόσκαιρον. He knew them to be but temporary, and to have an eternally bitter end in prospect....Therefore he suffered not himself to be dazzled by all the honours and luxury which his position offered him."

the author intends "sin" to signify more than a transgression of God's law. Michel, for example, defines the sin which Moses avoids in terms of refusing to live in solidarity with the people of God: "The content of this sin was separation from the people of God. 'See, then, how he calls it sin not to endure the like injuries together with one's brothers and sisters'."[107] As such, this helps the long-standing theological problem of Hebrews, namely its view of the impossibility of the restoration of the one who "sins" after coming to faith as well as relates the term specifically to the crisis facing the addressees. Sin occurs where fellowship with the people of God is refused or discontinued on account of the temptation to seek place or pleasure in the society of unbelievers. Sin occurs when one abandons "ill-treatment with the people of God" for the sake of honor as Christ's enemies define it and bestow it. Moses manifests faith in that he chooses maltreatment and dishonor in the world's eyes over honor before the human court, destined as it is to be overturned.

Moses' choice is motivated by his evaluation of the respective worth of the "treasures of Egypt" and the "reproach of Christ" (11:26). With his eyes firmly fixed on the reward (11:26b), he found that the latter constituted a greater treasure. Again one sees faith's reckoning of worldly realities in light of eternal realities at work, causing what entails reproach and dishonor before the world's court to be transformed into the path to honor before God's court. Scholars have offered numerous suggestions as to the meaning of the phrase τὸν ὀνειδισμὸν τοῦ Χριστοῦ.[108] The phrase

---

[107] Michel, *Hebräerbrief*, 273, quoting Theophylact (Migne, *PG* 125:356): ῞Ορα δὲ πῶς ἁμαρτίαν ὀνομάζει τὸ μὴ συγκακουχεῖσθαι τοῖς ἀδελφοῖς. So also Weiß, *Hebräer*, 605: "What is here called ἁμαρτία has thus a concrete form: the refusal of solidarity with the "People of God" who are suffering maltreatment." Ernst Käsemann (*The Wandering People of God: An Investigation of the Letter to the Hebrews* [Minneapolis, MN: Augsburg, 1984], 46) extends the meaning of "sin" in Hebrews to "slackening" in perseverance in faith.

[108] Lünemann (*Hebrews*, 684) suggests that "the sense is: *the reproach, as Christ bore it*, inasmuch, namely, as the reproach, which Moses took upon him to endure in fellowship with his oppressed people at the hand of the Egyptians, was in its nature homogeneous with the reproach which Christ afterwards had to endure at the hands of unbelievers, to the extent that in the one case as in the other the glory of God and the advancement of His kingdom was the end and aim of the enduring." Moses bore "the reproach of Christ" in that both Moses and Christ bore reproach for the same cause (such that Christ could also be said to have borne "the reproach of Moses"). Moffatt (*Hebrews*, 180) understands the phrase to refer to the "special obloquy in being connected with Christ," which, however, does not help much in understanding how Moses could have associated himself with Christ so as to bear the reproach of this association. Héring (*Hebrews*, 105) suggests that the author "sees in the suffering of the people a prefiguration of or an allusion to the suffering of Christ." Thus in joining

appears to have its roots in Psalm 88:51-52, in which the Psalmist claims to carry about in his bosom the reproaches directed against the Lord's Anointed: "Remember, O Lord, the reproach of thy servant (τοῦ ὀνειδισμοῦ τῶν δούλων σου); how I bear in my bosom the insults of the peoples, with which thy enemies taunt, O Lord, with which they mock the footsteps of thy anointed (οὗ ὠνείδισαν τὸ ἀντάλλαγμα τοῦ χριστοῦ σου; au. trans.)."

Whatever meaning is assigned to the phrase in Heb 11:24-26, however, must also accord with the use of the phrase in 13:12-13 where the addressees are given the exhortation to bear Christ's reproach as well: "So Jesus also suffered outside the gate in order to sanctify the people through his own blood. Therefore let us go forth to him outside the camp, bearing his reproach (τὸν ὀνειδισμὸν αὐτοῦ φέροντες)." This exhortation, moreover, recalls the former experience of disgrace which the addressees endured on account of their commitment to Christ, which in 10:33 includes reproaches, ὀνειδισμοί -- the reproaches which resulted from association with the name of Christ, and which was the common possession of many Christian communities (cf. 1 Pet 4:14-16; Matt 5:11; Luke 6:22). Therefore the complaint of the author of Psalm 68:8, 10 appears to come closer to the heart of our author's meaning:

> For it is for thy sake that I have borne reproach, that shame has covered my face (ὅτι ἕνεκα σοῦ ὑπήνεγκα ὀνειδισμόν, ἐκάλυψεν ἐντροπὴ τὸ πρόσωπόν μου).... For zeal for thy house has consumed me, and the insults of those who insult thee have fallen on me (οἱ ὀνειδισμοὶ τῶν ὀνειδιζόντων σε ἐπέπεσαν ἐπ᾽ ἐμέ).

Just as the authors of the synoptic gospels could place 68:10 in the context of Jesus' life, so the author of Hebrews could place 68:8 and 10 on Jesus' lips, who endured insult and disgrace for the sake of obedience to God. Those who hold God in low esteem (thus insulting God) insult and disgrace God's servants; nevertheless, just as Christ despised the honor-rating ascribed by unbelievers and bore the reproach which comes with obedience to God, so Moses and so the addressees are called to do. The phrase ὁ ὀνειδισμὸς τοῦ Χριστοῦ thus signifies first the reproach incurred through perseverance in the same obedience to God's call as exemplified by Jesus. It also signifies the hope that those who have thus shared in Christ's sufferings (here described as reproach) will also share in the exaltation and reward which Christ received (cf. 12:2; 2:10). In light of the promise ("for he was looking away to the reward"), Moses chooses to embrace the

---

himself to the people of God, who were suffering disgrace, Moses joins himself to a type of the future reproach of Christ.

reproach of Christ, that is, to choose the course of obedience to God even at the expense of being dishonored in the eyes of the world.

How, then, did Moses "despise shame"? He renounced the worldly honors into which he had been born (or, rather, adopted), and, in a manner analogous to the pattern of Christ, left a throne to take the form of a slave. He chose to be dishonored and reproached in the company of God's people, thus joining himself to their destiny, rather than to enjoy the pleasures afforded by a lofty status within the society of unbelievers, thus being joined with them in their destiny. Faith led him to choose temporary disgrace and to evaluate the honors of the world in light of God's reward. Finally, like Abraham and the patriarchs, he too leaves his native land -- Πίστει κατέλιπεν Αἴγυπτον (11:27) and joins the people of God in their wandering in order to attain the promised reward. Confronted with the example of Moses, the addressees may once more affirm their renunciation of their own status and accept the loss of their honor and place in society with joy, choosing to continue in their solidarity with the people of God by assembling together (10:25) and ministering to their marginalized brothers and sisters (13:3).

THE MARTYRS AND MARGINALIZED

The final group of heroes of faith consists of those who were martyred, tortured, or disenfranchised on account of their commitment and obedience to God. As such, they clearly form a gallery of figures who endured disgrace and outrage to their persons in their fulfillment of the requirements of faith. The list of these figures follows hard upon a summary of those who achieved mighty and miraculous things through the power of God (11:32-38):

> And what more shall I say? For time would fail me to tell of Gideon, Barak, Samson, Jephthah, of David and Samuel and the prophets -- who through faith conquered kingdoms, enforced justice, received promises, stopped the mouths of lions, quenched raging fire, escaped the edge of the sword, won strength out of weakness, became mighty in war, put foreign armies to flight. Women received their dead by resurrection. Some were tortured, refusing to accept release, that they might rise again to a better life. Others suffered mocking and scourging, and even chains and imprisonment. They were stoned, they were sawn in two, they were killed with the sword; they went about in skins of sheep and goats, destitute, afflicted, ill-treated -- of whom the world was not worthy -- wandering over deserts and mountains, and in dens and caves of the earth (RSV).

Those who suffered such horrible indignities for the sake of their commitment to God are indeed inseparable from those who achieved what might be considered greatness through faith. For the author, those who were "tortured to death, refusing to be released" on account of their devotion to the command of God are in no way inferior to those who "through faith conquered kingdoms" or "became mighty in war": all achieved greatness through their commitment to God, all are worthy to be held in honor and praised in remembrance.

At the head of the second group stand those who were tortured to death for the sake of a better resurrection. These are commonly and correctly identified as the martyrs who suffered under Antiochus IV.[109] That the author of Hebrews should include among his examples of faith this group of martyrs is not at all surprising, for they had served an important function as examples of commitment to God and Torah in Hellenistic Judaism. Indeed, their role as examples introduces itself into the very narrative of their sufferings. Eleazar (2 Macc 6:28) faces the torments with the intention that his death will "leave to the young a noble example (ὑπόδειγμα γενναῖον) of how to die a good death willingly and nobly

---

[109] The marginal reference in the Nestle-Aland text refers at this point to 2 Macc 6:18-7:42, where the story of the martyrdoms of Eleazar and the seven brothers is narrated. The emphasis throughout 2 Maccabees 7 on the martyrs' expectation of resurrection makes this a more than probable background for Hebrews. The author of Hebrews may also have been familiar with the story as told in 4 Maccabees 5 through 18. Several verses from this text are echoed in content and form within Hebrews. For example, 4 Macc 6:9 refers to Eleazar, tortured for his obedience to the Mosaic law, thus: ὁ δὲ ὑπέμενε τοὺς πόνους καὶ περιφρόνει τῆς ἀνάγκης. This bears a striking resemblance to Heb 12:2, where Jesus, persevering in obedience to God, ὑπέμεινεν σταυρὸν αἰσχύνης καταφρονήσας. Similarly, 4 Macc 17.4, where the author by a literary fiction encourages the mother of the seven martyred brothers to persevere (τὴν ἐλπίδα τῆς ὑπομονῆς βεβαίαν ἔχουσα πρὸς τὸν θεόν) bears a certain likeness in thought and vocabulary to Heb 3:6: ἐάν[περ] τὴν παρρησίαν καὶ τὸ καύχημα τῆς ἐλπίδος κατάσχωμεν; and Heb 3:14: ἐάνπερ τὴν ἀρχὴν τῆς ὑποστάσεως μέχρι τέλους βεβαίαν κατάσχωμεν.

Finally, the author of Hebrews gives the detail that these martyrs "did not accept release" from their torments, so that they might attain the better resurrection. In 2 Maccabees, the torments of Eleazar and the brothers commence only after they refuse to obey the tyrant. Once begun, they are uninterrupted. In 4 Macc 9.16, however, we do find the guards making the offer, "Agree to eat so that you may be released from the tortures (καὶ τῶν δορυφόρων λεγόντων ὁμολόγησον φαγεῖν ὅπως ἀπαλλαγῆς τῶν βασάνων)," and the third brother refusing this offer and urging the torturers to do their worst. Eleazar is also given a brief respite between tortures in which some members of the king's retinue seek to persuade him to eat and so save himself, an offer which is also refused (6:12-23).

(γενναίως) for the revered and holy laws (σεμνῶν νόμων; RSV)," a status which the narrator grants him in 2 Macc 6:31: "So in this way he died, leaving in his death an example of nobility and a memorial of courage (ὑπόδειγμα γενναιότητος καὶ μνημόσυνον ἀρετῆς καταλιπών), not only to the young but to the great body of his nation." The author of 4 Maccabees selects these martyrs as the noblest examples of those who died on behalf of virtue (1.8), whose story will motivate the hearers to "obey the law and exercise piety in every way" (18.1).

The author of Hebrews also harnasses the power of their story to drive his exhortation forward. Being tortured to death, besides being an experience of the extremity of physical pain, was an experience of utter degradation. The person was subjected to physical affronts, which one will recall involves a challenge to personal honor, but was denied any possibility for satisfaction, the reparation of honor, in this life. The text of 2 Maccabees 7 bears witness to this conjunction of pain and shame (not dissimilar from Heb 12:2!) when the author notes the mocking, scornful atmosphere of the torture of the seven brothers. 2 Macc 7:7 notes that "After the first brother had died in this way, they brought forward the second for their sport (ἐπὶ τὸν ἐμπαιγμὸν)." Similarly, the author records that "after this, the third brother was the victim of their sport (μετὰ δὲ τοῦτον ὁ τρίτος ἐνεπαίζετο)." The martyrs die amidst the scorn and mockery of their enemies, thus by all accounts they die a shameful death.

Nevertheless, they endure the pain and the shame. The author makes it clear that they had a way out from these extremities, a way back into ease and honor (one need only recall Antiochus' enticements to the martyrs to yield to him and enjoy a place in his rule). Like Abraham and the patriarchs, they could have returned and abandoned the journey which obedience to God required. Like Abraham, like Moses, and like Jesus, however, the martyrs fixed their eyes on the reward, here described as "a better resurrection."[110] Because they cherish the hope which God extends

---

[110] The martyrs' hope in the resurrection is a prominent feature of 2 Maccabees (cf. 7:9, 11, 14, 23, 29). In Hebrews 11:35, "better" indicates a comparison between the resurrection enjoyed by those who were brought back from the dead to a this-worldly existence (11:35a) and the resurrection anticipated by the martyrs, who awaken to the life of the eternal realm (11:35b). The former merely return by resuscitation to the life and enjoyments of this world, while the latter move beyond the earthly sphere to the life and joys of the world to come. Parallel comparisons within Hebrews, such as 10:34 (earthly property over against "better and lasting possessions") and 11:16 (an earthly homeland over against a "better, heavenly" one), reveal a consistent application of a modified Platonic dualism between the superior realm of the "real" and the inferior realm of the transitory "copies." Cf. also Josephus *Ap.* 2.217-218: "The reward for such as live exactly according to the laws, is not silver or gold; it is not a garland of

to the faithful, they are able even to refuse Antiochus' promises of honor and high status,[111] and persist in the course which brings them complete disgrace before the human court of opinion (specifically, Antiochus' court) yet which gains for them honor and life before God. Thus they replicate in their lives the choice of Moses, who similarly relinquished the enjoyment of a patron-client relationship with a human king in order to attain God's benefactions.

The martyrs are guided by different standards of worth, holding it to be of the greatest value to preserve obedience to God's Law and preserve themselves from sin or pollution (cf. 2 Macc 6:19-20, 28). While in the eyes of Antiochus, other non-Jews, and the Hellenizing Jews the martyrs are behaving contrary to standards of rationality and the love of honor, in their own eyes and in the sight of God their choice of resistance and their endurance of disgraceful treatment preserves their honor:

> But making a high resolve, worthy of his years and the dignity of his old age and the gray hairs which he had reached with distinction and his excellent life even from childhood (ὁ δὲ λογισμὸν ἀστεῖον ἀναλαβὼν καὶ ἄξιον τῆς ἡλικίας καὶ τῆς τοῦ γήρως ὑπεροχῆς καὶ τῆς ἐπικτήτου καὶ ἐπιφανοῦς πολιᾶς καὶ τῆς ἐκ παιδὸς καλλίστης ἀναστροφῆς), and moreover according to the holy God-given law, he declared himself quickly, telling them to send him to Hades. "Such pretense is not worthy of our time of life (οὐ γὰρ τῆς ἡμετέρας ἡλικίας ἄξιόν ἐστιν ὑποκριθῆναι)," he said, "lest many of the young should suppose that

---

olive branches or of smallage, nor any such public sign of commendation; but every good man ... believes that God hath made this grant to those that observe these laws, even though they be obliged readily to die for them, that they shall come into being again, and at a certain revolution of things receive a better life than they had enjoyed before" (Whiston translation).

[111] See, e.g., 4 Macc 8.5: "I encourage you, after yielding me, to enjoy my friendship (παρακαλῶ συνείξαντάς μοι τῆς ἐμῆς ἀπολαύειν φιλίας; NRSV)" -- the king's "friend" being an influential position. Similarly, Antiochus promises to become their patron, and thus replace God as the source of benefits and honor: "I can be a benefactor to those who obey me (δυναίμην...εὐεργετεῖν τοὺς εὐπειθοῦντάς μοι)." Cf. 2 Macc 7:24: "The youngest brother being still alive, Antiochus not only appealed to him in words, but promised with oaths that he would make him rich and enviable if he would turn from the ways of his fathers, and that he would take him for his friend and entrust him with public affairs (ἅμα πλουτιεῖν καὶ μακαριστὸν ποιήσειν μεταθέμενον ἀπὸ τῶν πατρίων καὶ φίλον ἕξειν καὶ χρείας ἐμπιστεύσειν; RSV)." In refusing to acknowledge the value of either honor or disgrace, and refusing to let consideration of these erode their constancy, the martyrs are much akin to Seneca's exemplar of the wise man (*Constant.* 13.2): "In the same spirit in which he sets no value (*nihilo aestimat*) on the honours they have, he sets no value on the lack of honour they show...."

> Eleazar in his ninetieth year has gone over to an alien religion, and
> through my pretense, for the sake of living a brief moment longer, they
> should be led astray because of me, while I defile and disgrace my old
> age (καὶ μύσος καὶ κηλῖδα τοῦ γήρως κατακτήσωμαι)."

They look not to the court of the unbelievers, but to the court of God, the
generations of the faithful, and their contemporaries in the faith for
recognition of their honor and praise of their choices. In 4 Macc 13.17,
the brothers look forward to a reward of honor after their struggles:
"Abraham, Isaac, and Jacob will welcome us, and all the fathers will praise
us (ἡμᾶς...πάντες οἱ πατέρες ἐπαινέσουσιν; NRSV)." Similarly, the
author accords their mother the status of "standing in honor before God
(ἔντιμος καθέστηκας θεῷ, 17:5)." Finally, in the memory of the author
and his audience, the martyrs are thought of as honored by God and as the
deliverers of their nation (17:20).

The Maccabean martyrs, therefore, are exemplars of those who
through faith "despised shame." Like Abraham, Moses, and Jesus, they
choose to embrace dishonor and refuse honor from the human court of
reputation in order to attain a place of honor before God. They do not
allow the social pressures of reproach or physical outrage to move them to
feel "shame" before (that is, respect for the norms and evaluations of)
those who do not share their commitment to God and hope of God's
reward. In this stance, they are joined by an unnumbered host of those
who "suffered mocking and scourging, and even chains and imprisonment.
They were stoned, they were sawn in two, they were killed with the
sword; they went about in skins of sheep and goats, destitute, afflicted,
ill-treated -- of whom the world was not worthy -- wandering over deserts
and mountains, and in dens and caves of the earth" (11:36-38; RSV).

The author combines a wide array of images, each of which contributes
to the overall picture of a group which is marginalized in the extreme,
having no place in society and exposed to every form of disgrace at
society's hands. This is explicitly the case for those who "suffered
mocking (ἐμπαιγμῶν)." Scourging was, of course, an experience of
disgrace both as an affront to one's person and as a token (indeed, a
stigma) of society's disapproval.[112] Bonds and imprisonment --
experiences close to the hearts of the addressees (10:34; 13:3) -- were also

---

[112] Cf. Prov 27:22 (LXX), which presents scourging as a dishonoring experience:
"even if you dishonor a fool in the midst of the council with scourges, you will still
certainly not remove his foolishness" (ἐὰν μαστιγοῖς ἄφρονα ἐν μέσῳ συνεδρίου
ἀτιμάζων οὐ μὴ περιέλῃς τὴν ἀφροσύνην αὐτοῦ; au. trans.).

considered dishonorable,[113] as were the various deaths which marked society's disapproval and rejection in the extreme. The inability to provide for one's needs, which again might reflect the situation of at least some in the community (notably those who have lost their property), also entails disgrace.[114] The description of the garments worn by some among this group speaks to the placement of these individuals in the margins of society.[115] Similarly, the author describes these figures as "wandering (πλανώμενοι)," placing them not in populated places like cities, towns, or even farms, but in the places signifying the opposite of social order and the rejection of society, "deserts, mountains, caves, and holes in the ground (ἐπὶ ἐρημίαις ... καὶ ὄρεσιν καὶ σπηλαίοις καὶ ταῖς ὀπαῖς τῆς γῆς)."[116] The addressees will be urged to join in this movement away from at-homeness within society near the end of the exhortation (13:12-14).

Within his catalogue of the dishonored and marginalized, the author introduces the striking evaluation, "of whom the world was not worthy (ὧν οὐκ ἦν ἄξιος ὁ κόσμος)." More than a "splendid aside" or a parenthetical remark,[117] this phrase encapsulates the reversal of evaluations of honor and disgrace which forms an essential part of the exhortation. This ironic statement of the relative worthiness of wanderers and world turns the norms of society upside-down. No longer are the faithful to be evaluated by the standards of the Greco-Roman society (the unbelieving world), but rather the world is to be evaluated by the standard of the faithful. The author of Hebrews thus effects a coup similar to that of Epictetus in his

---

[113] Recall the discussion of the community's experience in 10:32-34.

[114] Firstly, in that it indicates the utter lack of any sort of wealth, which was an important correlate of honor; secondly, in that the economic state of these "destitue" ones results from their own choices, motivated by faith. To unbelievers, then, they would have been thought to have "brought it on themselves," and so experience not only want but disgrace attached to self-inflicted loss (cf. Neyrey, "Poverty," 7).

[115] Cf. Neyrey, "Poverty," 3 n.12: "As the saying goes, 'clothing makes the man'. There are many examples of honor and status displayed in public by the clothing worn: the Essenes at Qumran symbolized their pursuit of radical purity by wearing the 'white robe' (Josephus *BJ* 2.129; Philo *De vita contemplativa* 66). Conversely, prophets like John the Baptizer identified their roles on the margins of society by wearing garments of skin, not cloth woven in households (Mark 1:6; see Heb 11:37-38; Zech 13:4; Josephus *Vita* 11)." So here in Heb 11:37b, the clothing carries associations with a specific social location.

[116] Cf. Malina and Neyrey, "Honor and Shame in Luke-Acts," 27: "Such physical mobility replicates the social behaviour that rejects ascribed status and implies a willingness to be deviant within the broader context. Yet the willingness to be deviant itself becomes a value worthy of honor within the group."

[117] Moffatt, *Hebrews*, 189; Attridge, *Hebrews*, 351.

discourse on the Cynic, in which the Cynic becomes the one who evaluates worth and the standard by which others are assessed.[118] That the world rejects, dishonors, marginalizes those who are committed to God does not effect a judgement against the faithful, but rather a judgement against the world.[119] Those who obey God, who seek God as their Benefactor, who take into account the unseen and future realities when evaluating and making choices are the ones who are equipped to make proper evaluations of the honorable and disgraceful, from which vantage point they critique the unbelievers.[120] No disgrace can justly cling to them, but must return to their detractors, to those who have violated God's order. From this perspective the sufferings themselves may be called "noble" (cf. 4 Macc 11.12), and the "shameful death" transformed into a "blessed death," thus a "noble death" (4 Macc 12.1).

How, then, do the martyrs and the marginalized "despise shame"? Renouncing the honors, status, and approval offered by the unbelieving society, they choose rather to endure reproach, outrage, and disgrace at its hands in order to maintain their integrity before God and attain what God has promised them. They reject the standards by which the world performs its evaluations of the honorable and disgraceful. Knowing these standards to be ill-founded and the resulting judgements to be unreliable guides to honorable activity, they remove themselves from sensitivity to the

---

[118] *Diss.* 3.22.63, 65: "But where will you find me a Cynic's friend? For such a person must be another Cynic, in order to be worthy of being counted his friend (ἵν' ἄξιος ᾖ φίλος αὐτοῦ ἀριθμεῖσθαι). He must share with him his sceptre [or staff] and kingdom, and be a worthy ministrant, if he is going to be deemed worthy of friendship (φιλίας ἀξιωθήσεσθαι)....Or do you think that if a man as he comes up greets the Cynic, he is the Cynic's friend, and the Cynic will think him worthy (ἄξιον ἡγήσεται) to receive him into his house?"

[119] Cf. Weiß, *Hebräer*, 623-24, who links this verse with 11:7 as "eine Verurteilung der Welt." The spirit is similar again to Epictetus, e.g., *Diss.* 1.29.50-54: "But the one who has authority over you declares, 'I pronounce you impious and profane'. What has happened to you? 'I have been pronounced impious and profane'. Nothing else? 'Nothing'. But if he had passed judgement upon some hypothetical syllogism and had made a declaration, 'I judge the statement, "If it is day, there is light," to be false', what has happened to the hypothetical syllogism? Who is being judged in this case, who has been condemned? The hypothetical syllogism, or the man who has been deceived in his judgement about it? ...But shall the truly educated man pay attention to an uninstructed person when he passes judgement on what is holy and unholy, and on what is just and unjust?"

[120] Cf. 4 Macc 11.4-6: "For what act of ours are you destroying us in this way? Is it because we revere the Creator of all things and live according to his virtuous law? But these deeds deserve honor, not tortures (ἀλλὰ ταῦτα τιμῶν οὐ βασάνων ἐστὶν ἄξια)!"

approbation or opprobrium of the world, and so are enabled to remain
steadfast with regard to God's norms and opinion.   As the martyrs
themselves were encouraged to imitate the faith of those who endured,[121]
now the addressees are urged to have the same faith.

4 The Example of the Community

The examples of despising society's negative evaluations for the sake
of a positive evaluation by God are prefaced strategically by the author's
use of the addressees themselves as exemplary in 10:32-34.   Abraham,
Moses, the martyrs, and Jesus are joined by the community itself as
witnesses to faith and examples to follow.   The author seeks to motivate
them to persevere in their former course and commitments, and not to fail
to achieve the reward which by their past actions have already all but won.

Such appeals to a group's own past achievements often serves as a
basis for encouragement to future endeavors.   At the climax of Tacitus'
Agricola (33-34), the general rallies his troops with the words: "The long
road we have travelled, the forests we have threaded our way through, the
estuaries we have crossed -- all redound to our credit and honour as long
as we keep our eyes to the front.... I would quote the examples of other
armies to encourage you.   As things are, you need only recall your own
battle-honours, only question your own eyes."   The rhetorical effect is to
motivate through instilling a sense of confidence that, as the group
succeeded in performing what was required before, so it would have the
resources and stamina to succeed again, as well as a sense of fear lest
former achievements and honor be marred by failure to act and persevere
in the present.   Dio affords a concisely drawn picture of this in his
paraphrase of *Philoctetes* (*Or.* 59.2): "This thirst for glory (φιλοτιμία) is
what leads even me to bear unnumbered woes and live a life of toil beyond

---

[121] Cf. 4 Macc 16.18-22: "Remember that it is through God that you have had a
share in the world and have enjoyed life, and therefore you ought to endure any
suffering for the sake of God.   For his sake also our father Abraham was zealous to
sacrifice his son Isaac; and when Isaac saw his father's hand wielding a sword and
descending upon him, he did not cower.   And Daniel the righteous was thrown to the
lions, and Hananiah, Azariah, and Mishael were hurled into the fiery furnace and
endured it for the sake of God.   You too must have the same faith in God and not be
grieved (καὶ ὑμεῖς οὖν τὴν αὐτὴν πίστιν πρὸς τὸν θεὸν ἔχοντες μὴ χαλεπαίνετε)."

all other men, accepting every fresh peril, fearing to mar the glory won by earlier achievements."[122]

The author of Hebrews, in drawing the addressees' attention to their former endurance and faithful action, harnasses the double power of this rhetorical device. Chrysostom, commenting on 10:32, emphasizes the aspect of encouragement: "Powerful is the exhortation from deeds [already done]: for he who begins a work ought to go forward and add to it....And he who encourages, does thus especially encourage them from their own example."[123] Calvin, himself trained in the classics and art of rhetoric, notes the appeal to the addressees' desire to preserve honor:

> For it is shameful, having begun well, to faint in the midst of the course; but baser still to go backwards when you have already made great progress....Moreover, he increases the effect of the exhortation by saying that they had performed glorious exploits even then when they were as yet raw recruits: the more shame then would it be if they should faint now after having been exercised by long practice.[124]

The author intensifies this by pointing out how the achievement of the goal is in clear view, within the grasp of the addressees if only they persevere (10:35-36).[125] He thus makes it a mark of honor for them to continue in, and a mark of dishonor to abandon, their former course of action.

That the "great contest" to which the author directs the readers' attention involved disgrace and loss of status has been demonstrated above. What is of importance to note here is that the addressees are commended specifically for their endurance ($\dot{v}\pi\epsilon\mu\epsilon\dot{\iota}\nu\alpha\tau\epsilon$) of this experience of dishonor and suffering (10:32). In the face of degradation and reproach, they chose rather to endure society's assaults of their honor rather than "shrink back" from the course which faith required, namely perseverance in the confession of Christ and solidarity with those who belonged to Christ. When threatened with the loss of their property, the markers of their status and place in society, they accepted such loss "with joy ($\mu\epsilon\tau\dot{\alpha}\ \chi\alpha\rho\hat{\alpha}\varsigma$)," for

---

[122] For a similar use of holding up a group's past as a model for reforming its present course of action, see Dio *Or.* 31.66-68.

[123] *NPNF¹* 14:461; Migne, *PG* 63.148-49.

[124] Calvin, *Hebrews*, 135, commenting on 10:32.

[125] Cf. Josephus *BJ* 6.38: "For shameful were it ($\alpha\dot{\iota}\sigma\chi\rho\dot{o}\nu\ \gamma\dot{\alpha}\rho$) that Romans ... should be outdone, either in strength or courage, by Jews, and that when final victory is in sight and we are enjoying the co-operation of God." The author of Hebrews likewise points to the availability of help from God, a topic intended to evoke confidence (cf. Aristotle *Rh.* 2.5.21), throughout the letter, notably at 4:15-16 and 10:19-23.

they placed value only on their "better and lasting possessions (κρείττονα ὕπαρξιν καὶ μένουσαν, 10:34)."

Here again one sees the influence of Platonic categories on the author's expression of the Christian's goal. Where in 11:16 the "heavenly" is evaluated as "better," here the "abiding" or "lasting" is evaluated as "better." The possessions which belong to the earthly realm are of less value than those which are afforded in the heavenly realm precisely because only the latter will "abide," or survive the eschatological removal of the "things that can be shaken" (12:27). Earthly possessions afford only "temporary" (πρόσκαιρος, 11:25) honor and enjoyment. The faithful, therefore, "looked away to the reward" (11:26) as did Moses, Abraham, the martyrs, and Jesus. Their "joy" at this loss was anticipatory, even as Jesus endured loss "in order to attain the joy that was set before him (ἀντὶ τῆς προκειμένης αὐτῷ χαρᾶς, 12:2)."

Such is the παρρησία which the author desires the addressees to continue to exhibit. Connected with the readers' joyful acceptance of the loss of status and place within society, this trait signifies more than "openness" or even "confidence." As elsewhere παρρησία is opposed to αἰσχύνη (Phil 1:20; 1 Jn 2:28), so it would profitably be opposed here, where the latter term would signify sensitivity to society's opinion. The community had been "bold" in the face of society's disapproval and its sanctions of reproach and punishment: they are called to continue in that "boldness" so that they may receive God's reward. Thus they will maintain their place among the people of faith, and not fall into the company of those who "shrink back" and lose God's approval (10:38).[126] In their own past endurance they have replicated the faith of Abraham, who relinquished his status in his homeland in order to attain new status as a citizen of God's city, and the faith of Moses, who chose disgrace and maltreatment in solidarity with God's people over ease and honor apart from them.[127] If they but take themselves as their examples and

---

[126] This "shrinking back" would entail the only true disgrace before the court of reputation formed by God and the believers. Cf. Epictetus' use of this sanction in his encouragement to persevere in the calling of the philosopher in *Diss.* 2.2.13: "Far be it from you to receive many blows and yet at the last give in!" Such a capitulation would be αἰσχρόν (2.2.14). Similarly he urges would-be philosophers (*Ench.* 29:1-3) to count the whole cost of the enterprise they are contemplating, lest they find it too difficult and "give up disgracefully" (αἰσχρῶς ἀποστήσῃ) or "turn back like children" (ὡς τὰ παιδία ἀναστραφήσῃ).

[127] Cf. Lane, *Hebrews 9-13*, 374: "The continuity in experience between Moses and the house church functions to reinforce a pattern of fidelity to God and the community that the writer wishes to promote in the congregation as belonging to the very nature of Christian faith."

persevere in their former faith and commitment (πίστις), they will exchange their temporary dishonor in the sight of the world for eternal honor before God.[128]

5 Conclusion

The author of Hebrews fills his exhortation with examples, calculated to rouse emulation and imitation, of those who have "despised shame." He seeks thereby to neutralize the addressees' re-awakening sensitivity to the society's opinion of their honor and what makes for honor. He seeks to dissociate them from attaching significance to society's grants of honor and disgrace, and thereby to insulate them from one of society's stronger means of enforcing adherence to its self-preserving values and goals.[129] This will lead to the community's continuing in a course which holds the danger for future hostility with the host society such as came to expression in the events described in 10:32-34, and such as may plausibly lead to the loss of life (12:4).[130]

---

[128] Cf. Philo, *De virtutibus* 37, where the Midianites exhort their women to seduce the men of Israel in order to preserve their nation: "And do not be afraid of the names of concubinage or adultery, as if they would bring shame (αἰσχύνην) upon you, but set against the names (ὀνόματα) the advantages which would ensue from the facts (ἐκ τοῦ πράγματος), by which you will change your evil reputation (ἀδοξίας), which will endure only for a day, into a glory which will never grow old or die (εἰς ἀγήρω καὶ ἀτελεύτητον εὔκλειαν)."

[129] Such a dissociation is prevalent in the Jewish and Christian traditions. Cf. Is 51:4-8, in which the people not devoted to God and looking forward to God's deliverance are excluded from the group of significant others that are to constitute one's "court of opinion." Their sort will come to an end quickly, while God's deliverance will be permanent. On this basis, the prophet exhorts the hearers not to respect their opinion or allow their reproaches to affect their commitment or behavior: "Hearken to me, you who know righteousness, the people in whose heart is my law; fear not the reproach of men, and be not dismayed at their revilings (μὴ φοβεῖσθε ὀνειδισμὸν ἀνθρώπων καὶ τῷ φαυλισμῷ αὐτῶν μὴ ἡττᾶσθε, 51:7)." Cf. also Jn 5:44 and 12:43, in which care for the opinion of unbelievers and desire for honor from such people is explicitly presented as a hindrance to faith or the confession of faith.

[130] So Michel (*Hebräerbrief*, 347) commenting on the exhortation to leave the camp and go outside to Jesus: "Just so it is certain that there, where hostility with the world breaks out, peace with God is truly to be found." In the case against Socrates, Plato provides further evidence that having a bad reputation with the members of one's society, or the populace, could lead to danger and hostility (*Crito* 44D: "But you see it is necessary, Socrates, to care for the opinion of the public (τῆς τῶν πολλῶν δόξης μέλειν), for this very trouble we are in now shows that the public is able to accomplish

Such a course leads to solidarity with Jesus and the replication of his faith.[131]   The author's use of the example of Jesus serves a function analogous to Dio's use of the example of Heracles in his discourse on virtue (*Or.* 8.28):

> As for Heracles, they pitied him while he toiled and struggled and called him the most 'trouble-ridden,' or wretched, of men; indeed, this is why they gave the name 'troubles,' or tasks, to his labours and works, as though a laborious life were a trouble-ridden, or wretched life; but now that he is dead they honour him beyond all others, deify him, and say he has Hebe to wife, and all pray to him that they may not themselves be wretched -- to him who in his labours suffered wretchedness exceedingly great.

Just as the honor in which Heracles is held ought to inspire the worshipers to endure hardships with a spirit of contempt for them (as did Diogenes, the hero of Dio's oration), so the honor in which Christ is held ought to inspire his followers to endure as he did, despising shame. By such a path of *imitatio Christi*, the addressees may aspire to attain the κρεῖττόν τι, the "something greater" which God has prepared for them (11:39-40). Christ's own attainment of honor -- the achievement of the "joy set before him (τῆς προκειμένης αὐτῷ χαρᾶς, 12:2)" -- should motivate the addressees faithfully to persevere in the "contest set before us (τὸν προκείμενον ἡμῖν ἀγῶνα, 12:1)" for the sake of the honor that awaits them as "partners with Christ (μέτοχοι τοῦ Χριστοῦ, 3:14)."[132]

The author encourages the addressees to pursue this goal and the honor it brings.   The greatness of the prize makes the means to attain it honorable, even if these include the experience of disgrace before the

---

not by any means the least, but almost the greatest of evils, if one has a bad reputation with it."

[131] Cf. Peterson, *Hebrews and Perfection*, 170: "The fact that Jesus 'despised the shame' of the cross and 'endured from sinners such hostility against himself' will have its own particular relevance for the readers, in view of their past experience (10:32-34), and what they may reasonably have expected again (10:35ff; 13:13)."

[132] Cf. Lünemann, *Hebrews*, 703: "For the immediate concern of the author must evidently be to point to the prize which Christ was to receive in return for His sufferings, in order thereupon further to indicate that to the readers likewise, upon their persevering in the conflict, the palm of victory will not be wanting." Cf. also Calvin, *Hebrews*, 170, commenting on 12:2: "Now he commends the patience of Christ to our notice on two accounts; because he endured a most painful death, and because he despised the shame. He then records the glorious end of his death, that believers may know that all the ills they endure will issue in their glory and salvation, provided they be followers of Christ."

world's court of opinion.[133]   Indeed, it transforms dishonor before the society into esteem before God and the community. He adds the promise of future reward and honor, which are attainable only by the person of πίστις, which in Hebrews combines "faith" in the reality and beneficence of God as well as commitment to persevere in answer to God's call. The author of Hebrews thus shares the conviction of Jews and Christians that those who trust in God will not fall into disgrace, but rather come into honor beyond measure.[134]   He uses the resources of his Jewish heritage, showing his readers that those who follow his exhortation will fulfill those central values better than those without the benefit of Christ. At the same time, he develops countercultural rhetoric in his manipulation of the relationship of the community to the society: "despising shame" is an essential prerequisite to fulfilling the requirements of faith, as the exemplars of faith in chapter 11 demonstrate.

Seneca writes in his *de Constantia* (19.2-3) about the effects of sensitivity to insult on one's performance in society:

> Otherwise, from the fear of insults or from weariness of them, we shall fall short in the doing of many needful things, and, suffering from a womanish distaste for hearing anything not to our mind, we shall refuse to face both public and private duties.... Liberty is having a mind that rises superior to injury, that makes itself the only source from which its pleasures spring, that separates itself from all external things in order that man may not have to live his life in disquietude, fearing everybody's laughter, everybody's tongue.

Mutatis mutandis, one encounters a similar danger in the situation addressed by Hebrews, namely that a return to sensitivity towards society's honor rating (and its use of dishonor as a negative sanction against those associated with the name of Jesus or the community of Christians) will lead

---

[133] It is this conviction that accounts for similar reversals of values throughout the early Christian literature. Cf. the striking passage in Acts 5:41, where the apostles, having been scourged as a sign of the authorities' disapproval, "rejoiced that they were counted worthy to suffer dishonor for the sake of the name [of Jesus]." Similar counter-evaluations appear in Matt 5:11 and 1 Pet 4:14-16, where suffering reproach for the sake of association with the name of Jesus is counted as making one "blessed (μακάριος)," that is, most to be envied (cf. Neyrey, "Poverty," 8-9).

[134] Cf. *Prayer of Azariah* 17: "there will be no shame for those who trust in thee (οὐκ ἔσται αἰσχύνη τοῖς πεποιθόσιν ἐπὶ σοί; RSV)." Rom 9:33; 10:11 and 1 Pet 2:6 all take up the promise of Is 28:16 (LXX) that "those who trust in him will not be put to shame," and apply it to trust in Jesus. 1 Pet 1:7 further promises that the tested and proven faith will redound to praise, honor, and renown before God's court for its possessor.

to the disruption of "faith" and the failure of the community to persevere in the activities required by faith.

The exemplars of faith have been chosen, and their stories fashioned, to address the community's situation and provide positive models for the course of action that faith (and therefore the attainment of the reward) requires. The community's own past record, however, provides a similar model for its present choices. They have endured the loss of their status within society, but, like Abraham, they are not to turn back from their pilgrimage in faith in order to regain honor and place within the unbelieving world, but rather continue one to the land of promise. Thus the author exhorts them: "Jesus also suffered outside the gate in order to sanctify the people through his own blood. Therefore let us go forth to him outside the camp and bear the abuse he endured. For here we have no lasting city, but we seek the city which is to come" (13:12-14).[135] Like the martyrs, they are not to accept release from the tension created between them and the host society on account of their commitment to God, they are not to seek re-enfranchisement in the Greco-Roman world. Rather, they are to continue in the society of their fellow-believers, not withdrawing from their assemblies (10:25) nor slackening in their care for and identification with those brothers and sisters who have come under society's fire (13:3). Like Moses, they are to continue in their choice of fellowship with the people of God, although this entails perpetual banishment from the honor and enjoyments offered by the society to its own. Like Abraham and Moses, once having left behind their homeland, their place in society, they are called to persist in their journey towards a better homeland.

---

[135] Cf. Delitzsch, *Hebrews*, 389-90: "The meaning is: therefore let us no longer continue in their society who have rejected the Lord Jesus, but go forth to Him outside the camp.... On the other hand, to forsake their company and communion for His sake is to involve ourselves not merely in future but in present shame or reproach; but this reproach is the reproach of Christ, a shame which we share with Him, and in bearing which we are made like Him." Cf. also Héring, *Hebrews*, 123: "This detail is also used for parenetical purposes. We too must 'leave the encampment', that is behave like pilgrims on the earth, like foreigners who must expect to be held in contempt, but always comforted by the hope of the country to come."

CHAPTER FIVE

Exchanging Grace for Wrath:
The Danger of Dishonoring God

The author of Hebrews seeks to move the addressees to "despise shame" by many positive models of those who have scorned society's estimation of them for the sake of achieving honor in God's sight. He also goads them in that direction through a fearsome presentation of the alternative -- despising or slighting God. For this author, there are only two options: one either honors and obeys God at the risk of dishonoring and provoking the world, or one honors and conforms to society at the risk of dishonoring and provoking God. Stated another way, one either seeks to gain security through adopting the representatives of the unbelieving society as one's patrons, or one attaches oneself to God and enjoys the benefits gained through Christ.

This brings us to the central question of Hebrews' Christology. Many scholars have inquired after what the author of Hebrews sought to accomplish through the comparisons of Christ with the angels, Moses, and Levitical Priesthood.[1] What is the purpose of the laudatory descriptions of Jesus which fill the so-called "doctrinal" sections, and how do the "hortatory" sections assist the scholar's appreciation of the author's Christology?[2] I argue here that such language expressing the greatness or superiority of Christ joins with the assertion of experiencing God as

---

[1] See, for example, P. E. Hughes' commentary (outlined in G. H. Guthrie, *The Structure of Hebrews*, 27), in which the structure is thematically divided by the demonstrations of Christ as superior to the prophets, angels, Moses, Aaron, and the Israelite cultus.

[2] F. Büchsel is credited with having first brought out the significance of the alternation between these two genres for understanding the argument of Hebrews (Guthrie, *Structure*, 9).

Benefactor through Christ and the dire warnings against acting so as to dishonor or affront the One presently known as Patron.

First, the author appears anxious to remind recipients of the supreme honor of Jesus Christ. He seeks to motivate the readers to resist adopting a course of action which would fail to return the proper honor to the One who occupies a place of supreme honor in the Jewish-Christian cosmos. He thus appeals to the Greco-Roman virtues of piety and justice, according to which one must give to each person his or her due.[3] Secondly, the author seeks to remind his readers that Jesus' exalted position enables him to exercise power and authority for their benefit at present, securing God's favor and benefaction ($\chi\acute{\alpha}\rho\iota\varsigma$) as their mediator. He appeals thus also to the central Greco-Roman virtue of gratitude, which demands that the Patron (both Jesus, who gains God's patronage for the believer, and God Himself) be honored. Danker's judgement that "ingratitude is the cardinal social and political sin in the Graeco-Roman world"[4] is well supported by contemporary sources.[5] Thirdly the author urgently warns the addressees to avoid behavior which would dishonor the Son and, through Him, God, thus turning benefaction and the promise of future benefaction into wrath and the promise of judgement. Heightening God's beneficence in Christ augments the horror and baseness of failing to return the proper honor and loyalty to God in Christ.

This combination represents another strategy used by the author to drive his exhortation and shape the response of the recipients. Here it is not a matter of appealing directly to their own honor, although this would be directly affected by their response, but rather a matter of delineating the

---

[3] Paul employs the topic of "justice" in Rom 13:7 when he advises, "Pay to all what is due them -- taxes to whom taxes are due, revenue to whom revenue is due, respect to whom respect is due, honor to whom honor is due."

[4] Danker, *Benefactor*, 436.

[5] Seneca (*Ben.* 3.1.1) claims that "not to return gratitude for benefits is a disgrace, and the whole world counts it as such (*Non referre beneficiis gratiam et est turpe et apud omnes habetur*)." On the other hand, "nothing is more honourable than a grateful heart" (Seneca *Ep.* 81.30). Dio (*Or.* 31.7) likewise states that gratitude is next to piety among the virtues, as well as an essential characteristic for those to show who desire future consideration by benefactors: "If we except the honours which we owe the gods, which we must regard as first in importance, of all other actions there is nothing nobler or more just than to show honour to our good men and to keep in remembrance those who have served us well.... For those who take seriously their obligations toward their benefactors and mete out just treatment to those who have loved them, all men regard as worthy of favour ($\pi\acute{\alpha}\nu\tau\epsilon\varsigma$ $\acute{\eta}\gamma o\tilde{\upsilon}\nu\tau\alpha\iota$ $\chi\acute{\alpha}\rho\iota\tau o\varsigma$ $\acute{\alpha}\xi\acute{\iota}o\upsilon\varsigma$), and without exception each would wish to benefit them to the best of his ability."

honor due to another and the consequences of failure in that regard.[6] The prominence of appeals to *pathos* in connection with whether one has made a proper or improper return to the Benefactor (particularly under the headings of "fear" and its antithesis, "confidence") demonstrates that the author believed the recipients would be deeply affected by such a demonstration of the honor due God and the danger and loss which one incurs if one chooses to dishonor Christ.

1 The Honor of Christ

The Christology of the Letter to the Hebrews is profoundly shaped by the exigencies of the situation which the author addresses. Recognizing this link, commentators use the author's particular discussions of the work and person of Christ as building blocks in the reconstruction of that situation, whether apostasy in the face of persecution, the attractiveness of Judaism, or simply moral lethargy and waning commitment. For example, William Lane writes that "the failure of nerve on the part of the community addressed, evidenced by the parenetic warning sections, occurred because of an inadequate christology.... They were prepared to abandon their confession because they had lost the realization of its significance."[7] The following investigation likewise probes the author's strategic use of his claims about and descriptions of Jesus, but from the more culturally apt angles of honor and patronage. The author seeks to establish in the minds of his audience the supreme honor of Christ, and from that starting point holds up two alternatives before them. The first is to continue to recognize this exalted person as their benefactor and their means of access to an even greater Benefactor. The second is to reject Christ as their benefactor, spurn his gifts, and incur the enmity of the One who upholds the honor of Christ, namely the Living God. The author depicts the honor of Christ largely under two headings, Son and High Priest, and, through the

---

[6] It is this aspect of honor to which B. Williams (*Shame and Necessity*, 80) so helpfully calls the scholar's attention: "It is natural, and indeed basic to the operation of these feelings, that *nemesis*, and *aidōs* itself, can appear on both sides of a social relation. People have at once a sense of their own honour and a respect for other people's honour; they can feel indignation or other forms of anger when honour is violated, in their own case or someone else's. These are shared sentiments with similar objects, and they serve to bind people together in a community of feeling." Cf. Aristotle *Rh.* 2.9.11: "If a virtuous man does not obtain what is suitable to him, we feel indignant. Similarly, if the inferior contends with the superior, especially among those engaged in the same pursuit."

[7] Lane, *Hebrews 1-8*, cxxxviii.

application to Jesus of certain psalms, also claims for him a place of highest standing in God's court.

THE HONOR OF THE SON

The author presents Jesus to his audience immediately as "Son," the bearer of the final word of God: "In many and various ways God spoke of old to our fathers by the prophets; but in these last days he has spoken to us by a Son (ἐν υἱῷ), whom he appointed the heir of all things, through whom also he created the world" (Heb 1:1-2). Specifically, Jesus is presented as the "Son of God," as the citations in 1:5 demonstrate.[8] As such, his honor derives from the honor of God, his Father. In the Greco-Roman world, one's honor rating depends largely on one's birth, whether into a family of high or low status. Sirach urges children to show honor to their parents at all times, since "a man's honor springs from his father's honor, and a mother in dishonor is a cause of reproach to her children (ἡ γὰρ δόξα ἀνθρώπου ἐκ τιμῆς πατρὸς αὐτοῦ, καὶ ὄνειδος τέκνοις μήτηρ ἐν ἀδοξίᾳ, 3:11)."

In their discussions of encomia, the rhetorical handbooks also demonstrate the connection between honor due the parents of the subject and the honor due the subject himself or herself.[9] In several orations, Dio of Prusa claims as his own the honors bestowed upon his father, grandfather, and brothers. Most strikingly, he links the showing of proper regard to himself as the truest display of respect for his father. In *Or.* 46.3-4, after Dio has been put on the defensive by a crowd of Prusans who suspect him of holding back grain in order to inflate market prices, he appeals to the honors won by his family for their contributions to Prusa, and exhorts the townspeople to be mindful of their debt to honor him now: "You should know, however, that these words of praise of yours are no use to [my father]; on the other hand, when you give your approval to me, his son, then you have been mindful of him too."

The author of Hebrews, in presenting Jesus first of all as "Son," is explicitly concerned with establishing Jesus' honor. The author of 2 Peter links the declaration of Jesus' sonship with a grant of honor from God, "having received honor and repute (τιμὴν καὶ δόξαν) from God the Father

---

[8] Jesus is referred to explicitly as the "Son of God" in Heb 4:14, 6:6, and 10:29.

[9] Cf. *Rhet. Her.* 3.7.13, where an element in the praise of an individual is the discussion of descent. Surviving encomia show that this advice was followed, as in Dio, *Or.* 29.2-3, in which Dio begins his funeral eulogy for the boxer, Melancomas, with the praise of his father.

when the voice was conveyed to him by the Supreme Glory: 'This is my Son, my beloved, in whom I am well pleased'."[10] The declaration of affiliation here, like the adoption formula in the enthronement psalm,[11] indicates God's public extension of God's rule and honor to the Son, Jesus, thus an investment of God's honor in the Son. Jesus has been granted a status superior to the status enjoyed even by the angels on the basis of his inheritance of this "better name." Moffatt insightfully notes that " ῎Ονομα ... carries the general Oriental sense of 'rank' or 'dignity'," for one's name, by indicating one's family, also indicated one's honor. The author uses the voice of two citations from the LXX to document the Divine investment of Jesus with this name of "Son" (1:5), after which he cites the command given to the angels to acknowledge Jesus' stature by offering him the προσκύνησις, which replicates in the posture of the body the assessment of relative honor and status.[12]

Jesus, as "Son," is also lauded by the author of Hebrews as the "reflection" or "effulgence of God's glory (ἀπαύγασμα τῆς δόξης)." Commentators and translations are divided as to whether or not ἀπαύγασμα is to be translated as "reflection" or "radiance/effulgence," and make their choice generally based on whether or not they read the second phrase "exact stamp of God's being (χαρακτὴρ τῆς ὑποστάσεως αὐτοῦ)" as a synonymous parallel. Either reading yields the sense that the Son is invested with the glory of God. But what is the "glory of God"? Understanding the meaning of the term δόξα for the author of Hebrews requires the exploration of the various meanings of this term in a variety of backgrounds. The close semantic connection between δόξα and τιμή in the "secular" Greek of the first-century C.E. appears nowhere more clearly than in Plutarch *Quaest. Rom.* 13 (*Mor.* 266F-267A):

> Why do they also sacrifice to the god called "Honor" with the head uncovered? One might translate Honor as "renown" (δόξα) or "honour" (τιμή). Is it because renown (δόξα) is a brilliant thing, conspicuous, and

---

[10] J. H. Neyrey (*2 Peter, Jude* [AB 37C; New York: Doubleday, 1993], 172) rightly emphasizes thia aspect of the text.

[11] Cf. Peter Wülfing von Martitz, *et al.*, "Υἱός, υἱοθεσία" (*TDNT* 8:334-399; Grand Rapids: Eerdmans: 1972), 350.

[12] Aristotle (*Rh.* 1.5.9) includes the *proskynēsis* among his list of honors as a barbarian sign of regard for those of high reputation. Similarly, Is. 49:23 uses it to express the promised future honor of the people of Israel over the kings of the Gentiles: "Kings shall be your foster fathers, and their queens your nursing mothers. With their faces to the ground they shall bow down to you (ἐπὶ πρόσωπον τῆς γῆς προσκυνήσουσίν σοι), and lick the dust of your feet. Then you will know that I am the Lord and that you shall not be put to shame (γνώσῃ ὅτι ἐγὼ κύριος καὶ οὐκ αἰσχυνθήσῃ)."

widespread, and for the reason that they uncover in the presence of good
and honored men, is it for this same reason that they also worship the
god who is named for "Honour"?

Plutarch binds δόξα and τιμή together as translation equivalents for a
single Latin word, and further provides insight into the conception of δόξα
in the ancient world. The imagery of "brilliance" or luminescence, of
visible spectacle, is used to capture for the senses the experience of
standing in the presence of someone who is widely held in high esteem.
Repute adds something ineffable to a person, something which reaches
beyond the physical space occupied by a person. Light and brightness
come to be used of this experience of something invisible yet nonetheless
experienced.

In LXX Esther, Δόξα signifies again the visible manifestation of honor
and status. Reputation and changes of status are accompanied by visible
signs or tokens of status, which makes it possible for Haman to display to
his family the "glory" with which the king had invested him: "And Haman
showed them his wealth, and the honor with which the king endowed him
(καὶ ὑπέδειξεν αὐτοῖς τὸν πλοῦτον αὐτοῦ καὶ τὴν δόξαν ἧν ὁ βασιλεὺς
αὐτῷ περιέθηκεν), and how he had advanced him above the princes and the
servants of the king" (Esth. 5:11; au. trans.). When troubled with the
news of the king's command, Esther prepares herself to pray and removes
"her splendid apparel (ἀφελομένη τὰ ἱμάτια τῆς δόξης αὐτῆς, 14:1)."
Her "garments of glory" were the visible manifestations of the dignity of
her rank, which she exchanged for garments of mourning. Honor
possessed translates into honor displayed, high rank into "glory." When
Esther at last goes in unannounced before the king, she sees him "seated
on his royal throne, clothed in the full array of his majesty, all covered
with gold and precious stones. He was most terrifying. And lifting his
face, burning with glory, he looked with intense anger" (15:6). The author
does not wish to depict a theophany, but rather convey an impression of
the powerful effect of the visible trappings of royal authority and status on
the subject. So impressive is the king's display that Esther exclaims "I saw
you, my lord, like an angel of God, and my heart was shaken with fear at
your glory (ἀπὸ φόβου τῆς δόξης σου, 15:13)." The king's "glory" was
nothing other than the impression of the trappings his authority and power,
hence his honor, upon the senses of the subjects. This "glory" takes on a
luminous, visible quality, but ultimately has its conceptual roots in the
display of honor, and so comes to be used metonymically for honor.

Commentators tend to drive a wedge between the meaning of δόξα in
secular Greek and in NT Greek, speaking in nebulous terms about the
word as designating "the supersensuous light and fire of [God's] own

nature thrown out for the purpose of self-manifestation to Himself," or the "divine reality or heavenly state."[13] Kittel claims that the use of δόξα in the LXX as "glory or honour ascribed to someone" or "reputation" is very rare, and that it more often denotes "power" or "splendour." He notes, however, that these latter traits lead to honor and prestige.[14] He allows it to mean "reputation," "splendour," or "the divine mode of being" in NT usage.[15] Given the background of the meaning of the term in secular Greek and the persistence of this meaning in the LXX, Heb 1:3 makes a claim about the honor of the Son. The Son reflects or shines with the visible manifestation of God's honor and authority, and hence is fully invested with the honor of the Father, God.

Jesus' dignity as "Son" is further enhance by a comparison with Moses in Heb 3:1-6. Attridge notes that the "assertion that Christ is 'superior' (κρείττων) involves one of Hebrews' most characteristic adjectives [cf. 6:9; 7:7, 19, 22; 8:6; 9:23; 10:34; 11:16, 35, 40; 12:24.]."[16] The comparison with Moses, like that with the angels and the Levitical Priesthood, does not necessarily imply a polemical purpose. Indeed, there are strong indications to the contrary. Michel notes with regard to the comparison of Jesus and Moses that "Hebrews might have higlighted Moses' unfaithfulness or his murmuring against God (Num 20:12): the faithfulness of Moses adds to the bargain. Hebrews also refrains from speaking as 2 Cor 3:7ff concerning the fading nature of Moses' δόξα (Ex 34:33ff.) as opposed to the abiding δόξα of Christ."[17] The author does not denigrate Moses in any way, but rather builds his comparison on a shared high regard for Moses. Christ's superiority to Moses aims not at disqualifying the latter as a servant within God's house, but rather at enhancing the honor of the former as Son over God's house (3:5).

The author thus engages in his comparison as part of his demonstration of Christ's honor, a practice well documented in the rhetorical handbooks.

---

[13] Delitzsch, *Hebrews*, 49; Attridge, *Hebrews*, 43. Cf. also Michel, *Hebräer*, 39: "δόξα is an expression of the divine mode of being.... This δόξα (בבוד) is God's self-manifestation (Exod 24:16; 33:18ff.; 40:34); it may also be an expression of God's person, a designation for God's own Self."

[14] G. Kittel, "Δοκέω, δόξα." (*TDNT* 2:232-255; Grand Rapids: Eerdmans, 1964), 243.

[15] Kittel, "Δοκέω," 247.

[16] Attridge, *Hebrews*, 47. Cf. Delitzsch, *Hebrews*, 58: "κρείττων, although not an unpauline word, is yet a *special* favourite with the writer of this epistle, generally used by him in the sense of superiority in goodness," or "in that of superiority in power."

[17] Michel, *Hebräer*, 96-97.

Aristotle (*Rh.* 1.9.38-39) instructs the would-be orator to include comparison as an essential feature of an epideictic oration:

> And you must compare him with illustrious personages, for it affords ground for amplification and is noble, if he can be proved better than men of worth. Amplification is with good reason ranked as one of the forms of praise, since it consists in superiority, and superiority is one of the things that are noble.

Seneca (*Ep.* 43.2) likewise points to the importance of comparison as a means of appraising the greatness of any one individual: "Any point which rises above adjacent points is great, at the spot where it rises. For greatness is not absolute; comparison increases it or lessens it." Based on the observation that "in encomia generally, the comparison serves not so much to denigrate the comparable figure as to exalt the subject of the discourse," Attridge surmises that the author's "contrast between Christ and Moses derives at least part of its force from the high regard in which Moses was held in the first century."[18]

A sampling of Hellenistic Jewish texts provides an overview of the estimation which Moses enjoyed. Sirach's hymn in praise of the Jewish heroes includes this portrayal of Moses:

> From his descendants the Lord brought forth a man of mercy, who found favor in the sight of all flesh and was beloved by God and man, Moses, whose memory is blessed. He made him equal in glory to the holy ones, and made him great in the fears of his enemies (ὡμοίωσεν αὐτὸν δόξῃ ἁγίων καὶ ἐμεγάλυνεν αὐτὸν ἐν φόβοις ἐχθρῶν). By his words he caused signs to cease; the Lord glorified him in the presence of kings. He gave him commands for his people, and showed him part of his glory (45:1-3; RSV).

The exaltation of Moses in the presence of kings and above the "holy ones" raises this servant of God to a high station in God's court. Josephus (*AJ* 3.38) speaks of Moses as "the one honored by God (ὁ ὑπὸ τοῦ θεοῦ τετιμημένος)." The author of Hebrews himself speaks of Moses as "faithful" or "reliable" (πιστός) to God (3:2) with regard to his service in God's house (3:5), for which he was indeed held in honor.

Starting from this positive commendation of Moses, the author declares that Jesus (explicitly named in 3:1) "has been deemed worthy of greater glory than Moses, in the same proportion as the builder of a house has greater honor than the house (πλείονος γὰρ οὗτος δόξης παρὰ Μωϋσῆν

---

[18] Attridge, *Hebrews*, 105.

ἠξίωται, καθ' ὅσον πλείονα τιμὴν ἔχει τοῦ οἴκου ὁ κατασκευάσας αὐτόν, 3:3; au. trans.)." The familiar acclamation "ἄξιός ἐστι..." or "ἄξιος εἶ..." (cf. Rev 4:11; 5:9-10, 12) implies that a value judgement has been made or acknowledged by those making the acclamation.[19] If the claim is true, then it belongs to "justice (δικαιοσύνη)" to render what is due, and to "just indignation (νέμεσις)" to enforce justice. Since the aorist passive may be described as a divine passive,[20] the author of Hebrews asserts indirectly that God has settled Jesus' claim to greater glory and honor. While Moses is given attestation as a servant in God's house (ὡς θεράπων, 3:5), the declaration of Jesus as Son indicates the surpassing honor and renown which is his due by divine decree.

JESUS' STANDING IN THE COURT OF GOD

Jesus' honor is also developed by the description of the prominent position he enjoys before God. The relative placement of bodies, as well as physical gestures, played an essential role in the enactment of honor and display of relative worth. The author of Hebrews weaves them both into his presentation of Jesus' honor. First, he repeatedly refers to Jesus as seated at the right hand of God (1:3; 8:1; 10:12; 12:2; see Ps 110:1).[21] In the ancient world, seating order was based on the appraisal of relative worth or honor. The most distinguished people enjoyed the best seats. This is most apparent in court stories, such as Esther, where sitting next to the king is a sign of high ranking, and where all the nobles have their place of sitting established by their rank: "After these things King Ahasuerus promoted Haman the Agagite, the son of Hammedatha, and advanced him and set his seat above all the princes who were with him (ὕψωσεν αὐτὸν καὶ ἐπρωτοβάθρει πάντων τῶν φίλων αὐτοῦ, 3:1 [RSV]; cf. 1:14)."

---

[19] Aristotle (*Eth. Nic.* 4.3.10), for example, explains that "'Worthy' (ἡ δ' ἀξία) is a term of relation: it denotes having a claim to goods external to oneself." The greatest of these external goods, he goes on to argue, is honor (ἡ τιμή), such that being said to be "worthy of honor" involves the social recognition of one's merit, achivements, and status.

[20] Cf. Weiß, *Hebräer*, 540.

[21] The prominence of citations from this psalm, and the large sections devoted to developing Jesus' position before God in light of this psalm has led G. W. Buchanan (*To the Hebrews* [AB 36; New York: Doubleday, 1964], xix) to argue that "the document entitled 'To the Hebrews' is a homiletical midrash based on Ps 110."

The instructions concerning taking the lowest seat at a banquet in Luke 14:8-10 bring the court practice into the everyday life of social gatherings:

> When you are invited by someone to a wedding banquet, do not sit down at the place of honor, in case someone more distinguished than you has been invited by your host; and the host who invited both of you may come and say to you, "Give this person your place," and then in disgrace you would start to take the lowest place. But when you are invited, go and sit down at the lowest place, so that when your host comes, he may say to you, "Friend, move up higher"; then you will be honored in the presence of all who sit at the table with you (NRSV).

By applying Ps 110:1 to Jesus, the author claims for him the place of highest honor in the Jewish-Christian cosmos,[22] namely a seat at the right hand of God.[23] Lane correctly observes that session at God's right hand "would convey to contemporaries an impression of the Son's royal power and unparalleled glory."[24]

The author includes a number of expressions which depict physical representations or enactments of the honor of Jesus. Pitt-Rivers noted "the intimate relation between honour and the physical person." Many rituals focus on the head of a person, which replicates the person's honor and status.[25] For example, "honor is displayed when the head is crowned, anointed, touched, or covered."[26] The author of Hebrews, again taking up citations from the Psalms, enhances Jesus' honor with the depiction of crowning and anointing. First, he adduces Ps 44:7 LXX to describe an anointing which sets Jesus above his peers (presumably the angels), and thus augments his dignity in comparison with theirs: "Thou hast loved righteousness and hated lawlessness; therefore God, thy God, has anointed thee with the oil of gladness beyond thy comrades (ἔχρισέν σε ὁ θεός ὁ θεός σου ἔλαιον ἀγαλλιάσεως παρὰ τοὺς μετόχους σου; au. trans.)." In a more extended discussion, the author applies Ps 2:6 to Jesus, by which

---

[22] In making this claim, it is apparent that the author is drawing on subcultural rhetoric (subcultural with regard to Jewish culture) to advance his demonstration of the dignity of the Son.

[23] It is a commonplace to note that "the right side is the side of honour" (W. Grundmann, "Δεξιός" [*TDNT* 2:37-40; Grand Rapids: Eerdmans, 1964], 38).

[24] Lane, *Hebrews 1-8*, 16.

[25] Julian Pitt-Rivers, "Honour and Social Status," 25.

[26] Malina and Neyrey, "Honor and Shame," 35.

he is awarded a crown as a result of his work while abased beneath the angels:[27]

> "Thou didst make him for a little while lower than the angels, thou hast crowned him with glory and honor (δόξῃ καὶ τιμῇ ἐστεφάνωσας αὐτόν), putting everything in subjection under his feet (πάντα ὑπέταξας ὑποκάτω τῶν ποδῶν αὐτοῦ)." Now in putting everything in subjection to him, he left nothing outside his control. As it is, we do not yet see everything in subjection to him. But we see Jesus, who for a little while was made lower than the angels, crowned with glory and honor (δόξῃ καὶ τιμῇ ἐστεφανωμένον) because of the suffering of death, so that by the grace of God he might taste death for every one. (2:7-9; RSV)[28]

From his place of highest honor, at the right hand of God, Jesus awaits the final subjection of all things (νῦν δὲ **οὔπω** ὁρῶμεν αὐτῷ τὰ πάντα ὑποτεταγμένα, 2:8). This includes the subjection of his enemies -- all those who have set or will set themselves in opposition to the Son rather than subject themselves to the Son -- as a footstool under his feet: "Sit at my right hand, till I make thy enemies a stool for thy feet (Κάθου ἐκ δεξιῶν μου, ἕως ἂν θῶ τοὺς ἐχθρούς σου ὑποπόδιον τῶν ποδῶν σου, 1:13; citing LXX Ps 109:1)." The placement of enemies under the feet is again a physical representation of relative status, and a sign of Christ's dominance. While the angels perform the *proskynēsis*, representing their voluntary submission, the enemies of Christ are involuntarily placed beneath the feet of their conqueror. The author places this day in the future, signalling that Christ, despite the high honor and status he enjoys presently before the court of God, looks forward to still greater prestige as

---

[27] Cf. Attridge, *Hebrews*, 72: "For Hebrews the psalm is not, primarily at least, a meditation on the lofty status of humankind in the created order, but an oracle that describes the humiliation and exaltation of Jesus....Being 'less than the angels' is now not the equivalent of being crowned with honor and glory, but is, rather, its antithesis."

[28] If the remainder of Ps 8:7 originally stood within the text, a possibility preserved in certain textual traditions, then one would have yet another declaration of authority and status: "You appointed him over the works of your hands." Calvin (*Hebrews*, 16) read this in connection with Christ's honor and what the author hoped to gain by dwelling on Christ's honor: "Again by another argument he proves that Christ must be obeyed, because the Father hath given him dominion over the whole world; an honour far removed from angels." Nevertheless, the author himself does not comment on this line in his application of the psalm to Jesus in 2:8b-9, although he does refer to the lines before and after it. As it would have aided his presentation of Jesus' dignity, it may be more reasonable to believe that the variant is not original to the text than that the author missed such an obvious opportunity.

his enemies are brought to acknowledge the worth which God declared the Son to possess.[29]

THE HONOR OF THE GREATER HIGH PRIEST

Hebrews is unique among the New Testament documents for its well-developed priestly Christology. Calling Jesus the "high priest of our confession" (3:1; cf. 2:17; 4:14; and 6:20) attributes to Jesus a great honor in addition to describing his activity within the Heavenly Sanctuary. The office of high priest was still held in deep regard during the first century C.E., even after the corruption which had eroded the office during the Macabean period. Josephus (*BJ* 4.164) calls the title of "high priest" the "most honored of revered names (τὸ τιμώτατον καλούμενος τῶν σεβασμίων ὀνομάτων)." Elsewhere (*BJ* 4.149), he refers to the office as "the highest dignity (τῆς ἀνωτάτω τιμῆς)." Similarly, Philo of Alexandria, far removed from the actual temple cult in Jerusalem, refers to the priesthood as an honor (cf. *Mos.* 2.142), even going so far as to claim that "the law invests the priests with the dignity and honour that belongs to kings" (*De spec. leg.* 1.142).

Why would the high priest be held in such high esteem, and be accorded the honors which belong to the chiefest of benefactors, namely kings? The Greco-Roman world as a patronal society may give an answer: the "broker" is a person who provides, for his or her clients, access to the goods and services of other benefactors. The broker stands as client to a greater person or as friend to persons of like and equal resources to himself; the broker provides a benefit in the form of access to other patrons, and so stands also as a benefactor. Relationships between deities and human beings were conceptualized in similar terms. The High Priest served as a broker of the benefits of God, the Patron *sans pareil*. Offering sacrifices as satisfaction for the affronts to the authority of God, he secured the Benefactor's favorable disposition (χάρις) and thus restored the nation's confidence in the hope of God's continued beneficence in God's dealings with the people.

The author of Hebrews claims the honor of this office for Jesus. He sets Jesus' appointment by God to the high priesthood parallel to his

---

[29] Similarly, as "heir of all things" (1:3) Christ has still not come into the fullness of his inheritance as Son, and so awaits still greater honor.

exaltation by God's declaration of his Sonship,[30] grounding both claims once more through Psalm 110 (LXX Psalm 109):

> And one does not take the honor (τὴν τιμήν) upon himself, but he is called by God, just as Aaron was. So also Christ did not exalt himself to be made a high priest (ὁ Χριστὸς οὐχ ἑαυτὸν ἐδόξασεν γενηθῆναι ἀρχιερέα), but was appointed by him who said to him, "Thou art my Son, today I have begotten thee"; as he says also in another place, "Thou art a priest for ever, after the order of Melchizedek."

The author is at pains to show that Jesus did not usurp this privilege for himself, thus making a false claim to an honor not his own, but rather was given this honor by the command of God just as Aaron had formerly received divine legitimation for his priesthood. Establishing the Son as perpetual high priest brought Jesus to his divinely appointed destiny, from which position he is able to benefit those who come to him: "He became to all those who obey him the source of eternal salvation (αἴτιος σωτηρίας αἰωνίου, 5:9)."[31] As high priest, Jesus has the capacity to be a benefactor, a cause or source (αἴτιος) of necessary goods and services.

As the author had previously compared Jesus to Moses, so he also constructs a much more highly developed comparison between Jesus' priesthood and the Levitical priesthood. Here the author's discourse becomes sharper. While the comparison with Moses did not detract from Moses' honor, the establishment of Jesus' priesthood means displacing the Levitical order: Jesus affords better and more reliable access to God, and

---

[30] Cf. E. Schweizer, *Lordship and Discipleship* (SBT, 28; Naperville, IL: Alec R. Allenson, Inc., 1960), 74: "The dignity to which the ascended Christ is appointed is strictly speaking no longer [we should rather say, not only] that of the Son but that of the High Priest of the order of Melchizedek."

[31] Jesus' induction into his heavenly priesthood has been seen by a number of scholars as his "perfection." This rather straightforward solution to the problem of "perfection" in Hebrews takes the activity of 5:10 (προσαγορευθεὶς ὑπὸ τοῦ θεοῦ ἀρχιερεὺς κατὰ τὴν τάξιν Μελχισέδεκ) as parallel and epexegetical to the cryptic participle of 5:9 (τελειωθείς). This position is favored by Attridge, *Hebrews*, 87: "Christ's perfecting, as developed in the text, may be understood as a vocational process by which he is made complete or fit for his office. This process involves, not a moral dimension, but an existential one. Through his suffering, Christ becomes the perfect model, who has learned obedience (5:10), and the perfect intercessor, merciful and faithful (2:17). Christ's perfection is consummated in his exaltation, his entry into 'honor and glory', the position where he serves to guarantee his followers' similar perfection." Lane (*Hebrews 1-8*, 122) offers a similar interpretation, adding the sense of "consecration to divine service" (e.g., as priest) which was a common use of "perfection" terminology (cf. *BAGD*, 810).

so leaves no place for the mediation effected by the Levitical high priest. Nevertheless, the honor of Christ as greater high priest is enhanced by the honor which attaches to the priesthood he replaces.

The founders of the Levitical priesthood were held in high esteem in the Hellenistic period. Sirach gives a prominent place to Aaron, with whom the priesthood was established, and Phineas, Aaron's grandson, renewed the priestly covenant through his demonstration of zeal for God:

> He exalted Aaron, the brother of Moses, a holy man like him, of the tribe of Levi. He made an everlasting covenant with him, and gave him the priesthood of the people. He blessed him with splendid vestments, and put a glorious robe upon him.... He added glory to Aaron and gave him a heritage....
>   Phineas the son of Eleazar is the third in glory (τρίτος εἰς δόξαν)... that he and his descendants should have the dignity of the priesthood for ever (Sir 45:6-7, 18-20, 23-24).

God invested Aaron with "glory," that is, with esteem and honor, and guaranteed Aaron's honor when he consumed Dathan, Abiram, and the company of Korah "in the wrath of his anger," a sign that God had taken their rebellion as an affront against God's own honor. Phineas, to whom the direction of the priesthood fell after Aaron, is ranked third in honor after Moses and Aaron, and his commitment to God confirmed for his descendants forever the honor of the offices of priests of God.

The author of Hebrews, however, introduces a new order of priest, namely the "order of Melchizedek." LXX Ps 109:4 announces the institution of a line of priests not from the tribe of Levi and the priestly line of Aaron and Phineas, but rather from the mysterious figure of Melchizedek. As an oracle of God, the psalm legitimates such a line of priests. The author of Hebrews uses it as an opening to read the story of Melchizedek's encounter with Abraham after the battle of the kings as a demonstration of the superiority of the order of Melchizedek over the order of Levi. Put succinctly, Abraham, the illustrious ancestor of Levi, acknowledges Melchizedek's greater dignity by giving him the tithe of the spoils and by receiving his blessing:

> See how great (πηλίκος) he is! Abraham the patriarch gave him a tithe of the spoils.... And those descendants of Levi who receive the priestly office have a commandment in the law to take tithes from the people, that is, from their brethren, though these also are descended from Abraham. But this man who has not their genealogy received tithes from Abraham and blessed him who had the promises. It is beyond dispute that the inferior is blessed by the superior (τὸ ἔλαττον ὑπὸ τοῦ κρείττονος εὐλογεῖται, 7:4-7).

Since Melchizedek tithed Levi, as it were, while he was still in the loins of his ancestor Abraham, Melchizedek's higher status has been proven. Jesus' order of priesthood has, therefore, a more distinguished founder than the Levitical order may claim.[32]

The author proceeds to contrast the strength of the Levitical Priesthood and the priest of the order of Melchizedek. The former, being mortal, "existed in great numbers, because they were prevented by death from continuing" (7:23) in the service of the priesthood. According to our author, only one priest of the order of Melchizedek is required, namely Jesus, who continues beyond the power of death. Jesus "abides forever, and holds his priesthood permanently" (7:24).[33] Jesus' priesthood is also founded upon a stronger and more reliable basis. Here the author adduces the prophecy of Jeremiah 31 (quoted in full in 8:8-12) concerning a promised new covenant which would supercede the old covenant, broken by the transgressions of Israel and Judah. This new covenant is based on the complete forgiveness of sins, something achieved by the priesthood of Jesus, but not through the priesthood instituted by Torah. The author charges both the Levitical priests and the Covenant upon which their priesthood rests with "weakness," that is, with being incapable of securing access to God and giving certain hope:[34]

> On the one hand, a former commandment is set aside because of its weakness and uselessness (ἀσθενὲς καὶ ἀνωφελές), for the law made

---

[32] Calvin (*Hebrews*, 79) sees very clearly that the author of Hebrews is primarily concerned about establishing the honor of the priestly order of Melchizedek: "The only cause that ought now to be considered, is that since the people offered tithes as a kind of sacred tribute to God, the Levites received them. Whence it appears that this was no small honour; because God in a manner appointed them in his own room. Therefore, in that Abraham, a most highly esteemed servant of God and a Prophet, gave tithes to Melchisedeck a priest, he confessed thereby that Melchisedeck excelled him in a degree of honour. But if the patriarch Abraham is held inferior in comparison of him, his dignity must be singular and transcendent. The appellation of patriarch was employed to enhance his honour: for it is in the highest degree honourable to Abraham to be called a father in the Church of God. The argument then is this: Abraham, who is more excellent than all the others, is yet inferior to Melchisedeck. Therefore Melchisedeck holds the highest place of honour, and is to be esteemed before all the sons of Levi."

[33] He holds his priesthood on the basis of "the power of an indestructible life" (7:16), a sign of great power regularly attributed to divinities and divinized heroes, cf. Quintilian *Inst.* 3.7.9: "Some again may be praised because they were born immortal, others because they won immortality by their valour."

[34] Cf. G. Stählin, "Ασθενής, etc." (*TDNT* 1:490-493; Grand Rapids: Eerdmans, 1964), 493, where the connotations of "impotence" and "incapacity" are developed.

nothing perfect; on the other hand, a better hope is introduced, through which we draw near to God (7:18-19).

Indeed, the law appoints men in their weakness (ἔχοντας ἀσθένειαν) as high priests, but the word of the oath, which came later than the law, appoints a Son who has been made perfect for ever (7:28).

Jesus' achievement of an "indestructible life" (7:16) makes him, in the eyes of the author, a more reliable and effective mediator: "he is able for all time to save those who draw near to God through him, since he always lives to make intercession for them" (7:25).

Finally, Jesus has the honor of serving in a greater and more distinguished sanctuary than the Levitical priests, who "serve a copy and shadow of the heavenly sanctuary (ὑποδείγματι καὶ σκιᾷ ... τῶν ἐπουρανίων)" made "according to the pattern (κατὰ τὸν τύπον)" which was shown to Moses on the mountain (8:5; cf. LXX Exod 25:40). Jesus, however, carries out his priestly activity in the "true tabernacle (τῆς σκηνῆς τῆς ἀληθινῆς), which the Lord pitched, not human beings" (8:2). The use of Exod 25:40 in Heb 8:5 affords "a happy opening by which the Platonic speculation enters our epistle."[35] The author of Hebrews places the historical, unfolding drama of redemption within the framework of Platonic dualism, here the notion that the earthly realities relate to the heavenly realities as shadow to object, as copy to original. The latter therefore manifest a "metaphysical" superiority. Williamson correctly observes that Jewish-Christian views of cosmology and God's redemptive activity in history intrude upon the static, unchanging notion of the ideal realm as found in Plato: "Plato's Ideal world is not a heaven that could be entered by Jesus; it can be penetrated only by the intellect."[36] Nevertheless, Jesus' resurrection is clearly interpreted as a translation from earthly realities to the heavenly types. From the abiding, heavenly realm, Jesus is now able to offer a superior service to his partners, who must continue on in the earthly realm.

The author therefore asserts throughout his discourse on the "better sacrifices" offered by Jesus that the Christians' high priest serves on their behalf in a "greater and more perfect tabernacle not made with hands (τῆς μείζονος καὶ τελειοτέρας σκηνῆς οὐ χειροποιήτου, 9:11; cf. 9:24)."[37]

---

[35] G. H. Gilbert, "The Greek Element in the Epistle to the Hebrews" (*AJT* 14 [1910] 521-32), 528.

[36] Williamson, "Platonism and Hebrews" (*SJT* 16 [1963] 415-24) 419.

[37] The rejection of the Jerusalem Temple as the exclusive residence of God, as well as the theme of the dwelling "not made with hands," are also found in Stephen's speech in Acts 7:48-50, which itself builds on Is 66:1-2. Both themes appear also in Paul's Areopagus speech in Acts 17:24-25.

These elements combine to depict Jesus as invested with "a more excellent ministry" than the Levitical priests exercise, "by as much as He is also the mediator of a better covenant, which has been enacted on better promises (ὅσῳ καὶ κρείττονός ἐστιν διαθήκης μεσίτης, ἥτις ἐπὶ κρείττοσιν ἐπαγγελίαις νενομοθέτηται., 8:6)." As a "Son made perfect forever (υἱὸν εἰς τὸν αἰῶνα τετελειωμένον, 7:28)," who "has taken his seat at the right hand of the throne of the Majesty in the heavens (ὃς ἐκάθισεν ἐν δεξιᾷ τοῦ θρόνου τῆς μεγαλωσύνης ἐν τοῖς οὐρανοῖς, 8:1)," Jesus enjoys a more exalted priesthood even than the Levitical priesthood. As the author goes on to demonstrate, Jesus alone succeeds where the many have failed.[38] Jesus, specifically in his office as priest after the order of Melchizedek (5:10), alone stands as the "source of eternal salvation" (5:9).[39] This argument provides a fine example of subcultural rhetoric -- the Levitical priesthood and its benefits, so central to Judaism, is surpassed in every way by the priesthood of Jesus and its benefits.

Jesus' honor as Son of God and as High Priest after the order of Melchizedek gives him a claim to the deepest respect and reverence. Before the court of God, his honor is acknowledged by the angels and symbolized in his session at the right hand of God, the seat of pre-eminence in the Jewish-Christian cosmos. It is none other than God who has conferred these honors upon Jesus, and so it is the duty of the just person to give to Jesus what is his due, lest he or she incur the indignation (νέμεσις) of the God who consumes the rebellious and disrespectful with the fire of his anger. The author stresses also, however, the benefits which may be enjoyed by those who continue in the course of action which honors the Son. Jesus' death, which was regarded as a disgrace by the unbelieving world (12:2), brought him the greatest honor, for it was his death that was the constitutive act of his priesthood -- the offering of

---

[38] This, too, marks Jesus out for special honor and renown, and the author's demonstration of this point follows precisely the instructions of Aristotle (*Rh.* 1.9.38) for the succesful encomium: "We must also employ many of the means of amplification; for instance, if a man has done anything alone, or first, or with a few, or has been chiefly responsible for it; all these circumstances render an action noble." Cf. also Quintilian, *Inst.* 7.16, who emphasizes the honor that springs from actions which are of benefit to others: "we must bear in mind the fact that what most pleases an audience is the celebration of deeds which our hero was the first or only man or at any rate one of the very few to perform...emphasizing what was done for the sake of others rather than what he performed on his own behalf."

[39] We have already seen in chapter four how this designation enhances Jesus' honor, following Aristotle, *Eth. Nic.* 1.12.8: "that which is the first principle and cause of things good we agree to be something honourable and divine (τὴν ἀρχὴν δὲ καὶ τὸ αἴτιον τῶν ἀγαθῶν τίμιόν τι καὶ θεῖον τίθεμεν)."

himself once-for-all (cf. 10:12, 14). Jesus' death became his initiation into the unique priesthood of Melichizedek, and that single sacrifice, the author claims, has an abiding effect. On the basis of that sacrifice, Jesus' priesthood brings access to the greatest of benefits for those who "draw near to God through him" (7:25).

2 The Son and Χάρις

The Mediterranean world of the first-century has been accurately described as a patronal society, in which the giving and receiving of benefactions was "the practice that constitutes the chief bond of human society" (Seneca *Ben.* 1.4.2). It is a description which continues to be applied to the Mediterranean societies of today, a testimony to the depth to which this practice was infused in those cultures.[40] This patronal society was supported by an infrastructure of networks of allegiance and favor, whether between equals (who called each other "friends," and for whom the dictum "friends possess all things in common" held true) or unequals (the patron-client relationship, where the language of friendship was, however, also commonly employed).[41] Saller observes that "precise evaluation and exact repayment of debt was rarely possible in the realm of day-to-day social favors."[42] The quotation from Seneca above supports his conclusion that it is precisely this imprecision in accountability that led these relationships to be ongoing, almost interminable. Mutual bonds of favor, and the accompanying bonds of indebtedness, provided the glue

---

[40] Cf. John Davis, *The People of the Mediterranean: An Essay in Comparative Social Anthropology* (London: Routledge & Kegan Paul, 1977), 146: "From the wholesale market in Athens to the desert of Western Cyrenaica, to the plains of southeastern Portugal, men take up postures of subordination in order to gain access to resources -- to market expertise, to water, to dried milk from welfare agencies. Submission to a patron is commoner and more widespread in the mediterranean than bureaucracy, or fascism, or communism, or any varieties of democracy: it can exist without any of them, and co-exists with all of them."

[41] R. P. Saller (*Imperial Patronage under the Early Empire* [Cambridge: Cambridge University, 1982], 8-11) notes the strong reluctance of writers (i.e., Seneca, Tacitus, Pliny the Younger, Suetonius, and Fronto) to designate themselves as *patrones* and their clients as *clientes*, preferring the ambiguous term *amici*, which did not draw attention to the socially inferior status of the client.

[42] Saller, *Patronage*, 16.

which maintained social cohesion.[43]   In such a society, gratitude would be an essential virtue, and ingratitude indeed the "cardinal social and political sin."[44]

An intimate bond existed between honor and patronage.   One main avenue for achieving honor in the Mediterranean world was through benefaction, a fact supported by the ability of φιλότιμος, meaning "love of honor" (hence, "ambition"), to mean also "generous."[45]   Danker's study of the benefactor is replete with inscriptions, notices of awards granted, and instructions for the public acclamation of those who have benefitted a collectivity such as a guild or city.   Dio's Rhodian Oration shows that honoring benefactors with statues in public places could fill a city with thousands of such honorary figures.   One's honor was likewise enhanced when one cultivated "a long train of client dependents."[46] Patrons gave access to goods, entertainment, and advancement.   One who received such a benefit accepted the obligation to "publicize the favor and his gratitude for it," thus contributing to the patron's reputation.[47]   The client also owed services to the patron, and could be called upon to perform most any task,[48] thus contributing to the patron's power base. A third figure in this network of patronage has been called the "broker," a term introduced into the discussion by Jeremy Boissevain: "Persons who dispense first-order resources [e.g., land, jobs, and the like] may be called patrons.   Those who dispense second-order resources [i.e., strategic contacts or access to patrons] are brokers."[49]   The term may seem modern, impersonal, and therefore inappropriate, but one must imagine the same personal relationship and duty between broker and client as between patron and client.   Indeed, the "broker" is not a third entity *sui generis*, but rather a "client to a patron and ... patron to a client."[50]   A broker

---

[43] Cf. J. D. Crossan's observation that "the web of patronage and clientage, with accounts that could never be exactly balanced because they could never be precisely computed, was the dynamic morality that held society together" (*The Historical Jesus: The Life of a Mediterranean Jewish Peasant* [San Francisco: Harper Collins, 1991] 65).

[44] Danker, *Benefactor*, 436.

[45] Danker, *Benefactor*, 328.

[46] B. Malina and R. Rohrbaugh, *Social-Science Commentary on the Synoptic Gospels* (Minneapolis: Fortress, 1992), 74.

[47] Saller, *Patronage*, 10.

[48] Malina and Rohrbaugh, *Commentary*, 74-75.

[49] J. Boissevain, *Friends of Friends: Networks, Manipulators and Coalitions* (New York: St. Martin's, 1974) 148.

[50] Crossan, *Jesus*, 60. Cf. also Davis, *People*, 134: "Characteristically, men are clients to those above them, while at the same time they patronise their inferiors."

may also simply be a friend of a similarly influential and well-endowed individual to whom he recommends a client.

The institution of brokerage, far from being a modern imposition on patronal society, is exceedingly well documented in the letters of Pliny the Younger, Cicero, and Fronto.[51]   Brokerage is an expectation among public figures.   Sophocles (*Oedipus Tyrannus* 771-774) provides a fine literary example of this in Creon's defense against Oedipus' charge of conspiracy to usurp the kingship:

> I am welcome everywhere; every man salutes me,
> And those who want your favor seek my ear,
> Since I know how to manage what they ask.

Creon enjoys the salutation of a patron, but his chief benefaction is access to Oedipus and favor from the king.   Many of Pliny's letters to Trajan document the former's attempts to gain imperial *beneficia* for his own friends and clients.   Particularly informative is *Ep.* 10.4, in which Pliny seeks from Trajan the grant of senatorial office for Voconius Romanus.[52] He addresses Trajan clearly as a client addressing his patron, and proceeds to ask a favor for Romanus.   Pliny's character is offered as a guarantee of his client's character, and Trajan's assessment of the second-hand client is inseparable from his assessment of Pliny -- indeed, Trajan's "favorable judgement" of Pliny (not Romanus) is the basis for Trajan's granting of this favor.[53]   Pliny's repeated attempts (*Ep.* 10.5-7, 10) to gain from Trajan a grant of Roman citizenship for his masseur, Harpocras, outlines a similar structure of relationships, wherein Pliny affords Harpocras access to the emperor, the fount of patronage, which he would never have enjoyed otherwise.

The correspondence of Fronto and Marcus Aurelius also abounds with examples of brokering by both parties.   In *Ad Marcam Caesarem* 3.2, the young Aurelius Caesar seeks favor for his friend Herodes Atticus from Fronto, before whom Atticus is shortly scheduled to appear in a legal case. What is particularly interesting to note in these letters is the way that indebtedness remains within each patron-client (or "friend-to-friend")

---

[51] G. E. M. de Ste. Croix, "Suffragium: From Vote to Patronage" (*British Journal of Sociology* 5 [1954] 33-48), 40.

[52] B. Levick, *The Government of the Roman Empire: A Sourcebook* (London: Croom Helm, 1985), 141.

[53] Such considerations in the patron-client exchange have an obvious corollary in the church's Christology and soteriology, wherein God, the Patron, regards Christ's clients (i.e., the Christians) not as their lives merit, but according to the merit of Christ.

relationship. Atticus will be indebted to Marcus, who in turn will be indebted to Fronto; similarly, in our earlier example, Voconius will be indebted to Pliny, who will, in turn, be indebted further to Trajan.[54] The broker, or mediator, at the same time incurs a debt and increases his own honor through the indebtedness of his or her client.

Brokerage occurs also between friends and associates in private life. In Paul's letter to Philemon, the apostle seeks to gain forgiveness for Onesimus, appealing to his convert on the basis of friendship: "So if you consider me your partner (κοινωνόν), welcome him as you would welcome me" (17). Philemon provides Paul with hospitality (22) and most likely financial patronage. Certainly he has provided such support for other believers (7). The householder who owns slaves and can provide generous support and the itinerant apostle are not social equals. Nevertheless, Paul regards such support as a due return for Paul's spiritual patronage, such that he may claim that Philemon's debt extends to his very soul (19). There is a sort of balance between their mutual benefactions typical of "friends" or "partners."[55] In asking a benefit for Onesimus, he is also asking a benefit for himself, and so uses the language of appealing for a benefit in v. 20: "Yes, brother, I would have this benefaction (ὀναίμην) from you in the Lord!" Paul would indeed find it beneficial to gain Philemon's permission to have Onesimus return to him and assist him; in all brokering activity, however, a favor done for someone else's client at the broker's request remains a favor also done for that broker.

Given the prevalence of the system of patronage in the Mediterranean world, it is logical that Jesus would be regarded as the patron of the Christian community. This is another expression of a wider tendency to conceptualize human-divine relationships by means of the language of patronage, seen, for example, in traditional Roman religion and in the

---

[54] Cf. also Saller, *Patronage*, 75, n.194: "That the mediators would have received the credit and gratitude from the ultimate recipient of the favor is clear from the last sentence of Pliny, *Ep.* 3.8, where Pliny secures a tribunate for Suetonius who passes it on to a relative, with the result that the relative is indebted to Suetonius who is in turn indebted to Pliny."

[55] The variety of benefits provided by the different partners in such a relationship made it impossible to calculate the debts or say when the debts had been mutually fully paid. Thus Crossan (*Jesus*, 61) observes: "The give-and-take of reciprocal and alternating indebtedness between social equals in which neither party could ever really be 'paid up' because any precise or exact computation of the 'balance sheet' was quite impossible supplied the moral cement for the edifice of patronal society." For the prominence of friendship *topoi* in the New Testament, see Luke T. Johnson, *Sharing Possessions: Mandate and Symbol of Faith* (Philadelphia: Fortress, 1981); *The Function of Possessions in Luke-Acts* (SBLDS 39; Missoula, MT: Scholars, 1977), 2-5, 32-36.

adoption of "patron deities" by individuals and collectives (e.g., guilds or cities).[56] The exalted status enjoyed by Jesus, which the author develops at such great length and detail, carries the promise of great benefaction and advantage for those who make themselves clients of the Son. The author's language emphasizes the patronal role of Jesus: he "helps (ἐπιλαμβάνεται) the descendents of Abraham" (2:16) and comes "to the aid (βοηθῆσαι) of those who are tempted" (2:18). He is thus the one to whom Christians are to look to supply what is wanting in their own resources. Christians, indeed, have been brought into his household (3:6), thus under the protection and provision of God through the Son.

BENEFITS PRESENTLY AFFORDED

The author speaks of Christ's death in terms of the numerous benefits this selfless act brings to those committed to Jesus, a fact which also develops the honor of Jesus.[57] As explored above, Christ's death became a tasting of death "on behalf of all (ὑπὲρ παντὸς)" by God's favor (χάριτι θεοῦ, 2:9). The shameful death on the cross (12:2) became the channel of God's beneficence, and a victory over the "one who held the power of death" delivered "those who through fear of death were subject to slavery all their lives" (2:14-15). The benefit most emphasized by the author of Hebrews, however, derives from Jesus' appointment as "high priest after the order of Melchizedek," through which consecration to priestly office "he became to all who obey him the source of eternal salvation" (5:9). This consecration, indeed, was Jesus' willingness to suffer pain and disgrace in obedience to God's will (10:12-18), whereby the tears and groans of the cross (5:7-8) became the path to honor and the source of Jesus' competence as patron for the community of faith (5:9). Jesus' chief gift is that he affords access to God. He is the broker, or mediator (μεσίτης, 8:6; 9:15;12:24), who secures favor from God on behalf of those who have committed themselves to Jesus as client dependents.[58]

---

[56] Cf. Saller, *Patronage*, 23.

[57] Cf. *Rhet. Her.* 3.7.14, in which an element of the encomium is to answer the question, "If he is dead, what sort of death did he die, and what sort of consequences followed upon it?" Giving one's life to secure benefits for others led to a most honored remembrance, as for the soldiers praised in Pericles' Funeral Oration.

[58] The basic meaning of μεσίτης as "one who establishes a relation which would not otherwise exist" (A. Oepke, "μεσίτης," *TDNT* 4.601) demonstrates the suitability of this term as a Greek equivalent of what Boissevain called a "broker" in patron-client relations.

Jesus provides the second-order resource of access to God as μισθαποδότης, "rewarder," allowing his clients, formerly separated from God by their sins, to approach God as their Patron rather than as the Judge of those who have affronted God through disobedience (cf. 10:30-31). Access to God as Patron and protector was a familiar *topos* of philosophical literature. Epictetus (*Diss.* 4.1.91-98), for example, speaks of the search for the best patron under whose aegis to travel through life - - one who could provide security against all assaults and in whom one could rely utterly not only for today but also tomorrow. His search leads finally and only to God: "Thus [the searcher] reflects and comes to the thought that, if he attach himself to God, he will pass through the world in safety."[59] Christianity, to use the expression of Barbara Levick, "gave access ... through an incorruptible intermediary, to a reliable authority, an important offering indeed in a patronal society.[60]

The author of Hebrews stresses that the benefit of such access to God cannot be attained through the mediation (brokerage) of the Levitical Priesthood, which is, within the biblical tradition, the only rival claimant of the ability to broker access to God. The author therefore increases the value of Christ's mediation by showing the limitations and ineffectiveness of the only alternative sanctioned by Scripture. The warrant for a new order of priest, after the order of Melichizedek rather than of Levi (Ps 110:4), indicates to the author that the Levitical priests could not fulfill their claim to provide access to God: "For if perfection were possible through the Levitical priesthood, ... what further need would there be for another priest to arise after the order of Melchizedek (7:11)?" The perfection required to come into the presence of God, is the perfection of the conscience of the worshiper -- a perfection the Levitical priests were not capable of providing (9:9). Both the Levitical sacrifices and Jesus' offering of himself have to do with providing satisfaction to God for the transgressions of God's commands (hence, affronts to God's honor and authority). The conscience (συνείδησις) becomes that which bears an "internal witness" to the fact that "defilement extends to the heart and mind."[61] An imperfect conscience, mindful of the affronts given to God, cannot stand before God in expectation of a benefit, but only in expectation of judgement and wrath. "Perfection" of conscience entails a decisive

---

[59] Cited in Levick, *Sourcebook*, 151.

[60] Levick, *Sourcebook*, 151.

[61] Lane, *Hebrews 9-13*, 225.

purgation of sins, such that the breach in the divine-human relationship is sealed and the possibility of favor restored.[62]

The annual offering for sin on the Day of Atonement, therefore, represents for the author not a decisive purging, but an admission that "the blood of bulls and goats" cannot take away sins (10:4). The very repetition of such sacrifices becomes proof of their inefficacy:

> The law ... can never, by the same sacrifices which are continually offered year after year, make perfect those who draw near. Otherwise, would they not have ceased to be offered? If the worshipers had once been cleansed, they would no longer have any consciousness of sin. But in these sacrifices there is a reminder of sin year after year (10:1-3).

Rather than removing the obstacle which stands in the way of the formation of a benefactor-client relationship with God, these sacrfices call attention to the obstacle, providing only a reminder (ἀνάμνησις) of sins.

The institutional form of the Levitical priesthood also hinders rather than secures the desired access to God. Describing the tabernacle's furnishings, the author writes (9:6-9):

> These preparations having thus been made, the priests go continually into the outer tent, performing their ritual duties; but into the second only the high priest goes, and he but once a year, and not without taking blood which he offers for himself and for the errors of the people. By this the Holy Spirit indicates that the way into the sanctuary is not yet opened as long as the outer tent is still standing (which is symbolic for the present age).

Access to God is strictly limited under these arrangements both in terms of personnel and frequency. Only the high priest may enter the inner sanctuary, and that only once a year. The priests busy with their duties in the outer tent (which would include receiving offerings from the people for the tabernacle and its priests) are viewed as a sort of impediment to unrestricted access to the sanctuary. Only with the removal of this system is the way into the sanctuary opened. Thus the Levitical priesthood provides only a "shadow of the good things to come" (10:1).

The author's purpose for dwelling on the failure of the Levitical priests is to exalt Christ's success, and to stress the uniqueness of the benefit made available by him to those committing themselves to him. Hence he underscores also the folly of relinquishing such an irreplaceable yet necessary gift by not continuing in loyalty and gratitude towards Christ.

---

[62] Lane, *Hebrews 9-13*, 224.

As Attridge comments, the author's "basic interest is to establish the significance of Christ for the present and future of his addressees by indicating the superiority of the Son to any other agent of God's purposes."[63] Christ alone is the effective broker of access to God as Benefactor. After Christ's death, there is the "introduction of a better hope through which we draw near to God," which necessitates the "setting aside of the former commandment because of weakness and uselessness" (7:18-19). This gives Jesus a claim to the greatest honor, gratitude, and loyalty. Before Christ's ministry, one only had recourse to the ineffective priests established by the Law; now after his death there is the possibility of unrestricted access to God following the perfection of the worshippers who draw near through Christ.[64] The "second order resource" of direct access to God would have been especially valued in a patronal culture where "face-to-face contact" with the patron was of special importance, giving one a greater hope of making a successful suit.[65]

Jesus makes this available through his superior priestly mediation, or brokerage, in matters divine. The author claims that Jesus has made the necessary purification for sins. Through the "sacrifice of himself" Jesus has decisively "put away sin" (9:26) and "obtained eternal redemption" (9:12; cf. also 1:3 and 2:17). Jesus' sacrifice, offered once for all (10:12), provides the cleansing of the conscience of the worshippers required, such that they might have confidence before God and assurance of divine favor:

> For if the sprinkling of defiled persons with the blood of goats and bulls and with the ashes of a heifer sanctifies for the purification of the flesh, how much more shall the blood of Christ, who through the eternal Spirit offered himself without blemish to God, purify your conscience from dead works to serve the living God (9:14).

Again, this perfection indicates the removal of sin. The author himself explicates his claim that "by a single offering he has perfected for all time

---

[63] Attridge, *Hebrews*, 55.

[64] The author of Hebrews has thus provided yet another component of the encomium in his discussion of Jesus' ministry, as Quintilian (*Inst.* 3.7.10) prescribes: "There is a greater variety required in the praise of men. In the first place there is a distinction to be made as regards time between the period in which the objects of our praise lived and the time preceding their birth; and further, in the case of the dead, we must also distinguish the period following their death." This "before and after" aspect is forcefully expressed in such passages as 7:18-19 and 11:39-40: "And all these, though well attested by their faith, did not receive what was promised, since God had foreseen something better for us, that apart from us they should not be made perfect."

[65] Saller, *Patronage*, 61.

those who are sanctified" (10:14) by referring to the promise in Jeremiah 31 that "their sins and their lawless deeds I will remember no more" (10:17). This proves for the author that Jesus' sacrifice has effected the final purgation of sins which leaves neither remembrance of sins (before God or in the conscience of the worshipper) nor the need for any further offering for sin. Only those who have been "perfected" stand beyond the need for future sacrifices. In Wisd 4:10-13, τελειωθείς ("having been perfected" 4:13) appears to be functionally equivalent to, and defined by, εὐάρεστος θεῷ γενόμενος ("having become pleasing to God," 4:10). Similarly, Jesus' sacrifice restores favor to the relationship of God and human beings, who now may stand before God as pleasing to God, and hence may stand in expectation of God's patronage.

Jesus has, through the veil of his flesh (10:20), entered the Heavenly Sanctuary to stand perpetually before God. According to the author of Hebrews, he has gone in before God as mediator on our behalf, and thus encounters the worshippers as broker of God's benefactions. "For Christ has entered, not into a sanctuary made with hands, a copy of the true one, but into heaven itself, now to appear in the presence of God on our behalf" (9:24). Jesus' offering of himself makes him the "mediator of a new covenant" (9:15), who fills this role precisely "in order that those who have been called may receive the promise of the eternal inheritance, since a death has occurred which redeems them from the transgressions under the first covenant" (9:15). The "promise" is a key term encapsulating the manifold benefactions gained through Jesus' brokerage (mediation).

Jesus does not, like the Levitical high priest, enter the Sanctuary only once annually, but rather stands there continually, having passed into the true Sanctuary of heaven. Further, he does not enter there on behalf of his clients who wait outside without access to God. Rather, Jesus' passage into the Heavenly Sanctuary opens up the way for believers to know and approach God as Benefactor and Patron.[66] Jesus has entered "as a forerunner for us" (6:20), as the author envisions the consummation of the Christian pilgrimage to be their entrance into the rest of the city of God in their heavenly homeland (11:14; 13:14). Such final access, however, follows upon the access which can be enjoyed now in this life:

> Since then we have a great high priest who has passed through the heavens, Jesus, the Son of God, let us hold fast our confession. For we have not a high priest who is unable to sympathize with our weaknesses,

---

[66] Cf. Danker, *Benefactor*, 319. Discussing Luke 18:18-30, Danker writes: "To know God is to recognize him as the Chief Benefactor, who will bestow 'treasure in heaven' on those who share their treasure on earth."

but one who in every respect has been tempted as we are, yet without sin. Let us then with confidence draw near to the throne of grace (τῷ θρόνῳ τῆς χάριτος), that we may receive mercy and find grace to help in time of need (ἵνα λάβωμεν ἔλεος καὶ χάριν εὕρωμεν εἰς εὔκαιρον βοήθειαν, 4:14-16).

Therefore, brethren, since we have confidence to enter the sanctuary by the blood of Jesus, by the new and living way which he opened for us through the curtain, that is, through his flesh, and since we have a great priest over the house of God, let us draw near with a true heart in full assurance of faith, with our hearts sprinkled clean from an evil conscience and our bodies washed with pure water (10:19-22).

The mediation of Jesus allows Jesus' followers to draw near to God, specifically looking to God as their benefactor.

A term of central importance for discourse about patronage is χάρις, equivalent to the Latin *gratia*, which covers a comparable range of meaning.[67] This term dominates an important transitional section of Hebrews, namely 4:14-16.[68] Heb 4:16 twice employs the noun χάρις, once to describe the "throne" (referring by metonymy to the One seated upon the throne), once to describe the expected result of such an approach. Usually translated as "grace," this word stands within the social-semantic field of patronage and clientage. Aristotle, for example, defines χάρις as "the feeling in accordance with which one who has it is said to render a service to one who needs it, not in return for something nor in the interest of him who renders it, but in that of the recipient" (*Rh.* 2.7.2). The word was, however, multivalent. In this passage from Aristotle, it refers to the act of conferring a benefit. It may also be used to refer to the proper return for a benefit, namely gratitude, as in Dio *Or.* 31.37:

For what is more sacred than honour or gratitude? (τί γάρ ἐστιν ἱερώτερον τιμῆς ἢ χάριτος;) Do you not know that the majority of men regard the Graces as goddesses? Therefore, if anyone mutilates their statues or overturns their altars, you hold this man guilty of impiety; but if injury or ruin is done to that very *grace* (χάρις) from which these goddesses have derived their name (Χάριτες) by anyone's performing a *gracious* act in a way that is not right, but in an ignoble, illiberal, and crafty manner showing rank ingratitude (ἀχαριστῶν) to his benefactors,

---

[67] Cf. Saller, *Patronage*, 21.

[68] The structural importance of this passage as both conclusion to the previous argument and introduction to the central argument has been carefully demonstrated by G. H. Guthrie in his published dissertation, *The Structure of Hebrews: A Text-Linguistic Analysis* (Leiden: E. J. Brill, 1994) 79-82, 103, 144.

can we say that such a man has sense and is more intelligent than his
fellows?

Finally, it may refer to the actual gift or benefit conferred, as in 2 Cor
8:19 where Paul speaks of the "generous gift" he is administering (i.e., the
collection for the church in Jerusalem). The claim of Malina and
Rohrbaugh that, "in the New Testament, the language of grace is the
language of patronage,"[69] is a quite welcome observation, placing the
nebulous and indefinite term "grace" into a definite social and lexical
province of meaning.[70]

Jesus' gift of access to God affords the community access to resources
for endurance in faith so that they may receive the benefactions promised
for the future, to be awarded before God's court at the end of the age.
The believers may draw near to God and expect to "receive mercy and find
favor" -- that is, the disposition of God to give assistance -- "to help in
time of need" (4:16). Such access would be expected to engender
confidence in the believers, giving them a hopeful orientation toward the
world. Aristotle (*Rh.* 2.5.16) again provides a definition: "Confidence
($\theta\alpha\rho\rho\epsilon\hat{\iota}\nu$) is the contrary of fear and that which gives confidence of that
which causes fear, so that the hope of what is salutary is accompanied by
an impression that it is quite near at hand, while the things to be feared are
either non-existent or far off." Through Jesus, the believers are brought
into the presence of God, near to One who has the will and power to
provide help.[71] Thus the believer has become a client of God, and may
say with the Psalmist:

> The Lord is my light and my salvation; whom shall I fear? The Lord
> is the stronghold of my life; of whom shall I be afraid? ... Though a
> host encamp against me, my heart shall not fear; though war arise
> against me, yet I will be confident (Ps 26:1, 3).

In emphasizing this benefit won by Christ for his clients, the author has
moved into the topic of Security, according to the author of the *Rhetorica
ad Herennium* the other component of "advantage" and goal of deliberative

---

[69] Malina and Rohrbaugh, *Commentary*, 75.

[70] Cf. also Danker, *Benefactor*, 437-38 on 2 Corinthians 8; also 451 on Gal 2:21.
Luke T. Johnson has reaped similar benefits in his culturally sensitive interpretation of
"grace" language in Luke-Acts (see, for example, *The Acts of the Apostles* [Sacra
Pagina; Collegeville, MN: Liturgical Press, 1992], 204 and *passim*).

[71] Cf. Aristotle *Rh.* 2.5.17: People may be made to feel confident "if remedies are
possible, if there are means of help, either great or numerous, or both."

oratory (together with honor).[72]   Their allegiance to Christ gives them access to the resources which will help them in the face of the exigencies of their life as Christians in society.

The relationship of human beings with their God thus takes a decisive turn in the ministry of Jesus. Under the Old Covenant and its ineffective brokers of divine favor, the people stand in fear of God, and cannot approach to stand in God's presence. Under the New Covenant, of which Christ is the Mediator, the believers find not fear but confidence to approach boldly, encouraged by the angels and souls of the righteous praising the Benefactor:

> For you have not come to what may be touched, a blazing fire, and darkness, and gloom, and a tempest, and the sound of a trumpet, and a voice whose words made the hearers entreat that no further messages be spoken to them. For they could not endure the order that was given, "If even a beast touches the mountain, it shall be stoned." Indeed, so terrifying was the sight that Moses said, "I tremble with fear." But you have come to Mount Zion and to the city of the living God, the heavenly Jerusalem, and to innumerable angels in festal gathering, and to the assembly of the first-born who are enrolled in heaven, and to a judge who is God of all, and to the spirits of just men made perfect, and to Jesus, the mediator of a new covenant (διαθήκης νέας μεσίτη), and to the sprinkled blood that speaks more graciously than the blood of Abel (12:18-24).

Apart from Jesus, there is no such access to χάρις, so that the hearers are powerfully motivated to remain loyal to their Patron in order to retain the benefits of his brokerage. Schweizer's striking statement thus appears to have considerable merit: "the sacrifice on the cross opens to the new High Priest the way to heaven. Strictly speaking the cross is therefore not the saving event itself, but the act that makes the saving event possible."[73] The cross represents the sacrifice offered by the Mediator of the New Covenant, which is a part of the larger picture of Christ as priest, where Jesus' saving power is most clearly located for the author of Hebrews.

---

[72] *Rhet. Her.* 3.2.3: "Advantage in political deliberation has two aspects: Security and Honour (*tutam, honestam*). To consider Security is to provide some plan or other for ensuring the avoidance of a present or imminent danger."

[73] Schweizer, *Lordship*, 72.

Excursus: Jesus' Sonship and Brokerage

The emphasis placed by the author of Hebrews on Jesus' "Sonship" also has important implications for Jesus' efficacy as a mediator of God's *beneficia*. In his attempt to discover "who possessed *gratia*" in the Roman imperial world -- that is, who was in a position to provide access to imperial *beneficia*, Saller points first to the imperial household: "When sons and grandsons existed, they *and their friends* were always natural candidates for the emperor's beneficence."[74] The close relatives of the emperor, especially his sons, were sought after as mediators of the emperor's favor: their close, familial relationship to the patron of the empire gave great hope of success. Saller points to the "two *commendationes* which Fronto sent to Marcus, requesting help in securing *beneficia* from [Antoninus] Pius for clients" (i.e., *Ad M. Caes.* 5.34, 37).[75] He concludes that "proximity (physical and emotional) was a critical factor in determining the channels through which imperial *beneficia* flowed."[76] Thus when the author of Hebrews presents Jesus as "Son" in 1:2, and constructs his comparison of Jesus with the angels in 1:4-14, his aim appears to be to emphasize the greater proximity of Jesus to God as mediator of divine favor. The angels, also familiar to the first-century Judeans and Christians as mediator figures, are strictly a second order of brokers when compared to the Son.

G. E. M. de Ste. Croix notes that any member of a great person's extended household could serve as a broker of that great person's favor. The list includes "his friends, who had the ear of the great man; their friends, even, at only one further remove; even the personal slaves of the great man, who often, for the humble client, could procure or withhold audience with the patron -- all these satellites shone with various degrees of reflected glory and were well worth courting."[77] Throughout Hebrews, one finds members of God's extended household at various degrees of remove, contrasted with Jesus, the Son. The angels are God's servants who are sent out to serve God's clients (i.e., "those who are about to inherit salvation," 1:14); Moses is a faithful, and hence trusted, servant in God's house (3:2). As a valued servant in the household, Moses would provide a certain level of access to the Patron of the house, namely God. The author stresses, however, that the believers have gained the Son as

---

[74] Saller, *Patronage*, 59 (emphasis mine).

[75] Saller, *Patronage*, 59.

[76] Saller, *Patronage*, 63.

[77] de Ste. Croix, "Suffragium," 41.

their patron and broker of God's favor: their access to favor is assured by the mediation of the one who stands in such close proximity to God that he bears "the reflected radiance of God's glory" (1:3). The author makes clear that Jesus' glory outshines that of the angels (1:5) and of Moses (3:3) on account of Jesus' closer proximity (i.e., relationship) to God, and hence Jesus provides greater surety of success in his brokerage.[78]

BENEFITS PROMISED FOR THE FUTURE

Access to God is a benefit enjoyed in the present, but also one pregnant with hope for the future. Jesus' death inaugurated the New Covenant, the goal of which is to bring "those who have been called" to that which is included in the "promise of an eternal inheritance" (9:14). The author speaks of the believers as "sons and daughters" (12:5-8; 2:10), who have, as such, the hope of inheritance. People who exhibit faith and perseverance "inherit the promises" (6:12); similarly, the author assures the "heirs of the promise" of the certainty of their hope (6:17). This inheritance is described succinctly as "salvation" (σωτηρία) in 1:14, and as the "reward" (μισθαποδοσία) in 10:35. The author fills out the content of this benefit with a number of images, all rather vague but nonetheless promising.

First, the believers have the promise of honor and the possession of that which inspires respect, as Jesus leads the "many sons to glory (πολλοὺς υἱοὺς εἰς δόξαν ἀγαγόντα)" (2:10). Hurst argues strongly for a link between "the extravagance of chapter one" and "the glory of mankind foretold in Psalm 8 and explored in chapter two."[79] The glory with which Jesus has been invested will be shared with all those who have remained "partners of Christ (μέτοχοι τοῦ Χριστοῦ, 3:14)" to the end. The author of Hebrews here introduces a familiar *topos* from Greco-Roman discussions of friendship. "Friends" hold possessions in common, and thus have fellowship (κοινωνία): although friends will not actually establish a

---

[78] T. H. Olbricht ("Hebrews as Amplification," 379) has recently suggested, based on a comparison with Isocrates' *Evagoras*, that the author's comparison of Jesus with the angels serves to highlight his "descent" (as a standard subheading of *encomia*) from a superior rather than an inferior divine being. While intriguing, this hypothesis does not capture the force of the declaration of Jesus as Son in a patronal culture, and also stands against the author's clear intention in every other comparison to show that Jesus' mediation is superior to the mediation provided by the Law, given by Moses (through angels), or the Temple priesthood.

[79] Hurst, "Christology," 163.

community of shared goods, they will place their goods at the service and disposal of one another.[80] As Christ's friends, the believers have access to the goods and services Christ can provide, notably to his mediation for God's favor; they likewise have the hope of sharing in Christ's inheritance when they, too, enter the heavenly realm where Christ "entered as a forerunner" (6:20). That is, the believers, as partners with Christ, have the hope of a share in Christ's honor, expressed as δόξα in 2:10. The believers will also receive the "better and lasting possessions" (10:34) for which they willingly allowed their worldly possessions to be taken from them, and to which their faith gives them a "title-deed."[81]

These possessions may be understood in light of the promise to the Wilderness Generation, that they would take possesion of the land of Canaan, or to Abraham, that his descendents would possess the land to which God had led him. Thus a more frequent image of the future benefit is that of a place which one may hold as his or her possession. The believers are presented with the promise of "rest" (κατάπαυσις), which still remains open since the orignal promisees did not attain God's goal for them (4:8-9). Those who persist in obedience (4:11) and who remain steadfast in faith (4:3) will enter that "rest," which *BAGD* suggests ought to be taken as an abstract term for a "concrete place of rest," i.e., the heavenly homeland (cf. 11:16). Those who have lost, or never attained, enfranchisement in civic rights are promised a "city" which God has

---

[80] Cf. Johnson, *Sharing Possessions*, 117-132 for an excellent discussion of the development of this ideal through the primary sources. Cf. also L. T. Johnson, "Friendship with the World/Friendship with God: A Study of Discipleship in James," *Discipleship in the New Testament* (ed. F. F. Segovia; Philadelphia: Fortress, 1985), 173 (and notes). Aristotle (*Eth. Nic.* 8-9) provides a helpful overview of friendship in the ancient world.

[81] D. R. Worley, Jr. (*God's Faithfulness to Promise: The Hortatory Use of Commissive Language in Hebrews* [Ph.D. diss., Yale University, 1981]) argues that the definition of "faith" in 11:1 answers directly to the believers' loss of property in 10:34 as a result of their loyalty to Christ and the Christian group. He cites (*Faithfulness*, 87) papyri where ὑπόστασις is roughly equal to ὑπαρξις (e.g., POxy II 237 p.176, in which ὑπόστασις appears to mean a property statement or title deed). He suggests (*Faithfulness*, 90-91) that the author of Hebrews may use ὑπόστασις in the sense of title deed in 11:1, linking his discussion of faith with 10:32-36 and the Christians' loss of property (and therefore abuse of their ὑποστάσεις -- title deeds). Based on the even wider occurrence of ὑπόστασις in papyri as a "bid," Worley favors this translation for "faith" in 11:1, yielding the following sense: "'Your property was confiscated. It went for the highest bid (ὑπόστασις). But remember that you have claim to a far better possession. Faith is your bid which guarantees your claim to the things you hope for'" (*Faithfulness*, 92).

prepared for God's clients (11:10, 16) -- a city of greater prestige and
security than any earthly city (13:14; 11:10), as it has been founded from
the abiding realm.   Finally, this future gift is called "an unshakeable
kingdom ($\beta\alpha\sigma\iota\lambda\epsilon\acute{\iota}\alpha\nu$ $\dot{\alpha}\sigma\acute{\alpha}\lambda\epsilon\upsilon\tau o\nu$, 12:28)," in which the believers will come
into the full inheritance of the children of God. This promised possession
is thus a share in the heavenly, abiding realm, which Jesus has entered as
a forerunner; as the realm of the eternal God, it has a greater value than
the imperfect, changeable earthly realm.[82]

The author assures the community that these promises are reliable on
three grounds. The first is the justice of God: "For God is not so unjust
as to overlook your work and the love which you showed for his sake in
serving the saints, as you still do" (6:10). Insofar as the believers have
followed God's commands with regard to caring for their brothers and
sisters, they may be assured of God's continued favor and hence of the
certainty that God will bring them to the promised reward. The second
assurance involves the honor of God in the oath sworn to Abraham, but
extending also to "the heirs of the promise" (6:17):

> For when God made a promise to Abraham, since he had no one greater
> by whom to swear, he swore by himself, saying, "Surely I will bless you
> and multiply you."   And thus Abraham, having patiently endured,
> obtained the promise. Men indeed swear by a greater than themselves,
> and in all their disputes an oath is final for confirmation. So when God
> desired to show more convincingly to the heirs of the promise the
> unchangeable character of his purpose, he interposed with an oath, so
> that through two unchangeable things, in which it is impossible that God
> should prove false, we who have fled for refuge might have strong
> encouragement to seize the hope set before us (6:13-18).

Pitt-Rivers explains how in disputes between persons an oath might be
"final for confirmation."   An oath "commits the honour of the
swearer...and aims to eliminate the ambiguity as to his true intentions. By
invoking that which is sacred to him ... he activates an implicit curse
against himself in the eventuality of his failure to implement his oath or,
at least, he assures that public opinion is entitled to judge him
dishonoured."[83] The reception of the promised benefaction by the faithful
is thus assured by the inestimable honor of God's own Self. The third
assurance is the succesful mediation of Jesus as high priest, already
explored in detail (cf. 6:18-19; 9:14).

---

[82] Again, the designation of these realms as the heavenly and earthly belongs to the
Jewish appropriation of Platonic categories. Cf. Johnson, *Writings*, 421.

[83] Pitt-Rivers, "Honour and Social Status," 34.

These benefits pertain directly to the believers' hope for their own honor in God's court, which will outshine the honor and renown they have sacrificed before the world's court for the sake of the "salvation" announced and procured by the Son (1:2; 2:3). They will be fully compensated for the possessions which they lost in the world, the loss of which brought also loss of status in society. In the beneficence of God, they will receive the "better and lasting possessions," and enjoy a place of rest in the city of God, together with the "glory" of the children of God. They have only to persevere until Christ's return, when he will come a second time not to deal with sin (as he had done previously), but to usher in the promised salvation (9:28).

RESPONSE

Since Jesus Christ gains for his clients what no other broker can -- not even the Levitical Priesthood with its noble ancestors and Scriptural legitimation -- one must necessarily make a proper response toward this Benefactor, and to the Divine Patron whose favor Jesus secures. This entails the demonstration of respect for the Benefactor, and acting in such a way as to enhance his honor. Certainly it implies avoiding any course of action which would bring him into dishonor, which would lead to the clients' exchanging favor for wrath, χάρις for ὀργή.[84]

Honor from those benefitted was the return expected for patronage. Danker, for example, cites a letter of Gnaeus Arrius Cornelius Proculus stating that "generous people are deserving of honor," and this was the majority opinion.[85] Aristotle (*Eth. Nic.* 8.14.2) speaks of the mutual obligations in an alliance between patron and client:

> Both parties should receive a larger share from the friendship, but not a larger share of the same thing: the superior should receive the larger share of honour, the needy one the larger share of profit; for honour is the due reward of virtue and beneficence (τῆς μὲν γὰρ ἀρετῆς καὶ τῆς εὐεργεσίας ἡ τιμὴ γέρας), while need obtains the aid it requires in pecuniary gain.

---

[84] This expression is taken from Clement of Alexandria's *Exhortatio* 9 (*ANF* 2:196; Migne, *PG* 8.196 C 3): "Look to the threatening! Look to the exhortation! Look to the punishment! Why, then, should we any longer change grace into wrath (τὶ δὴ οὖν ἔτι τὴν χάριν εἰς ὀργὴν μεταλλάσσομεν;), and not receive the word with open ears, and entertain God as a guest in pure spirits? For great is the grace of His promise, 'if to-day we hear His voice'."

[85] Danker, *Benefactor*, 436.

Friends exchanged reciprocal services, and such people enjoyed a mutual sense of partnership; between those who were not, the one party would enjoy the benefit, the other the "prestige" which came from "the ability to confer services which were highly valued and could not be remunerated."[86] The client was placed "in the very undesirable position of a debtor: and this feeling was worked off freely by showing respect for the benefactor." The client was expected to return this gift of honor not only in his or her own demeanor and actions, but in public testimony to the benefactor:

> The greater the favour, the more earnestly must we express ourselves, resorting to such compliments as: ... "I shall never be able to repay you my gratitude, but, at any rate, I shall not cease from declaring everywhere that I am unable to repay it" (Seneca, *Ben.* 2.24.2).

> Let us show how grateful we are for the blessing that has come to us by pouring forth our feelings, and let us bear witness to them (*testemur*), not merely in the hearing of the giver, but everywhere (Seneca, *Ben.* 2.22.1).

The author of Ephesians reflects this expectation in an exuberant exordium. The end result of God's provision in Christ is "the praise of the renown of God's gift that God freely bestowed on us (εἰς ἔπαινον δόξης τῆς χάριτος αυτοῦ ἧς ἐχαρίτωσεν ἡμᾶς) in the Beloved" (1:6; au. trans.); similarly, the redemption of the believers as God's own people leads to "the praise of God's glory" (1:14). The believers are themselves called to enhance God's glory as a result of receiving the promise of the inheritance, which is thus "for the praise of God's glory (εἰς τὸ εἶναι ἡμᾶς εἰς ἔπαινον δόξης αὐτοῦ, 1:12)."

The second quotation from Seneca above points to the second essential element of a proper response, namely gratitude. Gratitude, however, clearly signifies more than a subjective feeling. Seneca (*Ep.* 81.27) indicates the range of responses included under this term:

> No man can be grateful unless he has learned to scorn the things which drive the common herd to distraction; if you wish to make a return for a favour, you must be willing to go into exile, or to pour forth your blood, or to undergo poverty, or, ... even to let your very innocence be stained and exposed to shameful slanders.

---

[86] J. D. M. Derrett, *Jesus's Audience: The Social and Psychological Environment in which He Worked* (New York: Seabury, 1977), 41.

Gratitude such as Seneca describes involves an intense loyalty to the person from whom one has received beneficence, such that one would place a greater value on service to the benefactor than on one's place in one's homeland, one's physical well-being, one's wealth, and one's reputation. The bond between client and patron (or, one should add, between friends who share mutual beneficence) is thus truly the strongest bond in Greco-Roman society. Where the sanctity of gratitude is maintained,[87] it becomes the one support which remains after all other values and valuables have crumbled -- truly the cement of society which Crossan claimed it to be. Such, the author of Hebrews would claim, is the gratitude, the loyalty, which is due the Benefactor and Broker of God's favor, Jesus. When the authors concludes his exhortation in 12:28, he stresses this second sense of χάρις: ἔχωμεν χάριν, "let us show gratitude." Saller notes that such *amicitia*, indeed whether between equals or inequals, "was supposed to be founded on virtue (especially *fides*)."[88] It is this *fides*, or πίστις, to which the author of Hebrews enjoins his readers through both negative and positive models, through warnings and exhortations.

3 Exchanging Favor for Wrath: The Violation of the Patron

The author describes at such length the benefits which have been gained for the community by Jesus precisely because the addressees -- or, better, some members of the community -- are wavering in their commitment to their Patron. Indeed, the author presents them as if they are in danger of outraging the Son of God, of relinquishing their enjoyment of present benefits (e.g., access to God) and hope of future benefits (e.g., entering the promised rest) by provoking God's anger, and thus bringing upon their own heads God's satisfaction for affronts to his honor. The author presents them as if they are in danger of encountering God as Judge and Avenger, of receiving punishment, and hence disgrace, before his court at his coming, when every enemy will be subjected to Christ.

What actions or omissions of action would constitute such an affront? In what ways did the author believe certain members of the community to be falling short of making the proper return of honor and gratitude to their Patron? The answer to these questions is to be found in the examination of the negative examples and the warnings which figure prominently in Hebrews.

---

[87] One may here recall Dio *Or.* 31.37: "For what is more sacred than honour or gratitude (τί γάρ ἐστιν ἱερώτερον τιμῆς ἢ χάριτος;)?

[88] Saller, *Patronage*, 12-13.

NEGATIVE EXEMPLARS

As the author of Hebrews uses positive examples of faith as a means of arousing emulation in the addressees, so he also uses negative examples as a means of arousing fear in the addressees, lest they fall into the "same pattern (τῷ αὐτῷ ὑποδείγματι, 4:11)" and come to the same inglorious end. The author appears to share Quintilian's conviction that "examples are of the greatest value in deliberative speeches, because references to historical parallels is the quickest method of securing assent" (*Inst.* 3.8.36). Just as deliberation involves both recommending and dissuading, so both positive and negative examples are to be employed in order to gain the assent of the hearers that one course will lead to honor and safety, while another to disgrace and ruin.

An orator could expect negative examples to work powerfully upon the hearers' minds, and, if Aristotle is correct when he observes that fear is a more powerful motivator than honor (*Eth. Nic.* 10.9.4), to persuade more forcefully than positive examples which stimulate ambition. Josephus (*BJ* 2.397) depicts Agrippa II as capitalizing on the dissuasive power of fear in his appeal to the people of Jerusalem to restore the offerings for the emperor and repair the portico connecting the garrison's fortress to the Temple:

> There may be some who imagine that the war will be fought under special terms, and that the Romans, when victorious, will treat you with consideration; on the contrary, to make you an example (εἰς ὑπόδειγμα) to the rest of the nations, they will burn the holy city to the ground and exterminate your race.

The climax of Agrippa's speech is the threat that the people will themselves become an example (εἰς ὑπόδειγμα) to the rest of the Greco-Roman world, and that their remembrance will be marred by the disgrace of being a model of folly. Indeed, part of the force of a negative example derives from the shameful remembrance which attaches to the acts and choices of those who became paradigms of some vice. The greater part of the power of a negative example, however, is its ability to present the hearer with a picture of loss or suffering which the hearer will desire to avoid at all costs so as not to share in the same wretched fate. Plato gives expression to this in *Gorg.* 525B: "And it is fitting that everyone under punishment (τιμωρία) rightly inflicted on him by another should either be made better and profit thereby, or serve as an example (παράδειγμα) to the rest, that others seeing the sufferings he endures may in fear amend themselves."

The presence of a prominent negative example in Hebrews such as the exhortation based on the failure of the wilderness generation (3:7-4:13), accompanied by the less conspicuous but parallel example of Esau (12:16-17), shows that the author believes some members of the community to be in danger of choosing a course which will replicate in their lives the folly of these figures from the traditional past, and will incur similar and worse consequences. These examples, therefore, having been chosen because they speak directly to the situation of the hearers, afford an important window into the choices facing the members of the Christian group and the author's interpretation of those choices.

The Wilderness Generation

The single most developed example in Hebrews, combined with direct application to the situation of the recipients, is that of the wilderness generation in 3:7-4:11. The author moves into this passage immediately after the comparison of Christ and Moses in 3:1-6, which leads naturally into a comparison (of sorts) between the people led by Moses and the people led by Christ (cf. 4:2). The presentation of the wilderness generation begins with the citation of LXX Ps 95:7-11 in Heb 3:7-11, and the example is developed as an exegesis of this psalm text. Lane notes the liturgical use of this psalm as "a preamble to synagogue services on Friday evening and Sabbath morning," such that its contents were probably very familiar.[89] The MT of the Psalm directs the reader to the complaints of the wilderness generation over the lack of water at Massah and Meribah (Ex 17:1-7 and Num 20:2-13), while also alluding to the oath made by God in Num 14:21-23 in the wake of the rebellion. In the LXX, the Hebrew place names have been translated, such that the whole passage now refers to the single episode contained in Numbers 14, namely the peoples' refusal to take the land as God commanded on account of their fear of the inhabitants. That the author of Hebrews has this chapter chiefly in mind is demonstrated by several parallels. One would expect the oath of Num 14:21-23, referred to in the psalm (v. 11), to be mentioned by the author in his discussion (3:18). He also speaks of the "corpses" which fell in the wilderness (ὧν τὰ κῶλα ἔπεσεν ἐν τῇ ἐρήμῳ, 3:17), a direct reference to Num 14:29: "your dead bodies shall fall in this wilderness (ἐν τῇ ἐρήμῳ

---

[89] Lane, *Hebrews 1-8*, 85, citing I. Elbogen, *Der jüdische Gottesdienst in seiner geschichtlichen Entwicklung* (3rd ed.; Frankfurt: Kaufmann, 1931).

ταύτῃ πεσεῖται τὰ κῶλα ὑμῶν)."[90] Finally, while the psalm speaks of the people's having experienced God's benefits for forty years, after which God becomes angered with their persistent lack of trust (καὶ εἶδον τὰ ἔργα μου τεσσεράκοντα ἔτη: **διὸ προσώχθισα τῇ γενεᾷ ταύτῃ**, Ps 95:9-10; Heb 3:9-10), the author of Hebrews reverts to the original details of the Numbers narrative, in which God declares that the people shall know his anger for forty years. Thus Heb 3:17, "And with whom was he provoked for forty years? Was it not with those who sinned? (τίσιν δὲ προσώχθισεν τεσσεράκοντα ἔτη; οὐχὶ τοῖς ἁμαρτήσασιν;)" echoes Num 14:34: "According to the number of the days in which you spied out the land, forty days, for every day a year, you shall bear your sin, forty years, and you shall know the fierceness of my anger (λήμψεσθε τὰς ἁμαρτίας ὑμῶν τεσσαράκοντα ἔτη καὶ γνώσεσθε τὸν θυμὸν τῆς ὀργῆς μου)."

What, then, was the nature of this event which stands behind Heb 3:7-4:11? The author of Hebrews notes that "we have had good news preached to us, just as they also" (4:2), and indeed the Numbers narrative (14:6-8) contains a reiteration of the promise which God gave to the people:

> And Joshua the son of Nun and Caleb the son of Jephunneh, who were among those who had spied out the land, rent their clothes, and said to all the congregation of the people of Israel, "The land, which we passed through to spy it out, is an exceedingly good land. If the Lord delights in us, he will bring us into this land and give it to us, a land which flows with milk and honey (RSV)."

In effect, Joshua and Caleb preach the good news of God's promise to the wilderness generation on the eve of their rebellion. This promise was made by the same God who had delivered them from Egypt, even in the midst of the Red Sea. That deliverance made God the Benefactor of the people, as Philo (*Mos.* 2.256) indicates: "After this, what should Moses do but honour the Benefactor with hymns and thanksgiving (εὐχάριστοις ὕμνοις ψεραίρει τὸν εὐεργέτην)?" This same Patron had given the promise of land, an inheritance in Canaan, and had brought them safely to the very border.

---

[90] Possibly the author has in mind also Num 14:31-32, where this phrase is repeated in connection with the people's low evaluation of the prize they were abandonning: "But your little ones, who you said would become a prey, I will bring in, and they shall know the land which you have despised (καὶ κληρονομήσουσιν τὴν γῆν ἣν ὑμεῖς ἀπέστητε ἀπ' αὐτῆς). But as for you, your dead bodies shall fall in this wilderness (καὶ τὰ κῶλα ὑμῶν πεσεῖται ἐν τῇ ἐρήμῳ ταύτῃ; RSV)."

The day of their inheritance became the "day of testing" (τὴν ἡμέραν τοῦ πειρασμοῦ), in which the people manifested finally and fatally their distrust in the Patron's ability to provide. The damaging trait which characterizes the wilderness generation for the author of Hebrews is ἀπιστία, which is often translated as "unbelief" (cf. NASV; NRSV). The word belongs to a group of words signifying trust or reliability, such that Dio of Prusa delivers an oration on ἀπιστία (*Or.* 74) in which he recommends distrust of other people as a path to safety in human affairs. The companion oration, περὶ πίστεως, speaks of the burdens of being entrusted with some charge or responsibility. Danker catalogues several inscriptions in which πίστις refers to "that which is entrusted," such that "faith is required by the one who awaits fulfillment of the obligation that has been accepted by another."[91] In common Greek usage, then, πίστις refers both to the responsibility accepted by another to discharge some duty or provide some service and the affirmation of the reliability of that other in the person who awaits the fulfillment of the obligation. Πιστός describes the person who may be relied upon to carry out the obligation, who is "trustworthy." ᾿Απιστία may either signify the untrustworthiness of a base person or the feeling which ascribed unreliability to another, such that one neither entrusts that other with something nor trusts that other to fulfill an obligation.

The situation of the wilderness generation falls within the sphere of patronage, promises, and fulfillment of obligations. God has undertaken an obligation on behalf of the people, namely to bring them into the land which God would give them as an inheritance, and had provided many proofs of reliability (καὶ εἶδον τὰ ἔργα μου, 3:9). In light of the spies' report concerning the might of the native inhabitants of the land, however, they wavered in their trust, that is, doubted whether or not God would be able to fulfill his obligation (Num 13:31-14:4). Indeed, they ascribe to their Patron the base motive of treachery: that he intended to bring them to this place to die (Num 14:3). They abandon the prospects of the promise being fulfilled by setting in motion a plan to return to Egypt (Num 14:4), thus negating all the benefits God had already given them. They completely deny the validity of God's promise: "our children will become a prey" (Num 14:3, 31). Such distrust is interpreted by God as a test of God's reliability and ability to provide, which is nothing less than a challenge to the Benefactor, all the more inappropriate given the number

---

    [91] Danker, *Benefactor*, 352-53.

of tests God had allowed in order to stimulate trust (πίστις).[92] The response of the wilderness generation to the reiterated good news -- the promise of God (Num 14:6-9) -- is completely opposite to that of the prominent example of trust, namely Abraham, who elsewhere in the early Christian tradition (Rom 4:20) responds to the reminder of God's promise by trusting more and giving honor to the Benefactor even before receiving the benefit.

Distrust derives from a value judgement, specifically a low estimation of the honor and ability of the person whom one distrusts. Pseudo-Isocrates (*Ad Dem.* 22) advises his young friend thus concerning trust: "Consider that you owe it to yourself no less to mistrust bad men than to put your trust in the good (προσήκειν ἡγοῦ τοῖς πονηροῖς ἀπιστεῖν, ὥσπερ τοῖς χρηστοῖς πιστεύειν)." Distrust is the proper response to base persons, οἱ πονηροί. As such, the wilderness generation's response of ἀπιστία enacts a negative value judgement on God and insults their Patron, who alone is truly "good" (ἀγαθός). The Numbers narrative explicitly links distrust and the provocation which arises from contempt: "And the LORD said to Moses, 'How long will this people despise me? And how long will they not believe in me (ἕως τίνος παροξύνει με ὁ λαὸς οὗτος καὶ ἕως τίνος οὐ πιστεύουσίν μοι), in spite of all the signs which I have wrought among them?" (14:11).

The verb παροξύνω, often translated as "to urge, prick or spur on," or "to provoke, irritate, excite" (*LSJ*) carries definite connotations of contempt, such that the provocation would spring from the understanding that one has been slighted or insulted. This is most clear in LXX Ps 73:10 and 18, where παροξύνω is set in parallel phrases with the verbs ὀνειδιεῖ and ὠνείδισεν, and the object of the verb is God's "name." A name, as receptacle of honor,[93] is provoked only after and as a consequence of being despised or regarded with less honor than appropriate for the repute of the name. The action which is provoked will seek to restore the honor of that name. In LXX Ps 106:11, παρώξυναν is set in a phrase parallel to παρεπίκραναν, the objects of the verbs being the "words of God" and the "counsel of the Most High." A similar usage appears in LXX Is 5:24: "They have not desired the law of the Lord Sabaoth, but have despised the oracle of the Holy One of Israel (οὐ γὰρ ἠθέλησαν τὸν νόμον κυρίου σαβαωθ, ἀλλὰ τὸ λόγιον τοῦ ἁγίου Ισραηλ παρώξυναν)." Words, advice, and laws are disregarded, even despised, but not provoked. To

---

[92] Distrust and challenging God are linked also in Wis 1:2: "God is found by those who do not put him to the test, and manifests himself to those who do not distrust him (ὅτι εὑρίσκεται τοῖς μὴ πειράζουσιν αὐτόν ἐμφανίζεται δὲ τοῖς μὴ ἀπιστοῦσιν αὐτῷ)."

[93] Malina and Neyrey, "Honor and Shame," 33.

despise a person of honor, however, will provoke a response in defense of his or her honor. Finally, the verb is used to express the effect of Israel's idolatry upon the one true God. In Is 65:1-7, God's appeal to the Israelites is continually rejected while the people reach out to idols. Their spurning of God and adoration of other objects of worship, which amount to insults against God, constitutes a provocation of God:

> I spread out my hands all the day to a disobedient and hostile people (λαὸν ἀπειθοῦντα καὶ ἀντιλέγοντα), who walk in a way that is not good, following their own devices; a people who provoke me to my face continually (ὁ λαὸς οὗτος ὁ παροξύνων με ἐναντίον ἐμοῦ διὰ παντός), sacrificing in gardens and burning incense upon bricks; ... their iniquities and their fathers' iniquities together, says the Lord; because they burned incense upon the mountains and reviled me (ὠνείδισάν με) upon the hills, I will measure into their bosom payment for their former doings.

Thus when the wilderness generation are said to have provoked God (Num 14:11), the source of this provocation is the people's choice of a course of action which displayed contempt for God. Insofar as they withdrew their trust from their Benefactor, they declared God to be unreliable and unable to fulfill the obligation God had assumed in their behalf; they declare God to be base, and so repay their proven Benefactor with flagrant contempt.

The wilderness generation's disrespect for God appears also in its disobedience with regard to God's command to take possession of the land. In effect, disobedience enacts the rejection of the right and authority of the Patron to command obedience (an expected return for receiving benefits). Children who disobey the orders of their father show him disrespect, and threaten his honor in the eyes of others:

> When he commands his children and they obey him, his *power* is evident. In this situation of command and obedience, his claim to honor as father and head of the household is acknowledged; his children treat him honorably and onlookers acknowledge that he is an honorable father (see 1 Tim 3:4-5). Were his children to disobey him, he would be dishonored or shamed, for his claim would not be acknowledged, either by family or village. He would suffer shame, that is, loss of honor, reputation, and respect.[94]

In an analogous manner, disobedience to one's master was an action or omission of action striking at the honor and claim to authority of the master. It provoked the honorable person to seek satisfaction, and so to

---

[94] Malina and Neyrey, "Honor and Shame," 26.

regain his honor status (e.g., by punishing the disobedient). The honor of a deity was only clearly manifested by the loyalty and obedience of the worshipers, such that their disobedience harmed the respect which outsiders might have of the divinity, as Paul expresses in Rom 2:23-24: "You that boast in the law, do you dishonor God by breaking the law? For, as it is written, 'The name of God is blasphemed among the Gentiles because of you'." Respect for the Lord -- the fear which seeks to show proper honor so as not to provoke the greater power -- ought to lead to obedience and submission,[95] but the wilderness generation fear more the might of the natives of Canaan than the power of God. Joshua, one of the two spies, while not disputing the facts of the majority report nevertheless urges confidence in God's favor: "Only, do not rebel against the Lord (ἀλλὰ ἀπὸ τοῦ κυρίου μὴ ἀποστάται γίνεσθε·); and do not fear the people of the land (ὑμεῖς δὲ μὴ φοβηθῆτε τὸν λαὸν τῆς γῆς), for they are bread for us; their protection is removed from them, and the LORD is with us; do not fear them (ὁ δὲ κύριος ἐν ἡμῖν· μὴ φοβηθῆτε αὐτούς)." The people, however, begin to "rebel" or turn away from God (ἀποστῆναι), enacting their lack of honor for their Patron.

God's response is one of "wrath" or "anger" towards those who have been disobedient, who have trampled the promise, and faltered in their trust. Anger, according to Aristotle (*Rh.* 2.2.1), is aroused in response to a violation of the honor to which one believes oneself entitled: "Let us then define anger (ὀργή) as a longing, accompanied by pain, for a real or apparent revenge (τιμωρία) for a real or apparent slight (ὀλιγωρία)."[96] He explicitly mentions among various sort sof slighting which arouse anger the following: "Men are angry at slights from those by whom they think they have a right to expect to be well treated; such are those on whom they have conferred or are conferring benefits (εὖ πεποίηκεν ἢ ποιεῖ)...and all those whom they desire, or did desire, to benefit" (*Rh.* 2.2.8). This well describes the situation in Numbers 14. God's every act in the narrative has been to bring the people from a wretched into an enviable state, leading them from slavery to a land for their own possession. Those whom he desired to benefit, however, returned insult for favor, slighting God

---

[95] Cf. Sir 2:15-17: "Those who fear the Lord will not disobey (οὐκ ἀπειθήσουσιν) his words, and those who love him will keep his ways. Those who fear the Lord will seek his approval, and those who love him will be filled with the law. Those who fear the Lord will prepare their hearts, and will humble themselves before him."

[96] Thus Malina and Neyrey ("Honor and Shame," 46) are correct to include "nouns such as vengeance, wrath, anger" among "perceptions of being challenged or shamed."

through their distrust of God's good will and ability.[97]   In response to the challenges or tests with which the wilderness generation affronted God, the Psalmist declares in God's voice (3:10): "Therefore I was angry with that generation (διὸ προσώχθισα τῇ γενεᾷ ταύτῃ)."

The result of God's wrath is the people's loss of access to the promised benefit.   It is specifically out of God's anger that God swears the oath which excludes the rebellious generation from the promised land (3:11): "As I swore in my wrath, 'They shall not enter my rest' (ὡς ὤμοσα ἐν τῇ ὀργῇ μου: Εἰ εἰσελεύσονται εἰς τὴν κατάπαυσίν μου)."   The author of Hebrews ascribes this loss explicitly to disobedience and distrust (3:18-19): "And to whom did he swear that they should never enter his rest, but to those who were disobedient (τοῖς ἀπειθήσασιν)? So we see that they were unable to enter because of unbelief (δι' ἀπιστίαν)."   Numbers records an abortive attempt on the part of the people to recover the benefit they had forfeited.   Moses' report of God's response to their distrust left them in mourning.   When they realized their loss, they sought to regain their inheritance (Num 14:40-45):

> And they rose early in the morning, and went up to the heights of the hill country, saying, "See, we are here, we will go up to the place which the Lord has promised; for we have sinned." 14:41 But Moses said, "Why now are you transgressing the command of the Lord, for that will not succeed? 14:42 Do not go up lest you be struck down before your enemies, for the Lord is not among you. 14:43 For there the Amal'ekites and the Canaanites are before you, and you shall fall by the sword; because you have turned back from following the Lord, the Lord will not be with you."

The impossibility of a return to grace, that is, to the hope of the benefits which were once spurned, figures prominently in Hebrews.   Esau is permanently barred from his birthright once he trades it away (12:17), and the believers themselves are faced with the threat that, once they turn away from Christ and bring him dishonor, there is no repentance, no sacrifice,

---

[97] Again according to Aristotle, *Rh.* 2.2.3, "slighting (ὀλιγωρία) is an actualization of opinion (δόξα) in regard to something which appears valueless (μηδενὸς ἄξιον)....Now there are three kinds of slight: disdain (καταφρόνησις), spitefulness, and insult (ὕβρις)....He who disdains, slights, since men disdain those things which they consider valueless and slight what is of no account (ὅ τε γὰρ καταφρονῶν ὀλιγωρεῖ· ὅσα γὰρ οἴονται μηδενὸς ἄξια, τούτων καταφρονοῦσιν, τῶν δὲ μηδενὸς ἀξίων ὀλιγωροῦσιν)."   The relation between distrust and forming a negative value judgement of a person's character and worth has already been explored.   When a person of merit (e.g., the Divine Benefactor) is judged unreliable and untrustworthy, no small slight has been made.

that can restore their standing in God's favor (6:6; 10:26). The author does not mention explicitly the irrevocability of the loss of the wilderness generation. The finality of their rejection and the fulfillment of God's oath not to allow them to enter, however, is captured succinctly in the author's echo of Num 14:29: "And with whom was he provoked for forty years? Was it not with those who sinned, whose bodies fell in the wilderness (ὧν τὰ κῶλα ἔπεσεν ἐν τῇ ἐρήμῳ)?" (3:17). The reminder of their death "in the desert" recalls their failure to reverse their divinely decreed fate (4:6).

The wilderness generation stands as an "example of disobedience" (4:11), into whose pattern some of the addressees are in danger of falling. The distrust (ἀπιστία) of the wilderness generation stands in stark contrast to the trust (πίστις) exemplified by the people of faith in Hebrews 11. Indeed, faith in chapter 11 is defined specifically within the context of patron-client relationships: "without faith it is impossible to please God (χωρὶς δὲ πίστεως ἀδύνατον εὐαρεστῆσαι). For whoever would draw near to God must believe that he exists and that he rewards those who seek him (πιστεῦσαι γὰρ δεῖ τὸν προσερχόμενον τῷ θεῷ ὅτι ἔστιν καὶ τοῖς ἐκζητοῦσιν αὐτὸν μισθαποδότης γίνεται)." That is, faith looks to God as Benefactor with unwavering trust, and, further, faith perseveres in that commitment to the Patron and in the course which leads to the reception of the benefaction.[98] In the example of the wilderness generation, one finds a picture of a group brought to the very border of their promised inheritance, who at the last panic in the face of the native inhabitants, and withdraw their trust from God. They choose to act with fear and respect for the people over whom God had promised to give them victory, rather than in fear and respect for the God who promised them a lasting inheritance. *Mutatis mutandis*, this may well describe the situation of the addressees as perceived by the author. Having endured a period of wandering, as it were, in which they experienced the world's rejection and still held onto God's promise, some of the believers are wavering in their commitment at the very time when they are closer than ever to attaining what was promised. Some stand in danger of falling into distrust, of disobeying God by not continuing to assemble together to worship and by dissociating from those in need, of regarding more the opinion and hostility of society than of the God who promises them an unshakeable kingdom.

---

[98]   Cf. Derrett, *Jesus' Audience*, 44, in which the author defines faith as "unquestioning expectation of a benefit from Yahweh."

Esau

Much less fully developed, yet nevertheless relevent to the rhetorical strategy of the author and situation of the addressees, is the example of Esau, briefly sketched out in 12:16-17:

> See to it that ... no one be immoral or irreligious like Esau (μή τις πόρνος ἢ βέβηλος ὡς ' Ησαῦ), who sold his birthright for a single meal (ὃς ἀντὶ βρώσεως μιᾶς ἀπέδετο τὰ πρωτοτόκια ἑαυτοῦ). For you know that afterward, when he desired to inherit the blessing, he was rejected (μετέπειτα θέλων κληρονομῆσαι τὴν εὐλογίαν ἀπεδοκιμάσθη), for he found no chance to repent (μετανοίας γὰρ τόπον οὐχ εὗρεν), though he sought it with tears.

How is Esau "godless," or "profane" (βέβηλος)? The author points only to the single incident of Esau's exchange of his birthright for the bowl of lentils Jacob prepared (Gen 25:29-34). Esau probably did not regard the exchange seriously, although Jacob was clearly serious in his intentions to supplant his brother. While in the Genesis narrative it is Jacob's conspiracy with Rebecca which robs Esau of his birthright, in the tradition to which the author appeals Esau himself threw it away thoughtlessly in exchange for a single meal. His downfall is that he has no regard for God's promises and benefactions, represented here by his birthright as a son of Isaac, the son of Abraham. Thus Attridge writes: "the second epithet (βέβηλος) is another term that ultimately derives from the sphere of cult, although it can be applied more broadly as a term of moral opprobrium. It is readily comprehensible as a description of Esau, whose worldliness is manifested in a misplaced sense of value."[99] His incorrect evaluation manifests "a decisive contempt for the gifts of God."[100]

His choice of a single meal, to sustain him in his hunger, is a choice for the temporary safety and enjoyment which people of faith refuse in favor of persevering unto the attainment of the promises of God. Esau thus stands as a foil to Moses, who rejects the "temporary enjoyment of sin" and endures hardship (11:25) in order to attain the reward (11:27). Similarly, Esau makes the choice rejected by the mother of the seven martyred brothers (cf. 11:35), who "because of the fear of God ... disdained the temporary safety of her children." Faith values the promise of eternal reward over the attainment of temporary security, whereas Esau

---

[99] Attridge, *Hebrews*, 368.
[100] Lane, *Hebrews 9-13*, 488.

enacts a lack of faith, providing for safety today at the cost of eternal honor and blessing.

Perhaps he stands most closely as a foil to Jesus, with whose example his own is linked by textual proximity (12:2) as well as syntactic parallelism. Jesus is presented in 12:2 as choosing to endure the pain of the cross in order to attain the honor and joy set before him by God: "who for the joy that was set before him endured the cross, despising the shame, and is seated at the right hand of the throne of God (ὃς ἀντὶ τῆς προκειμένης αὐτῷ χαρᾶς ὑπέμεινεν σταυρὸν αἰσχύνης καταφρονήσας ἐν δεξιᾷ τε τοῦ θρόνου τοῦ θεοῦ κεκάθικεν)." Just as Jesus is praised, however, for submitting "to some disgrace or pain as the price of some great and noble object (ἐπαινοῦνται, ὅταν αἰσχρόν τι ᾖ λυπηρὸν ὑπομένωσιν ἀντὶ μεγάλων καὶ καλῶν),"[101] Esau is blamed for relinquishing a great and noble object so as to avoid a mild hardship: "ὃς ἀντὶ βρώσεως μιᾶς ἀπέδετο τὰ πρωτοτόκια ἑαυτοῦ" (12:16). Thus Esau gave up honor before God for the sake of avoiding temporary hardship.[102]

Here the author does make explicit what was only implicit in his exposition of the default of the wilderness generation, namely that once God's gift was despised and rejected it would be impossible to regain what was lost, or, rather, thrown away because it was lightly valued. Such comments in Hebrews have made the book somewhat unpopular in theological circles, and have caused commentators great difficulty on account of the apparent harshness of the author's words.[103] Nevertheless, the author claims no more than what was in keeping with the Greco-Roman ethos, as expressed, for example, in Dio *Or.* 31.65: "For to those who have not taken good care of a deposit entrusted to them nobody would thereafter entrust any of his own property; but those who insult their benefactors will by nobody be esteemed to deserve a favour (τοὺς δὲ ὑβρίζοντας εἰς τοὺς εὐεργέτας οὐδεὶς κρινεῖ χάριτος ἀξίους)."

The example of Esau is too carefully constructed as a foil to the example of Jesus in 12:2 and the example of Moses in 11:25 to be a warning included at random, as if the author was not sure of the target at

---

[101] Aristotle *Eth. Nic.* 3.1.7.

[102] Thus Chrysostom (*NPNF¹* 14:506; Migne, *PG* 63.214), commenting on 12:16: "'Who for one morsel of meat sold his birthright', who through his own slothfulness sold this honor which he had from God, and for a little pleasure, lost the greatest honor and glory."

[103] William Tyndale, for example, spends the whole of his prologue to Hebrews discussing these difficult passages and demonstrating that they are not inimical to the teaching of the gospel in other books.

which he was aiming. Rather, it appears that Esau serves as a possible pattern for the fate of some members of the community, who, having in mind the prospect of gaining temporary security in society by withdrawing from their confession of hope in Jesus, are on the verge of giving up the inheritance promised them Christ and confirmed by God (cf. 2:3-4). The author seeks to motivate them to reconsider, in light of the impossibility of a return to their spurned benefactor should they later repent after having dishonored him. He calls them to hold up again the promise of God and the prospects of re-enfranchisement in society, and re-evaluate their relative worth, lest they, too, follow through with their exchange.

WARNINGS AND EXHORTATIONS

The author of Hebrews perceives that the Christian community he addresses is in danger of dishonoring God in a manner similar to the wilderness generation and Esau. He therefore makes the addressees aware of the danger through a number of stern warnings designed to arouse fear and dread in the hearers of the consequences of pursuing a course which would provoke their Patron. These warnings, while calling for and advising against certain actions, also aim at appealing to the emotions of the hearers, and are thus an important part of the argument from *pathos*. The author could persuade an audience through presenting himself as a reliable authority and counsellor as well as by demonstrating his case through rational proofs. The counsellors in rhetoric recognized, however, that the successful orator also had to target the emotions of the hearers. Thus Aristotle writes (*Rh.* 1.2.5): "The orator persuades by means of his hearers, when they are roused to emotion by his speech; for the judgements we deliver are not the same when we are influenced by joy or sorrow, love or hate." Quintilian echoes this advice in his handbook (*Inst.* 3.8.12): "As regards appeals to the emotions, these are especially necessary in deliberative oratory. Anger has frequently to be excited or assuaged and the minds of the audience have to be swayed to fear, ambition, hatred, reconciliation." These experienced observers knew that a decision could be influenced by nothing more strongly than the passions, so that the strategic arousal of emotion became a key to persuasion.[104] The author's intentions of arousing emulation in 6:10-11 and 11:1-12:3 have already

---

[104] Cf. also Aristotle *Rh.* 2.1.8: "The emotions (*pathē*) are all those affections which cause men to change their opinion in regard to their judgements, and are accompanied by pleasure and pain; such are anger, pity, fear, and all similar emotions and their contraries."

been observed. He also makes extensive use of a contrasting pair of emotions, namely fear and confidence,[105] by means of which he alternately impels and entices his audience to persist in the course of faith, trust, and solidarity.

Following the initial presentation of Jesus and declaration of his dignity as the Son, in whom God now speaks, the author offers this exhortation (2:1-4):

> Therefore we must pay the closer attention to what we have heard, lest we drift away from it (Διὰ τοῦτο δεῖ περισσοτέρως προσέχειν ἡμᾶς τοῖς ἀκουσθεῖσιν, μήποτε παραρυῶμεν). For if the message declared by angels was valid and every transgression or disobedience received a just retribution, how shall we escape if we neglect such a great salvation (πῶς ἡμεῖς ἐκφευξόμεθα τηλικαύτης ἀμελήσαντες σωτηρίας)? It was declared at first by the Lord, and it was attested to us by those who heard him, while God also bore witness by signs and wonders and various miracles and by gifts of the Holy Spirit distributed according to his own will.

The introduction of this passage with the logical connector Διὰ τοῦτο commands attention. It suggests that this warning against "drifting away" from the message, and so "neglecting so great a salvation," is the goal of the preceding section. In 1:5-14, the author demonstrated at length that the dignity of the Son surpassed that of the angels. In this warning, he first notes that every act of willful neglect against the message delievered by angels (i.e., the Torah) received the punishment which justice demanded. That is, the honor of the angels could only be restored -- and it was necessary that it should be restored -- by means of the punishment of those who had shown them contempt. A greater punishment, however, must await those who "neglect so great a salvation" as was gained by the Son for his clients at such cost to himself.[106]

Dwelling on the honor of Christ in 1:1-14, therefore, enhances the severity of the insult offered to Christ when his message and gift are neglected. Inherent in the participle ἀμελήσαντες is the notion of showing contempt for the thing "neglected." Thus both Delitzsch and Lünemann offer a word indicating contempt as a synonym of "neglect" when

---

[105] Cf. Aristotle *Rh.* 2.5.16: "Confidence (θαρρεῖν) is the contrary of fear and that which gives confidence of that which causes fear."

[106] The author of Hebrews is not reticent to detail this cost. Salvation was gained at the cost of "enduring a cross" and the disgrace attached to it (12:2; 13:12), that is, nothing short of Jesus' own life (2:9; 9:12, 26; 10:10).

commenting on this verse.[107]   Perhaps this semantic relation is best demonstrated in a passage from Epictetus (*Diss.* 4.10.14), in which the philosopher expresses his hope that he will die while occupied with tending his moral faculty, so that he may the claim before God: "the faculties which I received from Thee to enable me to understand Thy governance and to follow it, these I have not neglected (τούτων οὐκ ἠμέλησα); I have not dishonoured Thee (οὐ κατήσχυνά σε) as far as in me lay." Neglect for God's gifts and revelation parallels dishonoring God.   To show such neglect towards the promise of the gospel, and hence to affront the bearer of that message, would put one in greater danger than those who transgressed the Torah.

L. D. Hurst offers the insight that "the emphasis of chapter one is the same as that of chapter two: it concerns a figure who, *qua* man, is exalted above the angels and leads those whom he represents, as their ideal king, to an appointed destiny."[108]   He concludes that "the point of the extravagance of chapter one is to lead the readers of the epistle to the glory of mankind foretold in Psalm 8 and explored in chapter two."[109]   It is true that the author of Hebrews enhances the value of the promised benefits and stimulates his addressees' hope for honor by first presenting an impressive portrait of Christ's dignity and then naming the believers as "partners of Christ" (3:14), or as "many sons" (2:10) who are destined to share the honor of the Son.   Nevertheless, it is also clear that the author has a second and more immediate purpose for chapter one, namely to strengthen the admonition against slackening in commitment to the message of Christ and to dissuade the wavering from falling away. He emphasizes Christ's honor in order to heighten the exigency of properly valuing the gift, of trusting the word of so great a benefactor, and of persevering in hope and firm commitment.

The second warning is built around the example of the wilderness generation, which in Psalm 95 is held up as a negative paradigm to each successive generation of worshippers. The danger facing the community is the possibility of apostasy, a choice which would follow from a faltering trust: "Take care, brethren, lest there be in any of you an evil, unbelieving heart (καρδία πονηρὰ ἀπιστίας), leading you to fall away (ἀποστῆναι) from the living God" (3:12; au. trans.). According to Danker, this καρδία πονηρὰ is a "base heart," which is "the root of a wicked life." Such a

---

[107]   Delitzsch, *Hebrews*, 97: "how shall we escape...if we shall have neglected or despised so great a salvation?"

[108]   Hurst, "Christology," 157.

[109]   Hurst, "Christology," 163.

heart is neither capable of virtue "nor of recognizing it in others."[110]
Hence the person having such a heart would not recognize the
trustworthiness of the God who gives such great promises in Christ, and,
distrusting God, would outrage the Deity. The author intimates that some
of the addressees may be in danger of "turning from the living God." This
phrase contains allusions to Jewish and Christian missionary language,
particularly with regard to the implicit distinction between the one, true and
"living" God and the many false, lifeless idols.[111] Since a great obstacle
to the addressees' regaining their standing in society is their avoidance of
all idolatrous activities, the author may be afraid that some of the
members, desiring to reduce tension between them and the unbelieving
society, are considering a return to engagement in the worship of idols
which formed a prominent part of most every civic, social, economic, and
political activity.

In light of the fate of the wilderness generation, who acted out their
disregard for God through distrust and disobedience, the author, in an
obvious appeal to their emotions, calls the addressees to be afraid (4:1):
"Therefore, while the promise of entering his rest remains, let us fear lest
any of you be judged to have fallen short (Φοβηθῶμεν οὖν, μήποτε
καταλειπομένης ἐπαγγελίας εἰσελθεῖν εἰς τὴν κατάπαυσιν αὐτοῦ δοκῇ τις
ἐξ ὑμῶν ὑστερηκέναι)." What causes fear is the presence of a highly
valued good, referred to by the catchword "rest," from which a person
may be excluded because of a lack of trust (4:2-3): "For we had good
news preached to us just as they did; but the message which they heard did
not benefit them, because it did not meet with trust in the hearers. For we
who have trusted enter that rest...." The author hopes that by inciting a
deep dread of provoking the Benefactor through distrust, the wavering
among the addressees will be motivated to confirm their endurance in hope
and trust in God. To "fall away" would be to dishonor God, and, as
Calvin comments, "too late will be their groans at the last, who slight the
grace offered now."[112]

The exhortation from the negative example of the wilderness generation
concludes with a peroration on the power of the word of God:

> For the word of God is living and active, sharper than any two-edged
> sword, piercing to the division of soul and spirit, of joints and marrow,
> and discerning the thoughts and intentions of the heart. And before him

---

[110] Danker, *Benefactor*, 318.

[111] Cf. 1 Thess 1:9: "how you turned to God from idols, to serve a true and living
God (θεῷ ζῶντι)."

[112] Calvin, *Hebrews*, 35.

no creature is hidden, but all are open and laid bare to the eyes of him (γυμνὰ καὶ τετραχηλισμένα τοῖς ὀφθαλμοῖς αὐτοῦ) with whom we have to do (RSV).

While this is often excerpted as part of a doctrine of Scripture, in its present context it constitutes a final and climactic warning as well as a transition to the return to the theme of Jesus the high priest in 4:14. The image created by these verses is that of a defendant being hauled before a judge, whose eyes can penetrate into the depths of the soul, and therefore guilt, of this defendant. Moreover, the term τετραχηλισμένα, usually translated "laid bare" or "exposed," refers more fully to the condemned criminal whose throat is exposed to the executioner's blade. It is thus an image crafted to strike fear in the hearts of the hearers, which the author strategically uses to move from the danger of refusing God's benefits and falling under the condemnation of God as Judge to the favor obtained by Jesus the high priest (4:14-16). In effect, the author juxtaposes here an image of God the Judge with the image of God the Patron in 4:16. All that separates these two images, and all that enables one to stand before God as Patron rather than as Judge, is the brokerage, or mediation, of Jesus. To lose this mediation through falling away would be to lose access to God's throne as locus of favor, gaining access once more to God's throne as site of judgement and execution.

Perhaps one of the most troublesome passages for the history of theological interpretation appears in 6:4-8, which constitutes a third section of strong admonition:

> For it is impossible to restore again to repentance those who have once been enlightened, who have tasted the heavenly gift, and have become partakers of the Holy Spirit, and have tasted the goodness of the word of God and the powers of the age to come, if they then commit apostasy (παραπεσόντας), since they crucify the Son of God on their own account and hold him up to contempt (ἀνασταυροῦντας ἑαυτοῖς τὸν υἱὸν τοῦ θεοῦ καὶ παραδειγματίζοντας). For land which has drunk the rain that often falls upon it, and brings forth vegetation useful to those for whose sake it is cultivated, receives a blessing from God. But if it bears thorns and thistles, it is worthless and near to being cursed; its end is to be burned.

While the author quickly encourages his audience after delivering these dire warnings that such could never be their fate, his words cannot have failed to have their impact (as they have upon generation after generation of readers). Indeed, by again arousing fear of the dread consequences of falling away, he helps assure that the faltering among the congregation will find the resources to persevere.

The passage contrasts the benefits which have been enjoyed by the believer (6:4-5), and which are full of promise for the future perfection of the gifts, with the strikingly inappropriate response of "turning away" from the one who has gained these gifts for the believer and "holding [him] up to public scorn."[113] The one who does not persevere in faith enacts contempt for the gifts gained at such cost to the Patron and shows a striking lack of gratitude, spurning the benefactor. After such an affront, there is no restoration.[114] The one who "shrinks back unto destruction" (10:39) has valued the benefits too lightly, since he or she refuses to endure what is required to keep them.

The verb ἀνασταυρόω may mean "crucifying afresh," yielding the sense that the apostate confirms the sentence with which the world disgraced Jesus (cf. 12:1-3),[115] or it may retain its primary meaning (*LSJ*) of "crucify." In this latter case, the sense might be taken after the manner of Gal 6:14, where one also finds the verb followed by a dative. The apostates will have then "crucified the Son of God to themselves," that is, they will have no possibility of future dealings with Jesus, and hence no possibility of restoration to favor. The author refers to Jesus as "Son of God" here for the rhetorical effect, as the hearer is not faced with the possibility of scorning Jesus *qua* human, but Jesus *qua* Son of God, whose honor is backed by the power of God.[116]

---

[113] Cf. H. Schlier, "Παραδειγματίζω" (*TDNT* 2:32; Grand Rapids: Eerdmans, 1964).

[114] Cf. Calvin, *Hebrews*, 66: "For it is unworthy of God to hold up his Son to scorn by pardoning them that abandon him." John Donne captures something of this in his poem, "The Crosse":

> Would I have profit by the sacrifice,
> And dare the chosen altar to despise?
> It bore all other sinnes, but is it fit
> That it should beare the sinne of scorning it?

[115] Public denial of Jesus (official, before a magistrate, or unofficial, before those who knew of one's former commitment) would signify such a re-evaluation of Jesus' value. Cf. Spicq, *Hébreux*, 154: "Official denial of the faith is an insult against Christ, casting upon him a scandalous disgrace."

[116] Héring, *Hebrews*, 46, seeks to soften the meaning of this troublesome passage thus: "It is therefore the impossibility of *repenting* which is being affirmed, and it is not a question of knowing whether fresh forgiveness can be obtained if one does repent....The many discussions about the possibility of renewed forgiveness are quite irrelevant to the question which is raised and resolved in this passage." Such may be a helpful comment for devotional appropriation of the text, but it quite misses the importance of the arousal of fear for the author's overall rhetorical strategy. It also obscures the extent to which the author models the relationship of God with human beings after patron-client alliances and the values and mutual obligations which maintain

The agricultural maxim which follows this warning is actually quite apt. Rain is regarded as a benefaction of God (cf. Matt 5:45b), which here looks for a proper return. God's gifts are to bring forth gratitude and loyalty toward God as well as useful fruits for the fellow-believers (e.g., the acts of service and love commended and recommended in 6:10). Such a response will lead to the consummation of blessing. The improper response of breaking with the benefactor, indeed, bringing dishonor to the name of the benefactor, leads to the curse and the fire, that is, exclusion from the promise and exposure to the anger of the Judge.

A fourth warning offers striking parallels to the third,[117] except that the author dramatically heightens the tone and seeks to augment the fear of his hearers still more when he delivers the admonition of 10:26-31:

> For if we sin deliberately after receiving the knowledge of the truth, there no longer remains a sacrifice for sins, but a fearful prospect of judgment, and a fury of fire which will consume the adversaries (φοβερὰ δέ τις ἐκδοχὴ κρίσεως καὶ πυρὸς ζῆλος ἐσθίειν μέλλοντος τοὺς ὑπεναντίους). A man who has violated the law of Moses dies without mercy at the testimony of two or three witnesses. How much worse punishment do you think will be deserved by the man who has spurned the Son of God, and profaned the blood of the covenant by which he was sanctified, and outraged the Spirit of grace (πόσῳ δοκεῖτε χείρονος ἀξιωθήσεται τιμωρίας ὁ τὸν υἱὸν τοῦ θεοῦ καταπατήσας καὶ τὸ αἷμα τῆς διαθήκης κοινὸν ἡγησάμενος, ἐν ᾧ ἡγιάσθη, καὶ τὸ πνεῦμα τῆς χάριτος ἐνυβρίσας)? For we know him who said, "Vengeance is mine, I will repay." And again, "The Lord will judge his people." It is a fearful thing to fall into the hands of the living God (φοβερὸν τὸ ἐμπεσεῖν εἰς χεῖρας θεοῦ ζῶντος).

The passage again compares infraction of the Mosaic covenant with transgression of the new covenant -- the "willful sin" of 10:26, a deliberate violation of the loyalty due the Patron who has struck up a better alliance with people. Just as the dignity of Christ exceeds that of Moses (cf. 3:1-6), so violations of that dignity will incur a greater punishment than even the "death without mercy" which fell upon those who disregarded Torah.[118] The author chooses the noun τιμωρία, indicating that the

---

such relationships.

[117] Cf. Lane, *Hebrews 9-13*, 291-92.

[118] Cf. Hering, *Hebrews*, 94: "If rebellion against the Law of Moses entailed in certain cases capital punishment, those who show contempt for Christ must expect the worst for stronger reasons. It is another example of the well-known argument *a minore ad maius*, very much in vogue among the Rabbis, and which had already been used in 2:2 in order to give an almost identical proof."

willful sin is indeed understood as a challenge to the honor of Christ, requiring the punishment of the offender for the maintenance of the dignity of the offended party.[119] The one who assaults the honor of Christ (rather than enhancing in every way possible the honor of his or her patron) becomes the target for divine satisfaction, the restoration of the honor of the Son. The offender, violating the dignity of the Benefactor, has a legitimate claim to only one object -- τιμωρία. He or she is "deemed worthy" (ἀξιωθήσεται) of this punishment by God, who has the power and authority to enforce the appraisal.[120]

The author goes on to portray a threefold offense against the honor of God, particularly heinous because such an assault violates the patron-client relationship, returning not gratitude but insult to the divine benefactor.[121] The author presents the apostate first as "the one who has trampled upon the Son of God (ὁ τὸν υἱὸν τοῦ θεοῦ καταπατήσας)." Again the choice of "Son of God" as a referent for Jesus heightens the impudence of the

---

[119] Cf. Aulus Gellius (*Attic Nights* 7.14.2-4) makes a distinction between various terms for "punishment": "It has been taught that there are three reasons for punishing crimes. One of these, which the Greeks call κόλασις or νουθεσία is the infliction of punishment for the purpose of correction and reformation, in order that one who has done wrong thoughtlessly may become more careful and scrupulous. The second is called τιμωρία....That reason for punishment exists when the dignity and prestige of the one who is sinned against must be maintained, lest the omission of punishment bring him into contempt and diminish the esteem in which he is held; and therefore they think that was given a name derived from the preservation of honour (τιμή)." I am indebted to J. Neyrey for drawing my attention to this passage.

[120] So Delitzsch, *Hebrews*, 188: "In ἀξιωθήσεται we are to understand God Himself as the ἀξιῶν by whom all actions are weighed and their worth determined, and the measure of penalty needed to vindicate the majesty of the law laid down." Cf. also Weiß (*Hebräer*, 540), who understands this verb as a divine passive denoting God's eschatological judgement.

[121] Calvin, *Hebrews*, 132-133, insightfully underscores this aspect of the passage: "Now it is more heinous to trample underfoot than to despise, and far other is the dignity of Christ than that of Moses....He enhances this ingratitude by a comparison of benefits. It is an exceeding great indignity to count an unholy thing the blood of Christ, which is the material cause of our salvation; but this do they that revolt from the faith....To do despite to Him [the Spirit of grace], by whom we are gifted with so many and so great benefits, is an impiety passing heinous....Wherefore no marvel if God avenge so severely blasphemies of this kind; no marvel if he show himself inexorable to them that have trodden underfoot Christ the mediator, who alone prevails with him on our behalf; no marvel if he stop the way of salvation to them that have spurned from them the one only guide, even his Holy Spirit."

offense and sets the affront within the context of God's honor[122] and hence God's desire for satisfaction from the offenders.[123] The verb itself is an expression of contempt in keeping with the tendency to describe acts of honoring and dishonoring through physical representations. It is, in effect, the opposite of worshiping, placing oneself at the feet of the Master (cf. the προσκύνησις of 1:6). Rather than taking one's proper place in submission and obedience to the Son of God, one treats him with the utmost scorn.[124] For Josephus (*BJ* 4.262), honoring and trampling form a pair of antonyms: the Temple is honored (τετιμήμενος) by foreigners but trampled on (καταπατεῖται) by the Zealots.[125] The author, in suggesting that the apostate "tramples upon the Son of God," creates a strikingly ironic and inappropriate image designed to make the hearers shrink from enacting such an affront. Indeed, the One who may be scorned now, and thus trampled, is the One who at whose feet all his enemies will be brought into subjection (1:13; 10:13).

The second and third phrases pertain more directly to disregard for the gifts of God and a rejection of the patron-client relationship with God through Jesus. The one who continues in sin (i.e., abandons the people of God, cf. 11:25-26) "has regarded as profane the blood of the covenant with which he or she was sanctified (τὸ αἷμα τῆς διαθήκης κοινὸν ἡγησάμενος, ἐν ᾧ ἡγιάσθη)." This blood constitutes the means by which believers were decisively restored to divine favor, by which the sins which stood between people and God were removed and forgotten, and by which the consciences

---

[122] Cf. Jn 5:22-23: "The father judges no one but has given all judgement to the Son, so that all may honor the Son just as they honor the Father. Anyone who does not honor the Son does not honor the Father who sent him."

[123] Delitzsch, 188, also appears to understand this passage in the context of a challenge to honor: "To trample Him under foot -- the gracious and almighty Heir of all things, who is now seated at God's right hand -- what a challenge to the Most High to inflict the severest and most crushing penalty!"

[124] So Delitzsch, *Hebrews*, 188: "Καταπατεῖν is not merely to reject or cast away as something unfit for use which men carelessly tread upon (Matt. v. 13; Luke viii. 5), but to trample down with ruthless contempt as an object of scorn or hatred (Matt. vii. 6)." Cf. also Spicq, *Hébreux*, 2.324: "In trampling Jesus, the apostate has professed the most injurious and flagrant contempt for the person of the Son of God. καταπατέω is a verb of scorn," used also in Matt 7:6 of the salt which has lost its savor, denoting metaphorically the scorn that shall be earned by the disciple without fervor.

[125] Cf. also 3 Macc 2:18 on the trampling of the Temple by the Gentiles. Indeed, such passages may be in the author's mind, for he has just completed his portrayal of Jesus as the better High Priest and better sacrifice, who has replaced the earthly Temple as the locus of intercession and way to gain the favor of God. The apostate, scorning Jesus, tramples the new Temple not made with hands.

of the worshippers were at last perfected. That is, the blood recalls Jesus' offering of himself once-for-all -- which is nothing other than his death on the cross (12:2) in obedience to God (10:5-9; cf. 5:8-10). This death constituted both his entrance into his eternal high priesthood (cf. 9:12) and the offering by which that priesthood sanctifies the people and perfects their consciences (cf. 9:14; 10:10, 14). The offense against this blood is a faulty evaluation,[126] manifested in the abandoning of the Christian community and assimilation into the unbelieving society. Those who do not persevere in loyalty to Christ, but rather dishonor him by manifesting distrust and forsaking the confession of hope, show that they do not value his blood as that which has gained access for them to the greatest of benefits and the greatest of Benefactors.[127] Such a failure to appreciate the worth of this gift would constitute a provocation of the benefactor who had been slighted by ingratitude and contempt for his gifts.[128]

Finally, the one who falters in trust and perseverance "has outraged the Spirit of grace (τὸ πνεῦμα τῆς χάριτος ἐνυβρίσας)." Spicq comments that "one could not make a more striking contrast than that between ὕβρις and χάρις,"[129] and indeed meeting favor and the promise of benefaction with insult is at once highly inappropriate and foolish. Dio expresses the society's condemnation of such a return, going so far as to call it "impiety (ἀσέβεια)": "But to commit an outrage against good men who have been the benefactors of the state (εὐεργέτας ὑβρίζειν), to annul the honours given them and to blot out their remembrance, I for my part do not see how that could be otherwise termed." Impiety can only lead to disgrace

---

[126] So Spicq, *Hébreux*, 2.324-25: "This scorn is completely conscious; the apostate has made a value judgement. ἡγέομαι does not have here its ordinary sense of 'drive, conduct', but rather 'believe, think' (XI, 11) and more precisely 'esteem, evaluate' (XI, 26).... The renegade has considered common or profane the blood of Christ which has sealed the new covenant."

[127] So Michel, *Hebräerbrief*, 236: "Whoever despises Christ also fails to appreciate the value of his blood."

[128] So Delitzsch, *Hebrews*, 189: "To treat this blood ... as the blood of an ordinary man, nay (as too likely), as that of a misguided or guilty criminal! -- what a profanation of the most sacred thing, what a provocation to the severest vengeance on the part of Him who has been thus treated with the blackest ingratitude!" Regarding the benefactions of a great person but lightly or of little value could easily provoke the wrath of the benefactor, whose honor alone should make every gift valuable. Hence the reaction of Brutus to the Xanthians (Plutarch *Brut.* 2.6-8): "The Xanthians ignored my benefactions, and have made their country a grave for their madness."

[129] Spicq, *Hébreux*, 2.325.

and the negation of confidence.[130] Such will be the fate, according to the
author of Hebrews, of those who outrage God's favorable spirit by
rejecting his gifts.[131]

Those who turn thus from God's beneficence in Christ encounter God
no longer as favorable Patron, but as Judge and Avenger: "For we know
him who said, 'Vengeance is mine, I will repay'. And again, 'The Lord
will judge his people'." The threefold challenge to God invites God's
response as Vindicator of the honor of the Son and the worth of the gifts
which have been scorned.[132] The prayers against God's enemies are now
extended to include those who have alienated themselves from God through
the same disregard for God shown by outsiders: "Remember this, O Lord,
how the enemy scoffs, and an impious people reviles thy name (ἐχθρὸς
ὠνείδισεν τὸν κύριον, καὶ λαὸς ἄφρων παρώξυνεν τὸ ὄνομά σου).... Arise,
O God, plead thy case (δίκασον τὴν δίκην σου·); remember how the
impious scoff at thee all the day (μνήσθητι τῶν ὀνειδισμῶν σου τῶν ὑπὸ
ἄφρονος ὅλην τὴν ἡμέραν)!" (LXX Ps. 73:18, 22). As God's enemies,
they can look forward only to ascribed disgrace (i.e., "punishment") before
the court of God on the day appointed for judgement.[133]

---

[130] So Prov 13:5: "The impious will be disgraced and not have confidence (ἀσεβὴς
δὲ αἰσχύνεται καὶ οὐχ ἕξει παρρησίαν.)."

[131] Cf. Chrysostom (NPNF[1] 14:458; Migne, PG 63.144): "'And done despite unto
the Spirit of grace.' For he that accepts not a benefit, does despite to the benefactor
(ὁ γὰρ τὴν εὐεργεσίαν μὴ παραδεχόμενος, ὕβρισε τὸν εὐεργετήσαντα)." Josephus (BJ
3.371-72) also uses this strategy in his attempt to dissuade his troops from carrying out
their suicide pact: "And God -- think you not that He is indignant when man treats His
gift with scorn (τὸν δὲ θεὸν οὐκ οἴεσθε ἀγανακτεῖν, ὅταν ἄνθρωπος αὐτοῦ τὸ δῶρον
ὑβρίζῃ;)? For it is from Him that we have received our being, and it is to Him that
we should leave the decision to take it away.... How can he who casts out from his
own body the deposit which God has placed there, hope to elude Him whom he has
thus wronged (ἀδικούμενον)?"

[132] Cf. Michel, Hebräerbrief, 236: "This threefold display of contempt for the Son
of God is understood as an affront to God (cf. 1 Cor 10:22)."

[133] Cf. 2 Esd 8:56-61: "They despised the Most High, and were contemptuous of
his law, and forsook his ways. Moreover they have even trampled upon his righteous
ones, and said in their hearts that there is not God -- though knowing full well that they
must die.... They themselves who were created have defiled the name of him who made
them, and have been ungrateful to him who prepared life for them. Therefore my
judgment is now drawing near." Cf. also 2 Esd 9:10-12: "As many as did not
acknowledge me in their lifetime, although they received my benefits, and as many as
scorned my law while they still had freedom, and did not understand but despised it
while an opportunity of repentance was still open to them, these must in torment
acknowledge it after death."

The author has designed this passage to lead the hearers to a feeling of deep dread, which he underscores explicitly in his text. Nothing remains for the apostate but "a fearful (φοβερὰ) prospect of judgment" (10:27), who will learn what a "fearful thing (φοβερὸν)" it is "to fall into the hands of the living God" (10:31). The passage forms a climax to the part of the argument from *pathos* which builds upon the "fear" of the audience. Aristotle (*Rh.* 2.5.1) defines fear (φόβος) as "a painful or troubled feeling caused by the impression of an imminent evil (κακοῦ) that causes destruction or pain." The author has provided the prerequisite for fear in his depiction of the coming of God as Judge and Avenger. Aristotle suggests (*Rh.* 2.5.3, 5) that fear can be aroused also by signs of impending danger, such as the "enmity and anger (ὀργή) of those able to injure us in any way...and outraged virtue (ἀρετὴ ὑβριζομένη) when it has power, for it is evident that it always desires satisfaction." In showing contempt for the Son of God, one knowingly incurs the wrath (ὀργή) of God, as anger is the expected response to a slight (all the more when one is slighted by those whom one desired to benefit); similarly the apostate has outraged the embodiment of the virtue of favor and generosity in insulting the Spirit of grace, and so can expect to be visited by an act of God's power seeking satisfaction. Fear is again heightened by the declaration of the impossibility of restoration (10:26), for after rejecting the brokerage of Jesus there remains no mediator who can regain God's favor for the transgressor.[134]

Having aroused such fear in his audience, he has prepared and motivated them to consider how to avoid the course of action which would offer such an affront to God and turn beneficence into anger. It is at this point that he reminds them of their former display of loyalty to Christ and to one another (10:32-34), and the trust and hope they showed as their status and property in the world were stripped from them. Such a stance manifested the "boldness" or "confidence" (παρρησία) which springs from commitment to the benefactor and to attaining the reward God promised. The admonition of 10:35 urges the addressees to hold onto precisely this stance as the means to retain the favor of the benefactor, and cautions against "shrinking back" as the act which would cause the loss of that favor:

> Therefore do not throw away your confidence, which has a great reward (μὴ ἀποβάλητε οὖν τὴν παρρησίαν ὑμῶν, ἥτις ἔχει μεγάλην μισθαποδοσίαν). For you have need of endurance, so that you may do

---

[134] Cf. Aristotle *Rhet* 2.5.12: Fear is aroused "also when there is no possibility of help or it is not easy to obtain."

the will of God and receive what is promised. "For yet a little while (ἔτι γὰρ μικρὸν ὅσον ὅσον), and the coming one shall come and shall not tarry (ὁ ἐρχόμενος ἥξει καὶ οὐ χρονίσει); but my righteous one shall live by trusting (ἐκ πίστεως), and if he shrinks back, my soul has no pleasure in him (ἐὰν ὑποστείληται, οὐκ εὐδοκεῖ ἡ ψυχή μου ἐν αὐτῷ)." But we are not of those who shrink back and are destroyed, but of those who have faith and keep their souls (ἡμεῖς δὲ οὐκ ἐσμὲν ὑποστολῆς εἰς ἀπώλειαν ἀλλὰ πίστεως εἰς περιποίησιν ψυχῆς, 10:35-39).

Throwing away their παρρησία and the reward which attaches to it would be to refuse the gifts of the benefactor, and hence to "do him despite." "Shrinking back" recalls the sin of the wilderness generation, who displayed their distrust of God and their disobedience by not pressing on in the journey to which God called them, but rather by seeking to turn back at the very threshold of the consummation of their hope and God's beneficence. For the addressees to shrink back now, that is, to seek to reacquire their place in the worldly homeland and ease the tension between their unbelieving neighbors and themselves, would mean that they would have "come short" of entering the promised rest (4:1) and, indeed, fallen short of God's gift ("ἐπισκοποῦντες μή τις ὑστερῶν ἀπὸ τῆς χάριτος τοῦ θεοῦ," 12:15). To fall short of God's grace, however, means (for those who have experienced God's benefaction, "who have tasted the heavenly gift," 6:4-5) to fall into God's anger.

A fifth warning against dishonoring God appears in 12:5-9. Citing Prov 3:11-12, the author admonished the reader not to "slight" the discipline of God:

You have forgotten the exhortation which addresses you as sons (ὡς υἱοῖς): "My son, do not regard lightly the discipline of the Lord (υἱέ μου, μὴ ὀλιγώρει παιδείας κυρίου), nor lose courage when you are punished by him. For the Lord disciplines him whom he loves, and chastises every son whom he receives." It is for discipline that you have to endure. God is treating you as sons; for what son is there whom his father does not discipline? If you are left without discipline, in which all have participated, then you are illegitimate children and not sons (ἄρα νόθοι καὶ οὐχ υἱοί ἐστε). Besides this, we have had earthly fathers to discipline us and we respected them. Shall we not much more be subject to the Father of spirits and live (οὐ πολὺ [δὲ] μᾶλλον ὑποταγησόμεθα τῷ πατρὶ τῶν πνευμάτων καὶ ζήσομεν)?

Proverbs understands divine discipline as a sign of God's love and acceptance; the author of Hebrews goes a step further. Taking the speaker to be God, he finds in this discipline a proof of the believers' adoption by God as sons and daughters. It is therefore a gift highly to be prized, not something "slighted" by being avoided as something grievous.[135] What constitutes the discipline which the author praises as a benefaction? It is the "hostility from sinners" which the believers endure as a result of committing themselves to the One who endured greater hostility (12:3), and whose endurance is held up as a model for those who follow Him and must persevere rather than "lose heart." It is the loss, degradation, and trials which believers must endure in their "contest against sin," that is, against the temptation to invest themselves again in the life of the world and sacrifice their exclusive commitment to Jesus and the community (the "people of God," 11:25). In effect, the author is telling them to value their experience of suffering, marginalization, and shame in a positive light according to the Christian construal of reality. Rather than being indications of rejection, these experiences are interpreted as assurances of inclusion among the children of God ("If you do not have that discipline in which all children share, then you are illegitimate and not his children," Heb 12:8). Treating these experiences as something to be avoided, in effect, amounts to slighting the parental discipline of the Lord and thinking unworthily of the honor of being a child of God.[136]

The addressees are warned, as has been noted above, against following the example of Esau, who had improperly evaluated God's gift and, exchanging it for a single meal, showed his contempt for his inheritance. 12:17 is an implicit warning that, like Esau, those who value too lightly their inheritance as children of God will not have an opportunity to return to their place in God's family (cf. 12.23, where the assembly of the saved are referred to as the "assembly of the firstborn").[137] Placing the proper value on God's promise goes hand in hand with accepting the "discipline" of the Lord, which fits the children for receiving their birthright.

Finally, the author admonishes the addressees again not to reject the message which they have received from the "one who speaks from heaven," recalling the initial admonition to pay closer attention to the message brought by the Son (2:1-4): "See that you do not refuse him who is speaking (Βλέπετε μὴ παραιτήσησθε τὸν λαλοῦντα). For if they did not

---

[135] Cf. Michel, *Hebräerbrief*, 296: "ὀλιγωρεῖν (in the NT used only here) = consider unimportant."

[136] Cf. Calvin, *Hebrews*, 171: "If the chastisements of God testify his love towards us, it is shameful that they should be regarded with disdain or aversion. For they must be exceedingly unthankful that endure not to be chastened of God to salvation; nay that spurn a token of his fatherly loving kindness."

[137] Cf. Calvin, *Hebrews*, 179: "Now because he warns all the despisers of God of the same danger, it may be asked whether no hope of pardon remain, if the grace of God has been received with contempt and his kingdom less esteemed than the world."

escape when they refused him who warned them on earth, much less shall
we escape if we reject him who warns from heaven" (12:25). Again the
situation of the addressees is juxtaposed with that of the wilderness
generation (cf. Ex 20:22). Neglecting or refusing the message again has
connotations of slighting the speaker,[138] which incurs a punishment from
which there is no escape.

In light of these warnings against dishonoring God and scorning God's
benefactions in Christ, what can be said to constitute the danger which the
addressees face, at least in the perception of the author? What constitutes
the dangerous affront to God and Son of God? The author indicates that
some of the addressees, whose commitment is wavering, are in danger of
forgetting the benefit which Christ has procured for them, and so develops
at length the uniqueness and irreplaceability of Jesus' brokerage which has
given the community access to God as their Patron. The time that they
have had to spend in their new status in society, as a result of their
degradation on account of their faith, must not be allowed to dim the
remembrance of this gift.[139] The fading of fervor for the benefits yet to
be enjoyed, coupled with the desire to regain the benefits of full
participation in the Greco-Roman society, leads to slackening in
commitment and the possibility that some will withdraw from the
community. The author interprets this as following the pattern of the
wilderness generation's disobedience, and as a course of action which sets
a low value on God's promises and the benefits gained by Christ at such
cost.[140]

One could readily compile a list of the phrases in Hebrews which
describe the course of action which the addressees must resist. Such a list
would include "shrinking back" (10:38), "falling away" (3:12; 6:6),
"drifting away" (2:1), "falling short" (4:1; 12:15). The author's
exhortations indicate the need for the opposite course to be adopted --

---

[138] So Gustav Stählin, "Παραιτέομαι" (*TDNT* 1:195; Grand Rapids: Eerdmans,
1964). Cf. also Lünemann (*Hebrews*, 719), who provides "despise" as a synonym for
"refuse" in his comment: "that ye turn not away from Him and despise Him."

[139] Cf. Seneca (*Ben.* 3.2.1; 3.3.1-2): "Who is so ungrateful as the man who has
so completely excluded and cast from his mind the benefit that ought to have been kept
uppermost in his thought and always before him, to have lost all knowledge of it?....
Busied as we are with ever new desires, we turn our eyes, not to what we possess, but
to what we seek to possess.... The desirability of other things assails our mind, and we
rush toward those, as is the way of mortals, who, having got great things, always desire
greater."

[140] Cf. Lane, *Hebrews 9-13*, 295: "Apostasy reaffirms the values of the world,
which permit those who stand outside the community to regard Jesus Christ with
contempt (cf. 6:6)."

"enduring" (10:36), "holding fast" (3:6, 14), "being diligent" (4:11; 6:11), "drawing near" (4:16; 10:22). In short, the addressees are faced with the alternatives of trust and sin, of remaining firm in their commitment to God or of falling away in the face of the pressures of the world.[141]

This slackening in commitment, like the shrinking back of the wilderness generation, is interpreted by the author as nothing less than apostasy. Indeed, the heightened tone of 10:26-31 leads many scholars to see apostasy in view, whether official renouncing of the faith or a quieter and less public withdrawal from community and dissociation from name of Christ (cf. 3:12; 6:6).[142] What else, indeed, would involve spurning God's gifts in the manner described in 10:29? To confirm those who remain steadfast and turn back those who are considering whether or not they would fare better if they make peace with the world, the author seeks to instill fear of the consequences of dishonoring God and Christ, such that the wavering will overcome their fear of or shrinking away from of the "hostility of sinners," and reminds them of the great benefits they stand to lose by failing to persevere in their commitment to Jesus and one another. Epictetus shows that the fear of dishonoring God can be used effectively

---

[141] Cf. Käsemann, *Wandering People*, 46: "Just as faith finds its own true charcter in perseverance, so sin finds its own in slackening."

[142] So Attridge, *Hebrews*, 292: "It now becomes clear that the object of this dire warning is not sin in general, but the sin of apostasy"; Michel, *Hebräerbrief*, 236: "Apostasy means crucifying the Son and putting him to shame (6:6), and is a sacrilege and affront to the Deity (ὕβρις)"; Héring, *Hebrews*, 94: "The mention of those who desert the assemblies is the first argument in its favour. For such people are in the process of turning their backs on Christianity. Then the expression '*hupenantioi*' (= 'opponents', v.27) confirms that rebels are under discussion. Similarly in v.29 the people who hold in contempt the precious blood of the Eucharist, who insult the Holy Spirit, bring us closer to this explanation. Finally the parallel with the situation described in 3[7ff] and in 3[15ff], where some rebel like the people in the wilderness, must not be forgotten. Thus, finally, we come to think that it is apostasy which is under discussion, and we then understand why the punishment is so terrible." Weiß (*Hebräer*, 605) focuses especially on whether or not one shows solidarity with the people of God: «What is here designated as ἁμαρτία has thus a concrete form: the renunciation of solidarity with the 'people of God' as they suffer maltreatment."

to lead hearers to adopt or preserve a certain ethos.[143]   The author of Hebrews makes extensive use of a similar strategy.

REMAINING IN GRACE

Having been warned of the dire consequences of dishonoring God, and thus becoming liable to God's anger (longing for satisfaction), the addressees might be expected to cling to those exhortations and counsels which speak of the way in which they might continue in favor, χάρις, before God.   They are urged to take the path of honoring God and the Son of God, which will lead to their continued confidence (παρρησία) and the reward it brings.   Unlike the wilderness generation, which allowed its regard for the inhabitants of the land to overwhelm its regard for God, the addressees are to show regard for God in all things, and not to fear others whose claims conflict with God's (13:6; cf. 11:23, 27; Matt 10:28).

They are urged to retain a firm trust in the promises and Promiser, thus honoring their Patron through showing absolute confidence (and affirming the Patron's reliability and ability to fulfill the obligations he has undertaken).   Sarah provides the model they are to follow in this regard, as her evaluation of the Promiser as reliable led to her reception of the promised blessing (11:11).   The declaration of 13:8, namely that "Jesus Christ is the same yesterday, today, and for ever (Ἰησοῦς Χριστὸς ἐχθὲς καὶ σήμερον ὁ αὐτὸς καὶ εἰς τοὺς αἰῶνας)," affirms his reliability.   Dio (*Or.* 74.21-22), in his oration on "distrust," presents the following as the greatest impediment to trust:

> What someone has said about Fortune might much rather be said about human beings, namely, that no one knows about any one whether he will remain as he is until the morrow (τὸ μηδένα εἰδέναι περὶ μηδενός, εἰ μέχρι τῆς αὔριον διαμενεῖ τοιοῦτος).   At any rate, men do violate the

---

[143] Cf. *Diss.* 2.8.13-14: "It is within yourself that you bear Him, and do not perceive that you are defiling Him with impure thoughts and filthy actions. Yet in the presence of even an image of God you would not dare to do anything of the things you are now doing.   But when God Himself is present within you, seeing and hearing everything, are you not ashamed to be thinking and doing such things as these, O insensible of your own nature, and object of God's wrath!" Cf. also *Diss.* 2.8.21: "Do you dishonour the workmanship of this Craftsman, when you are yourself that workmanship? Nay more, do you go so far as to forget, not only that He fashioned you, but also that He entrusted and committed you to yourself alone, and moreover, by forgetting, do you dishonour your trust?"

compacts made with each other and give each other different advice and, believing one course to be expedient, actually pursue another.[144]

The author asserts, however, that with Jesus there is no such variableness, such that he will indeed "remain as he is until the morrow" and through all tomorrows, and thus can be trusted never to violate his compacts made with his clients and partners (3:14). The addressees may thus hold fast to their confession of their hope -- a hope anchored in the efficacy of Jesus as Broker (3:6, 14; 6:19-20; 10:23).

In order to remain "in grace," the addressees must persevere in their commitment (10:36; 6:12), following the models of Moses (11:27) and Jesus (12:1-3), accepting the sufferings which, as divine discipline, make believers fit for the inheritance as sons and daughters, for "perfection" (cf. 5:8).[145] They are urged to draw near to God (4;14-16; 10:19-22) and find help from their willing Patron rather than to fall away, showing their distrust of their Patron to give adequate assistance for their need.

In sum, they are to return χάρις for χάρις, to show gratitude to God for the many benefits God has provided in Christ (12:28): "Therefore let us be grateful for receiving a kingdom that cannot be shaken, and thus let us offer to God acceptable worship, with reverence and awe (Διὸ βασιλείαν ἀσάλευτον παραλαμβάνοντες ἔχωμεν χάριν, δι' ἧς λατρεύωμεν εὐαρέστως τῷ θεῷ μετὰ εὐλαβείας καὶ δέους)."[146] They are called to give a just return to God for God's benefits, which will also assure that they retain their standing in God's favor: "For those who take seriously their obligations toward their benefactors and mete out just treatment to those who have loved them, all men regard as worthy of favour (πάντες ἡγοῦνται χάριτος ἀξίους), and without exception each

---

[144] Cf. also Dio *Or.* 74.4: "Accordingly, those who wish to live at peace and with some degree of security must beware of fellowship with human beings (εὐλαβεῖσθαι δεῖ τὴν πρὸς ἀνθρώπους κοινωνίαν).... For with human beings there is no constancy or truthfulness at all (οὐ γάρ ἐστι παρ' αὐτοῖς βέβαιον οὐθὲν οὐδὲ ἀληθές)."

[145] Cf. Peterson, *Hebrews and Perfection*, 175: "Suffering has an important role to play in enabling the Christian to reach his heavenly destination and the full enjoyment of the perfection achieved for him by Christ. The discipline of God serves as encouraging proof of sonship, as a means of developing the appropriate subjection to the person and will of God, and as a process by which God gives men a 'share in his holiness' and 'the peaceful fruit of righteousness'."

[146] Cf. Lane, *Hebrews*, 486: "the idiom ἔχειν χάριν τινί, 'to be grateful to someone', is well attested (BAGD 878 [5]) and in this context clearly means 'Let us be grateful to God'." The textual tradition, however, preserves a major variant suggesting that a number of scribes had difficultly understanding what aspect of "grace" was meant (whether "we have favor before God" or "let us be grateful to God").

would wish to benefit them to the best of his ability" (Dio *Or.* 31.37). One will recall, however, that gratitude means far more than a mere subjective feeling of thankfulness and the verbal expression of the same. Rather, accepting a benefit obligates one to show loyalty to the giver. Thus Danker writes: "That receipt of benefits from a head of state puts one under obligation and loyalty, is well understood in antiquity."[147] Obligating beneficiaries, he goes on to note, was an important part of Augustus' rise to power. Gratitude involves complete loyalty and commitment (cf. Seneca, *Ep.* 81.27).

Gratitude is linked with piety as the proper return to God for God's gifts, with gratitude as the door to offering "pleasing worship to God with reverence and awe." The addressees are called to return praise to the Patron, accompanied by service to the brothers and sisters (13:15-16): "Through [Jesus Christ] then let us continually offer up a sacrifice of praise (ἀναφέρωμεν θυσίαν αἰνέσεως) to God, that is, the fruit of lips that acknowledge his name. Do not neglect to do good and to share what you have (τῆς δὲ εὐποιΐας καὶ κοινωνίας μὴ ἐπιλανθάνεσθε), for such sacrifices are pleasing to God (τοιαύταις γὰρ θυσίαις εὐαρεστεῖται ὁ θεός)." There is a definite link between showing gratitude to God and giving assistance to one's fellows, between honoring God and serving others. Danker records an inscription in which service to the members of a guild is lauded as honor shown the patron deity of that guild:[148] similarly, caring for the needy clients of God honors the divine Patron.[149] They are thus to show the "same diligence" in serving the saints as formerly (6:10-11). Gratitude towards God must be expressed in the believers' continued effort to build community and maintain solidarity, while withdrawing from fellowship (10:25) and failure to serve the marginalized and imprisoned saints constitutes a violation of this basic virtue.

The addressees are thus to show God the honor due such a great Benefactor, and to maintain their loyalty toward Christ who gained access for them to God. For them, the honorable path (καλὸν) is to "be confirmed in grace": "for it is well that the heart be strengthened by grace, not by foods, which have not benefited their adherents (καλὸν γὰρ χάριτι βεβαιοῦσθαι τὴν καρδίαν, οὐ βρώμασιν, ἐν οἷς οὐκ ὠφελήθησαν οἱ περιπατοῦντες). We have an altar from which those who serve the tent have no right to eat" (13:9-10). These verses recall the contrast

---

[147] Danker, *Benefactor*, 450.

[148] Danker, *Benefactor*, 343.

[149] Cf. Prov 14:31, where honor of God must be reflected in one's relations to the poor and needy.

established by the author between the ineffective brokerage of the Levitical priesthood (the foods by which the adherents were not benefitted) and the successful brokerage of Christ, who gains access to God for his clients (figuratively, the right to eat at the altar of the Eucharist). The author's decision not to qualify χάρις in any way leaves its multivalence intact. The heart is strengthened by the favor of the Benefactor, and the confidence with which one may stand before God on account of Christ's mediation; the heart is strengthened by the gift itself; but the heart is also strengthened by gratitude. This gratitude is to become the foundation of the believer's life, in light of which he or she is to evaluate every option and make every decision. This gratitude is to keep the believer mindful of the benefits which have been enjoyed and which are still promised for the future for the one who perseveres in trust, and so will preserve the believer continually from slighting the gifts and dishonoring the Giver.

CHAPTER SIX

The Construction of an
Alternate Court of Reputation

Honor and shame have been shown to be powerful sanctions for and against certain actions and characteristics. Because honor and dishonor provide an important axis of value for most of the first-century inhabitants of the Mediterranean, and because it is the public, that is, the larger group or society, which grants honor or ascribes disgrace, adherence to the virtues and behaviors valued by the group are strongly reinforced by the social grant of honor or dishonor.[1] The discussion of this "public court of reputation" has recognized from its inception, however, that, in a complex society, "the individual's worth is not the same in the view of one group as in that of another, while the political authorities may view him in a different light again."[2] That is, there are as many "courts of reputation" as there are subgroups within a society, the values and evaluations between which groups will vary, sometimes insignificantly, sometimes widely. Whom one regards as one's "significant others" thus becomes very important, for one will seek to embody what the group of significant others value in order to be recognized, and to recognize oneself, as a person of worth.

---

[1] Cf. Pitt-Rivers, "Honour and Status," 27: "Public opinion forms ...'the court of reputation'...and against its judgements there is no redress. For this reason it is said that public dishonour kills." Cf. also H. Moxnes, "Honor and Shame: A Reader's Guide" (*BTB* 23 [1993] 167-176), 168: "Recognition from others is important. Although honor is also an inner quality, the value of a person in his or her own eyes, it depends ultimately on recognition from the group or from important people in society -- the 'significant others'."

[2] Pitt-Rivers, "Honour and Status," 22.

Minority cultures have therefore often sought to detach their members from regarding as significant others those who do not adhere to the values of the minority group.[3] It is a recurring theme of the writings of spokespersons for the philosophical minority cultures that the devotee of wisdom, truth, or philosophy, cannot allow himself or herself to be persuaded by the opinion of the multitude or influenced by the prospect of their approval or disapproval. Epictetus (*Diss.* 4.5.22) is exemplary in the manner in which he achieves this:

> What then? Do you want me to be despised? -- By whom? By men of understanding? And how will men of understanding despise the gentle and the self-respecting person (καὶ πῶς καταφρονήσουσιν εἰδότες τοῦ πρᾴου, τοῦ αἰδήμονος)? No, but by men without understanding? What difference is that to you? Neither you nor any other craftsman cares about those who are not skilled in his art.

People who share the philosopher's values (i.e., people of understanding) will support the philosopher in his or her pursuit of the goal of philosophy; those who do not share this quest cannot be relied on to give a proper evaluation of the behavior and the choices of the philosopher. Their low opinion ought therefore to have no effect on the philosopher's actions.[4] Similar strategies are apparent in minority cultures defined by ethnic-religious values, such as Judaism.[5] Deutero-Isaiah (51:7-8) exhorts his audience to remain steadfast in their commitment to living according to the norms of Torah, and not to be dissuaded from that path by the negative opinion of those whose commitment to Torah has eroded:

> Hearken to me, you who know righteousness, the people in whose heart is my law; fear not the reproach of men, and be not dismayed at their revilings (μὴ φοβεῖσθε ὀνειδισμὸν ἀνθρώπων καὶ τῷ φαυλισμῷ αὐτῶν μὴ ἡττᾶσθε). For the moth will eat them up like a garment, and the worm

---

[3] See the extensive discussion of this phenomenon in chapter 3 above.

[4] Cf. also Plato *Cri.* 44C: "But, my dear Crito, why do we care so much for what most people think (τῆς τῶν πολλῶν δόξης μέλει;)? For the most reasonable men, whose opinion is more worth considering (μᾶλλον ἄξιον), will think that things were done as they really ought to be." Seneca (*Constant.* 13.2, 5) likewise sets the "wise person" apart from and above the opinion of the lay person with regard to both praise and censure. See chapter 3 for a fuller discussion of these texts in the larger program of the authors.

[5] Cf. The undermining of the opinion of those who do not adhere to Torah-obedience in Wisd 2:1-23; 5:4-6; cf. also the overturning of Antiochus' evaluations of the martyrs' commitment to God and refusal of Hellenistic honors as folly and madness, and their end as disgraceful, in 4 Maccabees (discussed above in chapter 3).

will eat them like wool; but my deliverance will be for ever, and my
salvation to all generations.

The prophesied destiny of the people whose lives are not guided by
commitment to Torah -- namely, annihilation -- shows the error of their
judgement, and on the basis of their future ruin their present evaluations
of what is honorable and what disgraceful are set aside.

The purpose of neutralizing the opinion of those who do not adhere to
the values of the minority culture is, of course, to prevent the members of
that group from conforming to other values in order to gain approval and
honor in the eyes of the wider society. Much evidence has been gathered
from Hebrews showing that its author was concerned to effect this very
dissociation from society's values in its addressees.[6] When the author
encourages the readers to "despise shame," following the example of Jesus,
Abraham, Moses, the martyrs, and the community's own past, he seeks to
undermine the larger society's influence over the individual Christians.
Through a desire to be evaulated as an honorable person by the unbelieving
members of the Greco-Roman culture, the believer would be drawn to
perform those acts which the society viewed as honorable, such as
participation in traditional religions and emperor cult, and to desist from
those behaviors which the society regarded as deviant, such as adherence
to a depraved oriental cult (i.e., Christian congregations). If the believers,
however, can disregard society's evaluation of what is honorable and
disgraceful, and thus also the society's evaluation of the believers' honor,
then they will be free to persevere in their dedication to the Christian
minority culture's distinctive goals, values, and commitments.

An important corollary to this is the careful construction of an alternate
court of reputation, the body of those others whose opinion and approval
one should value and secure. In whose eyes are the addressees called to
seek to be recognized as honorable? Whose opinion and evaluation matter?
What actions or attitudes are defined as honorable? The author of Hebrews
throughout his letter points his addressees to God and to Christ as the
ultimate judges of worth. He also seeks to maintain a close-knit visible
court of reputation in the community itself. He reminds his audience of
the honor they are privileged to enjoy before this court of opinion, and
seeks to rouse their ambition by the promise of honors yet to be achieved
or bestowed before God. It is this honor that the addressees are to seek to
preserve and augment at all costs, avoiding those acts which will bring

---

[6] See the extensive discussion in chapter 4 of how Heb 10:32-12:3 contributes to
this end.

disgrace before this court and eagerly pursuing those behaviors which will result in the approval of fellow-believers and, ultimately, God.

1 The Divine Judge

Their belief in a personal God who was involved in human affairs and would one day rise up in judgement of humankind allowed Jews and Christians alike to regard God as a significant other whose approval or disapproval could be earned and experienced. While cultural anthropologists and those who have appropriated their work maintain that honor depends not only on the individual but on the society's recognition of that individual's claim to honor, the recognition of God alone could substitute for recognition by society. That is, the individual's conviction that she or he had done what was honorable in God's sight would allow that person to esteem herself or himself as a person of worth regardless of society's evaluation of that person's claim. This is especially prominent in the writings of Paul, who stresses that he seeks to please (i.e., gain the approval of) God and not human beings (1 Th 2:4; Gal 1:10). Not only the apostle and his team, but every true follower of God's Law acts so as to receive praise from God, and does not seek praise and respect from other people (Rom 2:29).[7]

The author of Hebrews shares this aspect of the common Jewish and Christian world view (thus once more demonstrating his ethnic subcultural relationship to Jewish culture), namely that God is the final Judge in whose sight one lives and with whose evaluation one must be ultimately concerned. This is grounded for the author of Hebrews not only in the future prospect of God's judgement of the world, but in the manifestation of Jesus as Son and Savior. Jesus' resurrection and exaltation proclaims not only the radical difference between God's evaluation and the world's, but also the ability of God's verdict to overturn the verdict of the lower court. Jesus, utterly humiliated in the estimation of the world by his shameful death on the cross (12:2), has been thought worthy by God of the

---

[7] Cf. Moxnes, "Honor and Righteousness in Romans," 70: "Paul loosens the granting of honour from the social group. 'Man', that is, the Jewish community, is no longer 'the significant other, in whose eyes approval is sought'. That is the prerogative of God alone." Corrigan ("Paul's Shame," 24) also notes prominently this aspect of Paul's construal of his honor: "When the apostle speaks of honor (*timē*) he is more concerned with the honor ascribed by God than he is with any honor that may be socially ascribed or achieved by people. God's activity and recognition count and not humanity's."

highest honor.[8] Jesus is thus named the "Son" of God (1:1-3), appointed by God to the dignity of "high priest after the order of Melchizedek" (5:4-6), and seated at the place of highest honor, at God's right hand (1:3), whence he awaits the subjection of all things (including his enemies, 1:13) under his feet (2:6-9). God's authority to overturn the verdict of society and power to enforce God's own evaluations of honor and disgrace elevate the divine opinion above all human courts of reputation (although, certainly, the believing community reflects the opinion of God and provides the visible counterpart to the divine court).

Free from the limitations of physical beings, God becomes the sole significant other whose sight extends beyond the reach of human eyes. Distinctions between private and public are meaningless before the all-seeing eye of the creator. The author's apparent digression in 4:12-13 on the efficacy of the word of God may be understood in light of this conviction:

> For the word of God is living and active, sharper than any two-edged sword, piercing to the division of soul and spirit, of joints and marrow, and discerning the thoughts and intentions of the heart (κριτικὸς ἐνθυμήσεων καὶ ἐννοιῶν καρδίας). And before him no creature is hidden, but all are open and laid bare to the eyes of him with whom we have to do (καὶ οὐκ ἔστιν κτίσις ἀφανὴς ἐνώπιον αὐτοῦ, πάντα δὲ γυμνὰ καὶ τετραχηλισμένα τοῖς ὀφθαλμοῖς αὐτοῦ, πρὸς ὃν ἡμῖν ὁ λόγος).

While this verse is popularly used to describe the power of the Scriptures, the author of Hebrews speaks of an extension or agent of God which calls all people to account before God (πρὸς ὃν ἡμῖν ὁ λόγος), whose sight

---

[8] As Delitzsch (*Hebrews*, 188) and Weiß (*Hebräer*, 540) argue that God is the agent of the "divine passive" ἀξιωθήσεται in 10:29, so one may see God again as the one who evaluates the relative worth of Jesus and Moses in 3:3, and who enacts that evaluation in the heavenly realm.

penetrates the deepest recesses of a person.[9] The emphasis in the author's argument is thus not a text but the God who speaks.

The author closes the letter by commending the addressees to God in the hope that the Deity will make them such as meet with divine approval: "Now may the God of peace who brought again from the dead our Lord Jesus, the great shepherd of the sheep, by the blood of the eternal covenant, equip you with everything good that you may do his will, working in you that which is pleasing in his sight ($\pi o\iota\hat{\omega}\nu\ \dot{\epsilon}\nu\ \dot{\eta}\mu\hat{\iota}\nu\ \tau\grave{o}$ $\epsilon\dot{\upsilon}\dot{\alpha}\rho\epsilon\sigma\tau o\nu\ \dot{\epsilon}\nu\dot{\omega}\pi\iota o\nu\ \alpha\dot{\upsilon}\tau o\hat{\upsilon}$), through Jesus Christ" (13:20-21). This is the common aim of all believers, as Paul expresses in 2 Cor 5:9-10: "whether we are at home [in the body] or away, we make it our aim to please God. For all of must appear before the judgement seat of Christ...." In parting, the author of Hebrews thus reminds his readers of whom it is they must please, whose praise or disapproval count above all others, and advises them in all their encounters as Epictetus (*Diss.* 1.30.1) advised his audience: "When you come into the presence of some prominent man, remember that Another looks from above on what is taking place, and that you must please Him rather than this man."

One's honor or lack of honor -- one's reputation -- was built upon the group's memory either of noble or base deeds enacted by the individual. If one was known as a person who had benefitted the public in some particular way, or who had fought bravely at such and such a place, the social remembrance of these deeds would perpetuate a good reputation, and reminding the public of these deeds could be expected to renew respect and honor. One's base or shameful deeds, similarly, would be recalled by the society as a warrant for showing dishonor, even as Oedipus is cursed always to be known for his incest and parricide. Where his deeds were remembered, his disgrace would be renewed. In Hebrews, it is God's memory which is of the greatest importance. God's remembrance of the believer's acts of love and service assures the believer of approval and future reward (6:10): "For God is not so unjust as to forget your work and

---

[9] The openness of all parts of a person's life to divine scrutiny is a familiar part of the Jewish tradition, as expressed in Psalm 139 or, succinctly, in Sir 23:18-19: "A man who breaks his marriage vows says to himself, 'Who sees me? Darkness surrounds me, and the walls hide me, and no one sees me. Why should I fear? The Most High will not take notice of my sins'. His fear is confined to the eyes of men, and he does not realize that the eyes of the Lord are ten thousand times brighter than the sun; they look upon all the ways of men, and perceive even the hidden places." One might be tempted to violate the norm of Torah if it were only a matter of escaping the notice and censure of the human court of opinion. Greco-Roman philosophers also found the omnipresence of God, and thus of God's sight, a useful support for the promotion of complete integrity in life. Cf. Epictetus *Diss.* 2.8.13-14, cited earlier.

the love which you showed for his sake in serving the saints, as you still do (οὐ γὰρ ἄδικος ὁ θεὸς ἐπιλαθέσθαι τοῦ ἔργου ὑμῶν καὶ τῆς ἀγάπης ἧς ἐνεδείξασθε εἰς τὸ ὄνομα αὐτοῦ)." Similarly, God's decision to forget the sins committed in the past removes the one true strike against the believer's honor which would have a lasting effect (10:17): "I will remember their sins and their misdeeds no more (καὶ τῶν ἁμαρτιῶν αὐτῶν καὶ τῶν ἀνομιῶν αὐτῶν οὐ μὴ μνησθήσομαι ἔτι)." This commitment not to remember allows the believers to stand before God's court of opinion with confidence, and heedless of any disgrace with which society might remember the deviant and marginalized community.

Finally, the references in Hebrews to the last judgement, when God will make known the divine evaluation of all people and actions, call the audience's attention to the ultimate importance of God as significant other. The author urges his hearers to increase their work of mutual encouragement and exhortation to good works -- the works which please God and bring honor before the divine court -- in light of the approach of the Great Assize, which is not depicted as remote but as an ever-nearer event on the horizon: "Let us consider how to stir up one another to love and good works, not neglecting to meet together, as is the habit of some, but encouraging one another, and all the more as you see the Day drawing near" (10:24-25; RSV). That day will signal the dissolution of the visible realm and the disclosure of the invisible world (12:26-27), and it is with regard to the values and promises of the latter that the person of faith acts and makes decisions (11:3, 7, 27). That day will be a day of reward and salvation (9:28) for those who have lived in the light of God's judgement, and so have sought to be pleasing to God, in which "each person will receive his or her commendation from God" (1 Cor 4:5); it will also be a day of disgrace for those who are evaluated by God as worthy of punishment (cf. 10:29; 10:30-31) for their transgression of the norms and standards which God has established.[10] From the author's point of view, fear of God's censure must outweigh fear of human society's censure, since the effects of the former are so much greater and lasting. The image of divine judgement becomes, thereby, a most powerful tool for strengthening commitment to group values over against society's values where these are in conflict.

Greco-Roman philosophers also appealed to this divine court as the ultimate sanction of the behavior and goals promoted by the particular philosophy, and the lever by which society's sanctions are moved aside.

---

[10] Again, the comments by Delitzsch (*Hebrews*, 188) and Weiß (*Hebräer*, 540) are instructive. It is God who evaluates the merits and claims to honor of all people, and whose evaluation leads to the final and enduring grant of honor or disgrace.

Plato (*Gorg.* 526D-527A), for example, pits this conviction against that of Callicles (the spokesperson for Greek society) that failure to excel in rhetoric so as to be able to defend oneself, one's friends, and one's kin in the law courts is a great disgrace and puts one in the danger of grave dishonor:

> I consider how I shall present my soul whole and undefiled before the judge in that day. Renouncing the honours at which the world aims, I desire only to know the truth, and to live as well as I can, and, when I die, to die as well as I can. And, to the utmost of my power, I exhort all other men to do the same. And, in return for your exhortation of me, I exhort you also to take part in the great combat (ἀγών), which is the combat of life, and greater than every other earthly conflict. And I retort (ὀνειδίζω σοι) your reproach of me, and say, that you will not be able to help yourself when the day of trial and judgement, of which I was speaking, comes upon you; you will go before the judge, the son of Aegina, and, when he has got you in his grip and is carrying you off, you will gape and your head will swim around, just as mine would in the courts of this world, and very likely someone will shamefully box you on the ears, and put upon you any sort of insult.

For Plato's Socrates, honor before the divine court is of greater value than honor before the human court of opinion, such that the latter is profitably renounced in order to concentrate undistractedly on how to attain the former. Similarly, the Jewish author of 2 Maccabees portrays the martyr Eleazar as regarding disgrace and pain before Antiochus' court as of no consequence when set against dishonor and punishment before God's court: "Even if for the present I would avoid the punishment of mortals, yet whether I live or die I shall not escape the hands of the Almighty" (2 Macc 6:26; RSV).

The author of Hebrews thus makes use of this tool, which is frequently employed by minority cultures as a means of preserving its distinctive values and commitments. Every aspect of the believer's life is open to divine scrutiny, and it is God rather than human society that one must please in order to gain lasting honor and avoid eternal disgrace. What Moxnes observed as true for Paul's cosmos is true also for the author of Hebrews: "It is before God's court that the final decision on honour or shame is made. Thus, the ultimate 'significant other' is God."[11] John Chrysostom, commenting on the "contradiction" of sinners endured by Jesus (12:3), by which he understands "the insults, the reproaches, the mockeries," expresses well the author's conviction: "Let it be granted us

---

[11] Moxnes, "Honor and Righteousness," 68.

to be approved in Heaven, and all things are endurable. Let it be granted us to fare well there, and things here are of no account."

Once more one may see the influence of Platonic dualism on the author of Hebrews, mediated, of course, through Hellenistic Judaism. The opinions derived from the visible realm are untrustworthy, based as they are on appearances (cf. 2 Cor 4:16-18), which are in turn grounded in the changeable, corruptible world. The knowledge derived from the contemplation of the eternal realities is superior and more reliable, based on the unchanging, incorruptible verities.[12] The pursuit of true and abiding honor, therefore, must not look to the opinions of those who evaluate by the standards of this shadowy reality, but rather to the opinion of the One who evaluates from the perspective of the eternal realities.[13] Just as Jesus, therefore, was not persuaded by the negative sanctions levelled against him in the course of his obedience to God, but rather looked only to God's approval and the honor which that would bring, so the addressees are urged to esteem God's approval above all else, which would lead them to continue also in obedience, that is, to value themselves according to the standards of the Christian culture.

2 The Community of Faith -- the Visible Court of Opinion

The earthly counterpart to the divine court of reputation is, for the author of Hebrews, the Christian community. It is in association with one's fellow Christians that one reinforces and has reinforced the distinctive values of that culture, commends and receives commendation for

---

[12] Cf. Johnson, *Writings*, 420: "The distinction is ... epistemological: the world of change allows only approximate perceptions, therefore, 'opinions'; but ideas can truly be 'known'." Cf. also Hurst, *Hebrews*, 9: "Since the world of sense-perception is in flux, it compares with the archetypal realm of ideas as a fleeting shadow compares with its object (cf. *Phaedo* 80b; *Tim.* 28a-29b)."

[13] Thus for Socrates, honor in the sight of those who evaluated only according to the world of shadows was without value. True knowledge without the honor or such people was incomparably better than knowledge only of the shadows accompanied by their high esteem: "And if they were in the habit of conferring honours among themselves on those who were quickest to observe the passing shadows and to remark which of them went before, and which followed after, and which were together; and who were therefore best able to draw conclusions as to the future, do you think that he [the person who had been exposed to the verities] would care for such honours and glories, or envy the possessors of them? Would he not say with Homer, 'Better to be the poor servant of a poor master', and to endure anything, rather than think as they do and live after their manner?" (Plato, *Republic* 516 B-D).

acting out these values and advancing toward peculiarly Christian goals. As long as one's fellow believers remain one's significant others, as long as interaction between Christians remains frequent and vibrant, the alternate court of opinion will remain strong and commitment to the group and its values will remain high. The author of Hebrews demonstrates a deep concern for the maintenance of this alternate court, especially in the light of waning commitment and interaction on the part of some, who have fallen into the habit (ἔθος) of "neglecting to meet together" (10:25). If the community does not remain strong enough to support its members' need for recognition of their worth, and does not provide a strong enough social base for mutual assistance, its members will be tempted increasingly to seek recognition and support from other groups, whether the Jewish communities or the Greco-Roman society. These members may extend their circle of significant others to Gentile "unbelievers," adapt themselves to the behaviors and goals valued by the dominant Greco-Roman culture, and return to the unbelieving society's definitions of virtues and direction of allegiances.

The author's exhortation, therefore, addresses this problem directly. The concluding parenesis (10:19-13:24) opens with a call to "draw near" to God through the way opened up by Christ. This approach occurs, however, in the worship of the common assembly, as προσερχώμεθα, "let us draw near," calls for the gathering of a congregation. This appeal is made explicit in 10:24-25:

> Let us consider how to stir up one another to love and good works (κατανοῶμεν ἀλλήλους εἰς παροξυσμὸν ἀγάπης καὶ καλῶν ἔργων), not neglecting to meet together, as is the habit of some (μὴ ἐγκαταλείποντες τὴν ἐπισυναγωγὴν ἑαυτῶν, καθὼς ἔθος τισίν), but encouraging one another, and all the more as you see the Day drawing near (ἀλλὰ παρακαλοῦντες, καὶ τοσούτῳ μᾶλλον ὅσῳ βλέπετε ἐγγίζουσαν τὴν ἡμέραν).

The author urges the members to interact more forcefully and in a specific way. They are to stir one another up and encourage one another with regard to holding onto their confession of the Christian hope (10:23), the mutual commitment of love, and the performance of good works. That is, they are to remind one another of what actions are valuable and praiseworthy within the ethos of the Christian alternative culture (which exhibits a subcultural relationship to the Jewish culture and a countercultural relationship to the Greco-Roman society), and to provide a strong social base to support continued pursuit of those actions and their goal ("hope").

Hebrews is thus concerned, in part, with reinforcing what Peter Berger calls a "plausibility structure," the social base which makes a particular world view tenable for an individual.[14] Beliefs, values, and hopes cannot exist in the typical human being without social reinforcement. "Put crudely, if one is to believe what neo-orthodoxy wants one to believe, in the contemporary situation, then one must be rather careful to huddle together closely and continuously with one's fellow believers."[15] *Mutatis mutandis*, the same holds true for any set of definitions of reality. In order to be tenable, the definitions (or counter-definitions) must be supported within a social group. Such social support, however, is not a necessity merely for cognitive reinforcement, but also for moral reinforcement. Filson writes about the author of Hebrews:

> He wants them to show solidarity...in regular assembling for common worship....He knows they need to keep the bond of Christian brotherhood strong especially in times when hostility from without actively besets them. They need the inner resources which can come only through common worship and mutual encouragement.[16]

Among these "inner resources," the sense of oneself as a person of value in the sight of others figures prominently among members of an honor culture.

Elsewhere in the New Testament, the congregation or community of believers is called specifically to show honor to each of its members on the basis of Christian values, and to resist making distinctions between degrees of honor based on the external society's criteria. Honor and recognition from society, lost through association with the Christian group and dissociation from traditional activities of "honorable" people, is to be replaced by recognition and honor within the group. Thus Paul advises, "love one another with mutual affection; outdo one another in showing honor" (Rom 12:10).[17] The society may honor the wealthy and place the poor below the rich in its estimation, but such worldly norms are not to pass into the Christian community (cf. Jas 2:1-7; 1 Cor 11:22).

Throughout the letter, the author of Hebrews expresses his desire that the community work hard to reinforce the commitment and behavior of its

---

[14] P. L. Berger, *The Sacred Canopy* (New York: Doubleday, 1967), 45.

[15] Berger, *Canopy*, 164.

[16] F. V. Filson, *Yesterday: A Study of Hebrews in the Light of Chapter 13* (London: SCM, 1976), 69.

[17] The reciprocity expressed in the first clause carries over into the second.

individual members. He frequently addresses the group in the second person plural to "watch" for signs of falling away in the individual:

> Watch out (Βλέπετε), brothers and sisters, lest there be in any of you (ἔν τινι ὑμῶν) an evil, unbelieving heart, leading you to fall away from the living God. But exhort one another every day (ἀλλὰ παρακαλεῖτε ἑαυτοὺς καθ᾽ ἑκάστην ἡμέραν), as long as it is called "today," that none of you may be hardened by the deceitfulness of sin (4:12-13; au. trans.).

> See to it (ἐπισκοποῦντες) that no one (μή τις) fail to obtain the favor of God; that no "root of bitterness" spring up and cause trouble, and by it the many become defiled; that no one (μή τις) be immoral or irreligious like Esau, who sold his birthright for a single meal (12:15-16).

The members of the community are collectively to take responsibility for the encouragement of each individual, to be accountable to and for one another, in order that no individual should begin to become detached from the group, that is, cease to regard the community as the body of his or her significant others, whose approval means life and self-respect. The author joins the community in this task in the hortatory subjunctive of 4:1: "Let us fear, then (Φοβηθῶμεν οὖν), lest while a promise of entering his rest remains, any of you (τις ἐξ ὑμῶν) be judged to have failed to reach it" (4:1). His work in the letter of reminding the addressees of their hope, their honor in Christ, the irrelevance of society's approval or censure, and the promise of honor before God for those who persevere, is to become the work of each member of the group in the enterprise of mutual encouragement.

The concluding chapter of Hebrews marks a return to the author's concern for the solidarity of the community: "Let brotherly love continue. Do not neglect to show hospitality to strangers, for thereby some have entertained angels unawares. Remember those who are in prison, as though in prison with them; and those who are ill-treated, since you also are in the body" (13:1-3).[18] With the exhortation to provide hospitality for travelling fellow-believers (probably missionaries or itinerant prophets), the author extends the court of opinion beyond the boundaries of the local Christian community to that of the broader Christian minority culture. His exhortations to familial love and to an intensification of solidarity where

---

[18] This exhortation builds upon the injunction implicit in the author's commendation of the examples of Moses (11:25) and the community's own past course of action (10:33). In all three places one finds self-denying solidarity with the marginalized members of the people of God commended as a mark of the "faith" that leads to honor before God and the redeemed community.

conditions are harshest aim directly at preserving the Christian community as a strong and sufficient body of significant others for the support of human life and the human need for approval and belonging.[19]

That the author himself forms an important part of this alternate court of opinion is evident. His censure, that is, his shaming of the addressees for their waning fervor and sluggishness (5:11-14) can be expected to have a powerful effect on them, namely, to stir them up to receive his encomium on the value of the benefit Christ attained for them and to respond as he directs.[20] Similarly, his praise of their former and present displays of love and service (6:9-10) and of their former demonstration of commitment even at great cost (10:32-34) is of sufficient weight to reassure the addressees of their worth and approval before God after the dire warnings of 6:6-8 and 10:26-31. The leaders of the local communities, to whom the believers are to subject themselves (thus showing honor to the leaders, but also placing a high value on their approval or censure) are also a part of this court of opinion (13:17).

Finally, the author broadens the picture of this court of opinion to include the community of faith throughout history. Those who have persevered in faith and received divine approval (11:1-40) are now the spectators of the earthly community's contest. They form an invisible court of opinion, an "encircling cloud of witnesses" (τοσοῦτον ἔχοντες περικείμενον ἡμῖν νέφος μαρτύρων, 12:1), whose approval and praise can

---

[19] Cf. Worley, "God's Faithfulness," 217: "What the author of Hebrews has attempted to do with commissive language is exhort his readers to a faithfulness before God and a dependability in brotherly love in the face of financial and social pressures, as well as a waning of Christian enthusiasms, which treaten the fellowship of the church and the readers' access to God." J. H. Neyrey ("Poverty," note 21) explores also the relationship between the creation of an artificial family of believers, material support, and moral support through showing honor within the group: "Time does not allow us to pursue the issue of 'fictive kinship' in relationship to the disciples of Jesus. Previous studies have tended to view it primarily in terms of the emotional and social advantage of association with Jesus, the 'group glue'. But might fictive kinship also function in the restoration of the kinship honor lost through loyalty to Jesus. Not only would fictive kin share material wealth (food, clothing, shelter) with the 'poor', but their honoring of them would begin to replace the shame experience by these 'poor' for their allegiance to Jesus."

[20] Cf. Moffatt, *Hebrews*, 70: "The author, himself a διδάσκαλος, as he is in possession of this mature γνῶσις, is trying to shame his friends out of their imperfect grasp of their religion"; also Calvin, *Hebrews*, 58: "This reproof hath in it no little pungency to rouse the Jews from their state of sloth. He says that it is out of all character and a shame that they should be in the elements when they ought to be teachers....To shame them all the more, however, he says the first principles, as if one said, the alphabet."

be won by those who run the race with the same faith and perseverance (6:11). The concept of such an extended community is not unknown in Jewish and Christian literature, and the prospect of the praise of those who have preceded the present generation could be valued as a great reward. In 4 Macc 13:17, for example, the seven brothers encourage one another to face the disgrace and agony awaiting them with this promise: "Abraham, Isaac, and Jacob will welcome us, and all the fathers will praise us (ἡμᾶς...πάντες οἱ πατέρες ἐπαινέσουσιν)." The believer stands thus not only within the earthly court of opinion, which may be small and insignificant in comparison with the unbelieving society, but before a vast assembly of significant others who award praise and censure on the basis of loyalty to Christ and obedience to God:

> You have come to Mount Zion and to the city of the living God, the heavenly Jerusalem, and to innumerable angels in festal gathering, and to the assembly of the first-born who are enrolled in heaven, and to a judge who is God of all, and to the spirits of just men made perfect, and to Jesus, the mediator of a new covenant, and to the sprinkled blood that speaks more graciously than the blood of Abel (12:22-24; RSV).

It is before this court that the believer is called to maintain and enhance honor, which will result in everlasting prestige.

3 The Basis of the Christian's Honor

Within the Christian court of reputation, honor is grounded upon a foundation significantly different from that recognized by Greco-Roman society.[21] For the author of Hebrews, the honor of the Christian rests upon the honor of Christ. The dignity enjoyed by the Son following his earthly ministry has already been explored at length (cf. 1:1-13; 2:6-9; 3:1-6; 10:12-13). One will recall that the author's development of the degree of this dignity served two rhetorical purposes: first, it made more fearsome the danger of offending such dignity; second, it enhanced the believers' dignity in so far as the honor of the Son foreshadowed the honor of the "many sons and daughters" of 2:10.[22] While the believers must wait for

---

[21] Such a distinction is commonly found in minority cultures and is often explicitly expressed, as in, for example, Epictetus *Ench*. 24.1 (see chapter three above).

[22] So Lane, *Hebrews 1-8*, 55: "God's fixed purpose is to lead many children to glory." Cf. 2 Th 2:14: "For this purpose he called you through our procalamation of the good news, so that you may obtain the glory of our Lord Jesus Christ." Cf. also Weiß (*Hebräer*, 205), who stresses the common destiny of the "Son," Jesus, and the

their final entrance into this "glory," living in the meantime as "sons without honor"[23] they already enjoy the dignity of being called sons and daughters by God.[24] Recalling the dictum of Sir 3:11, that "a man's honor comes from his father's prestige, and a mother in disgrace is a reproach to her children (ἡ γὰρ δόξα ἀνθρώπου ἐκ τιμῆς πατρὸς αὐτοῦ, καὶ ὄνειδος τέκνοις μήτηρ ἐν ἀδοξίᾳ; au. trans.)," the acceptance of the believer by God as a child of God's own family provides a firm and exalted foundation for the believer's honor and self-respect.[25] As Moxnes observed with regard to Romans, so one may conclude with regard to Hebrews: "the question of honour and shame is now a question of their relationship to Christ."[26]

The author closely links the exalted Christ and the believers by stressing the kinship which exists between them:

"many sons and daughters."

[23] So Moxnes, "Honor and Righteousness," 73.

[24] Cf. 12:5: "You have forgotten the exhortation which addresses you as sons and daughters (καὶ ἐκλέλησθε τῆς παρακλήσεως, ἥτις ὑμῖν ὡς υἱοῖς διαλέγεται)"; cf. also 12:7, "God is dealing with you as sons and daughters (ὡς υἱοῖς ὑμῖν προσφέρεται ὁ θεός)."

[25] On the basis of which, one would agree with Attridge's observation that "also in those texts that promise or describe the exaltation of the righteous, their status is marked by their being named sons of God" (*Hebrews*, 48). The notion of being the offspring of God figures prominently in Greco-Roman philosophical literature, the most famous example being, perhaps, Aratus, *Phaenomena* 5, cited in Acts 17:28. Epictetus (*Diss* 1.3.1, 4) promotes awareness of one's kinship with the divine as the true and most secure basis for self-respect, which consequently frees one from such heavy reliance on the lay society for recognition of one's worth and confirmation of self-respect: "If a man could only subscribe heart and soul, as he ought, to this doctrine, that we are all primarily begotten of God, and that God is the father of men as well as of gods, I think that he will entertain no ignoble or mean thought about himself.... Since, then, it is inevitable that every man, whoever he be, should deal with each thing according to the opinion which he forms about it, these few, who think that by their birth they are called to fidelity, to self-respect, and to unerring judgement in the use of external impressions (πρὸς πίστιν... καὶ πρὸς αἰδῶ καὶ πρὸς ἀσφαλείαν τῆς χρήσεως τῶν φαντασιῶν), cherish no mean or ignoble thoughts about themselves, whereas the multitude do quite the opposite." Awareness of this kinship with God, Epictetus argues (*Diss.* 1.13.3), transcends the false distinctions and inequalities created by human society: "Slave, will you not bear with your own brother, who has Zeus as his progenitor and is, as it were, a son born of the same seed as yourself and of the same sowing from above; but if you have been stationed in a like position above others, will you forthwith set yourself up as a tyrant? Do you not remember what you are, and over whom you rule -- that they are kinsmen, that they are brothers by nature, that they are the offspring of Zeus?"

[26] Moxnes, "Honor and Righteousness," 72.

For he who sanctifies and those who are sanctified have all one origin (ὁ τε γὰρ ἁγιάζων καὶ οἱ ἁγιαζόμενοι ἐξ ἑνὸς πάντες). For this cause he is not ashamed to call them brethren (δι' ἣν αἰτίαν οὐκ ἐπαισχύνεται ἀδελφοὺς αὐτοὺς καλεῖν), saying, "I will proclaim thy name to my brethren, in the midst of the congregation I will praise thee." And again..., "Here am I, and the children God has given me (' Ἰδοὺ ἐγὼ καὶ τὰ παιδία ἅ μοι ἔδωκεν ὁ θεός)."

Reinforcing the concept of kinship with Christ serves the author's program of reassuring his addressees of their honor as Christians, for, in first-century Mediterranean societies, "the advance of one member of an agnatic family would advantage all his kindred."[27] The common ancestry, namely belonging to the family of God as son and daughters, gives believers immense dignity, such that even the exalted Christ can claim them as brothers and sisters without damage to his own honor.[28] They are members of a household of which God is the head and over which Christ rules as Son and heir (3:6; 10:21), and as such share in the honor of the head of the house, who is most worthy of all of honor (3:3-4). Adoption into this family of God brings them also into the family of the noble and revered figures of sacred history, particularly Abraham, among

---

[27] Derrett, *Jesus's Audience*, 38. This passage also appeals to a friendship *topos* expressed in Aristotle (*Eth. Nic.* 8.12.3), in the middle of his discussion of friendship: "siblings love each other as being born of the same parents; for their identity with them makes them identical with each other (which is the reason why people talk of 'the same blood', 'the same stock', and so on). They are, therefore, in a sense the same thing, though in separate individuals." That Jesus and the believers have a common origin creates a strong bond, a close association between the two parties, such that a Mediterranean hearer would come to expect the relationship between Jesus and the believers as a relationship of friends, who share their assets, who assist one another. The passage also emphasizes the kinship (and therefore friendship) between believers, and thus contributes to the author's appeal for the believers sharing their goods with one another as any have need (13:16), continuing in close association (*syn-* compounds often appearing in friendship treatises) with the imprisoned and otherwise marginalized members (13:3), and maintaining familial love (13:1).

[28] Cf. Calvin, *Hebrews*, 21-22: "Now appropriately as well as significantly he says that he is not ashamed. For how great is the distance between us and him? Much, therefore, does he humble himself when he vouchsafes us the name of brethren; otherwise we are unworthy that he should esteem us beneath his servants. And this so high an honour vouchsafed us he enhances by a circumstance; for he that speaks is Christ, no more a mortal man in the form of a servant, but clothed with immortal glory after his resurrection: therefore this title has the same force as if he raised us into heaven with himself." Cf. also Moxnes, "Honor and Shame," 175: "It is their relationship to God that gives Christians their honor -- ascribed, not achieved, as 'children of God' (Rom 8:14-17; Jn 1:12-13)."

whose descendants the believers are now numbered (2:17). This "ideological genealogy"[29] enhances the believer's sense of honor, increasing the dignity they enjoy as members of the redeemed community.

The author further stresses the believers' connection with Jesus by calling them "partners with Christ" (μέτοχοι γὰρ τοῦ Χριστοῦ, 3:14). This enhances the believer's honor in two ways: first, the believer can expect to have a share in the honor and dignity which Jesus as Son has attained (cf. Mt 19:28; Jn 17:22); second, that the exalted Christ would associate with the believers so closely as to form a partnership demonstrates that they are regarded by him as honorable themselves.[30] The believers, as "partners in a heavenly calling" (μέτοχοι, 3:1),[31] share in the inheritance of the children of God. Like Jesus, the "heir of all things" (1:2), the believers are also heirs (1:14; 6:17; 9:15) who look forward to receiving their full honor and possessions in the kingdom promised by God (12:28).

Language of purification, sanctification, and forgiveness of sins (from the cultural resources of the author's Jewish heritage), all of which figures so prominently in Hebrews (particularly 7:11-10:18), also speaks to the believers of their honor. Before God's court, sins -- transgressions of God's commands -- result in the punishment of the transgressor, hence in his or her disgrace before God and the holy angels. They are affronts to God's honor which make one worthy, in God's estimation, of punishment (cf. 10:29). The author of Hebrews addresses his audience as "holy" (3:1), that is, as set apart from that which prevents one's coming before God. He reminds them of their purification in Christ (1:3; 2:17; 9:12; 10:22), of the cleansing of their consciences (9:14), indicating thereby the removal of the marks against their honor before God's court, such that they may now stand with confidence before God, and accept the full dignity of adoption by God (provided, of course, that they persevere in trust).

The believers' access to God is itself a high privilege, an honor which they enjoy through the work of Christ. Formerly, access to the throne of God was limited to the Jewish high priest alone. The architectural divisions of the Temple, from Outer Court to Holy of Holies, replicated the degrees of dignity enjoyed by all peoples. The Gentiles enjoyed the least; Israelites enjoyed limited privilege of access to the inner courts;

---

[29] Moxnes, "Honor and Shame, 142.

[30] Cf. Malina, *New Testament World*, 33-34: "In the Mediterranean world, no one would freely associate with you unless your honor rating were good, and so good name and prestige are the most valuable of assets."

[31] As "partners" with one another, the believers are called to be "friends," and thus to enact the ideals of friendship such as sharing their goods as any have need and holding to the same outlook (e.g., holding fast to the confession of the believer).

priests enjoyed the distinction of access to the Holy Place; the high priest alone enjoyed the privilege of access to the Holy of Holies, which set him above all fellow-Israelites in dignity.[32] The author of Hebrews, however, declares that God has conferred this dignity on the believers on account of Jesus' efficacious brokerage on their behalf. Christians may now approach the throne of grace (4:16) and "enter the holy place...by a new and living way which [Christ] inaugurated for us through the veil" (10:19-20). Indeed, according to the author the privilege now enjoyed by the believers surpasses the privilege enjoyed by the priests and all who participate in the Jerusalem Temple cultus: "We have an altar from which those who serve the tabernacle have no right (οὐκ ἔχουσιν ἐξουσίαν) to eat" (13:10). The believers thus enjoy a privilege, and hence a dignity, inaccessible to the most honored of non-Christians.[33]

Finally, the believers' honor is grounded in God's declaration of association with them, by which he commits to them a share in the divine honor and commits to preserve their honor as an extension of God's own dignity.[34] The believers are the "people of God" (4:9), that is, the "people called by God's name," and whose honor is thus bound up with God's. Their honor is thus guaranteed by God.[35] God declares this association with those who, like the faithful forebears, refrain from accepting any earthly homeland in favor of persevering in the quest for a home with God (11:16): "Therefore, God is not ashamed to be called their God (διὸ οὐκ ἐπαισχύνεται αὐτοὺς ὁ θεὸς θεὸς ἐπικαλεῖσθαι αὐτῶν)." Michel notes that οὐκ ἐπαισχύνεται does not give expression to an inner feeling, but to a public declaration or confession, God's testimony on

---

[32] Cf. Josephus *BJ* 4.164, 169 (cited above),

[33] Neyrey ("John 18-19") argues that "the shame of arrest, trial, and execution," it is hoped, "will wipe out Jesus' claim to any share in the limited honor available, and restore the prestige of the Temple aristocracy." According to the author of Hebrews, then, the opposite was in fact the result. In light of Christ's resurrection and exaltation (i.e., the vindication of his claim to honor), the prestige of the Temple aristocracy was added to the dignity of Jesus as High Priest, and thereafter to his brothers and sisters for whom he acquired this benefit.

[34] That this declaration of association brings honor to the believers was clearly recognized by John Chrysostom, commenting on Heb 11:16 (*NPNF¹*, 14:475; cf. Migne, *PG* 63.169): "Ah! how great a dignity! He vouchsafes 'to be called their God'."

[35] One will recall this assurance as expressed, for example, in Daniel's prayer (9:18-19): "O my God, incline thy ear and hear; open thy eyes and behold our desolations, and the city which is called by thy name.... Give heed and act; delay not, for thy own sake, O my God, because thy city and thy people are called by thy name."

behalf of the ancestors of faith.[36] This confession by God, which gives the believer his or her honor, answers the believer's confession that he or she is a "sojourner and foreigner on the earth."[37]

The author of Hebrews thus gives his addressees two powerful motivations to preserve their association with Christ, their obedience to God, and their enjoyment of the gift of access to the throne of God. First, to act so as to break these associations or refuse these gifts would be to incur the wrath of God, and to make oneself the object of divine punishment; second, to act so as to jeopardize one's association with Christ (and so with God), and to reject the gift of access to God, would be to strike a blow against one's own honor and dignity at its very foundations. Thus, the author seeks to motivate his audience to persevere in faith and obedience through both the arousal of fear and the consideration of honor.

The Reinterpretation of Disgrace

While, on the one hand, the author seeks to detach the addressees from the force of Greco-Roman society's evaluation of their experiences and attachments as disgraceful, he also seeks to provide an alternative interpretation of those experiences, an effort which serves to strengthen commitment to the Christian counterculture. In effect, he seeks to

---

[36] Michel, *Hebräerbrief*, 266: "ἐπαισχύνεσθαι in the context of acts of confession answers the ἀρνεῖσθαι of Mt 10:33. οὐκ ἐπαισχύνεται is thus an old circumlocution for confession, for bold and open declaration, and not a psychological feeling. God thus bears testimony (= μαρτυρεῖ) for the patriarchs, in that God takes their names into God's own self-identification (Gen 28:13; Exod 3:6)."

[37] That one's honor comes from bearing testimony to God, in effect, appears also in Epictetus, *Diss.* 1.29.44-49: "'Take a governorship'. I take it and having done so I show how an educated man comports himself. 'Lay aside the laticlave, and having put on rags come forward in a character to correspond'.... 'In what role, then, do you mount the stage now?' As a witness summoned by God.... What kind of witness do you bear for God? 'I am in sore straits, O Lord, and in misfortune; no one regards me, no one gives me anything, all blame me and speak ill of me'. Is this the witness that you are going to bear, and is this the way in which you are going to disgrace the summons (καταισχύνειν τὴν κλῆσιν ἣν κέκληκεν) which He gave you, in that He bestowed this honour upon you and deemed you worthy to be brought forward in order to bear testimony so important (ὅτι σε ἐτίμησεν ταύτην τὴν τιμὴν καὶ ἄξιον ἡγήσατο προσαγαγεῖν εἰς μαρτυρίαν τηλικαύτην;)?" Similarly for the believers, changes in status within Greco-Roman society do not alter one's essential dignity, for this resides not in the opinion of unbelievers and the possession of what is valued by them, but rather in faithful witness to the better hope which God provides for those who commit themselves to God as clients of the Deity.

transform the community's experience of disgrace into a claim to honor recognized by God and the whole Christian movement. Paul censured those whom he considered to be perverters of the gospel by claiming that they "boast in their disgrace" (Phil 3:19); the non-Christian members of the Greco-Roman societies could, however, level that claim against the Christian movement, since the followers of Christ considered as their most ennobling achievements the very activities and commitments which made them dishonorable in the eyes of unbelievers.

First, the author interprets the addressees' experience of hardship, loss of status and property, and endurance of continued reproach as a sign of their adoption into the family of God. The believers experience thus not society's rejection and censure, but God's acceptance and discipline (12:5-11), whereby they are fitted to receive their divine inheritance and enjoy the honor toward which God leads them (2:10):

> You have forgotten the exhortation which addresses you as sons (ὡς υἱοῖς) -- "My son, do not regard lightly the discipline of the Lord, nor lose courage when you are punished by him (μὴ ὀλιγώρει παιδείας κυρίου μηδὲ ἐκλύου ὑπ' αὐτοῦ ἐλεγχόμενος). For the Lord disciplines him whom he loves, and chastises every son whom he receives (ὃν γὰρ ἀγαπᾷ κύριος παιδεύει, μαστιγοῖ δὲ πάντα υἱὸν ὃν παραδέχεται)." It is for discipline that you have to endure. God is treating you as sons (εἰς παιδείαν ὑπομένετε, ὡς υἱοῖς ὑμῖν προσφέρεται ὁ θεός); for what son is there whom his father does not discipline? If you are left without discipline, in which all have participated (μέτοχοι γεγόνασιν πάντες), then you are illegitimate children and not sons (ἄρα νόθοι καὶ οὐχ υἱοί ἐστε). Besides this, we have had earthly fathers to discipline us and we respected them. Shall we not much more be subject to the Father of spirits and live? For they disciplined us for a short time at their pleasure, but he disciplines us for our good, that we may share his holiness. For the moment all discipline seems painful rather than pleasant; later it yields the peaceful fruit of righteousness to those who have been trained by it (12:5-11).[38]

The author encourages the addressees to regard their trials and the reproach acquired for Christ as a sign of their adoption by God -- precisely because they experience this discipline (παιδεία) at God's hands they can have assurance that they are indeed true sons and daughters, for whose

---

[38] Concerning the educative (rather than punitive) significance of suffering in Hebrews against the backgrounds of Jewish and Greco-Roman views of suffering, please see N. Clayton Croy, "Endurance in Suffering: The Example of Christ and the Educative Function of Suffering. A Study of Hebrews 12:1-13 and Its Religious and Philosophical Context" (Ph.D. dissertation, Emory University, 1995).

upbringing the Parent takes responsibility, and not illegitimate children (νόθοι) who have no claim to a share in the inheritance. Thus the trials by which the believers are "trained" (γεγυμνασμένοις) work for the believers' benefit (συμφέρον) and will yield its fruit. Only those who have become sharers in discipline (παιδείας ἧς μέτοχοι γεγόνασιν πάντες, 12:8) are also partners of Christ (μέτοχοι γὰρ τοῦ Χριστοῦ γεγόναμεν, 3:14) and sharers in the heavenly calling (κλήσεως ἐπουρανίου μέτοχοι, 3:1).[39]

Within the Jewish minority culture, the transformation of suffering and disgrace into a sign of God's favor was well-known. The author of Wisdom of Solomon (3:5) went so far as to recast death -- indeed the explicitly shameful death -- as divine discipline which tests and proves the worth of an individual. The final result is not disgrace in the eyes of society, but profit in being benefitted by God and honor in being proven worthy of God: "having been disciplined a little, they will be greatly benefitted, for God has tested them and found them worthy of himself (καὶ ὀλίγα παιδευθέντες μεγάλα εὐεργετηθήσονται, ὅτι ὁ θεὸς ἐπείρασεν αὐτοὺς καὶ εὗρεν αὐτοὺς ἀξίους ἑαυτοῦ; RSV)." The author of Hebrews shares this conviction, as he urges the believers to cherish their marginalization and censure by society as a process by which their worth is proven (and will one day be manifested to all) and by which they come into the closest possible relationship with their Benefactor.[40]

The second manner in which the author reinterprets the audience's experience of disgrace is through the image of the contest (ἀγών). When reminding the audience of their former experience of hardship in which they lost property (10:34), fell victim to public reproach (i.e., assaults on their honor, 10:33), yet nevertheless endured confidently and boldly stood by their fellows who were imprisoned and maltreated, the author uses the word ἄθλησις to sum up the entire chapter in the community's history. Chrysostom comments on the significance of the author's decision with regard to terminology: "Moreover he did not say 'trials' but 'contest', which is an expression of commendation and of very great praise (οὐκ εἶπε

---

[39] Cf. Worley, "God's Faithfulness," 55: "This mutual responsibility extends even to a shared suffering (10:34; 11:25; 13:3) in order that there might be a shared inheritance (11:9, 20, 21; 12:14-17)."

[40] Calvin, *Hebrews*, 171, commenting on 12:5, recognizes the connection between the signs of God's adoption and God's benefaction displayed in the believers' experience of suffering, such that he can accuse those who wish to avoid this marginalization as "unthankful" in light of the great benefits which they stand to receive by enduring: "If the chastisements of God testify his love towards us, it is shameful that they should be regarded with disdain or aversion. For they must be exceedingly unthankful that endure not to be chastened of God to salvation; nay that spurn a token of his fatherly loving kindness."

πειρασμοὺς ἀλλὰ ἄθλησιν, ὅπερ ἐστὶν ἐγκωμίου ὄνομα καὶ ἐπαίνων μεγίστων)."[41] Sensitive himself to matters of honor, Chrysostom perceives the author's strategic use of this image, by which he turns an experience of disgrace and marginalization into a competition for honor.

The author employs a more extended athletic image in the exhortation based around the example of Jesus in 12:1-4:

> Therefore, since we have so great an encircling cloud of witnesses (περικείμενον ἡμῖν νέφος μαρτύρων), let us also lay aside every weight, and the sin which clings so closely (τὴν εὐπερίστατον ἁμαρτίαν), and let us run with perseverance the race that is set before us (δι' ὑπομονῆς τρέχωμεν τὸν προκείμενον ἡμῖν ἀγῶνα), looking to Jesus the pioneer and perfecter of our faith, who for the joy that was set before him endured (ὑπέμεινεν) the cross, despising the shame, and is seated at the right hand of the throne of God. Consider him who endured (ὑπομεμενηκότα) from sinners such hostility against himself, so that you may not grow weary or fainthearted. In your struggle against sin (πρὸς τὴν ἁμαρτίαν ἀνταγωνιζόμενοι) you have not yet resisted to the point of shedding your blood.

While the "witnesses" are also examples of faith whom the addressees are called to imitate (cf. 6:12), Attridge is correct in noting that the author's description of these heroes of faith as a "cloud of witnesses" which encircles the believers conjures up the image of the spectators of competitions or games.[42] It is from the spectators and the judges that the champions desire to gain honor and among whom they wish to enjoy esteem; similarly the believers are set before those who have run the course with faith and before God, the judge of all, and it is before this arena that they are called to compete for honor (which, of course, all may win). Like runners in the games, they are called to lay aside every thing which might hold them back in the race, and to set aside "sin" as if it were a clinging garment, and hence an impediment to running the course.[43] Sin, indeed, appears as their antagonist (πρὸς τὴν ἁμαρτίαν ἀνταγωνιζόμενοι, 12:4) in this contest (ἀγών, 12:1), and as the runner must fix his or her eyes on the goal and avoid all distractions, so the believer is to fix his or her gaze on Jesus, who shows the way to victory (12:2).[44]

---

[41] Chrysostom on 10:32, *NPNF¹* 14:461; Migne, *PG* 63.149.

[42] Attridge, *Hebrews*, 354.

[43] Cf. Spicq, *Hébreux*, 2.385.

[44] So Spicq, *Hébreux*, 2.385: "The race begun, the athlete must not be distracted no matter what happens. He must not look either behind nor to either side, but rather

The athletic contest in the Greco-Roman world afforded the persevering competitor with an opportunity to achieve great distinction and prestige from his society. While monetary prizes were often given at games, the most valued prizes were the wreaths and proclamations given the winners, by which their reputation was greatly enhanced and their honor raised to new pitch. It is not surprising, therefore, that it became a metaphor commonly used by spokespersons of minority cultures.[45] By means of athletic imagery, they could portray the pursuit and achievement of the goals valued by their alternative culture as a path to acclaim and honor, and, for those within the minority group, turn experiences of hardship and deprivation into a noble endeavor. Just as athletes endured much pain and even humiliation on the way to victory, so the member of a low-status minority group could regard her or his suffering and humiliation as a sort of training for an honorable victory.

Athletic imagery is a favorite for Epictetus, who encourages the aspiring Stoic to endure hardships with courage and without dismay, since these are but the result of Zeus matching one up with a wrestling partner for training, the result of which will be a great victory: "It is difficulties that show what you are. Consequently, when a difficulty befalls, remember that God, like a physical trainer, has matched you with a rugged young man. What for? some one says. So that you may become an Olympic victor; but that cannot be done without sweat" (*Diss.* 1.24.1-2). Reputation, abuse, and even praise (δοξάριον, λοιδορία, ἔπαινος) are among those aspects of human experience listed as obstacles which can be thrown in the athlete's way, but which are despised and passed by on the way towards becoming "the invincible athlete" (ὁ ἀνίκητος ἀθλητής, *Diss.* 1.18.21).[46]

Both Epictetus and Dio Chrysostom speak of the life of the Cynic also as an athletic contest. Far from the normal channels of advancement in reputation and prestige, the Cynic's experience is nevertheless ennobled as

---

fix his gaze on the goal and dream of nothing but victory. Thus the Christian is to contemplate Christ unceasingly."

[45] For a detailed discussion, see the classic study by Victor C. Pfitzner, *Paul and the Agon Motif: Traditional Athletic Imagery in the Pauline Literature* (Leiden: Brill, 1967).

[46] Epictetus returns often to the problem of the experience of losing honor and encountering revilers, as again in *Diss.* 3.20.9: "Is it possible, then, to derive any advantage from these things? -- Yes, from everything. -- Even from the man who reviles me?-- And what good does his wrestling-companion do the athlete? The very greatest. So also my reviler becomes one who prepares me for my contest; he exercises my patience, my dispassionateness, my gentleness."

an "Olympic contest" (Epictetus *Diss.* 3.22.52), and his hardships, seen by more mainstream members of the Greco-Roman culture as tokens of the Cynic's depravity, are interpreted by the Cynic as the training ordered by Zeus (*Diss.* 3.22.56). Dio (*Or.* 8.11-13) describes the lifestyle of Diogenes of Sinope as that of one who competes in a contest, in which the antagonists are of the most difficult sort, namely hardships.[47] While the Cynic endures the loss of his reputation and status within society, he remains a "noble person":

> The noble man (ὁ γενναῖος) holds his hardships to be his greatest antagonists [which he engages] not to win a sprig of parsley...nor a bit of wild olive, or of pine, but to win happiness and virtue all the days of his life, and not merely when the Eleans make proclamation, or the Corinthians, or the Thessalian assembly, ... disclosing no weakness even though he must endure the lash or give his body to be cut or burned. Hunger, exile, loss of reputation (πενίαν δὲ καὶ φυγὴν καὶ ἀδοξίαν), and the like have no terrors for him; nay, he holds them as mere trifles, and while in their very grip the perfect man (τὸν ἄνδρα τὸν τέλειον) is often as sportive as boys with their dice and their coloured balls (*Or.* 8.15-16).

Athletic imagery was also in common use within the Jewish minority culture as a means of transforming the disgraceful and status-degrading experiences of the faithful Jews into an honorable competition which resulted in a reward before God. Athletic metaphors are particularly common in 4 Maccabees, an encomium of the martyrs which transforms their tortures into a contest (ἀγών) and the tyrant's hall into an "arena" of hardships (γυμνασία πόνων, 11.20).[48] The seven brothers are praised as "athletes" (ἀσκήτας) of religion and "contestants" (ἀγωνισταί)

---

[47] "And when a certain man asked whether he [Diogenes] too came to see the contest, he said, 'No, but to take part.'" Then when the man laughed and asked him who his competitors were, he said with that customary glance of his: 'The toughest there are and the hardest to beat, men whom no Greek can look straight in the eye; not competitors, however, who sprint or wrestle or jump, not those that box, throw the spear, and hurl the discus, but those that chasten a man (τοὺς σωφρονίζοντας).' 'Who are they, pray?' asked the other. 'Hardships,' he replied, 'very severe and insuperable for the gluttonous and folly-stricken men who feast the livelong day and snore at night, but which yield to thin, spare men, whose waists are more pinched than those of wasps.'"

[48] Cf. Thompson, *Beginnings of Christian Philosophy*, 64: "Both Philo and 4 Maccabees belong to a minority culture which was subject to persecution and acts of violence. Because they identified with this minority culture, the image of the contest was a useful way of giving a positive interpretation of the fate of their people."

competing for virtue. By means of this metaphor, the disgrace of punishment and mutilation becomes a contest for honor, in which even to compete is noble: "My sons, noble is the contest to which you are called (γενναῖος ὁ ἀγών, ἐφ᾽ ὃν κληθέντες) to bear witness for the nation. Compete zealously (ἐναγωνίσασθε προθύμως) for the ancestral law!" (16.16). 4 Macc 17:11-16 offers an extended athletic metaphor comparable in scope to Heb 12:1-4: In the divine contest (ἀγὼν θεῖος), Eleazar was the first contestant (προηγωνίζετο), the mother of the seven brother competed (ἐνήθλει), the seven brothers participated in the contest (ἠγωνίζετο·), and the tyrant was the antagonist (ἀντηγωνίζετο). Piety itself crowned, that is, honored the victors (θεοσέβεια...τοὺς ἀθλητὰς στεφανοῦσα). Also like the author of Hebrews, the author of 4 Maccabees (in the mouths of the seven brothers, 13.15) places only two options before his audience: "for great is the soul's contest (ψυχῆς ἀγών) and great the danger of eternal torment lying before those who transgress the commandment of God (κίνδυνος...τοῖς παραβᾶσι)." One either strives for honor before God or, yielding to the pressures of society (and its own promises of honor and approval, 4 Macc 8.5-7), incurs the danger shared by those who provoke God through disobedience.

The use of contest or athletic imagery opens up the way for the author's use of *topoi* pertaining to Courage, harnassing this greatly admired Greco-Roman virtue for the cause of perseverance in Christian community and activity. According to the author of the *Rhetorica ad Herennium* (3.2.3), "courage is the reaching for great things and contempt for what is mean; also the endurance of hardship in expectation of profit (*fortitudo est rerum magnarum appetitio et rerum humilium contemptio et laboris cum utilitatis ratione perpessio*)." The latter part of this definition describes a prominent part of the author's exhortation. Even as the heroes of faith endured, even as Jesus endured both cross and contradiction (ὑπέμεινεν σταυρόν, 12:2; ὑπομεμενηκότα ὑπὸ τῶν ἁμαρτωλῶν εἰς ἑαυτὸν ἀντιλογίαν, 12:3), so the addressees are to exhibit endurance in their contest (δι᾽ ὑπομονῆς τρέχωμεν τὸν προκείμενον ἡμῖν ἀγῶνα, 12:1). Their fortitude in faith will itself ennoble their lives as an expression of the most admired virtue; their endurance unto the end will attain for them the greater honors which God has reserved for the people of faith.

The third dominant way in which the author renders noble the experience of disgrace is through his use of Christ, Abraham, Moses, and the martyrs as examples (discussed above in chapter four). These figures establish a pattern by which the endurance of suffering and reproach leads to honor and joy in the heavenly homeland. Since the end is the enjoyment of privilege and reward before the court of God, the means to that end must also be considered honorable and full of promise. John Chrysostom underscores this in his comments on the relationship between the experience of Christ and that of the believers: "Seest thou that to suffer affliction is not the portion of those who are utterly forsaken; if indeed it was by this that God first honored His Son, by leading Him through sufferings?"[49] Christ's pioneering journey through sufferings and disgrace to the place of highest honor in the cosmos renders the sufferings and disgrace of Christians honorable, since they are promised a share in Christ's honor.[50]

For the author of Hebrews, even though obedience to Christ and solidarity with the believing community has led in the past and shall lead in the future to disrepute in the eyes of the world, these are the means by which one will come to stand in honor before God and not be put to shame on the Day of Judgement. By recasting these experiences as the discipline that leads to inheritance and the contest that leads to victory, and by pointing to the examples of those who have passed through suffering and disgrace into eternal renown, the author seeks to cause the addressees to regard their present status in a new light, namely from the perspective of the honor and joy they will have in the heavenly, and therefore eternally enduring, realm. Thus inspired, the believers will persevere in discipline (12:7), persevere in their contest against sin (12:1), and, following the examples of perseverance and faith (6:12), maintain their commitment to Christ and the community until the time of rewarding.

---

[49] Chrysostom on 2:10, *NPNF¹*, 14:384; Migne, *PG* 63.40: ὁρᾷς ὅτι τὸ παθεῖν κακῶς, οὐκ ἔστιν ἐγκαταλελειμμένων; Εἰδὲ τούτῳ πρώτῳ τετίμηκε τὸν Υἱὸν ὁ Θεός, τῷ διὰ παθημάτων αὐτὸν ἀγαγεῖν.

[50] Thus Calvin, *Hebrews*, 170, commenting on 12:2: "Now he commends the patience of Christ to our notice on two accounts; because he endured a most painful death, and because he despised the shame. He then records the glorious end of his death, that believers may know that all the ills they endure will issue in their glory and salvation, provided they be followers of Christ." The theme persists in modern scholars no less than in the ancient commentators, cf. Héring, *Hebrews*, 16: "And, strangely enough, what is true of the Man in the pre-eminent sense, applies to a certain extent also to men with a small 'm'. They must take up their cross and follow the Saviour, so that one day thay can share in future glory"; also Peterson, *Hebrews and Perfection*, 187: "The perfecting of Christ 'through suffering' provides a pattern for Christian discipleship. Christians share to a certain extent...the same struggle or contest that Christ endured and, because he pioneered the way, they have the prospect of enjoying his victory if they share his faith and manifest the same sort of perseverance in the face of hostility and suffering."

THE CHRISTIAN'S PROPER SHAME

Despite the author's desire to desensitize his addressees to the honor rating of the outside society, he clearly does not wish to render them "shameless." As he nurtures their desire for honor before God's court, he nurtures also their sensitivity to the opinion of those who form the truly significant others for the believers, namely the Christian group and its leaders. Within the framework of the values of the minority culture, the sanctions of "noble" and "base" are still expected to have an effect on the individual believers, urging them on to certain actions or dissuading them from certain behaviors. The addressees may be held accountable to the expectations of Christian leaders, and may be expected to respond to their censure, as in 5:11-14:

> About this we have much to say which is hard to explain, since you have become dull of hearing. For though by this time you ought to be teachers, you need some one to teach you again the first principles of God's word. You need milk, not solid food; for every one who lives on milk is unskilled in the word of righteousness, for he is a child. But solid food is for the mature, for those who have their faculties trained by practice to distinguish good from evil.

The author's goal in this passage is to cause the addressees to be zealous to acquit themselves of the charge that they are not ready for mature teaching. Rather than describing the actual conditions of the hearers (in which case the author's decision to go on to deliver the πολὺς λόγος καὶ δυσερμήνευτος λέγειν concerning Jesus as priest after the order of Melchizedek would be of questionable wisdom), the author seeks to rouse them to demonstrate with zeal that they are mature and ready to take on the responsibility of teaching what they have accepted as true rather than requiring further persuasion and instruction in the certainty of the gospel.[51] As teachers, of course, they become active participants in the

---

[51]   Thus Attridge (*Hebrews*, 157) argues that 5:11-14 is "an ironic *captatio benevolentiae*. The stance that 'this material is difficult because you are slow-witted', followed by the more positive remarks of 6:1-3 and 9-12, is designed to elicit the response, 'no, we are not dullards, we are ready to hear what you have to say'." Lane (*Hebrews 1-8*, 135) interprets the passage also not as an actual description, but rather as "irony, calculated to shame them and to recall them to the stance of conviction and boldness consonant with their experience." Héring (*Hebrews*, 43) also notes the discrepancy between the author's diagnosis of their spiritual immaturity and his decision to give them the "meat" of the teaching about Melichizedek, concluding that "no doubt he was trying to us a well-known pedagogic device to stir them to some exertion." The rhetorically trained Calvin (*Hebrews*, 58) also notes the rhetorical strategy behind this

maintenance of the counter-defintions and values of the alternate culture. Through this rebuke, the author hopes that his audience will lay claim to that wisdom which he claims they lack, and demonstrate their claim through persevering in the course of faithfulness to Christ.[52]

Peterson has noted another place in the letter where the author may be playing upon the addressees' sense of shame, namely 12:3-4: "Consider him who endured from sinners such hostility against himself, so that you may not grow weary or fainthearted. In your struggle against sin you have not yet resisted to the point of shedding your blood." While 12:4 has usually been taken merely as a source of information about the extent to which the addressees have suffered for their Christian convictions, Peterson suggests that "the writer is not *blaming* them for their failure to resist to the point of bloodshed but *shaming* them: their sufferings are much less than Jesus had to bear, and they are apparently ready to 'lose heart and grow faint'."[53] Failure to live up to the examples of those honored within the Christian minority group (e.g., Christ) provides a basis for feeling shame, just as following the example of those honored yields the praise of the other members of the community and the hope for honor before God.

The author nurtures the addressees' sensitivity to the honor rating of the Christian group also through praising their manifestations of virtues and behaviors valued within the minority culture, satisfying their desire for approval and pointing the way to the enjoyment of continued and enhanced honor. He praises particularly their acts of love and service, which give the addressees a claim to honor from God:

> God is not so unjust as to overlook your work and the love which you showed for his sake in serving the saints, as you still do. And we desire each one of you to show the same earnestness in realizing the full assurance of hope until the end, so that you may not be sluggish, but imitators of those who through faith and patience inherit the promises (6:10-12).

---

rebuke: "This reproof hath in it no little pungency to rouse the Jews from their state of sloth. He says that it is out of all character and a shame that they should be in the elements when they ought to be teachers....To shame them all the more, however, he says the first principles, as if one said, the alphabet." Delitzsch (*Hebrews*, 259) and Lünemann (*Hebrews*, 382) regard the passage as a description of the actual state of the hearers.

[52] It is only the mature who possess the faculties "exercised in distinguishing between the noble and the bad," which is precisely what the author of *Rhetorica ad Herennium* (3.2.3) names the faculty of "wisdom": "Wisdom is intelligence capable, by a certain judicious method, of distinguishing good and bad."

[53] Peterson, *Hebrews and Perfection*, 174.

The author likewise praises their former endurance of trials, reproaches, and loss for the sake of maintaining their hope for "better and lasting possessions," referring to the events by the honorable and encomiastic term ἄθλησις,[54] and transforming the endurance of marginalization into a demonstration of courage. Indeed, the author maintains that the committed believers have not fallen short with regard to any Greco-Roman virtue, but rather display wisdom (5:14), courage (10:32; 12:1-3), temperance (13:4-6), and justice (in the form of piety, giving to God what is due the Deity, 12:28). The believers above all demonstrate πίστις, which was a virtue recognized and valued in the Greco-Roman world long before it came to have a distinctively religious meaning. These virtues, however, are set by the author within the framework of the Christian world-construction and ethos, such that the perfection of virtue and complete commitment to the minority culture become one.

The author's praise, censure, encouragement, and admonitions model what the members of the community are to do as "teachers," as they encourage one another to persevere in faith, remind one another of the surpassing worth of their calling and the reward which their hope brings. While shameless with regard to the opinion of the unbelieving society, the believers are to display proper shame -- that is, sensitivity to one's honor rating -- within the Christian group, and thus to be held accountable to the group's values and commitments.

4 The Promise of Greater Honor

Quintillian (*Inst.* 3.8.12) claims that "appeals to the emotions ... are especially necessary in deliberative oratory. Anger has frequently to be excited or assuaged and the minds of the audience have to be swayed to fear, ambition, hatred, reconciliation." The preceding chapters have shown how the author's strategy includes rousing the addressees to fear, confidence, and emulation. He also calls the hearers' attention frequently to the magnitude of the reward which will greet those who have persisted in faith, thus appealing to their ambition, indeed providing a channel for their ambition so that they are not drawn by that same emotion back into the arenas provided by the unbelieving society for the fulfillment of φιλοτιμία.

---

[54] Recall Chrysostom on 10:32 (*NPNF*[1] 14:461; Migne, *PG* 63.149): "Moreover he did not say 'trials' but 'contest', which is an expression of commendation and of very great praise (οὐκ εἶπε πειρασμοὺς ἀλλὰ ἄθλησιν, ὅπερ ἐστὶν ἐγκωμίου ὄνομα καὶ ἐπαίνων μεγίστων)."

The author frequently employs the language of inheritance to achieve this end. The word group formed around the root κληρονομ- appears very prominently in Hebrews (eleven times -- proportionately the highest concentration of these words in the New Testament). This realm of discourse renders a double premium for the author's purpose. First, an unquestionable honor attaches to the status of the heir of a powerful or distinguished figure even before he or she inherited (cf. Moses' status as a "son of the daughter of Pharaoh," 11:24). Second, the heir looked forward to the greater honor he or she would enjoy when he or she came into the inheritance. Being named an heir by God, moreover, enhances this honor beyond all measure, such that John Chrysostom can say with regard to Esau's default that he "lost the greatest honor and glory."[55]

The nature of this inheritance is often described in general terms as the inheritance of salvation (1:14; 5:9; 9:28) or inheritance of "what was promised" (10:36; 6:12, 17; 9:15). Such non-specific terms can leave it to the hearer to fill in the details of the splendour of the inheritance, which will be nothing short of "glory" (δόξα, 2:10), the divinely appointed destiny of those who have honored their adoption by God.[56] Even as Jesus awaits the completion of his inheritance (i.e., "the subjection of all things," 2:6-9, and the "subjection" of his enemies "as a footstool under his feet," 1:13; 10:13), so the believers may eagerly anticipate their share in Christ's supreme dignity as his partners (3:14). The author enables the addressees to embrace their present circumstances as the prerequisite to the

---

[55] Chrysostom on 12:16, *NPNF¹* 14:506; Migne, *PG* 63.214.

[56] Thus Michel, *Hebräerbrief*, 78: "The ingressive Aorist ἀγαγόντα reveals the divine plan: the δόξα of the Son (2:7, 9) shall be the δόξα of humankind. πολλοὺς υἱὸς εἰς δόξαν ἀγαγόντα ought to be read as an epithet of God, derived from Palestinian-Christian theology. From this source came the connection between the Son and the sons [and daughters] (Mt 5:9, 45; Lk 6:20; 20:30)." Hurst ("Christology," 154, 163) echoes this view, as does Delitzsch (*Hebrews*, 117): "If Jesus, then, is 'Captain of their salvation' to the 'many sons' whom God is leading to 'glory', that 'glory' cannot be any or every kind of honour into which some of their number may have been brought before Christ's coming, but only that transcendent glory into which He, as the only Son in the absolute sense, is already entered, and to which, on the ground of the 'salvation' won by Him, God will ultimately lead the 'many sons'."

fulfillment of their ambition.[57]   Indeed, their trust in God's promises is
their "bid" or "title deed" to the full inheritance for which they wait.[58]

The prize for which the addressees are to strive is expressed also as
full access to God, namely, a place in the Heavenly Sanctuary. It is to this
place that their hope leads, and into this place that Christ went as a
forerunner on their behalf (6:19-20). As they, too, run their race, looking
ahead to the pioneer (12:1-2), they can look forward to attaining the prize
of entrance into this Sanctuary. This same goal is expressed by a variety
of terms. It is also called the heavenly "homeland" ($\pi\alpha\tau\rho\iota\varsigma$, 11:14-16) or
the sabbatical "rest" ($\kappa\alpha\tau\alpha\pi\alpha\upsilon\sigma\iota\varsigma$) which only the people of faith may
enter (4:3, 9). It is the city ($\pi\delta\lambda\iota\varsigma$, 11:16; 13:14) which God has prepared
and in which the believers will enjoy a better citizenship than in an earthly
city, and indeed nothing less than an "unshakeable kingdom" ($\beta\alpha\sigma\iota\lambda\epsilon\iota\alpha\nu$
$\alpha\sigma\alpha\lambda\epsilon\upsilon\tau\upsilon\nu$, 12:28), which is bequeathed to the faithful. The believers look
toward an inheritance in the eternal, heavenly realm. In pursuit of these
"better and lasting possessions" (10:34), of citizenship in the "better, that
is, the heavenly" homeland (11:16), the faithful will gladly suffer the loss
of earthly possessions or enfranchisement in an earthly city, for these are
of incomparably less value.[59]   It is in pursuit of this heavenly prize that
the addressees are called to exercise their diligence (4:11; 6:11).

Finally, the author speaks of the "reward" ($\mu\iota\sigma\theta\alpha\pi\upsilon\delta\upsilon\sigma\iota\alpha$) which God
will give to those who endure in faith and service. While the reward, like
the inheritance, is not highly specified by the author, its value relative to
any earthly rewards is established by Moses' choice of God's reward over
the promise of access to the "treasures of Egypt" (11:26). The satisfaction
of the believers' ambition is guaranteed by God's $\delta\iota\kappa\alpha\iota\upsilon\sigma\upsilon\nu\eta$, by which
God gives to each person the due recompense for his or her deeds ($\upsilon\dot{\upsilon}$ $\gamma\dot{\alpha}\rho$

---

[57] Cf. Moxnes, "Honor and Righteousness," 73: "Power in weakness, confidence
of honour while seemingly put to shame -- that was the paradox of Christian existence
in a Jewish and Greco-Roman environment....When Paul urges them to live a life
sharing the sufferings of Jesus ([Rom] 8.17), he asks them to live as 'sons without
honour'. Therefore, they look forward to the eschatological moment when they will
be glorified with Jesus. Then the entire world will recognize their honour."

[58] Worley, "God's Faithfulness," 92.

[59] The possessions which the believers lost in 10:34 are, like the title and wealth
that Moses renounced, of a "temporary" ($\pi\rho\delta\sigma\kappa\alpha\iota\rho\upsilon\varsigma$, cf. 11:25) nature, in contrast to
the "abiding" ($\mu\epsilon\nu\omega\nu$, cf. 10:34; 12:27) quality of their promised inheritance. While,
again, Platonic categories emerge in the author's expressions, they are completely
interwoven with eschatological categories -- "that which abides" is that which survives
the eschatological "shaking" of 12:27.

ἄδικος ὁ θεὸς, 6:10).[60] The author assures them not only in 6:10 but again in 10:35 that they have made a sufficient investment already to have a claim to honor before God's court, if only they persevere in the last stretch of the race. This reward is ultimately grounded in God's favor or beneficence (χάρις, 12:15), which assures those who remain faithful clients of God of their future enjoyment of the fruits of their endurance.

5 Threats to the Christian's Honor

Having given the Christian a new basis for his or her honor and dignity -- one which will survive society's assaults and the removal of all that belongs to the visible world (12:26-27) -- and held before the eyes of the addressees a prize worthy of their greatest ambition, he also arouses fear and caution in their hearts, by which he seeks to move them to safeguard their divinely given honor and their hope of greater privilege and prestige. It is not the experience of disgrace or loss of status in society's opinion which threatens the believer's honor; rather, only what jeopardizes his or her relationship with God, the source of the believer's honor, places that honor at risk. Hence, the threat to honor is not external but internal, where the believer's commitment and boldness waver. As much of this has already been discussed above in chapter five, a summary overview here will suffice.

The primary threat to the Christian's honor is the danger of provoking God through treating the gifts God made available through Christ with slight regard, that is, through valuing society's gifts above God's. Those who do not consider the benefits won by Christ to be of sufficient value to merit the cost of perseverance in faith, and who enact that evaluation through withdrawal from Christian activity and worship and conformity to the expectations of the unbelieving society, transform their divine Patron into Punisher and Avenger. Thus the author speaks of the punishment which will be incurred by those who neglect the message brought by the Son (2:3), who trample underfoot the Son and God's gifts (10:26-31). Those who act in this way have dishonored God, but have not challenged God's honor. "An offence given to an honourable man stained only the offender," and did not call for a riposte from the offended party, but rather

---

[60] Cf. *Rhet. Her.* 3.2.3: "Justice is equity, giving to each thing what it is entitled in proportion to its worth (*Iustitia* [=δικαιοσύνη] *est aequitas ius uni cuique rei tribuens pro dignitate cuiusque*)."

for punishment, which affirms the honor of the ofended one.[61] The impropriety of the challenge reveals the shamelessness of the offender, and hence his or her disgrace, which is enacted by means of punishment.[62]

Such an affront to God as rejecting God's gifts or disobeying God's call would entail violates the virtue of δικαιοσύνη, "justice" or "righteousness." *Rhetorica ad Herennium* (3.3.4) assists the modern reader in understanding what is meant by this virtue:

> We shall be using the topics of Justice ...if we show that it is proper to repay the well-deserving with gratitude;...if we urge that faith (*fidem*) ought zealously to be kept;...if we contend that alliances and friendships should scrupulously be honored; if we make it clear that the duty imposed by nature towards parents, gods, and the fatherland (*in parentes, deos, patriam*) must be religiously observed; if we maintain that ties of hospitality, clientage, kinship, and relationship by marriage must inviolably be cherished; if we show that neither reward nor favour nor peril nor animosity ought to led us astray from the right path.

Justice requires that the patron-client bond be held inviolate, that covenants be maintained by both parties, that proper honor and obedience (i.e., the fulfillment of the "duty imposed by nature") be shown toward the Deity. People of honor maintain this virtue, while those who violate justice demonstrate their own shamelessness.[63]

Distrusting the Benefactor also threatens one's honor, not only in that it deprives one of the dignity conferred by God and privileges yet to be awarded, but also in that it reveals the base character of the one who distrusts so honorable a Being. Danker has noted that the term καρδία

---

[61] Cf. Malina and Neyrey, "Honor and Shame," 30: "A superior's honor is simply not committed or engaged by an inferior's affront, although the superior has the power to punish impudence."

[62] Cf. Corrigan, "Paul's Shame," 26: "To challenge God and God's honor is always sinful because it is an inappropriate challenge....Sin as challenge exhibits humanity's sinfulness."

[63] Within Jewish literature, honoring the One God and having honor oneself are even more closely related. In Wis 15:10-12, for example, the author claims that the idol maker's, and the idolator's, life is of no value (that is, without honor), since they fail to honor the One God and exhibit a right estimation of life: "he counts it his glory that he molds counterfeit gods (καὶ δόξαν ἡγεῖται ὅτι κίβδηλα πλάσσει). His heart is ashes, his hope is cheaper than dirt, and his life is of less worth than clay (πηλοῦ τε ἀτιμότερος ὁ βίος αὐτοῦ), because he failed to know the one who formed him and inspired him with an active soul and breathed into him a living spirit. But he considered our existence an idle game, and life a festival held for profit, for he says one must get money however one can, even by base means."

πονηρά signifies a "base heart," the "root of a wicked life, which means that it is neither capable of *arete* nor of recognizing it in others."[64] When the author of Hebrews, then, warns his audience to be on guard against having a καρδία πονηρὰ ἀπιστίας (3:12), because of which one turns away from the Living God, he holds up distrust of God and lack of faith in God's promises as an indication of the baseness of the one who distrusts. Since God's reliability is unimpeachable, and distrusting the noble person is a sign of baseness, the believer can only lay claim to being a noble person as long as he or she continues to trust God and live out that confidence in God. The one who prefers to attain peace with society at the cost of what God has promised has made a disgraceful exchange, like Esau (12:16-17), of honor for temporary advantage. He or she has been "hardened by the deceitfulness of sin (ἵνα μὴ σκληρυνθῇ τις ἐξ ὑμῶν ἀπάτῃ τῆς ἁμαρτίας, 3:13)," which hardening represents nothing other than an insensitivity to disgrace before God's court, again, a mark of a base character and a strike against a person's honor.

Finally, the believer's honor would be in jeopardy if the Christian were to fail to attain the goal. The author admonishes the addressees to be afraid (Φοβηθῶμεν, 4:1) specifically of falling short of entering the rest which God has prepared as an eternal benefit for the faithful and obedient. Failing to persevere unto the attainment of the goal for which one began an enterprise would result in disgrace. Epictetus (*Ench.* 29.1-3) uses this commonplace in his admonition to count the cost of being a philosopher lest "you give up disgracefully (αἰσχρῶς ἀποστήσῃ)" or "you turn back like children (ὡς τὰ παιδία ἀναστραφήσῃ)." For the Christian, falling short of the goal of rest is equivalent to "falling short of the favor of God (ἐπισκοποῦντες μή τις ὑστερῶν ἀπὸ τῆς χάριτος τοῦ θεοῦ, 12:15). This conjures up similar commonplaces evoking disgrace. Aristotle (*Rhet.* 2.6.12) observed that people felt shame if they lacked

> a share in the honourable things which all men, or all who resemble us, or the majority of them, have a share in. By those who resemble us I mean those of the same race, or the same city, of the same age, of the same family, and, generally speaking, those who are on an equality; for then it is disgraceful not to have a share, for instance, in education and other things, to the same extent.

God's beneficence makes available to all believers a share in the honor of Christ, citizenship in the city of God, and better and lasting possessions: to fall short of these "honorable things" through one's own negligence or

---

[64] Danker, *Benefactor*, 318.

folly would indeed be perceived as disgraceful and a cause for feelings of shame.

By means of considerations and warnings such as these, the author of Hebrews urges his audience to care for their honor not before the world's court of opinion, but before the court of opinion constituted by the community of faith throughout the ages and by God, the judge of all. Having warned them of what they stand to lose, he trusts that they will avoid the shipwreck of their hope and maintain the honor they have been granted as children of God and heirs of the promised glory. For those who, despite these consideration, fall away and seek refuge once more in the court of the unbelievers, there remains nothing but the prospect of judgement and the ascription of lasting disgrace.[65]

6 The Path to Honor

Having called the readers' attention to those significant others in whose eyes one is to seek approval, given the addressees a firm basis for their claim to honor before that court, indicated the magnitude of the value of the reward for which they are striving, and alerted them to the sources of possible danger to their honor, all that remains for the author is to point the way by which his audience may pursue and attain the reward and dignity to which God has deigned to lead them. The author's exhortations, and the examples of behavior which result in honor, provide the details for a reconstruction of the path to honor along which he urges the community he addresses.

First, the believers are called to work to maintain the community as a body of significant others, as a counterculture within the Greco-Roman society. They are to continue ministering as before, showing diligence to the end in order to realize their hope (6:10-11). They are to continue to assemble together, resisting the social pressure to withdraw from associations with the Christian group (10:23-25), even in circumstances of disgrace. The parallels between the example of Moses and the exemplary use of the community's own past (11:25-26//10:32-34) underscore the importance of continued solidarity with people of God (cf. 10:24-25) in

---

[65]   Cf. Josephus *BJ* 2.396-97: "It were well, my friends, it were well (καλόν...καλόν), while the vessel is still in port, to foresee the coming storm, and not to put out into the midst of the hurricane to meet your doom. For to victims of unforeseen disaster there is left at least the meed of pity; but he who rushes to manifest destruction incurs opprobrium (προσονειδίζεται) to boot."

order to attain the promised reward (11:26//10:35).[66]   The author highlights this again in his concluding exhortation (13:1-6):

> Let brotherly love continue.   Do not neglect to show hospitality to strangers, for thereby some have entertained angels unawares. Remember those who are in prison, as though in prison with them; and those who are ill-treated, since you also are in the body.   Let marriage be held in honor among all, and let the marriage bed be undefiled; for God will judge the immoral and adulterous.   Keep your life free from love of money, and be content with what you have; for he has said, "I will never fail you nor forsake you."   Hence we can confidently say, "The Lord is my helper, I will not be afraid; what can man do to me?"

Here the author encourages the addressees to work to sustain the Christian community even beyond the local congregation through showing hospitality to travelling fellow-believers.   Christian cohesion will also benefit from the adherence of believers to the virtue of temperance, here encouraged in the form of restraint with regard to sexual desire and the desire for financial gain.[67]   The exhortation to be content with what they currently possess (ἀρκούμενοι τοῖς παροῦσιν, 13:5) cannot fail to recall to the audience their loss of possessions (10:34).   The author is not simply using a common *topos* of paraenesis, but has clearly constructed his exhortation with the community's circumstances in mind.   He thus urges them not simply to avoid greed, but rather not to seek to regain at the cost of losing their reward what they had lost for Christ's sake in previous times.   Their forebearance now will bring them better and lasting possessions in a country where their honor will be that of the children of God.

In addition to maintaining community, the believers must maintain uncompromisingly their orientation toward God and God's promise, and their detachment from the promises of society for those who assimilate to their values and commitments.   Thus the author offers repeated

---

[66] This comparison, toegther with the fulfillment of Jewish sacred history in the new Christian community, again reveals the subcultural relationship of the Christian community to the Jewish culture.

[67] Cf. *Rhet. Her.* 3.2.3: "Temperance is self-control that moderates our desires (*modesta est in animo continens moderatio cupiditatem*)"; 3.3.5: "We shall be using the topics of Temperance if we censure the inordinate desire for office, money, or the like."   With the enjoining of temperance, the author has encouraged the believers to pursue all four cardinal virtues of the Greco-Roman society, although transposed into a Christian framework.   The conviction that virtuous action leads to honor (cf. *Rhet. Her.* 3.2.3) has a place now within the believer's quest for honor, as the believer may still regard himself or herself as a virtuous person while remaining exclusively faithful to the minority culture.

exhortations to "hold fast" to the confidence, hope, and claim to honor ("boast") which God has given in Christ (3:6, 14; 10:23, 35), continually urging the addressees to "endure" and "persevere" (6:12; 10:36; 12:1, 7).[68] They are therefore called to continue worshiping together, looking after one another's needs, and bearing testimony to the better hope which accompanies serving God through Christ. Perseverance is coupled with faith (cf. 6:12), for it is the latter characteristic which enables the former and prevents external pressure and internal wavering from causing the believer to "shrink back" (10:38-39). Those who are "of faith" ($\dot{\epsilon}\kappa$ $\pi\dot{\iota}\sigma\tau\epsilon\omega\varsigma$, 10:38) trust their Benefactor to provide what was promised, and in granting God such a display of honor receive from God eternal honor and approval in return ("attestation," 11:2).[69] Faith involves choosing alien status now in favor of a better citizenship, choosing reproach and suffering with the people of God in hope of being granted the honor of the family of God at the Parousia, and looking forward to another Red Sea threshold, crossable only by the faithful.

To persevere in faith is thus to resist sin (10:26; 11:25; 12:4), and so maintain intact one's honor before God and the community of faith. It involves submitting to God's discipline ($\pi\alpha\iota\delta\epsilon\dot{\iota}\alpha$, 12:5-9) in order to be fitted for the honor of being a child of God, that is, it involves embracing marginalization with regard to the larger society, disgrace in world's court of opinion, and loss in this world for sake of attaining honor and gain before God. It is finally a voluntary act of "bearing Christ's reproach" ($\tau\dot{o}\nu$ $\dot{o}\nu\epsilon\iota\delta\iota\sigma\mu\dot{o}\nu$ $\alpha\dot{\upsilon}\tau o\hat{\upsilon}$ $\phi\dot{\epsilon}\rho o\nu\tau\epsilon\varsigma$, 13:13), of leaving one's place and status within society for the sake of clinging to the fellowship of those who share a common hope, common values, and common commitment.[70] From this

---

[68] The author thus enjoins upon the believers the demonstration of the virtue of Courage, cf. *Rhet. Her.* 3.3.5: "When we invoke as motive for a course of action steadfastness in Courage, we shall make it clear that...from an honorable act no peril or toil, however great, should divert us; death ought to be preferred to disgrace; no pain should force abandonment of duty;...for country (*patria*), for parents, guest-friends, intimates, and for the things justice commands us to respect, it behooves us to brave any peril and endure any toil."

[69] Cf. Sir 2:7-8: "You who fear the Lord, wait for his mercy; and turn not aside, lest you fall. You who fear the Lord, trust in him, and your reward will not fail ($\pi\iota\sigma\tau\epsilon\dot{\upsilon}\sigma\alpha\tau\epsilon$ $\alpha\dot{\upsilon}\tau\hat{\omega}$ $\kappa\alpha\dot{\iota}$ $o\dot{\upsilon}$ $\mu\dot{\eta}$ $\pi\tau\alpha\dot{\iota}\sigma\eta$ $\dot{o}$ $\mu\iota\sigma\theta\dot{o}\varsigma$ $\dot{\upsilon}\mu\hat{\omega}\nu$; RSV)."

[70] Cf. Filson, *Yesterday*, 61: the author "urges the Christians addressed to break ties with whatever would prevent full loyalty to the Christ who offered himself as the once-for-all sacrifice for sins....They must 'go forth', and since that will bring them under criticism, they must willingly bear the reproach that will come to them as they live in this new situation." Delitzsch (*Hebrews*, 389-90) also perceives a social component to the author's exhortation to go "outside the gate": "let us no longer

place of liminality, they join with the whole community of believers (cf. 1 Pet 5:10), indeed with Creation itself (Rom 8:17), in eager longing for the revelation of Christ, when they, too, shall be made to appear in their divinely given honor (cf. Col 3:4).[71]

The believers' path to honor is finally the path of two clearly recognizable virtues, namely piety and gratitude. The Christian's dignity is secure as long as he or she acts in accordance with the dignity of the One who gave him or her the gift of adoption into God's family (12:5), access to the throne of grace (4:16), and the promise of an eternal habitation (13:14). The recipient of these gifts is to show gratitude -- that loyalty which transcends considerations of one's own reputation and well-being (cf. Seneca, *Ep.* 81.27), and offer a return of praise and service to God and to fellow believers (12:28; 13:15-16). Pursuing this path, the Christian is assured of unimpeachable worth and dignity now, even in the midst of society's abuse and rejection, and of vindication and an "eternal weight of glory" (2 Cor 4:17; cf. Heb 2:10) when the time of God's judgement arrives.

---

continue in their society who have rejected the Lord Jesus, but go forth to Him outside the camp.... To forsake their company ... for His sake is to involve ourselves not merely in future but in present shame or reproach; but this reproach is the reproach of Christ, a shame which we share with Him, and in bearing which we are made like Him."

[71] So Moxnes notes, commenting on Romans ("Honor and Righteousness," 73): "When Paul urges them to live a life sharing the sufferings of Jesus ([Rom] 8:17), he asks them to live as 'sons without honor'. They look forward to the eschatological moment when they will be glorified with Jesus. Then the entire world will recognize their honour."

CHAPTER SEVEN

Conclusions

1 Primary Conclusions

Close attention to the author's use of honor and shame language contributes to an understanding of what J. H. Elliott phrased so well as the "manner in which the text is designed through the literary, sociological, and theological strategy of its author(s) to be a specific response to the specific situation of the intended audience as perceived by the author(s)."[1] This investigation of the Letter to the Hebrews has demonstrated several critical ways in which the author has used honor and shame language to drive his appeal. As in texts which promote adherence to the values and commitments of other minority cultures, whether Jewish communities or Greco-Roman philosophical schools, so the Letter to the Hebrews urges the Christians to "despise shame" before the eyes of the dominant culture whose values differ from or oppose those of the minority culture.

HONOR, SHAME AND THE SOCIAL FUNCTION OF HEBREWS

Through his presentation of the examples of Jesus and the heroes of faith and through his commendation of the community's former behavior, the author seeks to restore the addressees' detachment from society's pressure. The representatives of the dominant culture sought to exercise social control in the form of the negative sanctions of ascribed disgrace and marginalization, by means of which they sought to bring the Christians back into conformity with society's values and to the behaviors which

---

[1] Elliott, *Home for the Homeless*, 8.

maintain society's world view. The author, however, interprets endurance of such pressure as a contest to be won (such that endurance of loss ofstatus and honor in society's eyes leads to honorable victory in God's eyes) and as a form of discipline which confirms the Christians' status as heirs of God's promises. Where an action or endurance of an action is considered disgraceful by the society but honorable by God and the community, the Christian is called to disregard the estimation of honor by society in favor of preserving or enhancing honor in God's sight (as defined by the community's tradition and prophetic innovations within that tradition). The author thus seeks to stimulate solidarity among the addressees as the "people of God," even in conditions of "reproach," a partnership that leads to honor and favor (cf. 11:26).

While negating the social pressure exerted upon the believers by those outside the community of faith, the author also augments the pressure exerted from within. He urges the addressees to seek honor before the alternate court of opinion formed by God and the believing community, which is superior to the societal court by virtue of the former's belonging to the realm of that which remains fixed and eternal while the latter belongs to the transitory realm of that which shall one day be shaken and removed (12:26-28). This honor is attained through the demonstration of loyalty to the Divine Benefactor and perseverance in commitment to God and one's fellow believers. Indeed, one's own honor would be irreparably damaged if one were to "shrink back" in this contest and reject God's gifts (those received and those promised) in order to gain the approval of those outside. Such a course would show contempt for God, turning Benefactor into Punisher, and lead to the irrevocable loss of one's greatest claim to honor -- partnership with Christ as children of God, which leads to the inheritance of a place in the heavenly, abiding realm.

The author's use of honor and shame language, therefore, serves his aim of promoting solidarity within the Christian minority culture and increasing commitment to the values and behaviors of that alternative social group. The end result is the perseverance of the minority culture, the maintenance of its integrity as a group in the face of society's pressure (and internal response to that pressure) to conform to the larger social group. In a situation in which "the Church had to make up its mind whether its main interest would be to conciliate and conform to the community and its religious and social practices, or insistently preserve its distinctive life regardless of possible reactions against it from pagan neighbours," Hebrews seems to serve the latter goal.[2] Despite its

---

[2] Filson, *Yesterday*, 66.

eloquence, its cultured, literary Greek, Hebrews is less interested in making a place for Christianity within Greco-Roman society than Luke or even Paul.

HEBREWS AND THE TRAJECTORY OF POST-APOSTOLIC CHRISTIANITY

Elliott suggests that it is also part of the interpreter's task to determine "the intended and/or actual effect of the document upon the social condition, constitution, and interests of both author(s) and recipients within their larger social and historical contexts."[3] With Hebrews, without identifiable author, addressees, date, or destination, a close investigation of its effect is impossible. In a broader sense, however, one can see that the counter-definitions of honor forwarded in Hebrews and the emphasis on solidarity with believers who are victimized by the outside society became prominent features of the Christian counterculture. The journey of Ignatius from Antioch to his martyrdom at Rome, visited, attended, and given hospitality by Christians along the way, shows the willingness of the believers to "remember those in prison as though imprisoned with them" (Heb 13:3).

The martyr himself testifies (*Smyrn.* 10): "My life is a humble offering for you; and so are these chains of mine, for which you never showed the least contempt or shame. Neither will Jesus Christ in his perfect loyalty show Himself ashamed of you (οὐδὲ ὑμᾶς ἐπαισχυνθήσεται ἡ τελεία πίστις, ᾿ Ἰησοῦς Χριστός)." Similarly, he exhorts the Christians, "Let us show by our forbearance that we are their [i.e., the unbelievers'] brothers, and try to imitate the Lord by seeing which of us can put up with the most ill-usage or privation or contempt" (*Eph.* 10) and interprets his own imprisonment and public execution thus: "I have been deemed worthy to set forward the honor of God (ἠξιώθην εἰς τιμὴν Θεοῦ εὑρεθῆναι)" (*Eph.* 21). The dishonor ascribed the Christian counterculture by the members of the Greco-Roman society is thus embraced as a way of following the pattern of Christ, the road which leads to honor before God and the angels. Suffering indignities and the shameful death of a condemned criminal become a claim to honor ("I have been deemed worthy") within the Christian community, wherein martyrs are transformed into victorious champions of God's honor. Finally, in Lucian's famous passage, we find a description of the Christian community in the mid- second century which would have greatly pleased the author of Hebrews:

---

[3] Elliott, *Home for the Homeless*, 9.

The Christians...left nothing undone in the effort to rescue [Peregrinus]. Then, as this was impossible, every other form of attention was shown him....From the very break of day aged widows and orphan children could be seen waiting near the prison, while their officials even slept inside with him after bribing the guards. Then elaborate meals were brought in, and sacred books of theirs were read aloud....

Indeed, people came even from the cities in Asia, sent by the Christians at their common expense, to succour and defend and encourage the hero. They show incredible speed whenever any such public action is taken; for in no time they lavish their all.... (Peregr. 12; LCL)

2 Secondary Conclusions

HONOR/SHAME ANALYSIS AND NEW TESTAMENT TEXTS

This investigation has provided evidence for the fruitfulness of honor/shame analysis as a means of uncovering what a document seeks to effect in its readers. It has also advanced some methodological considerations for how to undertake such analysis. Seeking guidance not from cultural-anthropological analyses but rather from the authors of the rhetorical handbooks led to an awareness of how honor and dishonor were expected to influence the decision-making process of the Greco-Roman reader, and thus how this realm of discourse could be used to effect persuasion. A careful reading of several speeches and other texts from dominant and minority cultures within the Greco-Roman world confirmed the utility of the rhetorical handbooks as guides and refined the preliminary observations based on those theoretic works. This study also provided the groundwork for analyzing the social function of the use of honor and shame language in a discourse -- i.e., whether such language served to support the norms of the dominant culture or to create and maintain the boundaries of a minority culture and commitment to its norms.

This study has shown that honor and shame play a large part in the argument from πάθος in Hebrews, as the author rouses fear, emulation, and shame in his addressees to gain their consent. Considerations of honor and dishonor play a large role in the appeal to the λόγος of the hearers, as the author motivates the believers to faith and endurance through the promise of greater honor to come before the court of God. The depiction of Christ's dignity in Hebrews also serves this end positively, as the believers have a share in this dignity as "partners" or "children" as long as they remain committed to the Christian community and its values; it also serves as the basis for the many appeals to the emotion of fear, specifically the fear of violating the honor of such a powerful figure. Without forcing any part of the letter into an honor/shame framework, the prominence of this axis of value remains clear, and careful study of those passages where it does appear leads to a sharper focusing of the argument of the letter.

PATRONAGE AND HONOR: A CORRECTIVE EMPHASIS

This study has also provided something of a corrective to the view of Mediterranean cultures as primarily antagonistic, with people challenging one another in order to gain honor at every turn. Particularly in light of the importance of patron-client bonds in the Greco-Roman world, we should expect that the impulse to show honor to those from whom one seeks or receives favor should be equally, if not more, powerful. This is not absent in the work of, for example, Malina or Neyrey. It is, however, quite underemphasized, which has led to skewed applications of the model. The author of Hebrews seeks to remind the addressees of the surpassing value, indeed, ultimate superiority, of Christ, who has entered the heavenly (and therefore superior) sanctuary as an eternal high priest. It is Christ alone who gains access to a favorable standing before that court, who makes it possible for the believers to receive their promised inheritance in the lasting realm, and the discussion of Christ's superior mediation aims at provoking greater loyalty and gratitude to this great Patron. Indeed, it is in light of the favor that Christ has obtained at such cost to himself that apostasy appears as so reprehensible and damnable an act. Apostasy is equivalent to ingratitude, to dishonoring the Giver and Broker and despising gifts of greatest value for the sake of re-acquiring those of transitory value. By apostasy one removes oneself from favor, one cuts oneself off from access to the throne of favor. The unrepeatable nature of Christ's once-for-all offering makes the danger of apostasy even more horrifying, for the author extends no hope of a restoration to favor after Christ's mediation has been rejected. This investigation thus places the Letter to the Hebrews squarely within a culture "located at the crossroads of, on the one hand, honor and shame, and, on the other, patronage and clientage."[4]   At this juncture, honor is gained by showing honor and gratitude.

---

[4] Crossan, *The Historical Jesus*, 73.

HEBREWS AND COMPARATIVE LITERATURE

This investigation has shown that Hebrews bears a strong resemblance to protreptic literature, since the author is promoting a specific way of life and set of commitments. It differs from Epictetus' discourse on the calling of a Cynic in that Hebrews addresses those who are not about to embark on a new calling, but rather need to remain firmly committed to a way of life already chosen. This, too, is a prominent feature of protreptic discourses, which speak of the disgrace of taking up a task, only to abandon it when it proves too costly. The literature most fruitfully brought into comparison with Hebrews is the literature of minority cultures such as Judaism or philosophical texts. These writings demonstrate a consciousness of the need for insulation within the minority group against the effects of society's negative evaluation (and hence, low opinion) of the group's members. Both Stoic philosopher and Jewish martyr place no value on the honors or insults offered by the outsiders who speak for the dominant culture, but rather pursue what is noble within their counter-definitions of the honorable, and urge their fellow group members to do the same. This describes equally well the goal of the author of Hebrews.

HEBREWS' LOCATION WITHIN THE DOMINANT CULTURE

The author of Hebrews clearly reveals a subcultural relationship to Jewish culture. His use of the Hebrew Scriptures, exemplars from the Jewish tradition, and shared values place him within the frame of that culture. The subcultural relationship is captured in the repeated use of the word "better" (κρείττων). He claims, for example, that the Christian community is placed in a better position to fulfill the values of faith and obedience and inherit the benefits promised within the Jewish tradition. The Christians enjoy a more efficacious mediator of God's favor than the non-Christian Jews (8:6), one who offers "better sacrifices" (9:23); they stand under a "better covenant" (7:22), have a "better hope" (7:19), and rely on "better promises" (8:6). The author stresses that the Christian community has access to favor and benefits inaccessible to those who, although claiming the same Jewish heritage, have not placed their trust in the Son (13:10), the final articulation of God's will (1:1-3).

The relationship of the Christian community to the Greco-Roman society, at least as the author of Hebrews would like to shape that relationship, is countercultural. While the addressees are urged to withdraw from the dominant culture's definitions of honor, and from ties of patronage within the larger society which conflict with their higher bond of loyalty to the Divine Patron, the author clearly does not reject these axes of value. Patronage and honor remain central values and institutions within the Christian community, but are radically redefined and restructured.[5] Honor, the value which formerly supported the kinship and political structures of the dominant culture, has been transformed into the support for the fictive kinship within and commitment to the values of the alternative community.

Within the Christian minority culture honor and dishonor now function to motivate the pursuit of Christian virtues, the performance of deeds which demonstrate obedience to Christ, and to deter the wavering from falling away from his or her place in God's favor. Platonic metaphysics, transformed by Jewish cosmology, supports the author's claim that only the verdict of God's court is of real concern. Disgrace before the world's court as the price of honor before God's court is a price well paid, whereas the reverse transaction is as foolish as Esau's trade with Jacob (12:16-17). The believers have been brought into a new set of patron-client relationships with God, through Christ Jesus, the Mediator of God's favor. These networks of honor and shame, patronage and clientage serve now, however, to preserve the integrity of the minority group, enabling its members to maintain their commitment to its counter-ideals in the face of a dominant culture eager to assert the ultimacy of its own.

---

[5] Cf. K. Roberts ("Toward a Generic Concept of Counter-Culture," *Sociological Focus* 11 [1978] 112-113, quoted in V. K. Robbins, "Rhetoric and Culture," 454-55), who defines countercultures as "alternative minicultures" which reject "the norms and values which unite the dominant culture." In Hebrews, it is not a case of rejecting the values themselves, but of redefining their content so radically that a truly alternative culture emerges.

BIBLIOGRAPHY

Primary Texts and Translations

The Apostolic Fathers. 2 vols. Tr. Kirsopp Lake. LCL. London: Heinemann, and Cambridge, MA: Harvard University, 1912-13.

Apuleius. *The Golden Ass. Metamorphoses*. Tr. W. Adlington (rev. S. Gaselee). LCL. London: Heinemann, and Cambridge, MA: Harvard University, 1915.

Aristotle. *The Art of Rhetoric*. Tr. J. H. Freese. LCL. London: Heinemann, and Cambridge, MA: Harvard University, 1926.

Aristotle. *Athenian Constitution, Eudemian Ethics, Vices and Virtues*. Tr. H. Rackham. LCL. London: Heinemann, and Cambridge, MA: Harvard University, 19_.

Aristotle. *Nicomachean Ethics*. Tr. H. Rackham. LCL. London: Heinemann, and Cambridge, MA: Harvard University, 19_.

Biblia Hebraica Stuttgartensia. K. Ellinger and W. Rudolph, eds. Stuttgart: Deutsche Bibelgesellschaft, 1983.

[Cicero.] *Rhetorica ad Herennium*. Tr. H. Caplan. LCL. London: Heinemann, and Cambridge, MA: Harvard University, 1954.

Cicero. *Tusculun Disputations*. Tr. J. E. King. LCL. London: Heinemann Ltd., and Cambridge, MA: Harvard University, 1927.

Dio Cassius. *Roman History*. 9 vols. Tr. E. Cary. LCL. London: Heinemann, and Cambridge, MA: Harvard University, 1914-27.

Dio Chrysostom. *[Orations.]* 5 vols. Tr. J. W. Cohoon and H. L. Crosby. London: Heinemann, and Cambridge, MA: Harvard University, 1932-51.

John Chyrsostom. "Homiliae xxiv in Epistolam ad Hebraeos." Migne, *PG* 63 (1862) 9-256.

John Chrysostom. "Homilies on Hebrews." NPNF, Second Series, vol. 14. Edinburgh: T. & T. Clark, 1889.

Diogenes Laertius. *Lives of Eminent Philophers*. 2 vols. Tr. R. D. Hicks. LCL. London: Heinemann, and Cambridge, MA: Harvard University, 1925.

Early Christian Writings. Tr. M. Staniforth. New York: Penguin, 1968.

Epictetus. *The Discourses as reported by Arrian, the Manual, and Fragments*. 2 vols. Tr. W. A. Oldfather. LCL. London: Heinemann, and Cambridge, MA: Harvard University, 1925, 1928.

Eusebius. *The History of the Church*. Tr. G. A. Williamson. New York: Penguin, 1965.

Aulus Gellius. *The Attic Nights*. 3 vols. Tr. J. C. Rolfe. LCL. London: Heinemann, and Cambridge, MA: Harvard, 1927.

Isocrates. [*Works.*] vol. 1. Tr. G. Norlin and L. Van Hook. LCL. London: Heinemann, and Cambridge, MA: Harvard, 1928.

Josephus. *The Jewish War*. 2 vols. Tr. H. St. John Thackeray. LCL. London: Heinemann, and Cambridge, MA: Harvard University, 1927, 1928.

The Works of Josephus. Tr. W. Whiston. Peabody, MA: Hendrickson, 1987.

Lucian. [*Works.*] Vols. 1 and 5. Tr. A. M. Harmon. LCL. London: Heinemann, and Cambridge, MA: Harvard University, 1913.

Novum Testamentum Graece. Nestle-Aland 26th ed. Stuttgart: Deutsche Bibelgesellschaft, 1979.

Origen. *An Exhortation to Martyrdom, et al.* Tr. R. A. Greer. New York: Paulist Press, 1979.

_____. *Contra Celsum*. ANF, vol. 4. Edinburgh: T. & T. Clark, 1885.

Philo. [*Works.*] Vols 6-9. Tr. F. H. Colson. London: Heinemann, and Cambridge, MA: Harvard University, 1939-50.

The Works of Philo. Tr. C. D. Yonge. Peabody, MA: Hendrickson, 1993.

Plato. *The Dialogues of Plato*. Tr. Benjamin Jowett. With "The Seventh Letter." Tr. J. Harward. Chicago: William Benton, 1952.

Plato. *Euthyphro, Apology, Crito, Phaedo, Phaedrus*. Tr. H. N. Fowler. LCL. London: Heinemann, and Cambridge, MA: Harvard University, 1914.

Plato. *Lysis, Symposium, Gorgias*. Tr. W. R. M. Lamb. LCL. London: Heinemann, and Cambridge: Harvard, 1925.

Pliny the Younger. *Letters and Panegyricus*. 2 vols. Tr. B. Radice. LCL. London: Heinemann, and Cambridge: Harvard, 1969.

Plutarch. *The Parallel Lives*. 11 vols. Tr. B. Perrin. LCL. London: Heinemann, and Cambridge: Harvard, 1914-26.

____. *Moralia*. 15 vols. Tr. various. London: Heinemann, and Cambridge, MA: Harvard University, 1927-1976.

Quintilian. [*Institutes*.] Vol. 1. Tr. H. E. Butler. LCL. London: Heinemann, and Cambridge: Harvard, 1921.

Seneca. *Ad Lucilium Epistulae Morales*. 3 vols. Tr. R. M. Gummere. LCL. London: Heinemann, and Cambridge, MA: Harvard University, 1917-25.

____. *Moral Essays*. 3 vols. Tr. J. W. Basore. LCL. London: Heinemann, and Cambridge, MA: Harvard University, 1928-35.

Septuaginta. Alfred Rahlfs, ed. Stuttgart: Deutsche Bibelgesellschaft, 1979.

Suetonius. [*The Twelve Caesars*.] 2 vols. Tr. J. H. Rolfe. LCL. London: Heinemann, and Cambridge, MA: Harvard University, 1914.

Tacitus. *The Agricola and the Germania*. Tr. H. Mattingly (rev. S. A. Handford). New York: Penguin, 1970.

____. *The Annals of Imperial Rome*. Tr. Michael Grant. New York: Penguin, 1956.

____. *The Histories*. Tr. K. Wellesley. New York: Penguin, 1964.

Theophrastus. *Characters*. Tr. J. M. Edmonds. LCL. London: Heinemann, and Cambridge, MA: Harvard University, 1929.

Thucydides. [*Histories*.] Vol. 1. Tr. C. F. Smith. LCL. London: Heinemann, and Cambridge, MA: Harvard University, 1919.

Commentaries, Monographs, and Studies

Adkins, A. W. *Merit and Responsibility: A Study in Greek Values*. Oxford: Oxford University, 1960.

Anderson, B. W. *Understanding the Old Testament*, 4th ed. Englewood Cliffs, NJ: Prentice-Hall, 1986.

Anderson, C. P. "The Setting of the Epistle to the Hebrews." Ph.D. diss., Columbia University, 1969.

Anderson, H. "4 Maccabees (First Century A.D.). A New Translation and Introduction," pp. 531-564 in *The Old Testament Pseudepigrapha* (ed. J. H. Charlesworth). Vol. 2. Garden City, NY: Doubleday, 1985.

————. "Maccabees, Books of: Fourth Maccabees," pp. 452-43 in *The Anchor Bible Dicitonary* (ed. D. N. Freedman). Vol. 4. New York: Doubleday, 1992.

Attridge, H. W. *The Epistle to the Hebrews.* Philadelphia: Fortress, 1989.

————. "Paraenesis in a Homily (λόγος παρακλήσεως): The Possible Location of, and Socialization in, the 'Epistle to the Hebrews'." *Semeia* 50 (1990) 211-26.

Barrett, C. K. "The Eschatology in the Epistle to the Hebrews," in *The Background of the New Testament and Its Eschatology* (ed. W. D. Davies and D. Daube). Cambridge: Cambridge University, 1954.

Barucq, A. *Le Livre de Proverbes.* Paris: Gabalda, 1964.

Bengel, J. A. *Gnomon Novi Testamenti.* London: Nutt, Williams, & Norgate, 1862 [1759].

Berger, P. L. *The Sacred Canopy.* New York: Doubleday, 1967.

————. and T. Luckmann. *The Social Construction of Reality.* New York: Anchor, 1967.

Betz, H. D. *Galatians.* Philadelphia: Fortress, 1979.

Bickermann, E. J. "The Date of Fourth Maccabees," pp. 275-81 in *Studies in Jewish and Christian History.* Vol. 1. Leiden: E. J. Brill, 1976.

Boissevain, Jeremy. *Friends of Friends: Networks, Manipulators and Coalitions.* New York: St. Martin's, 1974.

Breitenstein, Urs. *Beobachtungen zu Sprache, Stil und Gedankengut des Vierten Makkabäerbuchs.* Basel/Stuttgart: Schwabe, 1978.

Bruce, F. F. *The Epistle to the Hebrews.* NICNT. Grand Rapids: Eerdmans, 1990 [1964].

Buchanan, G. W. *To The Hebrews.* New York: Doubleday, 1972.

Bultmann, Rudolf. "Αἰδώς." *TDNT* 1:169-171. Grand Rapids: Eerdmans, 1964.

————. "Αἰσχύνω, etc." *TDNT* 1:189-191. Grand Rapids: Eerdmans, 1964.

Calvin, John. *Calvin's Commentary on the Epistle to the Hebrews.* Tr. "by a beneficed Clergyman of the Church of England." London: Cornish and Co, 1842.

Campbell, John. "The Greek Hero," pp. 129-149 in J. G. Peristiany and J. Pitt-Rivers, *Honour and Grace in Anthropology.* Cambridge: Cambridge University, 1992.

Clarke, E. G. *The Wisdom of Solomon.* Cambridge: Cambridge University, 1973.

Collins, J. J. *Between Athens and Jerusalem.* New York: Crossroad, 1983.

Corrigan, G. M. "Paul's Shame for the Gospel." *BTB* 16 (1986) 23-27.

Cosby, M. R. *The Rhetorical Composition and Function of Hebrews 11 in Light of Example Lists in Antiquity.* Macon: Mercer University, 1988.

Crenshaw, J. L. *Old Testament Wisdom.* Atlanta: John Knox, 1981.

Crossan, John D. *The Historical Jesus: The Life of a Mediterranean Jewish Peasant.* San Francisco: Harper Collins, 1991.

de Ste. Croix, G. E. M. "Suffragium: From Vote to Patronage." *British Journal of Sociology* 5 (1954) 33-48.

D'Angelo, M. R. *Moses in the Letter to the Hebrews.* SBLDS 42. Missoula: Scholars, 1979.

Danker, Frederick W. *Benefactor: Epigraphic Study of a Graeco-Roman and New Testament Semantic Field.* St. Louis, MO: Clayton Publishing House, 1982.

Davis, John. *The People of the Mediterranean: An Essay in Comparative Social Anthropology.* London: Routledge & Kegan Paul, 1977.

Deissmann, A. *Light from the Ancient East.* Strachan; New York: Doran, 1927.

Delitzsch, Franz. *Commentary on the Epistle to the Hebrews.* 2 vols. Tr. T. L. Kingsbury. Edinburgh: Clark, 1871-72 [1857].

Derrett, J. D. M. *Jesus's Audience: The Social and Psychological Environment in which He Worked.* New York: Seabury, 1973.

DiLella, A. A. "Wisdom of Ben-Sira," pp. 931-45 in *The Anchor Bible Dictionary* (ed. D. N. Freedman). Vol. 6. New York: Doubleday, 1992.

_____. "Conservative and Progressive Theology: Sirach and Wisdom." *CBQ* 28 (1966) 139-54.

_____. "Sirach 10:19-11:6: Textual Criticism, Poetic Analysis, and Exegesis," in *The Word of the Lord Shall Go Forth: Essays in Honor of David Noel Freedman in Celebration of His Sixtieth Birthday* (ed. C. L. Meyers and M. O'Connor). Winona Lake, IN: ASOR-Eisenbrauns, 1982.

Dodds, E. R. *The Greeks and the Irrational.* Berkeley: University of California, 1966.

Droge, A. J. and J. D. Tabor. *A Noble Death: Suicide and Martyrdom among Christians and Jews in Antiquity.* San Francisco: Harper, 1992.

Duesberg, H. and P. Auvray. *Le Livre de L'Ecclésiastique.* Paris: Cerf, 1958.

Elliott, J. H. *A Home for the Homeless: A Social-Scientific Investigation of 1 Peter.* Minneapolis: Fortress, 1990 [1981].

Ellingworth, P. *The Epistle to the Hebrews.* Grand Rapids: Eerdmans, 1993.

Filson, F. V. *'Yesterday': A Study of Hebrews in the Light of Chapter 13.* London: SCM, 1967.

Ferguson, E. *Backgrounds of Early Christianity.* Grand Rapids: Eerdmans, 1987.

Foerster, W. "ἄξιος, etc." *TDNT* 1:379-380. Grand Rapids: Eerdmans, 1964.

Fox, R. L. *Pagans and Christians.* New York: Alfred A. Knopf, Inc., 1989.

Gilbert, G. H. "The Greek Element in the Epistle to the Hebrews." *AJT* 14 (1910) 521-32.

Gilbert, M. "Wisdom Literature," in *Jewish Writings of the Second Temple Period* (ed. M. E. Stone). Assen: Van Gorcum, and Philadelphia: Fortress, 1984.

_____. "4 Maccabees" pp. 316-19 in *Jewish Writings of the Second Temple Period* (ed. M. E. Stone). Assen: Van Gorcum, and Philadelphia: Fortress, 1984.

Gilmore, D. D. "Introduction: The Shame of Dishonor," pp. 2-21 in D. D. Gilmore (ed.), *Honor and Shame and the Unity of the Mediterranean.* Washington: American Anthropological Association, 1987.

Greeven, H. "Προσκυνέω." *TDNT* 6:758-766. Grand Rapids: Eerdmans, 1968.

Grundmann, W. "Δεξιός." *TDNT* 2:37-40. Grand Rapids: Eerdmans, 1964.

Guthrie, G. H. *The Structure of Hebrews: A Text-linguistic Analysis.* Leiden: Brill, 1994.

Hadas, Moses. *The Third and Fourth Books of Maccabees.* New York: Harper, 1953.

Hauck, F. "Κοινός, etc." *TDNT* 3:789-809. Grand Rapids: Eerdmans, 1965.

Hay, D. M. *Glory at the Right Hand: Psalm 110 in Early Christianity.* SBLMS 18. Nashville: Abingdon, 1973.

Hengel, Martin. *Crucifixion in the Ancient World and the Folly of the Message of the Cross.* Philadelphia: Fortress, 1977.

_____. *Judaism and Hellenism.* 2 vols. Philadelphia: Fortress, 1974.

Héring, Jean. *The Epistle to the Hebrews.* Tr. A. W. Heathcote. London: Epworth, 1970.

Hughes, Graham. *Hebrews and Hermeneutics.* SNTSMS, 36. Cambridge: Cambridge University, 1979.

Hughes, P. E. *A Commentary on the Epistle to the Hebrews.* Grand Rapids: Eerdmans, 1977.

Hurst, L. D. *The Epistle to the Hebrews: Its Background of Thought.* SNTSMS 65. Cambridge: Cambridge University, 1990.

_____. "The Christology of Hebrews 1 and 2," in L. D. Hurst and N. T. Wright, *The Glory of Christ in the New Testament: Studies in Christology.* Oxford: Clarendon, 1987.

Isaacs, M. E. *Sacred Space: An Approach to the Theology of the Epistle to the Hebrews.* JSNTSS 73. Sheffield: JSOT, 1992.

Johnson, L. T. *The Acts of the Apostles.* Sacra Pagina. Collegeville, MN: Liturgical Press, 1992.

_____. *The Writings of the New Testament: An Interpretation.* Philadelphia: Fortress, 1986.

_____. *Sharing Possessions: Mandate and Symbol of Faith.* Philadelphia: Fortress, 1981.

_____. *The Function of Possessions in Luke-Acts.* SBLDS 39. Missoula, MT: Scholars, 1977.

Käsemann, Ernst. *The Wandering People of God: An Investigation of the Letter to the Hebrews.* Minneapolis: Augsburg, 1984 [1961].

Kee, H. C. "The Linguistic Background of 'Shame' in the New Testament," pp. 133-148 in M. Black and W. A. Smalley (eds.), *On Language, Culture, and Religion: In Honor of Eugene A. Nida.* The Hague: Mouton, 1974.

Kennedy, G. A. *New Testament Interpretation through Rhetorical Criticism.* Chapel Hill, NC: University of North Carolina, 1984.

Kittel, Gerhard. "Δοκέω, δόξα." *TDNT* 2:232-255. Grand Rapids: Eerdmans, 1964.

————. "Θέατρον, θεατρίζω." *TDNT* 3:42-43. Grand Rapids: Eerdmans, 1965.

Klauck, H.-J. *4 Makkabäerbuch.* Jüdische Schriften aus hellenistisch-römischer Zeit 3.6. Gütersloh: Gerd Mohn, 1989.

Kraftchick, S. J. "Ethos and Pathos Appeals in Galatians Five and Six: A Rhetorical Analysis." Ph.D. dissertation, Emory, 1985.

Kümmel, W. G. *Introduction to the New Testament.* Nashville: Abingdon, 1973.

Kurz, W. S., "The Function of Christological Proof from Prophecy for Luke and Justin." Ph.D. dissertation, Yale University, 1976.

Lane, W. L. *Hebrews: A Call to Commitment.* Peabody: Hendrickson, 1985.

————. *Hebrews 1-8.* WBC 47A. Dallas: Word Books, 1991.

————. *Hebrews 9-13.* WBC 47B. Dallas: Word Books, 1991.

Lauer, S. "*Eusebes Logismos* in IV Macc." *JJS* 6 (1955) 170-71.

Lebram, J. C. H. "Die literarische Form des vierten Makkabäerbuches." *VC* 28 (1974) 81-96.

Levick, Barbara. *The Government of the Roman Empire: A Sourcebook.* London: Croom Helm, 1985.

Lindars, Barnabas. *The Theology of the Letter to the Hebrews.* Cambridge: Cambridge University, 1991.

————. "The Rhetorical Structure of Hebrews." *NTS* 35 (1989) 382-406.

Lünemann, Gerhard. *Kritisch-exegetischer Handbuch über den Hebräerbrief.* MeyerK 13. Göttingen: Vandenieck & Ruprecht, 1878.

Mack, Burton. *Rhetoric and the New Testament.* Minneapolis: Augsburg Fortress, 1990.

MacMullen, Ramsey. *Paganism in the Roman Empire.* New Haven: Yale, 1981.

Malina, Bruce. *The New Testament World: Insights from Cultural Anthropology.* Louisville: Westminster/John Knox, 1993 [1981].

_____ and J. H. Neyrey. "Honor and Shame in Luke-Acts: Pivotal Values of the Mediterranean World," in J. H. Neyrey (ed.), *The Social World of Luke-Acts: Models for Interpretation.* Peabody: Hendrickson, 1991.

_____ and J. H. Neyrey. "First-Century Personality: Dyadic, Not Individualistic," in J. H. Neyrey (ed.), *The Social World of Luke-Acts: Models for Interpretation.* Peabody: Hendrickson, 1991.

_____ and J. H. Neyrey. "Conflict in Luke-Acts: Labelling and Deviance Theory," in J. H. Neyrey (ed.), *The Social World of Luke-Acts: Models for Interpretation.* Peabody: Hendrickson, 1991.

_____ and R. Rohrbaugh. *Social-Science Commentary on the Synoptic Gospels.* Minneapolis: Fortress, 1992.

McCown, W. G. "Ό ΛΟΓΟΣ ΤΗΣ ΠΑΡΑΚΛΗΣΕΩΣ: The Nature and Function of the Hortatory Sections in the Epistle to the Hebrews." Ph.D. diss., Union Theological Seminary, Virginia, 1970.

Michel, Otto. *Der Brief an die Hebräer.* 12th ed. MeyerK 13. Göttingen: Vandenhoeck & Ruprecht, 1960.

Moffatt, J. *Hebrews.* ICC. Edinburgh: T. & T. Clark, 1924.

Moxnes, Halvor. "Honor and Shame." *BTB* 23 (1993) 167-176.

_____. "Honor, Shame, and the Outside World in Paul's Letter to the Romans," in J. Neusner, P. Borgen, E. S. Frerichs, and R. Horsley (eds.), *The Social World of Formative Christianity and Judaism.* Philadelphia: Fortress, 1988.

_____. "Honour and Righteousness in Romans." *JSNT* 32 (1988) 61-77.

Neyrey, J. H. "John 18-19: Honor and Shame in the Passion Narrative." *Semeia,* forthcoming.

_____. "Poverty and Loss of Honor in Matthew's Beatitudes: Poverty as Cultural, Not Merely Economic Phenomenon." An unpublished paper delivered at the CJA Seminar in October 1992.

_____. *2 Peter, Jude.* New York: Doubleday, 1993.

Nickelsburg, G. W. E. *Jewish Literature Between the Bible and the Mishnah.* Philadelphia: Fortress, 1981.

Olbricht, T. "Hebrews as Amplification," pp. 375-387 in *Rhetoric and the New Testament* (ed. S. E. Porter and T. H. Olbricht). JSNTSS 90. Sheffield: Sheffield Academic Press, 1993.

Peristiany, J. G. (ed.). *Honour and Shame: The Values of Mediterranean Society*. Chicago: University of Chicago, 1966.

Peterson, David. *Hebrews and Perfection: An Examination of the Concept of Perfection in the 'Epistle to the Hebrews'*. SNTSMS 47. Cambridge: Cambridge University, 1982.

Pfitzner, V. C. *Paul and the Agon Motif: Traditional Athletic Imagery in the Pauline Literature*. Leiden: E. J. Brill, 1967.

Pitt-Rivers, Julian. "Honour and Social Status," in J. G. Peristiany (ed.), *Honour and Shame: The Values of Mediterranean Society*. London: Weidenfeld and Nicolson, 1965.

Redditt, P. D. "The Concept of *Nomos* in Fourth Maccabees." *CBQ* 45 (1983) 249-70.

Riggenbach, E. *Der Brief an die Hebräer*. Leipzig: Deichert, 1922.

Robbins, V. K. "Rhetoric and Culture: Exploring Types of Cultural Rhetoric in a Text," in *Rhetoric and the New Testament* (ed. S. E. Porter and T. H. Olbricht). JSNTSS 90. Sheffield: JSOT, 1993.

_____. "Socio-rhetorical Criticism: Mary, Elizabeth, and the Magnificat as a Test Case," pp. 164-209 in *The New Literary Criticism and the New Testament* (ed. E. S. Malbon and E. McKnight). Sheffield: Sheffield Academic Press, 1994.

Roberts, K. A. *Religion in Sociological Perspective*. Chicago: Dorsey Press, 1984.

_____. "Towards a Generic Concept of Counterculture." *Sociological Focus* 11 (1978) 111-26.

Saller, R. P. *Imperial Patronage under the Early Empire*. Cambridge: Cambridge University, 1982.

Schlier, Heinrich. "Παραδειγματίζω." *TDNT* 2:32. Grand Rapids: Eerdmans, 1964.

Schmidt, T. E. "Moral Lethargy and the Epistle to the Hebrews." *WTJ* 54 (1992) 167-173.

Schneider, Carl. "Καταφρονέω." *TDNT* 3:631-632. Grand Rapids: Eerdmans, 1965.

Schneider, Johannes. "Τιμή." *TDNT* 8:169-180. Grand Rapids: Eerdmans, 1972.

_____. "ὄνειδος, etc." *TDNT* 5:238-242. Grand Rapids: Eerdmans, 1967.

Scholer, J. M. *Proleptic Priests: Priesthood in the Epistle to the Hebrews*. JSNTSS 49. Sheffield: JSOT, 1991.

Schürer, Emil. *The History of the Jewish People in the Age of Jesus Christ (175 B.C. - A.D. 135). A new English version* (ed. Geza Vermes, Fergus Millar, and Martin Goodman). Vol. 3, Div. 1. Edinburgh: T. & T. Clark, 1986.

Schweizer, Eduard. *Lordship and Discipleship.* SBT, 28. Naperville, IL: Alec R. Allenson, Inc., 1960.

Scott, R. B. Y. *Proverbs [and] Ecclesiastes.* Garden City, NY: Doubleday, 1965.

Seely, David. *The Noble Death. Graeco-Roman Martyrology and Paul's Concept of Salvation.* JSNTSS 28. Sheffield: Sheffield Acadmic Press, 1990.

Seesemann, H., and Georg Bertram. "Πατέω, etc." *TDNT* 5:940-945. Grand Rapids: Eerdmans, 1967.

Siebeneck, R. T. "May Their Bones Return to Life! -- Sirach's Praise of the Fathers." *CBQ* 21 (1959) 411-28.

Silva, Moisés. "Perfection and Eschatology in Hebrews." *WTJ* 39 (1976) 60-71.

Skehan, P. W. *Studies in Israelite Poetry and Wisdom.* CBQMS 1. Washington, DC: Catholic Biblical Association, 1971.

_____ and A. A. Di Lella. *The Wisdom of Ben Sira.* New York: Doubleday, 1987.

Snaith, J. G. *Ecclesiasticus.* Cambridge: Cambridge University, 1974.

Smend, R. *Die Weisheit des Jesus Sirach erklärt.* Berlin: Reimer, 1907.

Smit, J. "The Letter of Paul to the Galatians: A Deliberative Speech." *NTS* 35 [1989] 1-26.

Spicq, Ceslaus. *L'Épître aux Hébreux.* 2 vols. EBib. Paris: Gabalda, 1953.

_____. "L'Ecclésiastique," in *La Sainte Bible* (ed. L. Pirot and A. Clamer). Vol. 6. Paris: Letouzey et Ané, 1946.

Stählin, Gustav. "Παραιτέομαι." *TDNT* 1:195. Grand Rapids: Eerdmans, 1964.

_____. "ἀσθενής, etc." *TDNT* 1:490-493. Grand Rapids: Eerdmans, 1964.

Tcherikover, Victor. *Hellenistic Civilization and the Jews.* New York: Atheneum, 1977.

Thompson, J. W. *The Beginnings of Christian Philosophy: The Epistle to the Hebrews.* CBQMS, 13. Washington, DC: Catholic Biblical Association of America, 1982.

Thyen, H. *Der Stil der jüdische-hellenistichen Homilie.* Göttingen: Vandenhoeck & Ruprecht, 1955.

Toy, C. H. *The Book of Proverbs.* ICC. New York: Scribner's Sons, 1899.

Übelacker, W. G. *Der Hebräerbrief als Appel.* Stockholm: Almqvist & Wiksell, 1989.

van Geytenbeek, A. C. *Musonius Rufus and Greek Diatribe.* Assen: Van Gorcum & Co, 1963.

Vanhoye, A. *Le message de lÉpître aux Hébreux.* Paris: Cerf, 1977.

Weiss, H.-F. *Der Brief an die Hebräer.* 15th ed. MeyerK 13. Göttingen: Vandenhoeck & Ruprecht, 1991.

Westcott, B. F. *The Epistle to the Hebrews.* London: Macmillan and Co, 1920 [1889].

Wettstein, J. J. *H KAINH ΔIAΘHKH: Novum Testamentum Graecum,* etc. Vol. 2. Amsterdam: Dommer, 1752.

Wilken, R. L. *The Christians as the Romans Saw Them.* New Haven, CT: Yale, 1984.

Williams, Bernard. *Shame and Necessity.* Berkeley: Univeristy of California, 1993.

Williamson, Ronald. *Philo and the Epistle to the Hebrews.* Leiden: E. J. Brill, 1970.

_____. "Platonism and Hebrews." *SJT* 16 (1963) 415-24.

Winston, David. "Solomon, Wisdom of," pp. 120-27 in *The Anchor Bible Dictionary* (ed. D. N. Freedman). Vol. 6. New York: Doubleday, 1992.

Worley, Jr., D. R. "God's Faithfulness to Promise: The Hortatory Use of Commissive Language in Hebrews." Ph.D. diss., Yale University, 1981.

Wülfing von Martitz, Peter, *et al.* "Ψιός, υἱοθεσία." *TDNT* 8:334-399. Grand Rapids: Eerdmans, 1972.

Index of Modern Authors

333

Filson 286, 312, 315
Fox 153
Gilbert, G. H., 224
Gilbert, M., 108, 120, 122, 128
Grundmann, W., 218
Guthrie, G. H., 31, 33, 34, 209, 235
Hadas, M., 127-131, 133, 134
Hengel, M., 100-103, 108, 115, 167
Héring, J., 10, 156, 160,193, 208, 261, 262, 271, 301, 302
Hughes, G., 168
Hughes, P. E., 209
Hurst, L. D., 9, 10, 239, 258, 284, 305
Johnson, L. T., 5, 187, 229, 236, 240, 241, 284
Käsemann, E., 193, 271
Kennedy, G., 29, 32, 60, 61, 128
Kittel, G., 156, 215
Klauck, H.-J., 127, 130, 134
Kraftchick, S., 37, 42
Kurz, W. S., 29
Lane, W., 6-10, 28, 31, 33-35, 153, 155, 156, 158, 165, 168, 186, 204, 211, 218, 221, 231, 232, 246, 254, 262, 270, 273, 289, 302
Lauer, S., 131
Lebram, J. C. H., 128, 132
Levick, B., 228, 231
Lindars, B., 34
Lünemann, G., 158, 192, 193, 206, 257, 270, 303
Mack, B., 33, 37
MacMullen, R., 146, 149

Malina, B., 11, 14, 15, 18, 20-22, 24, 26, 65, 75, 80, 90, 137, 143, 158, 159, 200, 218, 227, 236, 249-251, 292, 308, 318
Michel, O., 6, 8-10, 168, 190, 192, 193, 205, 215, 265, 266, 269, 271, 293, 294, 305
Moffatt, J., 6, 8-10, 157, 158, 168, 169, 193, 200, 213, 288
Moxnes, H., 15, 21, 26, 178, 276, 279, 283, 290-292, 305, 313
Neyrey, J. H., 11, 14, 15, 18, 21, 24, 26, 80, 137, 143, 158, 159, 161, 162, 200, 207, 213, 218, 249-251, 263, 288, 293, 308, 318
Olbricht, T., 33-35, 100, 239
Peristiany, J. G., 13
Peterson, D., 7, 166, 177, 206, 273, 301, 303
Pfitzner, V. C., 138, 298
Pitt-Rivers, J. 13, 14, 18, 22, 25, 80, 81, 158, 178, 218, 241, 276
Redditt, P. D., 130, 131, 135
Robbins, V., 5, 27, 100, 320
Roberts, K. A., 320
Saller, R. P., 226, 227, 229, 230, 233, 235, 238, 244
Schlier, H., 261

Index of Texts Cited

Index of Subjects